CONTINENTAL PHILOSOPHY I

CONTINENTAL PHILOSOPHY I

Philosophy and Non-Philosophy Since Merleau-Ponty

EDITED BY HUGH J. SILVERMAN

ROUTLEDGE
New York and London

First published in 1988 by
Routledge
in association with Routledge, Chapman and Hall, Inc.
29 West 35th Street, New York, NY 10001
and in the UK by
Routledge
11 New Fetter Lane, London EC4P 4EE

Set in Linotron Palatino 10 on 12pt
by Input Typesetting Ltd, London SW19 8DR
and printed in Great Britain
by Billing & Sons Ltd, Worcester

Library of Congress Cataloging in Publication Data

Philosophy and non-philosophy since Merleau-Ponty/edited by Hugh J.
  Silverman
      p.   cm.—(Continental philosophy; 1)
    Bibliography: p.
    Contents: Philosophy and non-philosophy since Hegel/Maurice
Merleau-Ponty—Echoes/John Sallis—Sartre's last philosophical
manifesto/Peter Caws—Lacan and non-philosophy/William J.
Richardson—Foucault and the transgression of limits/Tony
O'Connor—Deleuze on a deserted island/Alphonso Lingis—The
adventures of the narrative/Stephen H. Watson—The origin and
end of philosophy/John Llewelyn—Philosophy as the heteronomous
center of modern discourse/John McCumber—Levinas/Robert
Bernasconi—The deaths of Roland Barthes/Jacques Derrida.
    ISBN 0–415–00178–1   ISBN 0–415–00179–X
    1. Philosophy, Modern—20th century.   I. Silverman, Hugh J.
II. Series.
B804.P535   1988
190'.9'04—dc19   87–27008
                                                             CIP

British Library Cataloguing in Publication Data

Philosophy and non-philosophy since
Merleau-Ponty.—(Continental philosophy;
1).
1. Philosophy, Modern—20th century
2. Philosophy, European
I. Silverman, Hugh J.   II. Series
190'.9'04   B804

ISBN 0–415–00178–1 (c)
     0–415–00179–X (pb)

CONTENTS

CONTENTS

5 Foucault

6 Deleuze

7 Lyotard

8 Derrida

9 Habermas

10 Levinas

CONTENTS

11 Barthes

INTRODUCTION

The beginning of *Continental Philosophy*? But is it a beginning? What is it to name what has already become a name? 'Continental philosophy' *as* philosophy has now come into its own – so why not give it a name and an avenue for expression? To name continental philosophy is to distinguish it from what it is not, to articulate its difference. It is not analytic philosophy; it is not process philosophy; it is not ancient philosophy, etc. This is not to say that it is opposed to other philosophies. Indeed not. Yet continental philosophy calls out for a space of its own. It already occupies such a space. In occupying a space of its own, continental philosophy claims an identity. It therefore seems to be *a* philosophy. But is it just another philosophy? Our first volume poses this question, while at the same time asking whether continental philosophy is itself philosophy in the pure, centered, self-defining sense. What is philosophy's relation to non-philosophy as posed by continental philosophy? Our enterprise begins with this question, a question that has long awaited an answer.

Continental Philosophy – we shall call it CP – recognizes that traditions such as phenomenology, existentialism, structuralism, semiology, semiotics, post-structuralism, hermeneutics, critical theory, deconstruction, archaeology, genealogy, libidinal economy, and post-modernism have undoubtedly established distinct terrains of their own. Nevertheless their collective philosophical practices can collectively be called 'continental.' These terrains are not exclusive – some have not yet been fully defined. Continental philosophy as a style of philosophizing has not closed itself off. In fact, continental philosophy operates in terms of an orientation toward openness. Just as continental

1

philosophy remains open to new formulations, new definitions, new orientations, *Continental Philosophy* shall not be limited by its own traditions. We seek to operate in terms of the tradition but not to be bound by it. CP acknowledges and assesses the shifting boundaries, foundations, and limits of established philosophical territories. Furthermore, CP aims to establish new directions and address crucial issues that set the pace for the practice of continental philosophy.

Continental Philosophy stresses current work drawing upon philosophical texts and traditions originating on European grounds (since Hegel, Marx, and Nietzsche). However, the principal focus of the series is on the Anglo-American context and its own philosophical activities, commitments, and concerns. Thus all articles will be written in English – only occasionally will translations be included. Contributions are addressed to an English-speaking audience and will be preoccupied with issues that arise for and out of that audience. Although different articles may employ different strategies, each volume will be oriented toward a chief concern in the Anglo-American philosophical community. In this respect our commitments are actively political. *CP* will demonstrate that philosophy is broader than – and in many cases other than – the ways it is commonly construed, and that there is a richness and profundity to a whole domain of philosophy that has for a long time operated outside the self-proclaimed mainstream. And yet as time has already shown, continental philosophy has come to achieve widespread expression, teaching, and effects throughout North American and British university settings. Continental philosophy is philosophy, academic, professional, and personal. It has sparked the minds of students, given new life to the meaning of philosophy in the curriculum, and offered a way out of the doldrums that philosophy has accomplished for itself in the past several decades. Continental philosophy is the new wave. It has embraced the relation between philosophy and other discourses as a real relation and not simply a detached observer reflection, analysis of propositions, or exercise in argumentation. Consequently, continental philosophy has become a vital and active force in Anglo-American philosophy today.

One might suppose that continental philosophy is that philosophy which is practiced primarily (or even exclusively) 'on the continent' of Europe. However, continental philosophy is no longer centered on the European continent. Rather it is dispersed across channels and oceans – both geographical and conceptual. Continental philosophy has achieved an originality and pertinence that has wandered far from France and Germany. It is to be found not only in Italy, Spain, and Austria, for instance, but it has also become a major philosophical force in the United Kingdom, the United States and Canada – significant traces being found in Ireland, Scandinavia, Latin America, and Asia as well. Decentered, dispersed, and disseminated, continental philosophy is rapidly achieving the status of the most substantial and alluring work in philosophy today. *Continental Philosophy* aims to serve as a vehicle for the articulation and expression of first-rate work done in this vein.

Continental Philosophy is not simply a collection of articles, a critical anthology, nor an academic journal. Each volume of essays constitutes a network of interlocking dialogical positions on a specified topic, figure, philosophical orientation, or complex of texts.

Our hope is to publish two volumes each year. Those in the odd-number series will focus on a theme or topic of contemporary philosophical interest. Those in the even-number series will be concerned with a major philosopher and a general orientation or movement associated with that figure. In each case, we will both invite and receive contributions from continental philosophers writing in the English-speaking context. Volumes will include essays by well-established, as well as younger, members of the continental philosophical community. The criteria will be consistency with the topic at hand, high quality, and effectiveness at addressing contemporary issues in continental philosophy. Each volume will be accompanied by a pertinent bibliography to assist readers in reviewing the broader context of the particular topic in question.

To inaugurate the series, we have entitled our first volume *Philosophy and Non-Philosophy Since Merleau-Ponty*. The motivation for this choice should be clear from a glance at the title of our first essay. When Merleau-Ponty set out to give a lecture course entitled 'Philosophy and Non-Philosophy since Hegel' at the *Collège de France* in 1960–61 he sought to raise the question of the very nature, function, and status of philosophy at that time. Furthermore, he saw a way to look at the whole philosophical tradition – emphasizing Hegel and Marx – but at the same time reading Hegel in particular through Heidegger's essay 'Hegel's Concept of Experience.' The choice of Hegel, Marx, and Heidegger set the parameters for the inquiry that he offered to his audience in that last year of his life. The course was not finished; he died in the spring of 1961. However, the theme of philosophy and non-philosophy, its relation to the tradition which names it, and its articulation in Merleau-Ponty's own enterprise is reiterated in a variety of ways in the quarter century that has followed.

Philosophy and Non-Philosophy Since Merleau-Ponty can be read as an homage to Merleau-Ponty. It could also be understood as an inquiry into the developments, wendings, and ruptures of continental philosophy since the year of Merleau-Ponty's death. We include a revised translation of Merleau-Ponty's course notes originally published over a decade ago. It will be evident that Merleau-Ponty himself was especially concerned with the limits of philosophy as it had come to be understood: reflection, analysis, overview thinking. Philosophy had in certain respects undermined its own opportunity to fulfill its mission, to enter into the texture of things, to interrogate them, to understand the workings of brute being. Merleau-Ponty found that Hegel – who, in announcing the end of philosophy, thought that it could be achieved – had set the stage for the inquiry. Hegel tried to bring experience into consciousness and consciousness into the resolution of the absolute. In all his wisdom, Hegel subsumed consciousness into absolute thought. However, absolute thought could no longer think. Consciousness, which Merleau-Ponty found to be so essential to philosophy in his earlier writings, was no longer a significant term for the interrogations into which he himself had moved.

Marx, by contrast, sought to enter into the political dimensions of the economic as they are lived by workers in their everyday experience. For Marx, life could not be identified with consciousness, much less with the absolute. Life would have to be characterized by conflict between whole classes on the basis of the oppression and the alienation that animate their relations. Merleau-Ponty would surely have brought his reading of Marx back into the reading of Hegel and ultimately into the contemporary understanding of political life. What is decisive for us is that Merleau-Ponty's reading of Hegel and Marx *via* Heidegger's insistence on thinking has opened up a vital question: What can philosophy be (and do) today? Or perhaps phrased differently: Is it possible for philosophy to be anything other than what it has made and makes of itself?

Our concern in *CP-I* is with the limits of philosophy: how philosophy has come to define itself, to give centrality to itself, and yet at the same time to undermine its possibilities, to decenter itself, to bring itself to the very brink of its own annihilation. However, this dissolution of philosophy is not to undo the practice of philosophy. Rather, it is to give focus to philosophy, its meaning, its activities, its future by asking what it is not. Not just any 'not,' but the 'not' of non-philosophy itself. Non-philosophy is not just everything else. For Merleau-Ponty, non-philosophy is experience, the living of the everyday, the primordial interrogation of what is visible, audible, expressible, interpretable. Out of the opposition of philosophy and non-philosophy (the *chiasm* as he called it) the identity of their difference comes into its own, the identity of what is not the visible, the audible, the expressible, the interpretable, but rather visibility, audibility, expressibility, etc., as they give shape to the philosophical enterprise that interrogates things.

CP-I sets out from the opening articulated by Merleau-Ponty. Our task has been to pose the question of the status of philosophy and non-philosophy since Merleau-Ponty. We have identified a number of the major figures from the European philosophical traditions since 1961. These constitute the topics for each of the essays included herein. Each figure is then assessed in terms of the question of the relation between philosophy and non-philosophy. Naturally, limitations of space and other factors have motivated the inclusion or exclusion of particular philosophers. There could have been essays on Adorno, Dufrenne, Gadamer, Serres, Marin, Taminiaux, Kristeva, Eco, Vattimo, and Irigaray, to name just a few. We nevertheless believe that a wide range of orientations, concerns, and commitments have been represented here.

Each of the essays is written by what could properly be called a continental philosopher whose primary context is the Anglo-

American scene. The only possible exception is the essay by Derrida whose reading of Roland Barthes is invaluable to the project as a whole. Nevertheless, Derrida often occupies an important place in the American academic scene not only by his writings but also by his person. We asked contributors not only to discuss the topic of philosophy and non-philosophy in terms of the figure in question but also to offer their own philosophical style as exemplary of continental philosophy. The range and quality of these essays is extraordinary. It serves as an excellent demonstration of continental philosophy as it is to be understood on the contemporary scene. The cohesiveness of continental philosophy is not in the imitation of a style, but rather in a certain orientation of thought, a way of asking about the activity and effects of philosophy, a commitment to the articulation of what governs the assumed, the expected, the all-too-transparent. Continental philosophy probes into the meaning, structures, and limits of thought itself, within the ongoing concerns, needs, desires, values, principles, concepts, language, and texts of everyday (philosophical) experience. As will be evident from a reading of these essays, the manner of articulating issues is both similar and different. What changes is the particular style and identity of the philosophical practice itself; what persists is the set of traditional texts, figures, and preoccupations that the contributors hold in common.

The contributors will understand what the others are about, what motivates their preoccupations, what underlies their questions, what pervades their thought. They will all be able to communicate at a level that does not undermine the project itself, that does not limit the inquiry before it gets started, that does not raise objections before frameworks and positions have been made evident. They will continue to set their own research programmes which carry on continental philosophy as philosophy itself. That they raise the question of non-philosophy does not mean that philosophy is not to go on. Quite the contrary, it is philosophy that is best equipped to ask about non-philosophy. Hence, here we ask about non-philosophy: What is it? Can it be? Should it be philosophy too?

Continental Philosophy is a series of books that are not books, a journal that is not quite a journal, a collection of essays that is not simply a collection of essays. We call this series *Continental Philosophy*. However, we are not as concerned to propose a name as to have an effect, to expand the space for writing, to write where writing is called for. We understand *CP* to be a multifaceted set of inscriptions – each set taking up a topic, elaborating its dimensions, pushing it toward its limits – all with the multiplicity that characterizes contemporary continental philosophy.

Continental philosophy is no longer a unified scientific program as Husserl had set forth. It can no longer simply inquire about perception as if it were a phenomenon, or an entity, or a wall that makes noise. Continental philosophy cannot still think of structures, frameworks, centers as if they were the only concern. With its communicative competences, its textual readings, its liminal meditations, its libidinal economies, continental philosophy scans the surfaces of things in order to go deeper into their being. Continental philosophy is not afraid of its own methodologies or its stylistic flourishes. Continental philosophy is not afraid to say what it means, to have something to say in all domains of human endeavor, artistic, scientific, textual, political, or otherwise. Continental philosophy wants to understand, wants to interpret, to make sense, to know, to be able to act – it is not afraid to say so; it should have no phobias about its practices. Often continental philosophy declines to make political moves that will bring it hegemony on the academic scene – there is too much to explore, to ask about, to understand to seek office for the sake of control, for the sake of the office, for the sake of power. At the same time, office, control, power, and understanding are all vital concerns for continental thinkers. Yet to omit the political is to omit the activity. And hence these polygrams, these volumes, these sets of essays, are eminently contemporary, persistently in the vanguard of philosophical thinking, unabashedly seeking to say and write what demands to be said, what demands to be written. The time for this new phase in continental philosophy has come into its own; with this inaugural volume *Continental Philosophy* begins to come into its own.

Hugh J. Silverman, *Editor*

Chapter 1

PHILOSOPHY AND NON-PHILOSOPHY SINCE HEGEL[1]

Maurice Merleau-Ponty

PART ONE: HEGEL*

No battles occur between philosophy and its adversaries. Rather what happens is that philosophy seeks to be philosophy while remaining non-philosophy, i.e. a 'negative philosophy' (in the sense of 'negative theology'[2]). 'Negative philosophy' has access to the absolute, not as 'beyond,' as a positive second order, but as another order which must be on this side, the double – inaccessible without being passed through. True philosophy scoffs at philosophy, since it is aphilosophical.

According to Hegel, one attains the absolute by way of a phenomenology (the appearance of mind; mind in the phenomenon[3]). This is not because the phenomenal mind is on one level of a scale, after which one moves on to the absolute, but because the absolute would not be absolute if it did not appear as absolute. From a certain point of view, phenomenology is the whole truth.

Introduction to the phenomenology of mind

For Marx, the realization of philosophy is its destruction as an independent philosophy [philosophie séparée] (Hegel is to be understood here).

Kierkegaard advances further, for philosophy is sacrificed. Philosophy masks the whole of existence [l'existence intégrale] which 'includes' other existences and surpasses[4] them from within, that is, it transforms them into one [chapter]. A relationship with the absolute cannot be realized except in an existence which is not whole [*l'existence non intégrale*] but which is narrow and [therefore] profound.

This anti-philosophy is above all anti-system – against Hegel the scholar – not against the Hegel of 1807 and earlier.

Nietzsche's Preface to the second edition of Joyful Wisdom *(1886)*[5]

Every philosophy is life and the life of the body 'ends up fulfilling the need to write ideas across the sky in cosmic capital letters.'[6]

> After such self-interrogation, such self-temptation, one learns to take a more subtle view toward what has been philosophy up to the present. We can guess better than before which are the involuntary detours, the circumvented routes, the side lanes, the resting places, and the places of thought where the happy sufferers are driven and transported precisely because they suffer. . . . All philosophers until now have never concerned themselves with 'truth' but with something else, – let us say, health, the future, growth, power, life. (*FW*, pp. 9–10; trans., pp. 34–5)

A philosopher

> simply cannot keep from transposing his states every time into the most distant form of the spiritual – this art of transfiguration is precisely philosophy. We others are not free to separate the body from the soul, as the people are wont to do; we are even less free to divide soul from spirit. We are not thinking frogs, nor are we objective and registering mechanisms with their innards in refrigeration. We constantly give birth to our thoughts out of pain, and, like mothers, endow them with all we have of blood, heart, ardor, joy, passion, agony, conscience, fatality. For us, life consists in continually transforming all that we are into clarity and flame, just as it transforms everything that we touch.
>
> . . . Only great pain is the ultimate liberator of the spirit, being the teacher of *the great suspicion* . . . [which] compels us, we other philosophers, to descend into our ultimate depths and to put aside everything good-natured,

everything that would impose a veil, that is mild, that is medium, – things in which we may have formerly placed our humanity. I strongly doubt that such pain makes us 'better', but I know that it makes us more profound. One emerges as a different person out of these dangerous exercises in self-domination, and with a few more question marks in addition. Above all, one emerges with the *will* henceforth to question further, more deeply, severely, harshly, evilly and quietly than one had questioned heretofore. The trust in life is gone; life itself has become a *problem*. (FW, pp. 11–12; trans., pp. 35–6)

But one should not imagine that all this should necessarily make us misanthropic! Even love of life is still possible, only one loves differently. Our love is like the love for a woman whom we suspect. . . . However, the attraction of everything problematic, the joy caused by the x, is so great in such more spiritualized and more intellectual men that this pleasure flares up again and again like a bright blaze over all the distress of what is problematic, over all the danger of uncertainty, and even over the jealousy of the lover. We know a new happiness. (FW, pp. 12–13; trans., pp. 36–7)

One returns *newborn* from such abysses, from such severe sickness, also from the sickness of severe suspicion. One returns as if one had shed one's skin, more ticklish and malicious, with a more subtle taste for joy, with a tenderer tongue for all good things, with a merrier spirit, with a second dangerous innocence in joy. One returns more childlike and yet, at the same time, a hundred times more subtle than one has ever been before. . . . No, we no longer find pleasure in things of bad taste, this will to truth, to 'truth at any price', this youthful madness in the love of truth: we have too much experience for that, we are too serious, too merry, too burned by fire, too *profound*. We no longer believe that truth remains truth when the veils are withdrawn; we have lived too much to write this. Today we consider it a matter of decency not to wish to see everything naked, or to be present at everything, or to understand everything and to 'know' everything. . . . One should have more respect for the bashfulness with which nature has hidden behind riddles and multiple uncertainties. Perhaps truth is a woman who has reasons for not letting us see her reasons? . . . Ho, those Greeks! They knew how to live. What is required for living is to stop courageously at the surface, to hold on to the skin, to adore appearance, to believe in forms, sounds, words, in the whole Olympus of appearance! These Greeks were superficial, – *out of profundity*! (FW, pp. 14–15; trans., pp. 37–8)

COMMENTARY

When detached from life, philosophy is a panacea: a search for 'sunny places of thought.' Philosophy is a 'transfiguration' of what we live, a 'transfiguration' of sadness and of suspicion, for life is a 'problem'. – At the end of this awareness [*clairvoyance*], there is no misanthropy and hatred for life, but rather *another* love, 'a new happiness.' – 'Abyss' and 'regeneration.' – Second innocence. – Truth is only a hidden truth. – Do not seek to 'see' everything 'in its nakedness,' to 'know' all – to be superficial through profundity (Apollo and Dionysus).[7]

We find here the idea that there is a philosophy that does not question enough, which flees from questioning into 'sunny places' – all philosophy is a 'transfiguration' (cf. Marx). We discover that true philosophy is beyond: great suspicion, abyss, a-philosophy through infidelity to what we live. We realize that this does not end with 'full knowledge' (a new positivism), nor with despair, but with the will to appearance. – For Hegel, appearance and profundity are not contraries. – Nietzsche maintains the quality of the 'philosopher' [in]* the absolute of appearance.

If we have time, we will examine:

(a) The connection that Heidegger thinks he brings with his *Denken* to this movement towards a surpassing of metaphysics, towards philosophy a-philosophy

(b) A text from Sartre's *Critique of Dialectical Reason*, to see if Marx is the unsurpassed philosophy, as Sartre claims, or if Marx is a moment in the history of a-philosophy.[8]

Problems linked to what is within [the world of experience], what is
beyond, and their relationship*

1 The problem of Christianity. – Philosophy as the negation of
   a detached philosophy; religion as the death of God. – Death
   of God: Hegel's word, Marx's theory of ideologies, Kierkegaard's Pharisean Christianity, Nietzsche's word. – This does
   not mean (according to Heidegger): *es gibt keinen Gott*.⁹ – It
   does mean: the absolute must be thought by a mortal (capable
   of dying). This is not death in the sense of beings which are
   merely alive and which are uprooted from existence by an
   external cause. Rather it is death in the sense of human
   death, prefigured in man because conscience¹⁰ (*Er-innerung*) is
   negativity offered as proof of itself. – The absolute requires
   all that in order to avoid being 'solitary' and 'lifeless' (Hegel).¹¹
The question of Christianity in the second sense.
2 The problem of humanism. – Humanism must also involve a
   kind of anti-humanism. Are the Dostoevskian superman and
   the Nietzschean overman¹² to be understood as man replacing
   God (mystique of the Superman), – or do Being and man
   belong to one another¹³ without the possibility of thinking
   their relationship only from man's point of view? The relationship is the appropriate domain of philosophy – beyond all
   anthropology.

Our procedure will be to explain the last four paragraphs of
Hegel's Introduction to the *Phenomenology of Mind*. But first we
will analyze what precedes with reference to some passages.

I

Philosophy has no knowledge¹⁴ by which it can gain the
absolute. Philosophy is (irreducibly) the revealing¹⁵ of
phenomena, the presence of the absolute.

Philosophy goes 'to the thing itself' – but if this movement
is established by 'understanding' [*Erkennen*], it is conceived
either as an instrument or as a medium through which the thing
itself is visible to us. – Whence the question of the critique of
'understanding'¹⁶: can consciousness acquire '*what is in itself*' by
this instrument, through this milieu? – With the question posed
in this way, the response is necessarily that 'there is a strict line
of demarcation separating *understanding* and the absolute.'¹⁷

For, the instrument modifies the thing. The milieu alters its image. The means runs counter to the end. There would have to be no means: 'what is non-sensical lies in our making use of any means at all' (*Holz*, p. 106; trans., p. 8).

Would we say that the action of the instrument cuts off the result? – But then we find ourselves back again before the initial problem: How does one grasp the absolute? If the instrument is only a trap, like lime for ensnaring birds, bringing the absolute closer to us but without being able to enter into it, then the instrument becomes a kind of derision. The absolute defies all activities of 'understanding.' It serves only 'to bring forth a relationship which is immediate and thus effortless' and would be powerless 'if it (the absolute) were not, in and for itself, already close to us of its own accord' (*Holz*, p. 106; trans., p. 9).

Would we say that 'understanding' is corrected through a medium by taking into account the refraction of light rays? But 'understanding' is not a certain refraction of light. It is light itself, 'the ray of light itself through which the truth touches us' (*ibid.*), and if we subtract this light, 'understanding' indicates nothing more to us than an empty spot or a pure directionality (*ibid.*).

A philosophy of 'understanding' (whether instrument or medium) destroys itself by placing philosophy and the absolute side by side. The relation to the absolute must be preliminary to 'understanding.' Such a relation must pass by another route whether the absolute be 'already in our midst,' or whether it be the light itself which reveals it.

The critical attitude of 'understanding' involves a distrust or knowledge [*savoir*] which 'takes up *its* work and actually understands without any such hesitations' (*ibid.*). But this distrust is presupposed and is not true radicalism. It presupposes a 'representation' of 'understanding' as a medium and instrument and 'a difference [*Unterschied*] between ourselves and this understanding' (*FW*, p. 107; trans., p. 10). It also presupposes the disjunction between 'understanding' and the absolute, and therefore the immanence to the 'understanding' of a truth at the moment when it is spoken outside of the absolute. All this is not a 'fear of error,' but a 'fear of truth' . . ., resistance to the truth.[18] – True radicalism will not be just this distrust, but also a 'distrust of distrust.'

A 'difference' between ourselves and 'understanding' must not be presupposed.[19] We must seek an 'understanding' which is [identical with]* ourselves (our being).

In reality, we must begin with the fact that 'the absolute alone is true' or 'the true alone is absolute' (*Holz*, p. 107; trans., p. 10).

This appears to be a dogmatic leap into the absolute; a proposition not proven. That is:

1 The leap is implicated into our existence as a distrust of distrust, as a knowledge which becomes, in fact, *Weltthesis*: the identity of our being and knowing [*connaître*].

2 The proof will be given by whatever follows, that is, by our history, by revealing a mind-phenomenon, a life which makes itself knowledge, and therefore a knowledge which gives itself life.

In a sense, it is a circle – the beginning is the end – but it is a conscious circle.[20]

'The "absolute," "understanding," etc., are words which presuppose a signification, which has yet to be acquired' (*Holz*, p. 107; trans., p. 11).

We must understand the relation between 'understanding' and the absolute as given in our life (hence an absolute which will also be 'understanding'). We must truly recast the concepts of subjectivity and objectivity, absolute and knowledge according to their contact with our life. We must take science within us in its nascent state; 'science, in that it appears, is an appearance itself' (*Holz*, p. 108; trans., p. 12).

The fact of knowledge is not like a simple fact (as in Descartes) which can be placed alongside any sort of false knowledge, and which has certainty in that it is a simple thought. However, the fact of knowledge delimits an appearance of knowledge 'as it is in and for itself' and takes recourse in the 'presentation of knowledge as a phenomenon (of appearing knowledge); experience of its own self' (*Holz*, p. 109; trans., p. 13).

Phenomenology is this self-presentation of mind, an appearance which is not an effect of the absolute, but the absolute itself. – In that respect, philosophy is experience.

II

1 Philosophy is not 'understanding' but [it wishes]* to redefine everything with our being as its point of departure. Our life of understanding opens onto 'the thing itself.'

The distinction between the understanding [*connaissance*] and the absolute (the critical attitude) is a false radicalism. It presupposes:

[a] the understanding as instrument: either that this instrument alters the absolute (and on that basis, how do we even have a notion of an absolute?) or, if it is only a trap like lime for ensnaring birds, it presupposes a relation which is 'immediate and thus effortless' and that the absolute 'in and for itself is already with us of its own accord;'

[b] the understanding as medium: this 'milieu' is truth coming in contact with us, 'the ray of light itself through which the truth touches us.'

Therefore, this fear of error invokes a critical examination of 'understanding' against these *Vor-stellungen* (external representations of the 'understanding'). – 'This is the error itself.' – In other words, we are within truth; – or, to put it another way: the 'understanding' is not distinct from us, and we are not distinct from the 'understanding.' There is no 'difference between us and this understanding.'

And this understanding which we are, is also understanding of the absolute, since, if one denies it (Descartes),[21] it must be affirmed that knowledge is true at the moment when one says that it is outside the absolute and hence outside the true (Holz, p. 107; trans., p. 10). And what does this 'other truth' mean? Absolute, understanding: 'words which presuppose a signification which has yet to be acquired.' There is knowledge [*savoir*], a science 'which takes up its work and actually understands without any such hesitations.'

Thus, there is the fact of understanding which we are and which is in contact with the absolute. –

Only the absolute is true, *das Absolute allein wahr*; only the true is absolute, *das Wahre allein absolut*. This implies that the absolute within us is internal to the truth, that there is an absolute which is nothing other than our truth, and which is not separated from 'understanding.'

16

The attitude here is not dogmatic. On the contrary, it is the true radical, critical attitude. By it, we commit ourselves to 'giving' the concept of the absolute, 'understanding,' the objective, the subjective 'to give this concept' (Holz, p. 108; trans., p. 11) rather than presupposing what everyone knows or assuming the concept that we already have of it.

We begin with the true as absolute and with the absolute as true. We start from a knowledge [connaissance] which can only form a unity with our being as a knowing being [être sachant]. This knowledge cannot correspond to 'science making its appearance' (Holz, p. 108; trans., p. 12) as a nexus of knowledge and absolute, of our Being and the Being. – We must grasp this nexus fully and not in the emptiness of 'representations' [Vorstellungen].

2 Revealing the phenomenon is presence of the absolute.

The phenomenon ('science making its appearance') is Erscheinung ('manifestation'). – The science is that which 'appears,' 'which is not yet rendered explicit and developed in its truth.' It is not yet freed from the 'Schein.'[22] – It cannot simply free itself as 'assurance' (Holz, p. 108; trans., p. 12) certainty of thought (in the Cartesian sense), certainty 'dried of its Being [Sein]' – for another Being, that of false knowledge, is worth precisely as much. Similarly it is undesirable to make reference in false knowledge to any misgivings (or presentiment) that it might have about itself. This would still be to refer oneself to a Being (the presentiment). It is false knowledge to refer to oneself as 'science making its appearance,' to refer to a 'bad' mode of its Being, to refer to its manifestation (Erscheinung) and not to itself, a science, 'as it is in and for itself' (Holz, p. 109; trans., p. 13).

Science must be shown to manifest itself with reference to science in and for itself. – This occurs through the presentation (Darstellung) of science while it is appearing, that is, while it proves itself to be a science, the 'presentation of appearing knowledge' presenting itself, exposing itself in the name of science. (That is, not only the Cogito, but a Cogito which includes both itself and the false.)

This 'presentation' is no longer science 'in its free form,' but the pathway (Weg) of 'natural consciousness' which strives toward true knowledge, – or the soul's road towards the explicit

Geist through stations which are prescribed for it by its nature. – This pathway is experience (*Erfahrung*), complete within itself, realizing the understanding (*Kenntnis*) of 'that which is it in-itself' (*ibid.*).[23]

Science here is in the process of manifesting itself. That is, it proves itself to be a science by taking up what goes before it, conserving it and surpassing it. Now there is a question of its identity in this becoming, because it develops itself, and because this departure is a return to that which it is in its pure state, as pure 'knowledge' [*Wissen*].

Life makes itself into knowledge, – and perceives itself in such a way that it is a knowledge that becomes life.

The juncture of the two, the overthrowing of one in favor of the other, is a manifestation of knowledge. – When there is an identity of the phenomenon and of the absolute, the phenomenon, i.e. the way, is precisely the absolute (in and for itself) or its presence. And reciprocally the absolute is the phenomenon since it is that which 'is in and for itself.'

Presence of the absolute and revealing the phenomenon are synonyms because the absolute is the subject, self-consciousness, and the phenomenon represents the becoming of this self-consciousness. The phenomenon and the absolute are linked, because every phenomenon represents the relation to itself, and because the absolute is itself, that is, relation to itself.

Every phenomenon [is] a 'presentation of appearing knowledge': an exposition of knowledge in the process of manifesting itself. – Here exposition means exteriorization, revelation, and what is not secondary in relation to knowledge. What is appropriate to knowledge is to manifest itself as knowledge. – Whence:

(a) The phenomenon is a 'figure' (*Gestalt*) and not 'free' knowledge. – It is 'figurative' knowledge. – Thus the relation to a *Gestalt* [is]* knowledge of something. – But this knowledge of something is self-knowledge: what I see, in these phenomena, are figures of a relation to myself. – Consciousness of something is self-consciousness (once it is decoded).

(b) Inversely, self-knowledge (either in equilibrium with itself, or as absolute) does not truly rejoin itself except in departing from itself. To attain the absolute is nothing other than to decode completely the 'appearance.' – An absolute knowledge does not prove itself to be absolute except in manifesting itself, in being born into phenomena.

The relation between phenomenology and absolute knowledge (metaphysics) is the relation between perception and the thing: partial perception is not simply reconciled with the thing. In order to be total, it must be partial. This is at least the case if one considers the 'vertical,' present world – and an 'understanding' which is not distinct from our being. Phenomenology uncovers this order where to be with the thing and to be with oneself are synonymous, – where the linking of 'figures' leads to the Self. This order is the same thing as the Self, and is not a prolegomenon to metaphysics. Inversely metaphysics here is nothing other than a taking possession of what appears.

Phenomenology is the total part: the whole system under a certain relation. – What is restrictive in the 'appearance' (which is *only* a manifestation) is in reality not a hindrance, but the accomplishment of an absolute which is entirely a manifestation of the self, subjectivity.

We must now specify the nexus, the 'chiasm'[24]: relation to the self/relation to the external.

3 The structure of consciousness as a fundamental law of the phenomenon and of self-presentation (*Holz*, p. 109; trans., p. 13ff.): the movement from 'appearing knowledge' to 'knowledge.'

'Natural consciousness' (*natürliches Bewusstsein*) is not real accomplished knowledge (for example, when living in a society, a religion is not knowledge in its truth). – However, taking itself for real knowledge, 'natural consciousness' is the concept of knowledge, a non-realized concept, and one which will be realized only by sacrificing this deceitful positivity, 'loss of itself' (*Holz*, p. 109; trans., p. 13), recognition of its non-truth.

There is a natural consciousness which is naturally unconsciousness (cf. Marx; and Freud), naturally mystified. This is 'consciousness': consciousness of the external. It appeals to the truth, but can only happen unexpectedly by negating and tearing it apart. The immediate is deceitful.

The movement from there to truth. We note the difference between this movement and that of Descartes. – The pathway is that of doubt or even despair. Cartesian doubt, however, leads to a restoration of truth in the initial sense (by God), whereas here, doubt – the whole history of consciousness – inserts itself into truth ([since]* the object and work of consciousness reflect each other exactly). An intuition of the non-truth of the immediate and an intuition of a higher truth than what follows is the carrying out (*Ausführung*), of knowledge, – consciousness at work on the self (*Bildung*).[25] The school of truth is not the place for doubt, which converts everything into *my thoughts*. Skepticism, which is no more careful with my opinion than that of others, does not give precedence to my principles over those of others. It does not take refuge in my thoughts, but attaches itself neither to me (thought of understanding), nor to authority, but to the content, to its 'necessities' (*Notwendigkeit*), and to its cohesion (*Zusammenhang*).

This consciousness, which forms itself, cultivates itself, or works itself, is a negation (since the immediate is recognized as untrue). It is a negation which does not reach the 'pure nothingness' (*Holz*, p. 110; trans., p. 10) but attains the 'nothingness of that from which it results' (*Holz*, p. 111; trans., p. 16) and which is, therefore, in the end, 'the actual result' (*ibid.*). Once nothingness has been determined and that which has a content has been determined, the previous truth is therefore not a 'void' (*Abgrund*) (*ibid.*) but a movement (*Uebergang*) to a new form, its true surpassing. Question: But then could anything ever be achieved from this movement? Would it not be necessary for the negation to be absolute, a negation without context which disclaims itself (a negation of the negation)? Therefore it would no longer be necessary 'to go out beyond itself' (*ibid.*). 'Knowledge' would find itself. The concept would correspond to the object, [and back again]* to the concept. Sartre's solution would be to sacrifice the for-itself so that the in-itself might be: the nothingness is not anything.[26] For Hegel, this would be an impossible solution, since 'consciousness' (thrust into the apparently solid reality of the immediate, into its flesh), which, we would say, *is only* its own concept, a projection of itself, a being in the distance, is not its own self-realization. We must also say that if 'consciousness' is its own concept, the concept is intentional with all its force. 'Consciousness' projects itself into that of which it is conscious and, therefore, 'out beyond itself.' It is within its Beyond: spatial perception, for example, is 'of the beyond' [*von Jenseits*]; it forces itself

20

beyond the limited segment. 'Consciousness' is violence done against itself, passion by itself, self-destruction ('consciousness therefore suffers violence at its own hands, a violence through which it destroys for itself any limited satisfaction') (*Holz*, p. 111; trans., p. 17). Hegel condemns the nihilist solution that would conclude on this account that the self and others are guilty of vanity. This solution which depends on vanity detaches itself from all content and 'bereft of all content, finds itself no more than a barren "I" ' (*Holz*, p. 112; trans., p. 18), remains in 'being-for-itself' (*ibid.*). Judgment [*l'entendement*], skepticism, pure nothingness, are always 'I.'

But then, if 'consciousness' is, by definition, outside of itself, a hole, (and it does not feel that it can even find repose in nothingness) why isn't all consciousness unhappy?[27] How can there be access to the absolute?

4 The problem of the standard of measurement [*mesurant*] and what is measured [*mesuré*].[28] – The exchange between the standard of measurement and the measured or 'experience' [*Erfahrung*] (*Holz*, p. 112ff.; trans., p. 18ff.).

'Presentation' is science entering into knowledge in the process of appearing. 'Presentation' tests (*Prüfung*) this knowledge which supposes a 'standard of measurement' [*Masstab*] (*Holz*, p. 112; trans., p. 12) that is applied to it. This 'standard of measurement' is taken as 'essence' or 'in-itself.' Now, since science only appears, from where will we take the 'essence' (the essential as opposed to the inessential)? (How can consciousness learn? Either it knows or it does not know.)

'Consciousness' distinguishes from itself something to which it relates – this 'something' [*etwas*] is 'something' *for consciousness*. This being of something for consciousness (*für ein anderes*) is what we call 'knowledge.' But what is known is also presented as being outside this relation. And that is what is called 'truth' [Wahrheit] or 'being-in-itself.' All this is taken as a phenomenon, an 'appearing.' Here, we philosophers interrogate ourselves about 'the truth of knowledge.' We are therefore questioning what 'knowledge' is in itself. But this inquiry, this 'in itself' of 'truth' is the 'for us' which we attain. Its supposed 'in itself' is not the truth, but our knowledge of this truth. We therefore do not have any standard of measurement which we could introduce here; and when we apply such a standard to nascent knowledge, it will perhaps be refused.

Nevertheless, consciousness is what we study, and we are the standard of measurement, which is consciousness. Philosophy is already in life. 'Since consciousness provides itself with its own standard, the investigation will be a comparison of consciousness with its own self' (*Holz*, p. 113; trans., p. 20). The *mesurant–mesuré* distinction is internal to consciousness. Being for the other is its own, and this other for consciousness is not only other in consciousness, but other in itself. Consciousness is knowledge, *Wissen*; it is truth. In that consciousness declares itself 'in itself' or 'true' we have the standard of measurement which it brings along to measure its own knowledge.

The 'concept' [*Begriff*] can be called 'Knowledge'; 'truth' or 'Knowledge' can be called the object – the examination (*Prüfung*) of the correspondence between the concept and the object occurs in consciousness. Inversely, the concept can be called the essence or the in-itself of the object (the consciousness-object) and the object can be called the examining, philosophical, consciousness, since that is what we examine. When examining the 'philosophical consciousness,'[29] we make it appear before 'natural consciousness' and we seek its being for natural consciousness.

The two presentations are 'the same' [*dasselbe*], – exchanging their roles; natural consciousness and philosophical consciousness are object and subject for each other. We philosophers do not bring our standards of measurement, our 'thought' [*Gedanken*] and our inventions. We seize the thing (*die Sache*) 'as it is in and for itself' (*Holz*, p. 114; trans., p. 21), that is, absolutely.

III

1 para. 13[30]: Knowledge is experience. The absolute is the reversal of roles between the measured and the standard of measurement; para. 14: Experience, Ambiguity, Dialectic.

2 paras 15 and 16: However philosophy is not a 'pure act of observation' [*reine Zusehen*] (*Holz*, p. 114; trans., p. 21).

1 PARAS 13 AND 14[31]

But if a contribution (addition, or *Zutat*) by us becomes
superfluous, it is not simply in connection with the concept
and the object that the standard of measurement and what
is to be examined are already present in consciousness.
We are also spared the effort of comparison and preparation
for examination (*Prüfung*). And therefore, since
consciousness examines itself, what remains for us, on this
side of the investigation too, is simply the pure act of
vision* (*reine Zusehen*). For consciousness is, on the one
hand, consciousness of the object and, on the other,
consciousness of itself; it is consciousness of what is true to
it, and consciousness of its knowledge of this truth. Since
both are before the same witness (for consciousness, *für
dasselbe*) consciousness itself is a comparison; whether its
knowledge of the object corresponds or fails to correspond
with this object will be a matter *for consciousness* itself.

To be sure, the object seems to be for consciousness only
as consciousness knows it; consciousness seems, as it
were, unable to get behind the object (*dahinter*) in order to
see it, *not as* it is *for consciousness*, but as it is *in itself*.
Therefore consciousness also seems unable to examine its
own knowledge by comparing it with the object. But the
difference between the in-itself and the for itself is already
present in the very fact that consciousness knows an object
at all. With respect to consciousness, something is the *in-
itself*, but the knowledge or the being of the object *for*
consciousness is still another moment. It is upon this
differentiation, which exists and is present, that the
examination (*Prüfung*) is grounded. And if, in this
comparison, the two terms do not correspond, then it seems
that consciousness will have to change its knowledge in
order to conform with the object. In the transformation of
knowledge, however, with respect to consciousness the
object itself becomes something which has in fact been
transformed as well. For the knowledge which existed was
essentially a knowledge of the object: with change in the
knowledge, the object also becomes an other, since it was
an essential part of this knowledge. Hence it comes to pass

23

for consciousness that what had been *in-itself* is not in-itself, or, in other words, what was *in itself* was so only *for consciousness (für es an sich was)*. When therefore consciousness discovers that its knowledge does not correspond with its object, the object itself will also give way. In other words, the standard of the examination is changed if that whose standard it was supposed to be fails to endure the course of the examination *(Prüfung)*. Thus the examination is not only an examination of knowledge, but also of the standard used in the examination itself. *(Holz,* pp. 114–15; trans., pp. 21–3)

This *dialectical* movement, which consciousness exercises *(ausübt)* on its self – on its knowledge as well as its object – is, *in so far as the new, true object emerges to consciousness* as the result of it, precisely that which is called *experience.* In this connection, there is a moment in the just mentioned process which must be articulated further so that new light may be cast on the scientific aspect *(die wissenschaftliche Seite)* of the following presentation *(Darstellung).* Consciousness knows *something,* and this object is the essence or the *in-itself.* But this object is also the in-itself for consciousness; and hence the ambiguity *(Zweideutigkeit)* of this truth comes into play. We see that consciousness now has two objects; one is the first *in-itself (Ansich),* the other is the *being-for-consciousness* of this *in-itself.* The latter seems at first to be merely the reflection of consciousness into its self, a representation *(vorstellen)* not of an object, but only of its knowledge of the first object. But, as already indicated, the first object is transformed for consciousness in this very process; it ceases to be the *in-itself* and becomes with respect to consciousness an object which is the *in-itself* only *for it.* And therefore it follows that this, the *being-for-consciousness of this in-itself (das Für-es-sein dieses Ansich),* is the true, which is to say that this true is the *essence* or consciousness' new *object.* This new object contains the annihilation *(Nichtigkeit)* of the first; it is the experience constituted through that first object. *(Holz,* p. 115; trans., pp. 23–4)

Literal commentary on paragraphs 13 and 14

The development from 'consciousness' to knowledge occurs without our adding anything (*Zutat von uns*). This is true not only because the standard of measurement and the measured are both present in consciousness,[32] but also because there is no basis for comparison; when the self is examined by itself, there is only pure intuition (*reine Zusehen*), pure insight (*spectacle*). In effect, consciousness is itself the comparison to be made, on the one hand, with the object, on the other hand, with the knowledge consciousness has of it. Since these two moments are for consciousness, for the same consciousness (*für dasselbe*), they are therefore grasped at once as to whether they coincide or not. One could say that consciousness, on the contrary, cannot pass behind itself (*dahinter kommen*) in order to rejoin the in-itself and confront the in-itself with the knowledge that it has of it. However, from the very fact that consciousness is consciousness of an object, consciousness does have a dual reference. Its double reference is

1 to that which is in-itself for consciousness and
2 to that which for consciousness is the knowledge or the being of the object for consciousness (*das Sein des Gegenstandes für das Bewusstsein*).

Because there are two references, there is an 'examination', [*Prüfung*]. Thus there is a duality in the undivided nature of the process (intentionality).

If consciousness cannot determine any correspondence between the in-itself and the knowledge of the in-itself, one could be led to believe that knowledge must model itself after the object. (Here the problem is how consciousness can learn anything.) But this change in 'knowledge' (toward the true) also entails a change in the object, for the initial 'knowledge' was essentially linked to the object. If 'knowledge' changes, the object changes. The initial object which could pass for the 'in itself' becomes 'an in itself for consciousness.' The object, the in-itself that was a standard of measurement, is modified by the fact that the measured does not remain stable. The proof is therefore equivocal [*à double sens*]: the measured according to the standard of measurement and vice versa (cf. Lévi-Strauss).[33]

1 This exchange is dialectical. An action of A on B is also an action of B on A. Furthermore, the action is a self-regulated

25

movement [*automovement*].[34] Consciousness as a relation to its object is its own modification of itself.

2 This dialectic is 'experience' (pure 'vision,' concrete without discourse) because it creates for itself the new truth (by its content), without our bringing anything to it. Only experience, that is, the productive incorporation of a being [*l'assomption effective d'un être*], can make way for a dialectic, because it alone is an openness onto something that can reveal itself, something that is profound and latent, and something that can therefore give way to the *ek-stasis*[35] out of which a truly *new* [form]* will arise.

3 The consciousness in question here, i.e. experience, is 'ambiguous' [*zweideutig*]: a reference to an 'in itself' and a reference to the 'being for consciousness of this in itself.'

The introduction of this second element (self-consciousness) modifies the object itself. It becomes the second object, an object established by evidence. This second object, which annuls the first *is* the experience of the one on the other. (The second is nothing other than the first which has become its truth, and which is other in becoming the second. Thus the exchange of the In-itself-in-itself with the In-itself-for-us is an exchange which supposes that consciousness or 'experience' is at the same time the relation to the self and the relation to a transcendent, and that it is both – not alternatively, – but simultaneously. This is to say that latent intentionality calls for reversals and not dependence in the unitary sense direction[36] of a noema in relation to noesis.

Thus it seems that dialectic (if it is defined entirely in this way) could be, essentially, phenomenology (in the Hegelian sense), that is, the relation to the self in relation to a transcendent [object]* and vice versa. This dialectic is an intertwining[37] of subject and object, because they are abstract moments of an 'experience'. – Since the dialectical movement is a movement of content, it is not 'given' by consciousness; it exists only as content in relation to someone who experiences and lives it. No dialectical movement is possible without the duality: relation to the thing and relation to the Self. – To put dialectic back on its feet again would be to destroy it. We forget that it is Hegel who said deliberately that dialectic is the world stood on its head. Philosophy – that is, access to the absolute – appears to be essentially experience. Philosophy is an entering into phenomena in order to take part in their maturation and in experience. This is its character because in the relation of *experiri* with existing things, we can participate in the advent[38] of knowledge.

Correlatively, surpassing is conceived above all as conservation. The true (the standard of measurement) is already there, before the beginning. The beginning is the end or the result. The creation of the new, the *Bildung*, is the rendering explicit of what was already there.[39] Nevertheless the movement, as we have described it, includes a meta-empirical aspect.

2 PARAGRAPHS 15 AND 16 (HOLZ, PP. 115–17; TRANS., PP. 24–6)

In this presentation of the course of experience, there is a moment in virtue of which it does not seem to be in agreement with the ordinary use of the term 'experience.' This moment is the transition from the first object and the knowledge of that object to the other object. Although it is said that the experience occurs in this other object, here the transition has been presented in such a way that the knowledge of the first object, or the being-for-consciousness of the first in-itself becomes the second object itself. By, contrast, it usually appears that we experience the non-truth of our first concept in another object, such that we discover, in an accidental and extraneous manner, that what rises from us (i.e. falls on our side) is the pure *apprehension* of what exists in and for itself.[40] From the viewpoint of the present investigation, however, the new object shows itself as having come into being through a reversal (Hyppolite calls it 'conversion')[41] of consciousness itself. This way of considering the content (*der Sache*) is our contribution. When viewed in this way the sequence of experience constituted by consciousness is raised to the level of a scientific progression and only what the philosopher is in the process of considering is for consciousness (*Bewusstsein*).

As a matter of fact, the circumstance which guides this way of observing is the same as the one discussed with regard to the relationship between the present inquiry and skepticism. In every case, the result which emerges from an untrue mode of knowledge must not be allowed to dissolve into an empty nothingness (*leeres Nichts*) but must of necessity be grasped as the nothingness of that whose result it is, a result which contains what is true in the previous knowledge. Within the present context, this circumstance occurs as follows: when that which first appears to consciousness as the object sinks to the level of knowledge of the object, and when the in-itself becomes the being-for-consciousness of the in-itself, then the new object *is*. And with this new object a new form of consciousness also makes its appearance, a form whose essence is constituted by something else. This circumstance guides the entire succession of forms of consciousness in its necessity. But it is this necessity alone – or the *birth* of the new object, presenting itself (*darbietet*) to consciousness without the latter's knowing how this happens to it – which occurs for the philosopher, as it were, behind the back of consciousness. A moment which is both in-itself and for-us is thereby introduced into the movement of consciousness, a moment which does not present itself (*darstellt*) for the consciousness which is engaged (*begriffen*) in the experience of itself. But the *content* of what is born before the eyes of the philosopher exists for consciousness, but the philosopher comprehends only the formal aspect (*das Formelle*). That is, for consciousness, what is born in a pure state is nothing but an object. For the philosopher it exists at once as movement and as becoming.

This, then, is the necessity in virtue of which the present road toward science is already a *science*. And, at the same time, in accordance with its content, it may be called the science of the *experience of consciousness*.

[para 16]* According to the concept of experience, consciousness creates an experience of itself which in itself grasps (*begreifen*) nothing less than the whole system of consciousness or the whole realm of the truth of mind. The concept of experience thus entails the moments of truth presenting themselves, not as abstract, pure moments, but

as they are for consciousness, or as this consciousness itself appears in its relationship to them. Presenting themselves in this way, the moments of the whole are *forms of consciousness*. And in driving itself toward its true existence, consciousness will reach a point at which it casts off the semblance of being burdened by something alien to it, something which is only for it and which exists as an other. In other words, at that point where its appearance becomes equal to its essence, consciousness' external presentation of itself will therefore coincide with this very same point in the authentic science of mind. And, finally, when consciousness itself grasps this, its essence, it will indicate the nature of absolute knowledge itself.

Literal commentary on paragraphs 15 and 16

'Experience' has just been described as the revealing of knowledge. Philosophy, however, is not experience in the ordinary sense. Experience in the ordinary sense uncovers the non-truth of its point of departure by the truth of another object which substitutes for it.

Here, on the contrary, the experience, which was described, makes the new object emerge from the negation of the previous one by the work accomplished on the previous object. Experience produces its appearance as a result and surpasses the previous object by conserving it in its truth.[42] What the philosopher adds is this necessity apperceived in the unravelling of experience. The philosopher sees a 'reversal [*Umkehrung*] of consciousness'[43] while in common experience one sees an object emerge without knowing how it comes to pass [*lui advent*]. The philosopher goes behind the back of consciousness. Unlike the view of the man who simply lives, the philosopher's view of experience is not consciousness grasping successive objects (according to the irreversible noetic–noematic correlation). Rather experience is viewed from where what was an object (in-itself) can become consciousness (*an sich für es*), where what was consciousness can become an object, and where there is a reversal [*inversion*] of consciousness. Common consciousness is 'engaged' in experience, and thought through experience 'is caught up in the experience itself' (*Holz*, p. 116; trans., p. 25). The philosopher thinks the experience. – The implication is that content and the formal aspect are distinguished anew. The way, if it is going somewhere,[44] if it has a direction, is already science and the experience of consciousness is not the content of this science.

Thus, experience contains everything, the entire realm of mind, determined in a particular fashion, i.e. by 'figures of consciousness.' A moment comes precisely within this experience when 'consciousness' comprehends itself in its own truth, reintegrating the object into itself. Its own nature, which is to manifest, becomes equivalent to all that is essential and thus leads to absolute knowledge, that is, the knowledge which is absolute and the absolute which is knowledge.

IV

1 The absolute and us: its parousia[45] – an und für sich bei uns – *the chiasm*.

From the beginning, the absolute: 'was already in and for itself close to us of its own accord.' From the absolute to us, the whole intermediary is 'the ray of light through which the truth touches us' – the intermediary is not the 'difference between ourselves and this understanding.' – Consequently, only the absolute is true, and only the true is absolute. – This does not signify a dogmatism (an external link: 'knowledge'-absolute) but on the contrary an internal and reversible relation (without hierarchy) between true knowledge and absolute knowledge. The absolute is in the nature of the knowledge, and knowledge is in the nature of the absolute. – What is given is their relationship, from which 'subject' – 'object' must be clarified.

2 The absolute

The absolute is in the nature of the knowledge. The absolute is subject, not 'object' (not 'in itself,' that is, not 'for us'). The absolute is 'for-itself.' If it is 'in itself,' it is 'in and for itself'; that is, its repose in itself depends upon what it is for-itself. The only true 'in itself' is 'for itself'; but that means non-coincidence. That which the subject knows is nothing other than itself – 'self-knowing Spirit' [*Sich selbst wissends, Geist*], but it objectivates itself [in the process].

THE PHENOMENON

Here we are not told what this absolute is, since that would run counter to the starting point. As to the notion of phenomenon, in considering human history and our own, we see 'appearing' there a 'knowledge.' – And the absolute would be this 'knowledge for itself.' Everything that is produced is never anything but a *'Gestalt'* (a form, which is related to something else, hence, not 'free'; which has not yet overcome itself; and which does not quite know itself fully yet). This follows from the unique nature of 'knowledge,' for example, as in the Greek city-state, or in Christianity.[46]

Why is the form related to something else? Because it is engulfed, non-transparent to itself, but, according to its very nature, it is in the process of 'appearing.'

However this whole variety is nothing but a series of variants on the relation to Self. But the relation to Self is unachieved. It 'appears,' that is, before us. The knower is not that which he knows and vice versa. One can 'present' it, and recount it like an external event.

Yet, as the form unravels itself, its relatedness allows one to say that what follows is the truth of what precedes. Thus it is both accumulation and elucidation, not a blind process. So it 'returns into itself,' becomes itself. Its 'appearance' [*Erscheinung*] undoes itself from the *Schein*.[47] At the same time, as the 'I' which contemplates it, I perceive that I am not other than it. The form becomes the Self that knows itself and becomes me while I become it. There is an appearance (that is, an external manifestation) of the knowledge which is absolutely know ledge. Every phase of this absolute knowledge passes from one into the other (its beginning into its end, its end into its beginning), and what passes into me is like my passing into it. At this decisive moment where knowledge 'making its appearance' [*le savoir auftretende*] comprehends itself (*begreift*) 'as it is in and for itself,' we have arrived at the absolute.

The Hegelian notion of phenomenon [incorporates]* the mind as phenomenon. The for-itself is viewed from the outside, appearing, and, to that extent, not fully for-itself. Yet the for-itself is already the for-itself, since otherwise, while on the way toward self and toward the other, it would never become for

31

itself. – Identity both departs from the self (*erscheinen*) and returns into the self.[48]

The phenomenon is not the object, nor is it the subject. It is not the object in that it concerns me: in presenting it, I understand myself. It is not the subject in that it still has to become for itself. The phenomenon is the hidden frame of 'subject' and 'object' – object returning to itself, subject outside of itself.

The only justification for the absolute is the conquest of this order of the phenomenon, the presentation of its relatedness. This justification is not a demonstration but rather an 'automonstration'[49] of the becoming-absolute of the phenomenon (the becoming-phenomenon of the absolute by its own movement).

3 Phenomenon and the structure of consciousness. – The movement from the phenomenon to knowledge.

The starting-point: 'natural consciousness' – knowledge of the external – believes that it comprehends the external and truly believes that it possesses the external. But how would 'natural consciousness' possess it if it is already the external? Perhaps it is only my dream – total skepticism: I know my thoughts as little as I know things (Montaigne?).[50] What there is, is *work*, not according to my rules, but according to the context, knowledge at work according to its necessities and its 'cohesion' [*Zusammenhang*]. Thus negation, which is the 'actual result,' is negativity that is not 'pure nothingness' [*reine Nichts*] and not 'void' [*Abgrund*], but movement to the truth of . . . (cf. Husserl: all blocked perception is replaced by a true one).

This movement is set in motion by a consciousness of the external *per se*.

Consciousness of the external is its own concept, that is, 'beyond itself'; it is above itself, 'goes out beyond itself' – the Hegelian equivalent to intentionality. – In this sense, consciousness destroys itself in order to realize itself: 'consciousness therefore suffers violence at its own hands, a violence, through which it destroys any limited satisfaction for itself.'

But this must be clarified further, for one could object that consciousness is impossible, a failure in principle, being both a crack and an overhang.[51] One could offer the objection that one is tempted to direct at Husserl: consciousness is consciousness of something, always noetic-noematic correlation, – but how can consciousness have its noema if it does not possess itself as noesis? Now if it possesses itself as noesis, consciousness can therefore take itself as an object (reflection) and, to the extent that there is not always a correlation in one noetic–noematic direction, reversibility is possible. This is precisely what Hegel will say: consciousness is this reversibility, this exchange. (In Husserl, intentionality also has this meaning[52].)

THE MEASURED AND THE STANDARD OF MEASUREMENT [*Mesuré et mesurant*]

A knowledge, which turns out, in fact, to be knowledge, is put to the test (*Prüfung*) that is, a standard of measurement which is essential or 'in itself,' is applied to it. From where can the standard be taken? Answer: it is already in consciousness.

The relation to 'something' [*etwas*] is for 'consciousness.' The being of 'something' for consciousness (*für ein anderes*) [is] 'knowledge.' But this something is also thought as outside of this relationship to consciousness, i.e. as 'truth' or 'being-in-itself.' When the philosopher questions himself about the truth of 'knowledge,' about the 'in itself' of 'knowledge,' we will obtain nothing but its 'being for us.' The enterprise appears absurd. These are our measures which we apply to our 'knowledge'; and perhaps our 'knowledge' declines to judge them. But philosophy is possible because the object to which we are applying ourselves here is consciousness, and because this object is identical with our measures. The consciousness which we take from 'knowledge' and from its truth cannot deform it because, in this case, consciousness is acquainted with consciousness. 'Since consciousness provides itself with its own standard, the investigation will be a comparison of consciousness with its own self.' The standard of measurement is not external to what is measured. Consciousness comprehends the being-for-another of knowledge as consciousness itself. The fact that, by reflecting on 'knowledge,' consciousness makes it a being-for-another does not diminish its value, since this being-for-another is consciousness.

Here the dichotomy 'knowledge' – 'in itself' is dissolved and the 'knowledge' of philosophy rejoins the 'in itself,' because it is the 'in itself' of 'knowledge.' Reflection is a return to the unreflected.[53] In Hegel, if one calls 'concept' the 'knowledge,' and 'truth' or 'essence' the object, then the object is the proof of the concept. Consciousness is not detached from its object by this structure since the object is restricted to presenting itself as having a view 'for consciousness,' but one which the object could dispute. For consciousness is its relation to the object – and the proof of their correspondence is part of the definition of consciousness. In other words, one could equally well reverse the situation by calling 'concept' the essence or the in-itself under consideration (the 'knowledge' which I strive to evaluate), and by calling the object this 'knowledge' in that I examine it and in that it becomes in that way 'for an other.' Thus the concept is proof of the object.

> We see clearly that both are the same; but what is essential is to retain for the whole investigation the fact that the two moments, *Concept and Object, being-for-another* and *being-for-itself*, themselves fall within the knowledge which we are studying. We therefore do not need to bring along standards or to apply our preconceived ideas and thoughts throughout the entire course of the investigation. On the contrary, in leaving them along the way, we come to examine them as the thing is in-itself and for-itself. (*Holz*, p. 114; trans., p. 21)[54]

The exchange between the standard of measurement and the measured, in reflection, creates a situation in which the object measures the subject as much as the subject measures the object, and one in which we are therefore at the absolute.

The narrow relationship between phenomenology and philosophy is self-confirming. Even the structure of consciousness is such that:

1 absolute knowledge is available to us (with respect to knowledge, there is not relativity in one's comprehension of oneself); and
2 absolute knowledge in a sense precedes itself, since the measured is also the standard of measurement.

Thus the notion of the phenomenon as neither object nor subject – as mind appearing, for-itself seen by another – turns out to be from the outside, and must be taken as it *presents* itself. [This notion] which is itself bound up with the true structure of consciousness, – a reversibility of measured standard of measurement which makes the apprenticeship of consciousness and the appearance of knowledge possible – leads immediately to a relation with the absolute.

4 *Subject–object relativization.* – *They are both 'for the same'* [für dasselbe]. – *Consciousness is* ek-stasis.

PARAGRAPHS 13 AND 14

para. 13: We cannot even say that a distinct act of comparison has been added to 'consciousness,' for it is consciousness of both the object and itself and the split between the two. Consciousness itself and the object are 'for the same.' Consciousness conceals any reference to the 'back' of the object, and to the sides where the object escapes it. One doesn't even have to say that consciousness rectifies its 'knowledge' according to the object. The object precisely as object was exactly correlative to 'knowledge' and when 'knowledge' changes, the object also becomes another. In truth, consciousness goes to test the object (the standard of measurement) by knowledge (what is measured), just as much as the measured is tested by the standard. Consciousness, the true progress of knowledge, does not consist in the external comparison of the two terms, but in the 'mutual encroachment' [*Ineinander*] of object–knowledge, noeses–noemata, which give birth to each other. (Cf. Lévi-Strauss's double critique, – and in general the relationship between objects and research.)[55] Therefore, the idea of consciousness is not a 'meaning-giving act' [*Sinngebung*], but an adequateness in the manifestation – philosophy [is] 'pure vision' [*reine Zusehen*].

para. 14: This movement (which is internal to consciousness) is 'dialectical,' in the sense of reciprocal action, transition of one into the other, 'being-for-another', and therefore a movement which starts itself again. This dialectic is linked to the structure of consciousness. It is 'experience' [*Erfahrung*] in the sense of someone's experience, for example, in the course of which the object and knowledge modify one another. The dialectic is a movement of content, its opening onto . . . its truth, is without any contribution from us. This is only possible when the dialectic has the phenomenon as its base. Because it is 'experience', the contact with something which can reveal itself remains latent. Therefore it can give rise to *ek-stasis*.[56]

An ambiguity of the true: the in-itself becomes in-itself-for-us, that is, object-subject. The progress of 'knowledge' is a surging of a new object. The ambiguity is essential to the dialectic and the 'experience' for the object passes into the subject and conversely. There is no immanence; there is truly apprenticeship. – 'experience' is a solution to the dilemma: either one knows or one does not know.

The movement seems certainly not to be connected with consciousness in the sense of immanence, but rather with consciousness as this same consciousness *for which* the in-itself and the in-itself-for-itself exist simultaneously. It is certainly not connected with the 'meaning-giving act' [by a subject]*, but with consciousness as the identity of savage consciousness and reflected consciousness. The movement comes from the content, but from the content inasmuch as there is 'experience.' To put dialectic back 'on its feet' again would be to destroy it. Philosophy seems to have entered into the phenomena. But then there is para. 15.

V

February 20, 1961
Reread the translation of para. 13.

COMMENTARY

The development 'consciousness'-knowledge, the 'knowledge making its appearance' or the 'knowledge' that 'comes forward' operates without any contribution or addition from us (philosophers). This occurs not only because consciousness is a comparison of the self with the self (as stated in *Holz*, p. 113; trans., p. 20), and does not receive its standard of measurement from the outside ('provides itself with its own measure'). This could be the banal theme of immanence, where we ask only those questions which we can resolve. The interrogation is the contrary of an affirmation in the process of determining itself; the battle is a victory; there is an underestimation of the investigation; dogmatism. But for a more profound reason, there is not even any comparison, since the self puts the self to the test, but as pure vision, *reine Zusehen*. It is truly a self-presentation of 'knowledge,' and not a 'meaning-giving act' by us.

For it is not necessary to imagine consciousness either as a relation to the pure exterior, or as a pure relation to the self, or as the summation of the two (consciousness of the true plus consciousness of the knowledge of the true). Consciousness is the third and unique aspect for which the first two (the true and knowledge of the true) are distinguished by abstraction. This means that there is no true and no knowledge of the true. There is only one single term, and a second which is the same, and a third term, which is: openness onto . . ., examination of the self in the presence of. . . . An openness before that which was knowledge can become an object, and that which was true can be restored to the level of simple 'knowledge'. Consciousness must not be thought alternatively as a relation to the self and a relation to another, but as the locus of a single explosion which produces selfness and consciousness of something. Consciousness serves neither as positive nor as negative, but as negativity at work – thus one cannot truly speak of consciousness as either an entity or as a *négatité*.[57]

If that is achieved, we escape from the banality of immanence. The immanentist objection is that the reference to the true in-itself is illusory; consciousness can only aspire to that which *is* in-itself *to it*. Consciousness cannot go behind the object that offers itself. It tries to catch a glimpse of the object itself. But since consciousness cannot comprehend my old sport jacket as it is in my absence, consciousness cannot go behind itself as an appearance of the 'phenomenon making its appearance'. [Thus], there is no knowledge where one could compare the self with the self, [since] all objects would be relativized into knowledge. This would be true of all knowledge, even knowledge of future objects. Hegel rejects this objection. If the immanentist were right, there would be no consciousness at all. Never would the words 'in itself' or being-in-itself, 'knowledge' or being-for-consciousness have any meaning for us. From the moment that there is consciousness ('already in the fact that consciousness knows an object at all' (*Holz*, p. 114; trans., p. 23), there is a meaning for the in-itself, or the true, and a meaning for being-for-consciousness, or knowledge. The truth is not that there is only knowledge or that there is only the in-itself or the object, but that there is the one and the other is a kind of precession, or gravitation, exchange or reversibility.

We could ask ourselves if we are not, in that way, both 'consciousness' and 'self-consciousness,' two abstractions that designate the two sides of 'the same' [*dasselbe*]. The Self (and philosophy) is neither receptivity, nor 'meaning-giving act' ('our contribution'), but the spontaneous articulation of a 'pure vision.'

End of para. 13: what has happened to the self's 'putting itself to the test' or the self's placing itself in question?

How does consciousness learn something? This seems to occur either in the reception of the object (but then how does it search [for the object]) or else by reminiscence and contribution of itself (but then how is it ignorant [of the object]?). It seems that the solution is either to deny knowledge or to deny non-knowledge.

A relation to an external transcendent [object] or, on the contrary, a relation to an immanence (philosophical dogmatism) are, in reality, equivalent. We must not say: I learn by changing my knowledge to conform with the object; nor must we say: I learn by elucidating a knowledge which corrects the object. The truth is that I form my knowledge according to the object, and I model the object according to knowledge, because there is no knowledge that is purely knowledge nor any object that is purely an object. [Consciousness is]* neither the subject nor the object, but the work of one against the other. For example, the minute that I 'correct' my knowledge according to the object, the object is also changed. The change deposits a layer of disillusionment in the object, even if it is the object which teaches that suddenly it is not the same as it was a while ago. Compare this to when I learn the truth about someone after coming to know him. The change in my knowledge is also a change in the object, since this enemy today is no longer my friend of yesterday. It would be false to say that the friend of yesterday is the enemy today or that my friendship has given way to hatred. What is excluded is not annulled, not even in the object. There is no absolute error. Essence does not substitute for appearance. Appearance becomes essence and the true is what 'has been' or 'has occurred' [*ist gewesen*]. It is essential to 'knowledge' to be 'knowledge making its appearance'.

Thus, the phenomenological theme (*erscheinende Wissen*, the blossoming of knowledge) seems to imply an overthrowing of philosophy. There is no absolute *Ansich*, and no absolute *für uns*, for the same reasons, i.e. their reciprocal relativization, their 'mutual intertwining' [*Ineinander*]. This means that the very dimension of the absolute is to conceive in a fashion other than the way philosophy has done until now. The absolute is neither 'free' knowledge (that is, without attachments, without an outside, without adherence to the in-itself), nor 'free' object (that is, purely an object, without adherence to knowledge), but the *Ineinander* of the two. The (ultimate) formula: 'the absolute is the subject' does not mean that there is only a subject. The 'free' is freedom of the free and the related. The absolute is the 'sameness' of the absolute and the relative. The true subject is the subjectivity of the subject and the object. There is an absolute 'lifeless' and 'alone' which is not the absolute. True philosophy does not go 'behind': behind the 'appearance' and behind the one which is in the world. Philosophy cannot conceive the absolute except as the other side of the 'appearance' or the phenomenon.

WHENCE PARA. 14

Translate para. 14 – Of major importance [is]:

1 What we call dialectic. – Its activity is a movement which consciousness exercises on itself. The reaction of 'knowledge' on the object and of the object on 'knowledge' is the metamorphosis of one into the other. Thus we have self-movement which is consistent with the structure of *ek-stasis*. Its product is the movement which makes the new true object 'surge forth.' Surging forth implies discontinuity, 'pure vision' and not 'our contribution'. It is a newness created by the surpassing, but a surging forth which con-firms [*a-vère*] what preceded, and which therefore has its cohesion and its 'necessity,' i.e. reason and knowledge. The subject has become object and vice versa or they have exchanged places.

2 Dialectic understood in this way is 'experience', that is, a relation to the being which is pre-objective, a relation to a being in which we are *begriffen* (*Holz*, p. 116; trans., p. 25),

i.e. taken or thought. To think the other is to be thought by him.

Why must dialectic be 'experience'? Because it is not 'our contribution' or 'meaning-giving act,' but only 'for us'; because it is the self-movement of the preobjective and presubjective content; because it is *reine Zusehen*, vision, 'knowledge making its appearance' inside an outside, a 'related' inside; and because it would be nothing of the sort if it were immanence. Between immanence and the relation to an external transcendent, horizon and richness, the fecundity of a content is not a dried up *object*.

3 Dialectic understood in this way is 'ambiguity' [*Zweideutig-keit*]. This must be understood if the 'the scientific side' of the 'presentation' that follows (from the phenomenon) is to be placed in a new 'light.' A new idea of light is at work here. The true is of itself 'ambiguous', for it must be 'essence' or 'in-itself' and cannot be such while it is 'for the consciousness of the in-itself,' that is, not 'in-itself.' (Compare this with Kierkegaard's pharisaism: from the moment that I say that I am Christian, I am no longer what I say I am).[58] The 'polysemy' [*Vieldeutigkeit*][59] is not a shadow to eliminate true light. The true cannot be defined as coincidence and outside of all difference [*écart*] in relation to the true. All relation to an 'in-itself' (the first object) includes an inevitable relation in which this 'in-itself' is for me and destroys the first object. This 'in-itself' transforms the first object into a second one. But one would say that this is not a second object. Only the reflection of consciousness on itself adds to the object my knowledge of it. The limits of the subjective and the objective remain well defined. Yet this 'reflection' becomes the 'true,' the truth of the first openness onto an object, and, in this respect, the essence as opposed to the appearance, – the object. In determining the state of my knowledge, the state of the object (the state of the motives for my naive experience), I integrate these motives into the domain of the object. I annul the first object as something abstract, and I bring about a new object. Hegel says that this is 'the experience produced by that first object' (*Holz*, p. 115; trans., p. 24). An 'experience' [signifies] this incorporation of an object. Because the experience incorporates the object most, the object works on the experience

40

('through it' – an understanding which is not distinct from our being). As such it is generative of truth, of an object to the second power, an object of the object, a truth of the truth.[60] Truth and knowledge are inseparable from a reciprocal 'concept' [*Begriff*] where the object 'comprehends' [*begreift*] me no less than I do it.[61] – Philosophy is inseparable from the phenomenon. (Compare this to modern phenomenology and the discovery of latent or operant intentionality, including the reversal of the relation to the self and the relation to the other. It is not only the uni-directionality of noesis–noema.)

It seems that dialectic is certainly not a fact of consciousness in the sense of a spiritual motive, – for then it would be 'our contribution.' But it is also not an objective movement (and for the same reason). Dialectic is a *movement of content*, that is, of our new ontological milieu, which is the 'experience' and which does not occur without a relationship to someone who experiences. [Dialectic] is not a property of consciousness, rather consciousness is the property of dialectic. Dialectic has consciousness. (It appears unthinkable without consciousness, for the production of the new object occurs through consciousness, – but it is an opaque consciousness, i.e. experience).[62] To 'put it back on its feet again' would be to destroy the 'presentation' of science, of productivity. When Marx says this, does he misunderstand Hegel? No, Hegel himself also said that dialectic is the world stood on its head.

LITERAL COMMENTARY ON PARAGRAPHS 15 AND 16

para. 15: The experience which Hegel discusses here [is not] experience as it is commonly understood. As commonly understood, experience externally and accidentally finds the new object that devalues the old. In our sense, on the contrary, the knowledge of the old object becomes the new object. For example, what I projected about this friendship, once projected before me in the object, becomes the truth of this friendship. Now this presupposes an *Umkehrung* (reversal, conversion) of consciousness. The object becomes subject and vice versa. There was mystification; there is demystification. I was walking on my head; I now stand erect on my feet. How is this possible?

The philosopher must be supplying something (*unsere Zutat*) which guides the experience towards its truth.

If there is to be philosophy and not skepticism, past experience must not fall into the nothingness, the present must be a result and the truth of the past, what was in-itself and what has become being for consciousness, no matter what this thing may constitute, must be the new object, and necessity must be the genesis of it. Whence, [we encounter]* the disjunction between consciousness 'comprehended' [*begriffen*] in experience and philosophy which 'comprehends' [*begreift*] the becoming. Human experience is only the content; – philosophy is only 'the form'. But then, from the philosophical point of view, the path towards science is already science, and the experience of consciousness is only the content of this science. Is this not a reversal of the *pro* to the *con* in relation to what precedes? – 'Our contribution' – Why pass through phenomenology if the goal is a science which hangs over experience (as 'the form' hangs over the 'content'). [Whence] Logic. – For Heidegger the genetive 'science of experience' [*Wissenschaft der Erfahrung*] is neither objective nor subjective. It is speculative, dialectic, that is, the chiasm of the two movements.

The answer[63]: phenomenology contains all of mind, but under a particular determination. The moments [of each determination] are not 'pure.' Rather they are as they are for consciousness (*Bewusstsein*) or in that they are terms of reference from consciousness, such that they are 'figures of consciousness' [*Gestalten des Bewusstseins*]. The consciousness which considers them feels itself linked to another, an external world, in which 'knowledge' is not quite what appears. Then comes a point where the 'figure' is entirely included, where it comprehends itself, where what appears regains its center, where the phenomenon passes into the absolute and shows the nature of the absolute.

This means that there is something other than consciousness of the external world. However nothing is outside of 'consciousness'. This something other is attained when 'consciousness' is equal to its outside, when it coincides with knowledge of itself. This self-knowledge is not the attribute or property of consciousness. No such property or attribute pertains to that which has self-knowledge and which turns out to start only from self-knowledge. For the same reason (necessity, continuity, conservation of the truth of the past), experience must be a 'concept', but 'concept' must be experience. – The equilibrium of 1807.[64]

GENERAL COMMENTARY ON PHILOSOPHY AND NON-PHILOSOPHY

Phenomenology poses the problem of a consciousness that understands itself. [Such a consciousness has]* two sides: on the one hand, there is discontinuous, skeptical experience; and on the other hand, experience which is only for the form and in which the standard of measurement is never put to the test.

Philosophy was defined in 1807 as this double critique of experience by the concept and the concept by experience. We exclude impressionism and dogmatism. – But these dangers exist to the second power:

1 One has recourse to experience as dogmatism (a judgment of history – the facts show that. . ., I did not say it, the things did. Consider, for example, the 1937 trials).[65]

2 One has recourse to the concept as skepticism (*I think that* this experience is absolute – *that* I have attained the essence there – that 1937 [is] history in its nakedness). But can any such experience coincide with the essence? A consciousness that is truly consciousness of itself is empty – 'nothing' – All full consciousness is related.

Phenomenology and logic represent these two dangers. There is no solution as long as we remain at the antithesis: subject–object or consciousness of the external world–consciousness of the self. Hegel has surpassed this antithesis for a moment in his analysis of the Third Term. But he re-establishes the 'contribution' of philosophy. Therefore his very recourse to the phenomenon is the most violent dogmatism. The others no longer know what they think. The philosopher understands them better than they understand themselves.

In that respect, he aggravates the situation. His successors will protest against his dogmatism (Kierkegaard and Marx), and against his skepticism or his conciliation (Marx and Kierkegaard). He necessarily collapses the 'alienation' [*Entäusserung*].[66] He takes the bourgeois state for the State. He takes established religion for the truth, – *praxis* must be absolute. But these philosophers as well, in their opposition to Hegel, have the same oscillation between dogmatism and skepticism. The problem of a philosophy which *might be* non-philosophy remains *in toto* as long as one thinks *consciousness* or 'object' [*Gegenstand*].[67]

VI

Lecture of March 6, 1961

We have shown that only the truth is absolute. The true: only that which turns out to be (work, becoming, experience) is absolute. There is no external relationship with the absolute, no instrumental means of joining it. There is no introduction to the absolute: we are there.

There is only a manifestation (*Erscheinung, Offenbarung*) of the Free, of identity with the self, of 'knowledge,' of science in the Cartesian sense, of certitude. The manifestation is the externality of 'knowledge making its appearance' and 'knowledge.' But this exteriority is not an accident of 'knowledge.' The 'ambiguity' is not to be understood 'as a lack of univocity, but as a characteristic of consciousness in its essential unity' (*Holz*, p. 155; trans., p. 95).[68] Consciousness is equivocal, not in the skeptical sense, but because it is a reversal (*Umkehrung*) (derived from its 'perversity' [*Verkehrtheit*]), because in this movement, concept and in-itself exchange their roles and the truth manifests itself, because consciousness becomes what it is, i.e. its concept. The concept makes the free, delivered *sense* (the 'as,' the being of what is) appear.[69] As long as consciousness is 'consciousness,' it 'does not accept the "as" ' (*Holz*, p. 160; trans., p. 104). It carries a horizon or a 'background' [*Hintergrund*] which it has not explored. In order that it become itself, consciousness must tear itself away (*Zerrissenheit*): 'a mended stocking is better than a torn one; not so with self-consciousness' (*Holz*, p. 127; trans., p. 44).

But this tearing is its realization –

the presentation of appearing knowledge is not a path travelled by natural consciousness. But it is also not a way which distances itself gradually from natural consciousness in order to close itself off, at a determined point along the way, somewhere in absolute knowledge. This presentation

is none the less a path. However, it instantly moves 'in-
between' here and there, opening itself up between natural
consciousness and science. (*Holz*, p. 132; trans., p. 53)

'If one were able to speak even here of a pathway, then the
absolute only departs from the path to the extent that it *is* the
way' (*Holz*, p. 151; trans., p. 85).

It is essential to the absolute that it include this self-presentation, for self-presentation is the living truth, experience which
gives the absolute-subject life. 'The representation of the object
represents the object, although this fact is not grasped in
thought' (*Holz*, p. 163; trans., p. 108). Since it is preontological,
natural consciousness aims at going beyond the 'object' [*Gegenstand*] (but for Hegel, it will not discover 'what is distinguished
in the distinguishing' [*Holz*, p. 153; trans., p. 90] except on the
side of the 'subject'). – 'Experience [is] the word of Being' –
'the name of the Being of that which is' (*Holz*, p. 166; trans.,
pp. 113–14); the new object is 'the truth of the true being of
what is, the appearing of appearing things' (*Holz*, p. 170; trans.,
p. 120); it is experience itself. Here Hegel approaches the
surpassing of subject–object. (The Third Term, 'for the same,'
includes the 'in-itself' and the 'for us' and thus beyond.) –
'Experience' is therefore 'the existence of the absolute' (*Holz*,
p. 171; trans., p. 122). 'Experience is the Being of that which is'
(*Holz*, p. 175; trans., p. 130). Phenomenology [?] in the kingdom
of the mind. Phenomenology and science are 'the same'
(included in 'the same') (*Holz*, p. 179; trans., p. 136). *Wissenschaft der Erfahrung des Bewusstseins*[70]: the genitives are subjects
as much as objects, the reversal indicates the dual relationship
of 'that which is' and 'Being,' a dual relationship which 'opens'
(*Holz*, p. 182; trans., p. 140) onto Being – dialectical-speculative
genitives. – 'Phenomenology itself is Being, according to whose
mode the Absolute is with us in and for itself' (*Holz*, p. 187;
trans., p. 148). This mode of Being according to which the
absolute is beside us in and for itself has a need to avoid being
alone and 'lifeless.' – 'For man there is no introduction to the
Being of that which is, because man's nature, his life, led in the
accompaniment of Being, *is* itself that accompaniment' (*Holz*,
p. 189; trans., p. 150). Natural consciousness was not introduced into the absolute, it is there. Its only obligation is to

recognize the constitutive 'perversity' [*Verkehrtheit*], which 'we, in this experience, may also be what our Being *is*' (*Holz*, p. 190; trans., pp. 151–2).

All this is in the text. True philosophy is non-philosophy, – which is to enter into the profundity of 'experience' [*Erfahrung*].

But the absolute is also true. The absolute alone is true. Nothing that is related is true. No consciousness of the external world is true. No 'figure' is true.

Experience in the ordinary sense [is] an external encounter of a new object with a forgetting of the former – [whence] skepticism. The second object is not an interiorization of the first object; rather it is – a 'pure comprehension' of what is in and for itself. For example, mastery (and its complications) disappear. [Whence] the truth of slaves, stoicism, Christianity. – To move from there to metaphysical experience, a conversion is necessary. This conversion is a reversal by which what was 'for me' is objectivity. What was 'in itself' is subjectivity. Otherwise consciousness makes itself into a 'figure.'[71]

Now, in the eyes of consciousness, this is not taken into experience. There is a disjunction between lived 'content' and its 'form' or 'pure originating' or becoming. Slaves do not know that they make the future and surpass the master.

In short, experience [is] necessary, but not sufficient. Experience must be understood – which requires 'conversion' or 'reversal.' – The ground of natural consciousness is in reality the 'foreground of light' (*Holz*, p. 164; trans., p. 113). To convert this ground into a figure, truly to know what 'appears,' the 'self-manifestation' of the 'appearance' or the 'appearance' of the 'appearing,' is the contribution of the philosophical gaze that transforms into a 'for us' (philosophers) what is in itself a consciousness in relation.

But there seems to be a dilemma here: either experience is truly assumed and is errant, skeptical; or it is understood, transformed into its truth, but then surpassed. The claim that experience introduces itself at this second order is the greatest dogmatism; for this is a dogmatism disguised in the movement of things.[72]

Read text para. 16.

HEGEL'S SOLUTION

But where will the philosopher establish external standards of measurement for experience? He does not contribute anything; his contribution is precisely the renunciation of all contribution so that the 'appearance' of the 'appearing' will show itself (*Holz*, p. 174; trans., p. 127). We have said that no consciousness was cut off from this reverse side of things, which the philosopher sees. What is 'behind the back' of consciousness is only that the true characters in the drama are not the 'figures' among which it plays, but the moments of a unique Self. Experience itself metamorphoses itself into absolute knowledge. Phenomenology eliminates itself and the 'presentation' interiorizes itself. Simply from the fact that the *point* where experience attains this level is defined by coincidence, the philosopher reveals himself

1 as allowing an understanding of himself and all the rest,
2 as not a local event in the middle of everything,
3 as rather always having been in another mode of Being, and
4 as even giving reasons for his becoming.

The relationship of envelopment, however, remains reciprocal. The 'reversal' is in the nature of consciousness. The moments of the truth of Mind are in experience, not in a *pure* (*reine*) state, but as in a mirror: 'as they are for consciousness (in the eyes of this consciousness of the external world, in the face of an external 'presentation') or as this consciousness arises in relation to them.' With phenomenology, structures of consciousness of the external world appear and create the dialectical movement in consciousness without knowing exactly why, – without taking possession of its own reversal, of its own chiasm, of the autogenetic movement that traverses it. But this movement (which is consciousness) *pushes* consciousness toward its true Existence (that is, toward its existence as revealed to itself). At a certain point, it knows that it is not consciousness of an *external world*, that it is conscious of itself, that the 'presentation' is a presentation of self to itself, that 'appearance' [*Erscheinung*] is equivalent to 'essence' [*Wesen*], to the thing itself, and therefore that it coincides with the same point of knowledge appropriate to Mind. Thus consciousness 'designates' absolute knowledge. The absolute is not therefore the object to be contemplated before itself or before the philosopher; when it was that, it was no more than the mind-phenomenon. This mind-phenomenon perceives that it is mind in and for itself. From the fact that the meaning of experience and its truth is, in the end, only the full identity of the Self, and from the fact that the secret of things is simply that Being is the Self (the 'formal,' i.e. structural, secret, which all experience confines in what is ontological), one could say that the philosopher does not reveal this secret to mankind, that it is also latent in humans, and that it receives its rigorous, naked, direct, (*and ordinarily retrospective*) formulation from the philosopher. In the same way, we can say that all men, except the philosopher, are in error, and that they are all in the same truth as he is. The philosophical 'meaning-giving act'[73] does not go to any other source than the very form of experience, which emerges when consciousness puts down its presumed intentionality, in order to discover *itself* as that which it sought, and at the same time, as absolute.

The Hegelian absolute (what the philosopher sees behind the back of consciousness taken in experience) is of such a nature (the pure core of the Self, which tears itself away, which does not have *its own* Concepts or Ideas, which however does have the Ideas and the Concepts that we all have, and which, once it is seen from the outside, in the object, is what we hold before our eyes as the 'figures' of the mind-phenomenon), that one cannot understand it as *behind the back* of consciousness occupied with their own experience. The Hegelian absolute is in their hearts and in their reports. The 'divine universal man' as an 'element' (Hyppolite), in which self-consciousness of the absolute is possible, is not the external consciousness of the 'divine universal man.'

Without the rest, this Hegelian absolute, which is complete nothingness, would be 'lifeless' and 'alone'. Therefore it is not to be thought separately – 'The mode of Hegelian thought itself . . . this circularity of thought or this finality of the self.'[74] – 'The true is the self's becoming, the circle which presupposes and which has, at the beginning, its own end as its goal and which is only effective by means of its developed actualization and by means of its end.'[75] Thinking the absolute is not only thinking the absolute but also everything else and again the absolute from everything else, and so forth. The circle is constituted by what there is. Furthermore, it is true at the same time that

1 phenomenology encompasses everything; and
2 everything is affected by an indication of externality, since consciousness is in the process of conquering it.

Consequently, besides phenomenology, there will be a system of 'science', specifically Logic. Logic is Hegel's metaphysics, where discontinuous experience is surpassed,[76] where truth develops in itself and for itself. – One could say that Logic is 'the presentation of God as it is in its external essence before the creation of Nature and a finite mind.'[77] – But Hegel does not accept the creation; this is thus his way of saying that logic is abstract, a methodical abstraction. In fact, at first it is objective (Being, Essence) and then subjective (Concept); it encompasses therefore the Self-Being distinction. – 'Self-certainty is *immanent* in truth.'[78] Logic presumes the phenomenology which has shown that Self and Being are identical.[79] Inversely, it presumes the absolute-subject in order to place the genesis of experience in perspective. In 1807, while having phenomenology open onto 'science', Hegel conceives their relationships as circular. In 1802, he had said, 'the world of philosophy in itself and for itself is an inverted world' – 'Natural consciousness immediately entrusts itself to science. It is a new effort for natural consciousness to walk on its head, which it does without knowing what impels it to do so.'[80] For science, ontic consciousness is the inverse of itself. – 'Phenomenology' is created in order to transform one into the other. It is not, therefore, a simple reference to an external regulation of logic, by which consciousness will walk on its head. (Hegel 1807, no more than Marx, would not want to 'walk on his head.' He sees that better than Marx, for the head is the *Object* as well.) One could say that this circular solution is ambiguous (*Vieldeutig*) with a conscious ambiguity which has no lack of univocity. In *Phenomenology*: 'man kills his own death and is uprooted by the absolute – the absolute separates out death' – 'God is dead. This means everything except "there is no God" ' (*Holz*, p. 186; trans., p. 147).[81]

Is the Hegelian solution stable? Or is there a good ambiguity? Doesn't the solution always move toward the equivocal? It was not so with Hegel. In the first edition, the fragment which is translated without a title is subsequently called the 'Introduction.' Hegel himself no longer holds the view that there is no 'introduction' to the phenomenology of mind, which *is* the presence of the absolute. In 1817, at the time of the *Encyclopedia*, phenomenology again becomes a discipline, i.e. a part of science. It can no longer be 'the whole of the system from a certain point of view' (Hyppolite). In 1807, a relationship of *Ineinander*, a concentric condition, a reciprocal envelopment, then gives way to the enveloping thought of the 'positively rational' – or of the speculative.

'Identity of identity and identity of non-identity' eventually subordinates *difference*. This is inevitable as soon as [the difference]* ceases being experience and becomes *signification*, something spoken (oldness),[82] that is, as soon as it ceases reconsidering itself, thinking itself as encompassed by an englobing: the present vertical world. At this point it is presumed to have totalized, included *everything*, surpassed *everything*.

The risk implies a return to skepticism, to dogmatism, – or rather to the two.

The absolute [can be]* considered as expressing itself on the same account in everything that is, 'the enduring' (because what is, is all that can be). Thus the bourgeois State and established religion are thought as an expression of the absolute, which they obviously are, but in [connection?] with another future. – Hegelian reconciliation: the worst stupidities are treated as historical barriers, because that is what they are. The absolute empties itself, becomes indifference and pure conservation, because its tie with the vertical world of experience is released. We repress this skeptico-dogmatism in the name of a nominal absolute. The absolute is practically the empty 'nothing' of skeptics, and the world is practically the positivity of all that 'endures' while in 1807 the negative was at work.

I have said that the movement of experience to things spoken is inevitable. But this means that in a sense philosophy negates itself in formulating itself (what Kierkegaard will call Pharisaism)[83]; at least this occurs when philosophy converts itself into contemplated significations. – The dissociation: 'the enduring' – the empty absolute, the disjunction in the order of phenomena was inevitable with a philosophy which remained a philosophy of consciousness, of representation and of the 'subject'. – Hegel admirably deepened these notions, made them supple, showing the paradoxical relationships between consciousness and the object and its metamorphoses. But in conserving the relation to the Self and the relation to the external world, he could not avoid the fact that the double envelopment was equivocal, and that the fissure appears at the level which phenomena must seal. Perhaps it is here that Hegel has not succeeded in his desire to link philosophy and non-philosophy.

Will Marx succeed better? If one accepts this appreciation of Hegel, the perspective in which he is placed here, it is to be feared that Marx will not succeed any better. As Kierkegaard claims to have experienced with the present age against the established State and established religion, Marx reopens the vertical world onto the future, but he does not interrogate Hegel about what truly caused the ruin of the enterprise. What Marx questions was not necessarily responsible for the dislocation. In terms of this misunderstanding, he picks up certain mistakes that Hegel made, sometimes reproducing Hegel poorly.

VII

March 13

The alternative is that experience or enveloping thought does not exist in principle. Moreover clarity is not placed on experience. Experience itself demands the reversal which makes it true. Inversely, what does absolute knowledge know? That all 'figures of consciousness' are 'self-consciousness'? But it knows this only by experience and on the way. The truth is that which has become. The 'end' and the 'means' are interdependent, – the end is the integral of the different experiences. The expression: 'there is self-consciousness' has no meaning, if not as a totalization of this movement. And the totalization must also appear. – Therefore the truth is not *only*: there is 'self-consciousness',[84] but also there is 'self-consciousness' appearing in that which is other than itself and which *is* only in revealing itself there. – To submit experience to an external regulation (to a 'meaning-giving act' by a 'self-consciousness for us', for a philosopher who will identify with God, or – what turns out to be the same – with a process in itself behind experience, 'in-itself') will be to walk on one's head. By definition, the Hegelian absolute is In and For-itself. It is neither on the side of the In-itself, nor on the side of the For-itself, as they present themselves on the level of 'consciousness' (that is, at the same time correlative and destructive of one another). If it is truly In-itself/For-itself and not the pursuit of the In-itself by the For-itself, a movement from one to the other, it is such only in the context of experience. It is the limb and face of experience, the manifestation of the intimacy of the one and the other which 'consciousness' never succeeds in attaining. In the movement of experience, which brings understanding, we reach the absolute which is not something behind it or under it, but which is a water-mark within it and which exists only as a water-mark.[85] The negativity of the *Phenomenology of Spirit*, which does not reappear again in the same role in subsequent writings, is a negativity which works, which is negativity only when it is in practice and which eliminates the immanence–transcendence alternative in philosophy. Philosophy is the recognition of this negativity which is only a negativity when at work, that is, when in contact with the Being which it sets to work.

The rigorous solution – should we even say solution, that is, the end of interrogation by a positive response?

The 'ambiguity' of consciousness is not eliminated by the experience which reveals its 'perversity' [*Verkehrtheit*] and which realizes the 'reversal' [*Umkehrung*]; for the external cannot be eliminated. The absolute knowledge which I have become remains a 'figure of consciousness' and does not reabsorb itself as such. Hence it never ceases to be 'consciousness'. – In this respect, there is no 'definitive recovery.'

Ambiguity is not a lack of univocity. Ambiguity is 'good.'[86] This poses no problems if 'ambiguity' is present as such. Here the absolute appears as the light of truth which penetrates the thickness of experience, and which unites the relativized subject and other. But if it is formulated in terms of 'consciousness', it is equivocal.

In truth, we have experience of knowledge and knowledge of experience. These two faces of ambiguity are abstractions. The absolute is that which is between the two: the transformation of one into the other. But this cannot be maintained except in contact with experience, with the 'vertical' world (of which the absolute is its 'profundity').[87] The very formulation of this living 'ambiguity' makes experience disappear. The formulation transforms it into something said, into the positive, and makes the negative disappear in the 1807 sense — it restores the truth of identity. The Hegelian philosophy of 1807 (like Kierkegaard's Christianity)[88] excludes the utterance. Once uttered, it returns to identity.[89] Speculation separates itself from dialectic, that is, the absolute [is] conceived as absolute negation or as absolute affirmation [*position*] (the 'positively rational' in *The Encyclopedia*). In any case, the absolute is taken as thinkable separately: whence, skepticism (the empty 'nothing') and dogmatism ('enduring' is entirely positive). Here we have a mixture of indifference and conservatism. The bourgeois State and established religion are thought to be the only expressions of the absolute. Experience is localized. The Hegelian reconciliation would then be that there is no more living communication between the absolute and history.

The conclusion:

1 Either, if consciousness protects its rights, if it falls back into abstract positivism or negativism, and if it creates a disjunction at the level of phenomena (the *Phenomenology* becoming a part of science again, and our text becoming an 'Introduction'), then one no longer has 'the whole system from a certain point of view' (Hyppolite) – ; or

2 philosophy can be left unformulated;

in any case philosophy is whatever succeeds in passing for a notion of consciousness.

Have others succeeded better than Hegel in maintaining the link between philosophy and experience?

Marx certainly had every intention of doing so (in the early manuscripts of 1843–4). He reactivated the philosophy of right. But in the end did he do so? What he criticizes in Hegel includes: the theoretical attitude, the exhaustibility of philosophy, the return to phenomenology, *praxis* contra *theoria*, the search for a thought-action which does not have the positivity of all thought, the *profane* character of all action, and the exteriority of all action. (Marx therefore remains faithful to the negativity of 1807.) Fine, but then Nature (a dead end) also returns to the 'reversal' of Hegel's dialectic. A return to the object. Now, to get there, he must make use of the Hegelian Concept, of Hegel's Logic. At the moment that he believes he has inverted Hegel, he takes up the Hegelian mode of thought (applied to the analysis in *Capital* where the self-destruction of all 'enduring' is inscribed). What transpires then is a polemic against idealism, accompanied by a counter-idealism and a return to Hegel's logic.

PART TWO: MARX[90]

March 20, 1961

The texts to be considered are the 'Introduction' to *A Contribution to the Critique of Hegel's Philosophy of Right* (which was written in 1843 for the *Franco-German Yearbooks*) and the *Economic and Philosophical Manuscripts of 1844*.[91]

Before translating the text, we must indicate:

1 why we are studying it;
2 what questions we must ask about it (particularly in relation to our problem of 'Philosophy–Non-Philosophy') and;
3 how and in what terms can this Hegelian problem also be addressed to Marx.

The Hegelian Marx (the 'Young Hegelian') was associated with the movement to *reform* Hegelian philosophy, which included principally Feuerbach.[92] In what sense do we mean *reform* here? We shall see.

Then Marx dissociated himself from Feuerbach in his *Theses on Feuerbach* of 1845, written six months after *The Holy Family* (1844). Perhaps he was dissociating himself from all philosophy. In the 'Preface' to *A Contribution to the Critique of Political Economy* (1859), Marx says that, with *The German Ideology*, he wanted to 'liquidate traditional philosophical consciousness.'[93]

But when he writes the afterword to the second edition of *Capital* (1875), he once again praises Hegel against his critics. He even coquettishly restates the first book of *Capital* in Hegelian form. He writes that one day it must be explained that Hegel's *Logic* has given a true account, but in a mystifying form.

The usual interpretation delineates three stages:

1 the pre-Marxist and 'philosophical' period (Feuerbach);
2 the break with philosophy as a form of alienation (the critique of other types of alienation is extended to philosophy);

3 the transition to science and 'scientific socialism' based on a
scientific analysis in *Capital*.

Two problems arise from this classification:

1 At the time of the first period, views which are very different
from those of Feuerbach are mixed with ideas characteristic
of Feuerbach. For example, in our text, destruction must be
the realization of philosophy and realization must be the
destruction (of truth and falsehood in philosophy) and not
simply a return to speculative philosophy.

2 If socialism is 'scientific,' how and why can Hegel's dialectic
in the *Logic* be valid? How and why can it become an empirical
truth drawn from fact? (Engels) This removes the whole foundation of 'comprehension' – or rather, on the contrary, it is
recovered from Hegelian logic and placed in absolute
objectivism.

Marx did not write his own *Logic*. Marxists claim that *Capital*
serves this purpose. But *Capital* goes from essence to appearance, reconstructs experience out of essence, and implies a
Hegelian logic.

In its totality, it is Hegelian from one end to the other.

But, first, consistent with the *Phenomenology*, in 1843–4 there
are some humanist, Feuerbachian themes. In the end, they are
more consistent with the *Logic*. (*Capital* follows an order which
is the inverse of that in the *Phenomenology*, i.e. from essence to
appearance.)

This is not a movement from philosophy to science; rather it
is a movement from 'direct' philosophy (man, nature, Feuerbach) to another conception of philosophy (man, and nature
which achieves itself through the experience of capitalism).
Once this experience is understood, and leads to the concept,
it reveals the proletarian class which is the historical formation
in which the understanding of capitalism is realized. There is
then an identification of the one who thinks the functioning of
capital with this historical formation. This historical formation
therefore, which reveals *the point* corresponding to Absolute
Knowledge, is knowledge making its appearance. *Capital* relates
to the intuition of the proletariat as Hegel's logic relates to the
Phenomenology.

Marx does not say this but it amounts to a *utilization* of Hegel's
logic without specifying its relation to facts. We would like to

ask him, as he asks Hegel: Is the relation of a 'logic of the thing in question' [*Logik der Sache*] or a 'question of logic' [*Sache der Logik*]? If it is a *Logik der Sache*, why is there a logic of content?

Furthermore, he reviews Feuerbachian critiques of Hegel in their most extreme form. These are not dialectical, but they include a reversal of speculative philosophy, and a replacement of idealism with materialism.

With Lukács, the 'return' cannot consist simply of a reversal of signs.

Materialism, as opposed to idealism, does not account fully for what *Capital* introduces as essence-ideas. Furthermore, in a dialectical philosophy, what is surpassed is the very opposition between the thing and the idea. Hegel does not withdraw any of his 'spontaneous movement' [*Eigenbewegung*][94] from History to give it to the Absolute or to Self-Consciousness. (He has explicitly stated that the philosopher comes after history and the passions, and contemplates them.)

Being so disposed, we arrive at the question of the Absolute and the question of philosophy.

If, as has been stated above, philosophy is experience understood and passed on to the concept, if the absolute is a form of self-presentation, an apperception that consciousness comprehends the self in an external form; or, at least, if the absolute is the movement of truth that carries this movement of consciousness along with it and makes it possible (Hegel), then when Marx wants to return to immediate philosophy (nature, man, 1844) with Feuerbach, he gets lost along his own way, and falls back outside the Hegel who had characterized sense-certainty as abstract. And when he believes that he has abandoned 'philosophy' (with *Capital*) in reality he rediscovers it, since he sensed it in defending Hegel.

When he engages in a polemic with idealism, as a 'war of the gods,' and against the personal union of the philosopher with God, this must not be understood as a kind of positivism, in which 'the idealist joke' is empty of meaning, but as the truth of this philosophy 'in mystical form.' This is not like the movement of philosophy to 'non-philosophy', but like the negation of the philosophy which realizes 'non-philosophy'. Of course, it is no longer necessary that 'the world become philosophy' but rather 'philosophy must become the world.'[95]

Marxist *praxis* is the inheritor of 'self-consciousness'. The Marxist 'sacred cow' is totality: the alienation of alienation, or the action of revolutionizing – an action which is never only mine, whence the return to transcendent problems.

Thus what remains to be done is a study of the philosophy in Marx's *Capital*. There we will find what Marx has been able to say about philosophy. We must also take into account what the human experience of capitalism and Marxism has revealed after Marx.

Our two texts are once again:

1 The very Feuerbachian manuscripts of 1844. Here we must ask to what extent the ideas of nature and history, which these manuscripts express, are pre-Marxist and pre-Hegelian.
2 The 'Introduction' of 1843, which is remarkable for its precociousness and permanent value. This text contains:
   (a) A reference to man, not as directly received, but as the 'human world.'
   (b) A view of speculative philosophy as ambiguous: false and true, true and false precisely as an abstraction – and not only, as Feuerbach said, false in that it is abstract.
   (c) A derivation of *praxis* coming out of speculation – as speculation that is negated, but realized.
   (d) A positive evaluation of philosophy – as, in a certain respect, the germ of life and the point of departure for the Revolution, – the head of the Revolution with the proletariat as its heart.

What is lacking is the idea of a concrete-economic analysis, showing that the proletariat is the philosophical god. But perhaps this intuition is the best document of Marxist philosophy. It would then be sufficient to reconnect this intuition concerning *praxis* and the proletariat to the objective structures of *Capital* and to the 'comprehension' of *Capital* in order to obtain the philosophy of *Capital*.

April 10, 1961

The 'Introduction' to *A Contribution to the Critique of Hegel's Philosophy of Right.*

The following issue arises: Hegel envisaged (on the level of 'phenomena') the identification of philosophy and non-philosophy, Absolute and 'appearance' of the Absolute. Then he subordinated a dialectic of consciousness to a movement of truth.

Didn't Marx follow an analogous route? In that respect, he was a Hegelian from head to toe. Specifically, the movement from the young Marx to *Capital* is not so much a movement from philosophy to science as it is a movement from *Phenomenology* to *Logic*.

What confuses things is the approval at first given to Feuerbach. Feuerbachian themes arise in the *Economic and Philosophical Manuscripts*. The role of the idea of nature appears, which is not Hegelian. And Marx engages in a polemic against Hegel in the name of embodied man [*l'homme sensible*] and 'non-philosophy.' But, from the beginning, Marx is profoundly Hegelian.' And, later, it is not Hegel from whom he distances himself, but from direct philosophy.

Thus we must show that for Marx, as well as for Hegel, the failure to reunite philosophy and non-philosophy, which he wanted in the first place, is due to a domination of the philosophy of the concept over a philosophy of 'experience' (*Capital*).

We must first show this in Marx: Hegel is imbued with it (similarly the efforts of direct philosophy describe the 'here – there is'). The notion of *praxis* as inheritor of absolute knowledge is elaborated here. This is the unity with a form of existence (the proletariat) which is the presentation of a true society and the true man.

The 'Introduction' to *A Contribution to the Critique of Hegel's Philosophy of Right*.[96] The issue here is to 'critique' Hegel, and to reform speculative philosophy (Feuerbach and the Hegelians). But in what sense is he to be criticized?

I THE PROBLEM

1 The historical situation of Hegel's philosophy is equivocal, i.e. both true and false (*MEGA*, pp. 612, 38–613; IntroCHPR, p. 249).

2 We would be right to want to deny philosophy. But we do so only by surpassing it, or by surmounting it (*aufzuheben*) (*MEGA*, pp. 613, 21–613, 40; IntroCHPR, p. 250).

3 We would be right to want to realize philosophy. But we do so only by surpassing it (*aufzuheben*) (*ibid.*).

4 The critique of the philosophy of Right is equivocal like the

philosophy of Right itself. It is both *pro* and *con*. *Pro*, as a critical analysis of the Modern State. *Con*, in the sense that this State is illusory [*un fantasme*]. – Germany, for example, is outside and above the Modern State (*MEGA*, pp. 613, 40–614, 22; IntroCHPR, p. 250).

5 The problem is to find a *praxis* (because it is not a question of theorizing here, for Germany itself is backwards) which expresses the profundity of the philosophy of Right and thus the future of mankind. [The problem is]* to surpass the Modern State and, at the same time, the defects [*l'écharde*] of the Modern State, represented by a backward Germany. The two are related.

This *praxis* will be both the realization and the surpassing of the philosophy of Right. *Praxis* is the head and heart of the Revolution. (An unequal development arises here, particularly in connection with the idea of Revolution. In order to indicate the appearance of the revolutionary idea, compare this with the text of the appendix to Marx's thesis on the Hegelians.)

[This question of *praxis* can be considered according to the same five levels]*

1 The philosophy of the historical situation in Germany, and the philosophy of Right (as an 'oneiric history' [*Traumgeschichte*] of the Germans). Philosophy in Germany is a lived 'natural history' [*Naturgeschichte*] just as mythology for primitive man is a lived 'pre-history' [*Vorgeschichte*]. The philosophy of Right is contemporaneous with the 'official' Principles of the Modern State. It is associated with a backward German historical reality, and is its 'abstract continuation.'

This ambiguous situation (a *de facto* backwardness with a boldness of thought) means that the future is neither in the immediate negation of historical reality, nor in the immediate realization of an already surpassed philosophy.

2 Therefore we would be right to want to negate the philosophy. But by this negation we cannot overlook it, since philosophy is part of the German reality. It is even the only germ of life in Germany. It cannot be surpassed without being realized. Practice must realize philosophy.

3 Inversely, we would be right to want to realize philosophy (the Hegelians, the partisans of 'critique' who measure things against the idea). But we forget that philosophy belongs to

this German world, and that it is its 'imaginary complement' [*l'idéelle Ergänzung*]. We will not realize it, except in denying it 'as philosophy.'

4 Marx's enterprise is a critique of Hegel. This critique is 'both' [*beides*]: destruction and realization. Here we find consciousness of the modern State and its infrastructure, and also a negation of this consciousness inasmuch as it is satisfied with itself and its 'theoretical' status.

The picture of the modern State, its 'truth,' is possible in Germany, *because* Germany is backward (because the *ancien régime* is artificial and without conviction; and because the power of the industrial nation is not the result but the condition of its development).

This 'truth' is at the same time an illusion. The modern State, as Marx describes it, is a fiction.

The philosophy of Right – and its critique – is equivocal.

[It presents]* the idea that the truth, *qua* expressed, formulated, conceptualized truth, is associated on its own with falsehood. Truth is necessarily not a reflection of that which exists in the same place, but rather an illusion of it, – and even an illusion in relation to England and France. – Philosophy is

1 a part of a historical whole and
2 the content, the mask, 'the abstract continuation,' – and the truth as an illusion.[97]

5 What can be done in the face of this ambiguity? A critique that will also be ambiguous implies a break. Change is necessary. *Praxis* (in contrast to philosophy as sleep) is necessary. But it must be a *praxis* that employs the highest of principles[98] (which could not be any less true than philosophy, but which could be more true), a *praxis* that indicates the future and is thus above the illusion of the modern State.

II   THE SOLUTION

1 The Proletariat *qua* '*formation*' of existence is the presentation of truth (*MEGA*, pp. 619, 37–620, 10; IntroCHPR, p. 256). This was the case before the period of economic and political analysis beginning in 1844.

2 The thought which recognizes this is the realization, and not simply the elimination of the philosophy of Right (*MEGA*,

pp. 620, 41–621, 10; IntroCHPR, p. 257). It is the Hegelian sense of 'experience'.

Next time, we will explore the following two questions: What does Marx have against Hegel? What philosophy does he put in the place of speculation?

April 17, 1961

We have examined the problem of the eminently dialectical relation between philosophy and historical reality ('non-philosophy'). This is not a simple parallelism in the form of either reflection or mystification.

1 Hegel's philosophy is not a reflection of a backward Germany and it is not a simple falsehood or mask of this Germany. It is a theory of the modern State. In Germany, the germ of life is in one's head.

2 Hegel's philosophy is not a simple reflection of modern States either. Nowhere does a State actually become what Hegel says it is. Nor is he presenting a falsehood; his philosophy is the spirit of a time without spirit.

Philosophy is an 'oneiric history,' imaginary history – like religion. But dreams have an historical function, – like the 'pre-history' characterizing the myths of primitive peoples, – they constitute a 'post-history' [Nachgeschichte].

Dream and reality are in a dialectical relationship with one another. The dream is part of human reality. Philosophy qua philosophy is also part of human reality.

What must be done to escape this equivocation?

If one wants simply to realize philosophy out of the Modern State, Germany remains backward. For this philosophy is the 'imaginary complement' of this backwardness, and the radicalization of philosophers remains verbal. To realize philosophy directly is to annul it, and also to maintain everything at the status quo. Therefore, are we going to turn our backs on philosophy? Will we throw ourselves into pure action (praktische Partei)? But this still runs counter to what one would wish; it is to forget that philosophy is part of the German reality – that it is the living part. In its absence, there would be action without principles.

In place of this realization which destroys and this destruction which maintains, a realization-surpassing is necessary. In place of a dialectic that does the opposite of what it wants to do, a dialectic which obtains 'both' [*beides*] (cf. Plato's 'the two'). Note, for example, Péguy's *Clio*[99] in which the 'scandal,' the failure of all public life becomes a 'mystery,' i.e. a beneficent paradox: 'a justified scandal.'

This is precisely the problem that Marx poses for himself. The proof appears in the appendix to his doctoral thesis (written in 1839–41) on the Hegelians.[100]

Already, then, Marx takes a position against the reformers of Hegel. These are Hegelians who wish

1 to maintain Hegel's philosophy as such, and
2 to realize it.

According to the second group, Hegel's only failing was to 'accommodate' himself to his philosophy – all he would have to do is apply it, to realize it – which is a 'non-philosophical' way of criticizing Hegel. There is no 'moral' fault here. The fault must be in the very principle of philosophy as separate philosophy, as *utterance*, as 'comprehension' [*Begreifen*]. Their Hegel was 'science in the making.' 'The last drop of his intellectual heart's blood aspired to the extreme limits' of this science (*MEGA*, p. 63; *CW*, p. 84). Hegel (i.e. dialectic) must be criticized philosophically

1 more profoundly, more faithfully, and
2 by remaining faithful to him, by remaining a philosopher oneself.

– Hegel is fufilled when he is criticized (parricide). – These Hegelians [commit] the inevitable error of unsuccessful emancipations – emancipations that are a form of dependence. – The theoretical spirit becomes 'practical energy,' 'will,' but this *praxis* itself is fully impregnated with theory: 'the praxis of philosophy is itself theoretical.' In what respect? In the respect that one wants to replace philosophy by 'Critique,' which 'measures the individual existence by the essence, the particular reality by the Idea' (*MEGA*, p. 64; *CW*, p. 85). It is also true that immediate realization is a poor theoretical spirit. This is a theoretical spirit since we make reference to concepts, but it is a perverted theory, since the concepts lose their value and their truth [when]* employed immediately.

When philosophy turns against the world which it criticizes (the backward German reality), it becomes 'one side' of the world. Its relationship to the world is a 'relation of reflection' of it, one tension against another (here Hegel is quite right to oppose himself to the Hegelians who want to 'apply' him): 'What was inner light has become consuming flame turning outwards. The result is that the world has become philosophical, philosophy also becomes worldly,'[101]

> 'that its realization is also its loss, that what it struggles against on the outside is its own inner deficiency, that in the very struggle it falls precisely into those defects which it fights as defects in the opposite camp. . . . That which opposes it and that which it fights is always the same as itself, only with factors inverted' (*MEGA*, pp. 64–5; *CW*, p. 85).

(Here, there is a will to realize ends and the ideas that destroy them.) – This is the immediate will. – It is empty, hollow. It combats its own emptiness in the world. It combats itself. The immediate will's action is in disagreement with itself. As a lack of the world, it is in profound agreement with backwardness and can bring nothing to it. Under the flag of realization, this immediate will ruins philosophy without any gain for itself. There is a commitment which is profoundly theoretical, precisely because it is the immediate negation of the world. – Therefore, there is a low estimation of the relation between philosophy and the thing. It is 'perverted in itself.'[102]

On the philosophers' side of consciousness, this attitude of 'Critique' is equivocal. There are two contrary unreasonable demands: 'one turned against the world, the other against philosophy itself. . . . Their liberation of the world from non-philosophy is at the same time their own liberation from . . . philosophy. . . .' (*MEGA*, p. 65; *CW*, p. 86). Philosophy's weariness is still philosophy. The replacement of the philosophy-system by the 'act' and by the 'immediate energy of development' proves that 'from the theoretical perspective (*sic*) they have not yet emerged from that system' (*ibid.*). The Hegelians actively sense their opposition 'with the plastic self-equality [*der plastischen Sichselbstgleichheit*] of the system' (*ibid.*), – and do not take into account that, in denouncing it purely and simply, they do not truly change anything. Philosophy is destroyed only if it is realized.

This equivocation of the young Hegelians ends finally in two opposing philosophical tendencies:

1 the liberal party that wants to apply philosophy ('Critique');
2 the opposition party, Positivist Philosophy, which presents the 'non-concept' of philosophy, 'the moment of reality,' as essential.

'Each of these parties does exactly what the other wants to do and what it itself does not want to do' (*ibid.*). 'Critique' ruins philosophy, while it wants to 'realize' it. – 'Positive philosophy' (Schelling? Feuerbach? the 'practical' political party?) conserves the ideology-masks, because it wants to destroy them physically, immediately.

What is the difference between this text and our own? The two unilateral, immediate, non-dialectical attitudes are brought back to a common principle in 1839–41. It is a false freedom with respect to Hegel, whether one wishes to apply it, or whether one wishes to replace the 'concept' by an act. The immediate 'energy' of development is not dialectical but a 'reflexive' relationship.

The result is philosophy-world. – Hegel's true freedom is Hegelian, dialectical, and does not turn its back on philosophy, or criticize the world from the heights of philosophy, which returns to the same. – The Hegelian attitude applied to the history of Hegelianism consists in understanding it dialectically.

1 There is first of all a 'perverted' relationship of philosophy-world which 'appears'. A tension of abstract opposition [exists]* between them.
2 This becomes an opposition of philosophical consciousness with itself.
3 Finally, there is a division and a doubling back of philosophy, which interiorizes its opposition to the world.

The conclusion of the 1839 dialectical analysis is that there are two tendencies (both false) to be placed in the same bag. The tactical rallying to the 'liberal party', to the extent that it is 'the party of the concept', conserves philosophy immediately, while the other side is 'perversion' in its pure state: *Verrücktheit* (breakdown, madness). This leads to the position of waiting for a realization which might not be the destruction [of philosophy].*

The diagnosis (that each one does the contrary of what he wishes) remains in 1843. But, instead of saying that they are both wrong (and for the same reason, which is false emancipation, and a poor critique of Hegel), Marx adds: they are both right. One must both destroy and realize. This is what he proposes to himself in making himself a critic of the philosophy of Right.

Why?

At the end of 1842, a violent reaction occurs. Frederick William IV announces the suppression of certain journals notably, beginning in January 1843, the *Deutsche Jahrbücher*, edited by Arnold Ruge, and beginning in April 1843, the *Rheinische Zeitung*, edited by Marx. In September 1843, Marx writes to Ruge: 'a general anarchy rages among the reformers . . . each is obliged to admit to himself that he no longer has a very clear notion as to what the future must be.' The 'liberalism' of the Hegelian State is a myth. It is illusory to want to put the State back on its path of freedom again. – Feuerbach recommends an alliance of German theory and French practice. – Marx senses the necessity of moving away from an attitude disposed toward waiting. What is needed is a revolutionary dialectic which puts the State back on its path, a driving force towards historical evolution, – since the State turns out to be revolutionary.

Whence, it is *no longer* the case that the philosophical party and the practical party are both wrong (above all the practical party). The attitude of non-engagement [can no longer continue].* They are both right. It is all the same, since Marx continues to say that each one, powerless to do what it wishes, does what the other wants. Thus they are right, but one cannot disengage their truth while surpassing them. Simply put, the positive formula indicates that one must take a position in the matter.

This position will be, at the same time, for philosophy and for practice, ceasing to be external to one another in a 'relation of reflection.' Practice will be that which implies the true realization of philosophy (a theory that is the true destruction of itself as a separate theory) where the light of philosophy is rediscovered. This practice therefore incorporates philosophy in its entirety, and, in this sense, destroys it, truly surpasses it, because it contains it.

Thus we can consider (1) *praxis* and (2) a *praxis* which holds the promises that philosophy can give:

1 'By the single fact that it is the determined opponent of the previous form of German political consciousness, the critique of the speculative philosophy of Right does not become lost in itself, but in the tasks which can only be solved in one way: through *praxis*' (*MEGA*, p. 614; IntroCHPR, p. 157).

We go against the German political consciousness as a 'point of honor,' and as an ideological justification of a backward reality. The task is to transform the German reality, to pass on to action, to an action that is not a hidden theory (as before), but which changes the world.

2 But, the difference between it and the practical political party which has forgotten the philosophy in action (and in this respect it remains 'theoretical' and was an intellectual's *praxis*, anti-philosophy and hence philosophy), – is that it must deal with an action that realizes philosophy. Is this therefore compelling the State to apply Hegel's principles? No, this is impossible in the backward State of Germany. And, moreover, Hegel's principles are not applied anywhere. – Hegel's realization will not consist in *reforming* the real according to its concepts, but in instigating the transformation of this reality by itself, in seeking the principle of surpassing and of negative work within itself, which Hegel's philosophy of Right seeks in the Spirit.

'The question is: Can Germany attain a practice *according to the highest of principles*, that is, a revolution that raises it not only to the official level of modern nations, but to the human level that will be their immediate future' (*MEGA*, p. 614; Intro CHPR, p. 251).

An action according to the highest principles, i.e. one which realizes not less, but more than the principles of the Hegelian State. – These principles always remain 'official,' i.e. masks, and in Germany, they cannot have this official existence. They cannot realize themselves there except by surpassing themselves as principles. They animate a historical movement which realizes in concrete men and makes a society not less advanced, but more advanced than the English and French societies. Thus they become the model for the future of these actual societies.

How is such philosophical action possible? Particularly in Germany? Practically speaking, Germany has not even attained the level that it surpasses theoretically. It must therefore cross not only the limits of its own reality, but also the limits of modern States. Since this is the case, Germany does not appear to offer the 'radical' needs which would make this radical revolution possible.[103]

Where is the positive possibility of German emancipation?[104] The answer: it is precisely in the formation of an absolutely lost class, the proletariat. He also gives a definition of the proletariat.[105]

The work of the negative to an extreme in the proletariat will amount to the dialectical union of the proletariat and philosophy.[106] The proletariat is the *Weltgeist*, the historical figure of the *Weltgeist*. – The proletariat (as defined above) in its seizure of power is the advent [*l'avènement*][107] of negativity and of the universal, since it cannot save itself except by saving man, and by surpassing itself as a class, in creating a society without classes. But this imposes a condition on revolutionary *praxis*: even if it is a *praxis* animated by the negativity of the proletariat, and, in that respect, a philosophical *praxis*. It is not action, in the pragmatist sense of success, nor in the relative and 'realist' sense of attaining certain particular ends, certain goals by any means, but a *praxis* which is not *poèsis*, but which is the integration of all means, – with means and ends in dialectical interdependence. – It is a refusal to opt for Being or Doing; one is not to be preferred over the other. They are indivisible in *praxis*. – It is a refusal to opt for moralism or cynicism. *Praxis* is not an empirical action in this respect. Properly speaking, it has no *goal*; rather it is a 'manner.' It is an action that is done for nothing (empirical or positive) and for everything (the universal and man). *Todo y nada*. – The proletarian 'mystery of existence,' *Geheimnis seines eigenen Daseins*[108] (*MEGA*, p. 620; IntroCHPR, p. 256). – The philosophical function of the proletariat is to command its economic function.

Such is the philosophico-political attitude.

More specifically, what 'philosophy,' what conceived superstructures, what conceptual preparations will make this *praxis* possible? We will examine this in the *1844 Manuscripts*, where Marx offers his phenomenology. Here conceptual preparations go before the practical recognition of the proletariat as a carrier of the universal. What is in question here is a 'philosophy' which is not a philosophy of consciousness, but a philosophy of man incarnate.

Just as Hegel makes phenomenology a part of knowledge as soon as he installs himself there, Marx will view these essays as preparatory once he has installed himself through them in the becoming of truth, i.e. in *Capital* and its self-surpassing.

Future lectures:

April 24: *1844 Manuscripts*

May 2: Afterword to *Capital*

May 8: a text by Kierkegaard and one by Nietzsche

April 24, 1961[109]

(Read *MEGA*, pp. 620–1; IntroCHPR, p. 257)[110]

Praxis bears *its own* theory, – man is the supreme being for man. This is a theory that surpasses the modern as the modern surpasses the Middle Ages, a theory that is *fundamental* and universal – what philosophy is in words, the proletariat is in act. This theory expresses 'the mystery of existence.' – The 'secret' or speculative mystery (negativity) is passed on to the proletariat. Note that in *Capital*, there is the mystery of 'reification' [*Verdinglichung*] where the proletariat and the *praxis* which it is (as negativity) and which it defines are the realization of philosophy. *Praxis* is not the fabrication of a certain result, for example, a technical tool of Power, but a practice, a mode of historical existence (universal and fundamental). *Praxis* is not defined by deliberate ends, but by a movement of history (the industry that creates the proletariat) extended into the re-creation of human society. – Evidently what is necessary is a political technique to illuminate the *de facto* proletariat. But the last measure will always be the mystery of negativity and the negation of the negation which is the idea of the proletariat. It is an action that is an action for all (the universal, mankind), because it is, in a sense, an action for nothing and for no *particular* interest.

Philosophy is the conceptual preparation for this historical adherence. Concepts such as positive and negative, universal, *Grund* (fundament), history, man, nature, mind, contribute to the science of historical experience. This is why Marx treats them in 1844.

We see that Marx's concept of the proletariat as 'self-consciousness' is prior to the experience of 'advanced' countries and prior to an extensive reading of Hegel's sources. This is no argument against his position. It only shows that Marx is a philosopher. He will remain such since *Capital* was interrupted before he began treating classes and the proletariat. However an analysis of the structure of *Capital* reveals the same metaphysical mechanism: that of a reality which 'surpasses' itself, and in which *Capital* contradicts itself. Here, we pass from reality (*Capital*) to appearance (the proletariat). As in Hegel's *Logic*, 'becoming truth' is substituted for 'becoming consciousness,' but it is still philosophy and still Hegel. Under the guise of philosophy's abandonment, it is the most audacious philosophy: a philosophy which hides itself in 'things' and which is masked by an apparent positivism. It is a philosophy to the very extent that it does not wish to be one. Inversely, the declared philosophy of 1844 is not far from the concrete.

Why then do we have this change, these declarations concerning the abandonment of philosophical consciousness?

1 Because what must be understood, particularly after 1848, is the weight of things in the sharpest sense and *their* movement. Thus *Capital* founds proletarian philosophy in the movement of things.

2 Because the sense of political practice leads to a consciousness of separation between the *de facto* proletariat and its philosophical and historical function. Action is the strategy and the technique of the reversal of capitalism. (Whence) the objective analysis. From this point of view, the sketches of 1844 appear too 'immediate,' schematic. One cannot 'realize' only half. But what must be realized, by the analysis of *Capital* and through action, is always precisely the play of negative and positive.

April 24, 1961

The *Economic and Philosophical Manuscripts* of 1844.[111]

1 The critique of Hegel. – Let us leave aside for the moment the Feuerbachian critique (returning, subject-object), and the superficial critiques of 'idealism' which 'surpass' history and remove its 'spontaneous movement' from it. This leaves the following:

(a) The critique of philosophical exhaustiveness in the name of *Dasein* (*MEGA*, I, 3, p. 165; *EPM*, p. 394). Here negation and confirmation in philosophy render real modes of existence equivocal in philosophical existence.

(b) The critique of the pretension of 'self-consciousness' that it is other than itself. Here the pretensions of pure 'knowledge' permit one to identify objectification and alienation. – This is related to the very essence of Hegel's philosophy (negativity) and not to 'accommodation' (*MEGA*, I, 3, pp. 163–4; *EPM*, pp. 392–3).

(c) The critique of the negation of negation and of the equivocal 'surpassing' (*MEGA*, p. 164; *EPM*, p. 393).[112]

However, the negation of negation is a good description of Human Prehistory (*ibid.*) Marx is a positivist for a far-off future, beyond communism. Communism is a negation of the negation depending upon a future positivism (*MEGA*, p. 125; *EPM*, p. 348).

(d) Similarly, Marx accepts the idea of the alienation of the subject in the object, but not as a definition of 'objectivity' [*Gegenständlichkeit*]. Rather as an episode of it, since non-alienating objectification (the positivist perspective) will follow.

This is the critique of Hegelian alienation. We must add the alienation of alienation; in short, a negation which is carried away absolutely into the positive.

(e) The critique of nature according to Hegel.

This summarizes everything that precedes: the critique of 'knowledge,' speculation, negation of the negation, and alienation (*MEGA*, pp. 170–2; *EPM*, pp. 398–400).

2 Efforts at a Marxist philosophy.

(a) 'Surpassing' [*Aufheben*]. The negation of negation must be maintained. However, the surpassing must be a true one and not a conserving negation (i.e. in raising the object to the level of thought). It is an abstraction of an abstraction. In an *alienated language*, 'thought' is this negation of a negation which is the being-object of man, of his 'essence' and positive humanism (*MEGA*, pp. 166–7; *EPM*, pp. 395–6).

(b) Nature before and after pre-history.

Here we must study the relationship among the concepts: nature, man, history, *praxis*.

Man is viewed as a sensuous-objective being (*MEGA*, p. 160; *EPM*, pp. 389–90). Man is also viewed as a social, historical being inasmuch as he is non-alienated [*désaliené*]. – This is his *nature* and nature becomes man through him – the nature–history relation becomes dialectical (*MEGA*, pp. 115–16; *EPM*, pp. 344–5 and *MEGA*, p. 160; *EPM*, pp. 389–90). Such is the critique of Hegelian negativity (Spirit). It involves reform (a final and primordial positivism) and, consequently, the elaboration of the concepts: man and nature.

What remains to be appreciated is the exact relationship between Marx and Hegel, and between Marx and Feuerbach. Is this the return of Hegel, as Feuerbach says? Or is Marx introducing something else? And, as a function of that, what is the relationship here with Marx's final thought?

May 2, 1961

THE MARXIST CRITIQUE OF HEGEL

1 Philosophical 'thought' [*Denken*], as exhaustiveness, as unconditioned thought, as identical to the thing itself, is equivocally both destruction and conservation:

> This unstable being, in the real existence (*wirklichen Existenz*) of human attitudes, is hidden (their existence is blind). It is only visible and revealed (*Offenbarung*) in thought and in philosophy. Thus my true religious being-there (*Dasein*) is my being-there in the philosophy of religion. My true natural being-there is the being-there in the philosophy of nature. My true human being-there is my philosophical being-there. Similarly, the true existence of religion, the State, art, nature is the philosophy of religion, nature, the State, art. . . . Thus, it is only as philosophy of religion that I am truly religious and thus I deny real religiosity and the really religious man. But, at the same time, I confirm them, partly in my own being-there, that is, in the alien being-there which I oppose them with, for this is merely their philosophical expression, – and partly in their particular and original form, for apparently, there are also no others (than me). They are all allegories and hidden variants under

sensuous mantles of their authentic and true being-there, i.e. my philosophical being-there. (*MEGA*, p. 165; *EPM*, pp. 394–5)[113]

For Marx, philosophy is equivocally both phenomenology and also speculation. 'To understand' is taken as 'seizing the truth of. . .'. In other words:

(a) this means denying art, nature, religion, the State in their immediate form, – destroying them –, transforming them into their truth, which is other than what they are.

(b) It also means being what they are, since this form is only its philosophical expression and they are allegories, emblems of this truth, and hence true.

But didn't Marx say that there must be both destruction and realization? Yes, but in the end, philosophy does neither destruction nor conservation or maintenance. – It engages in pseudo-destruction and pseudo-conservation, with each serving as no more than an alibi to escape the other. – We do not reproach philosophy for ambiguity, but rather for bad ambiguity.

How does philosophy develop a bad ambiguity? Like the *Denken* of the overview, exhaustive, possessing the thing 'in thought,' philosophy, wanting to be all, is nothing; it does not inhabit the things it discusses, – and, since it is not anything in particular, it is not even opposed to that which it critiques. It is neither yes nor no; it is not no, because it is not yes. Philosophy has no enemies, nor does it have any friends. It has no friends because it has no enemies. It lacks everything, both the particular and the universal. By contrast, it must have both. This thought will not have the character of an overview, the pretense of living at a distance, of seeing, haunting, contemplating – which is a yes under the flag of a no, and a no under the flag of a yes. By contrast, what is needed is a manner of thinking which is at the same time concrete and universal, in which the yes will be a no, and the no an unequivocal yes. It is not a question of returning behind Hegel, for example, towards a philosophy that renounces its comprehension of non-philosophy or towards a non-philosophy that will take non-philosophy (art, religion, nature, the State) without criticism. The problem is to succeed at that which it lacks, to create a concrete philosophy that is truly concrete.

2 To be more precise, Marx criticizes the pretensions of philosophical *Denken* for remaining at home in what is other than self, for being contained in itself and possessing its contrary, – surpassing its contrary from the inside or for understanding it from the outside, without experience. The problem is to rediscover philosophical proximity and distance: philosophy's state of being nowhere and everywhere.[114] There are two conditions to this:

1 Consciousness, – particularly 'self-consciousness,' – must not be given the power to carry its contrary in itself and to be at home with its inverse.

2 An illusory all-powerfulness – a negativity that is so total that it founds and digests everything and nothing, – must not be fabricated in the name of 'knowledge.'

In this discussion, we find a compendium of all the illusions of speculation. First, self-consciousness is at home without its being-other than self as such. This is true – if we create an abstraction of Hegelian abstraction here and replace self-consciousness with *man's self-consciousness* (which is at home in its being-other than self). This implies, for one thing, that consciousness, – knowledge *qua* knowledge, thinking *qua* thinking, – presumes that it is immediately other than itself, sensuousness, reality, life, thought which, by thinking, overreaches itself (*sich überbietende*) (Feuerbach). This aspect (of the doctrine) is implied in that consciousness as the simple consciousness (of the external) (*Bewusstsein*) is not offended by alienated (*entfremdeten*) object-being (*Gegenständlichkeit*), but by the object-being as such.

Secondly, this implies that to the extent to which man in his self-consciousness has recognized and surpassed (*aufgehoben*) the spiritual world or the general spiritual being-there of his world as self-exteriorization of himself (*Selbstentaüsserung*), he nevertheless reconfirms it in this externalized form. He passes it off as his true being-there. He restores it and presumes that he is at home in his being-other as such. Thus, for example, after having

73

surpassed religion and recognized it as a product of self-externalization, he finds that he has nevertheless been confirmed in religion *qua* religion. Here is the root of Hegel's false positivism or of his merely apparent critique. It is what Feuerbach calls the positing, negating, and restoring of religion or theology, – but it needs to be understood in a more general fashion. This is to say that reason is at home in non-reason *qua* non-reason. The man, who has recognized that he leads an exteriorized life in law, politics, etc., in fact leads his true human life in this externalized life as such. Self-affirmation (*Selbstbejahung*), self-confirmation in contradiction with itself and with the knowledge and the essence of the object is therefore true knowledge and true life.

Therefore there is no longer any question about a compromise on Hegel's part with religion, the State, etc., since the falsehood here is that of its very (philosophical) progress. (*MEGA*, pp. 162–4; *EPM*, pp. 392–3)

[We must]* relate the critique of pure 'knowledge' and pure 'thought' – as they outdo themselves and realize their own surpassing – with the problem of what carries the dialectic, namely, sensuousness, reality, life, nature, man bringing 'self-consciousness' but not created by 'self-consciousness' as it 'outdoes' itself.[115]

This 'self-consciousness' is in the midst of things and does not produce things. It is a negativity which permeates things that are already there [*déjà là*] and does not manipulate them from itself.

The problem of alienation appears as a movement from the self into the other who denies the selfness [*ipséité*] of the first. For Hegel, this movement is coextensive with objectivity, where 'self-consciousness' is pure subject. The relationship 'self-consciousness'-object must be thought, though it does not necessarily involve a contradiction, or the genesis of an antagonist.

The problem of the 'surpassing' has already been discussed. Hegel's progress (i.e. thinking negativity) is responsible for equivocation in the 'surpassing.' For thinking, 'surpassing' can only reinforce critique, criticize critique, that is, a 'false positivism,' which re-establishes that which had been criticized under the aegis of extracting the truth.

3 Marx and Feuerbach as critics of Hegel.

In this text; the problem of negation appears as a central item in Hegel's Marxist critique. The questions of 'materialism' or 'idealism,' of a 'returned' or 'rectified' dialectic are all subordinated to this problem of negation. One must achieve a conception of negation (and of the negative-positive relation, of alienation, of 'surpassing') which is not the pseudo-destruction and pseudo-conservation that one obtains in replacing the thing by the thought of the thing.

In all this, there is not a word against the idea of negativity. The Feuerbachian critique of Hegel is very different from this. In his *Thesis*, Feuerbach says:

> The method of the reformative critique of speculative philosophy as such does not differ from the method already used in the *Philosophy of Religion*. It is sufficient to transform the predicate into the subject, and, once it is a subject, it can be transformed into an object and a principle – thus it is sufficient to invert speculative philosophy. In this way we obtain the naked, pure and simple truth (*die blanke Wahrheit*).[116]

Although Marx has sometimes taken up these formulae, they do not express his thought or at least not for very long. 'Direct thought (*die Direktheit*) – the conscious elimination of all mediation – eliminates dialectic by means of Hegelian idealism.'[117]

We can observe Feuerbach's temptation (the Feuerbachian return) and Marx's reaction in his assessment of Feuerbach:

> When he opposes negation of the negation, which goes under the pretense of being the absolute positive, with the positive which is based on itself and positively grounded in itself . . . Feuerbach interprets negation of the negation as philosophy in contradiction with itself, as philosophy affirming theology (surpassing, etc.) after having denied it, and hence affirming it in opposition to

itself. The positing or self-affirmation and self-confirmation which resides in the negation of negation (for Feuerbach) becomes a positing which is not yet sure of itself, which is preoccupied with its opposite, which doubts itself and requires a demonstration, which therefore does not prove itself through its being-there, and which is not admitted. It is therefore directly and immediately counterposed to that positing which is sensuously ascertained and grounded in itself. (*MEGA*, pp. 152–3; *EPM*, pp. 381–2)

This [is] where positivism is tempted [to move]* against negativity. Therefore it is the temptation of a non-dialectical philosophy. But Marx pursues this further:

Since Hegel understood the negation of the negation, from the aspect of the positive relation contained within it as the only true positivity and from the aspect of the negative relation contained within it as the only true act and self-confirming act of all being (*Selbstbestätigung alles Seins*), he simply discovered the abstract, logical, speculative formula for the movement of history. This movement of history is not yet the real history of man as a presupposed subject, but the act of his creation, the history of man's emergence. (*MEGA*, pp. 152–3; *EPM*, p. 382)

Feuerbach with his positivism, or his humanist and immediate philosophy, does not account for history, or man as making himself across history. In so doing, he creates himself as subject and becomes 'self-consciousness'.

Yes, Hegel was wrong in extracting nature or man (or religion, art, law) from thought. This is no reason to simply overthrow Hegel – just because he makes nature or man the subject and consciousness the predicate. (One could equally well make law or religion the subject and Spirit the predicate, the positive the subject and the negative the attribute.) This would be to misunderstand the problem. – The problem is to have a conception of the negative that does not transform nature, man, and history into abstractions, a conception of the negative which is in their very fabric, and particularly in that of history. Marx would argue that when Feuerbach affirms matter, he is not a historian. When he recognizes history, he is not a materialist. For Marx, a historical materialism is a concrete conception of negativity and of the negation of a negation. It is a correct formula, but an algebraic one with respect to the *movement* of history.

In this spirit, Marx tries, in the 1844 *Manuscripts*, to elaborate his philosophy and his dialectic. He tries to redefine the concepts of nature, man, and history, to 'realize' the Hegelian 'surpassing' and negation. – It is a dialectic that will no longer be a history of consciousness, not even a history of man (Feuerbach), but 'a History of Being' [*Seinsgeschichte*].

SKETCH OF A MARXIST 'HISTORY OF BEING'

We no longer start from *Denken* or pure 'knowledge', i.e. the equivocal relation consciousness(*Bewusstsein*)-object, becoming finally self-consciousness and absolute self.

Where, then, do we start? From nature or from man? We no longer start from pure nature, [which] by itself is not man. And man taken positively will not be a valuable philosophical principle. Man himself is not two natures, but a double nature: 'Both the material of work and man as subject are the result as well as the starting point for the historical movement' (*MEGA*, pp. 115–16; *EPM*, p. 349).

Marx's sketch of philosophy is essentially dialectical, i.e. nature, man, and history are all understood, not as substances definable by a principal attribute, but as movements without a locatable discontinuity, where the other is always involved. – There is no cleavage between matter and idea, object and subject, nature and man, in-itself and for-itself, but a single Being where negativity works. – Therefore, nature will not be defined as a pure object, externality, but as the 'sensuous', carnal, nature in the way we see it. Natural beings have an internal relation where the relation between some of them and others is predetermined. Man will be defined neither as a pure subject nor as a fragment of nature, but by a sort of coupling of 'subject-object' with two sides; a relation to an object, or an active object, and also a relation essentially to another man, a generic being (*Gattungswesen*), 'society'.

This latter relation is a transformation and a continuation of the natural relation of living beings with external beings. History in this sense is the very flesh of man.

Man is immediately a natural being (*Naturwesen*). As a natural being and a living natural being, he is, to an extent, equipped with natural powers and vital forces. He is an active natural being. To an extent, it is as a natural, corporal, sensuous, objective (*gegenständliches*) being, a suffering (*leidendes*) being, conditioned and limited like animals and plants. In other words, the objects of his drives exist outside man as objects independent of him. . . . That man is a living, real (*wirklich*), sensuous, objective being with natural powers means that he has real, sensuous objects as the *object of his being* (*Wesens*) and of his vital expression (*Lebensaüsserung*). . . . To be objective, natural, and sensuous and to have one's object, nature, and sense (*Sinn*) outside oneself,[118] or even to be oneself object, nature, and sense for a third (being)[119] in one and the same thing (*ist identisch*). Hunger is a natural need. It therefore requires a nature and an object that is outside itself. . . . The sun is an object for the plant, an indispensable object, which maintains (*bestätigend*) his life, just as the plant is an object of the sun, an externalization (*Aüsserung*) of its life-awakening power and its objective essential power. A being which does not have its nature outside of itself is not a natural being. . . . A non-objective (*ungegenständliches*) being will be a non-being (*Unwesen*).
Imagine a being which is neither an object itself nor has an object. In the first place, such a being would be the only being (*das einzige Wesen*); no other being would exist outside it. . . . *For as soon as there are objects outside of me, as soon as I am not alone, I am another*, a reality other than the object outside of me. For this third object, I am therefore a reality other than it, in other words, its object. (*MEGA*, pp. 160–1; *EPM*, pp. 389–90)[120]

Man is therefore a suffering being (*leidend*) and, because he feels his suffering, he is a passionate being (*leidenschaftliches Wesen*).

But man is not only a being of nature. He is a being of human nature, that is, a being which is for himself (*für*

sich selbst seiendes Wesen) and therefore a generic being
(Gattungswesen).[121]. . . Therefore human objects are not
natural objects such that they offer themselves immediately.
The human sense *(der menschliche Sinn)* as it is immediately,
objectively, is not human sensibility. . . . Neither objective
nature, nor subjective nature is immediately and
adequately present to the human being. Just as everything
that is natural must be born, man too has his act of birth
(Entstehungsakt): history. But history is an act of birth that
is known *(gewusste)*. Consequently, it is an act of birth that
consciously surpasses itself as an act of birth *(als
Enstehungsakt mit Bewusstsein sich aufhebender Entstehungsakt
ist)*. History is the true natural history of man. (*MEGA*,
p. 162; *EPM*, p. 391)

Nature is transformed into history by sensuous-practical man.
Nature, which comes to be for itself, and therefore realizes itself
in destroying itself, maintains itself while surpassing itself. And
carnal, 'material,' history serves as its clutch to connect up with
natural forces and as a continually 'objective' movement that is
its 'steering wheel.'

This is quite Feuerbachian, but with the added dimension of
history as that which produces man and is produced by him.
Here then Hegel with his negativity descends into the flesh of
the world.

But the philosophical problem was, then, the exact status of
this negativity, which is no longer the absolute Self, and which
floats above nature.

If one holds oneself [to that negativity]*, after all it comes
from Hegel, it is an act of birth which 'surpasses itself' as an
act of birth, because it is 'for itself.' Is this not the access to the
known, to 'knowledge?'

But in introducing the concept of nature, Marx denies himself
the possibility of letting negativity float into the air. He maintains, against Feuerbach, the negation of Hegelian negation as
an abstract formulation of history before the birth of man. But
this negation of the negation is the installation of man's positive
Being or of a second nature. This is why Marx praised Feuerbach
for having taken the positive resting in itself as a principle.
Marx only reproached him for not envisioning the mediations

that precede him. Marx himself envisions the 'surpassing' of history by itself: the 'self-surpassing' as a blossoming of man's 'true essence':

> If I know religion as alienated human self-consciousness, this does not mean that religion is already self-consciousness, but that it is an alienated self-consciousness. Thus I know that the self-consciousness which belongs to the essence of my own self is realized in an annihilated, surpassed, religion, but not in religion itself. In Hegel, therefore, the negation of the negation is not the realization (*Bestätigung*) of the true essence by a negation of an apparent essence. It is the realization of a pseudo-essence or a self-estranged essence. The alienation occurs across its negation or the negation of this essence appearing to be objective, residing outside man, and independent of him and its transformation into the subject. (*MEGA*, p. 164; *EPM*, p. 393)

The relation with the external is a problem in that this relation can no longer be the passing from the negative to the positive, as in Hegel, where there is an alienation of the negative in the positive. This means that the two terms are relativized, that, therefore, the negation of the negation is a denial of alienation [*désaliénation*], establishing a relation devoid of contradiction with the positive. In relation to the 'surpassing' problem, this means that a man who has 'appropriated' his essence for himself received grounding and produces a new state of man in equilibrium with himself.

Therefore, we have the Hegelian negation of negation taken in its positive sense:

> In grasping the positive sense of the negation which has reference to itself, even if once again in estranged form, Hegel grasps man's self-estrangement, alienation of being, loss of objectivity and loss of reality as self-discovery, manifestation of being, self-objectification and self-realization. In short, he sees labor – within abstraction – as man's act of self-creation. (*MEGA*, p. 167; *EPM*, p. 395)

The positive moments of the Hegelian dialectic . . . (a)

'surpassing' as an objective movement, which re-absorbs alienation into itself. That is the insight, expressed within alienation, into the appropriation of objective being by surpassing its alienation. It is an alienated institution of the real objectification of man. (*MEGA*, p. 166; *EPM*, p. 395)

Whence negativity (and notably the negation of the negation) is only the contrary of man's 'true essence' which has never been, but which will be. Positive, simple nature is not only at the origin but also at the end:

atheism as the surpassing of God is the emergence of a theoretical humanism. Communism as the surpassing of private property reclaims true human life as man's property, the emergence of practical humanism. In other words, atheism is the humanism mediated with itself by surpassing religion; communism is humanism mediated with itself by surpassing private property. Only by surpassing this mediation (a surpassing of a surpassing) – which is nevertheless presupposed to be human – will positive humanism, which originates in itself be born. (*MEGA*, p. 167; *EPM*, p. 395)

More precisely, the description of a future to man's true self-possession (assumed by the concept of nature) supports the previous phase of a negative negation of the negation.

When the essentiality of man and nature has become 'practically and sensuously' visible . . . the inquiry into a foreign being above nature and man becomes practically impossible. Atheism as the negation of this inessentiality no longer makes any sense. . . . Socialism *qua* socialism no longer needs such mediation. It begins with the theoretically and practically sensuous consciousness of man and nature as essential beings (*als des Wesens*). It is man's positive self-consciousness, which is no longer mediated by surpassing religion, just as real life is man's positive reality, which is no longer mediated by surpassing private property or communism. Communism is the act of positing, negation of the negation, and therefore the real phase, necessary for the next (*nächste*) historical development in the emancipation and recovery of mankind.

> Communism is the necessary form and the dynamic principle of the nearest (*nächste*) future. But communism is not as such the goal of human development – the form of human society. (*MEGA*, p. 125; *EPM*, pp. 357–8)

This is the face which communism turns toward a 'beyond' (its side where negation of the negation is positive): the 'positive surpassing' of property, the genuine appropriation of the human being –

> the genuine dissolution of the opposition between man and nature, and between man and man, the true resolution of the opposition between existence and essence, between objectification and self-realization (*Selbstbestätigung*), between freedom and necessity, between individual and species. It is the problem of history resolving and knowing itself as such (*er ist das aufgelöste Rätsel der Geschichte und weiss sich als diese Lösung*). (*MEGA*, p. 114; *EPM*, p. 348)

Thus Marx [is different from] Feuerbach, [different from] immediate positivity. But the domain of negativity is enclosed on both sides by Nature and Equality with itself. This is the resolution of the historical enigma (or prehistorical enigma – which is where Marx's reservation lies).

It is also true, as Lukács has said, that even if this 'direct thought' is rejected in the distant future, it colors the whole dialectic which depends on it. 'Direct thought' gives its state to the *Aufheben* and to work as the possibility of *whatever appears* [*n'importe quoi*], as the absolute recreation of the world and man. Is it not also the elimination of dialectic along with Hegelian idealism?[122] 'It would be dangerous to understand Engels' sentence as if standing again on materialist feet in Hegel's philosophy involved only a reversal of philosophical signs.'[123]

Hyppolite comments in *Logique et Existence*:

> Marx adds this historical dimension to Feuerbach. He therefore rediscovers more or less the Hegelian dialectic in the concrete conflicts of history, but he refuses to reduce the positive to the negation of the negation. . . . Man's objectification is not an alienation for him, since the object determined is not negation; it comes first. History then, has created conflicts and will put an end to them.[124]

82

The first positivity of nature must be substituted for the negation of the negation. Man must be understood subjectively out of this positivity. (*LE*, p. 238)

> Human nature will then manifest itself after the resolution of historical conflicts. Positivity comes first, positivity will be last, and this positivity must not have any cracks in it – it must not have anything negative. (*LE*, p. 239)

Since then, *praxis* has ceased to be an openness, an action which does everything, because it is not particular and because it is animated by the class which is its own self-surpassing. *Praxis* becomes the technique of this class power. – It implies a return to the positive by the Party and the dictatorship. This is certainly efficacity, but is it a realization of negativity?

Ironically, in a sense, positivism produces the same result as absolute negation or Hegel's absolute negative, i.e. a hidden sense of history, a combat of gods – Stalinism and Hegelianism. One could even say that Hegel maintains more of the sense of negativity and tension.

Is there a coming to consciousness [*prise de conscience*] in existence today? Non-antagonist oppositions are recognized in soviet society, oppositions which are no longer presented as steps toward nature.

Philosophy and non-philosophy: a detached philosophy always reappears in disguise. What is needed is a negation of the negation which we do not fix either in negativism or positivism.

(Texts from *Capital* and from the introduction to *A Contribution to the Critique of Political Economy*.) – The renunciation of philosophy must be a consciousness of these difficulties in the nature/history opposition.

Chapter 2

ECHOES: PHILOSOPHY AND NON-PHILOSOPHY AFTER HEIDEGGER

John Sallis

First, some stories.

The first an old story, told in late antiquity by Ovid. It is a story that is almost too familiar to bear retelling, a story too in which an overarching purpose or meaning seems too readily discernible, its depth too near the surface, perhaps nothing but surface, like a mirror, lacking the space in which to resound. Yet suppose one were to listen to it now with postmodern ears as it echoes across that expanse of two millennia, the space of – almost – the entire history of metaphysics.

It is the story of Echo.

Once Juno had come to the mountains looking for Jove, her purpose to expose him in his amorous pursuits among the nymphs. She was, however, intercepted by the nymph Echo, who chattered away at her until those nymphs who had been in Jove's company had time to flee. Thanks to Echo's speech, Jove's deeds went unexposed. But Echo paid dearly for having tricked the goddess. Juno punished her by depriving her of the power of originating speech. Henceforth:

> She liked to chatter,
> But had no power of speech except the power
> To answer in the words she last had heard.[1]

Henceforth, Echo's speech was limited merely to repeating what someone else had just said. It was as though her voice were no longer her own, as though it were taken over by the words of others, expropriated.

Recounting thus how Echo had come to be deprived of living speech, the story tells, then, of her futile efforts to make love

84

to Narcissus, a design which she could carry out only by repeating to the beautiful youth certain tail-end fragments of his own speech. Narcissus's response was the same as in every other case, the same as, finally, in the case of every other: he repulsed her, retreated before her, retreated finally into his own self-enclosing gaze:

> But he retreated:
> 'Keep your hands off,' he cried, 'and do not touch me!
> I would die before I give you a chance at me.'[2]

All that she ever said thereafter was – repeatedly – 'I give you a chance at me.' Finally, she disappeared from sight:

> Her body dries and shrivels till voice only
> And bones remain, and then she is voice only
> For the bones are turned to stone. She hides in woods
> And no one sees her now along the mountains,
> But all may hear her, for her voice is living.[3]

In the end she is nothing but the words of others, a voice that is the death of the living voice.

Or the life of the dead voice. For there is another story about Echo, told a few centuries later by Longus.

Now Echo has come to sing and to play the pipe and the lute. Daughter of a nymph, she had been taught by the Muses and, once she had grown up, she had come to sing with them and to dance with the nymphs. The story tells, then, of how she provokes the wrath of Pan, who envied her music while, on the other hand, being enraged by the way in which she, in love with her virginity, fled all males, whether men or gods, giving him thus no opportunity to enjoy her beauty. The story continues:

> Therefore he sends a madness among the shepherds and goatherds, and they in a desperate fury, like so many dogs and wolves, tore her all to pieces and flung about them all over the earth her yet singing limbs. The earth in observance of the nymphs buried them all, preserving in them still their music, and they by an everlasting sentence and decree of the Muses breathe out a voice.[4]

A maniacal, Bacchic frenzy. Echo, her voice, her music, dismembered – like Dionysus – and dispersed, scattered, disseminated, yet sounding forth still from beneath the earth, unseen.

Another story, in a quite different setting. It is a story of wandering alone in the Alps under a sky so clear that the sunlight has almost the same intense transparency as in Sicily or even Greece, the same burning intensity yet cooled, or rather masked, by the fresh mountain air. The story tells of climbing over a ridge and then down into a high valley. Boulders are strewn here and there, reminders of deafening avalanches; but now only the occasional tinkle of a cowbell is to be heard. Nothing else. It is partly for this reason that listening proves so exceptional here, because there is almost nothing to hear; but also because the valley, encircled by snow-covered peaks, forms a kind of open enclosure into which one's voice can expand and resound. Here monologue and its interiority are unthinkable. Instead, the voice is drawn out into a space which, rather than being simply filled by the sound of the voice, claims it and in a sense takes possession of it. Here there is a spacing that disperses the voice while also giving back its sound, that multiplies it while also letting its sound echo back as if from other voices. Hearing the echo, one then experiences silence, not as the mere opposite of speech or sound but as the open space of the voice.

Wandering through the open, drifting just now away from stories about Echo, the discourse drifting now toward some other genre. Toward what? Perhaps toward philosophy? Or perhaps toward its other, another of its others, toward non-philosophy? In any case it is time to listen to the philosophers, to what some of them have said about philosophy and non-philosophy. Let us, then listen to the voices – echoed across the space of historical and linguistic differences – the voices with which philosophy has addressed its other.

Parmenides, received by the goddess: 'It is necessary that you shall learn all things, as well the unshaken heart of well-rounded truth as the opinions of mortals in which there is no true belief'.[5]

Plato – or rather, Socrates, alluding to Homer, speaking to Theodorus on the occasion of meeting the Stranger from Elea:

However, I fancy it is not much easier, if I may say so, to discern this kind than that of the gods. For these men – I mean those who are not feignedly but really philosophers – appear disguised in all sorts of shapes, thanks to the ignorance of the rest of mankind, and visit the cities, beholding from above the life of those below, and they seem to some to be of no worth and to others to be worth everything. And sometimes they appear disguised as statesmen, and sometimes as sophists, and sometimes they may give some people the impression that they are altogether mad.[6]

Hegel, introducing his and Schelling's *Critical Journal of Philosophy* in 1802: 'Philosophy is by its nature something esoteric . . . it is philosophy only by being opposed to the understanding and therefore still more to common sense . . . in relation to the latter the world of philosophy is in and for itself an inverted world'.[7]

Finally, Merleau-Ponty, just before his death, in his last course 'Philosophy and Non-philosophy since Hegel': 'True philosophy is non-philosophy – which is to enter into the profundity of "experience".'[8]

But what, then, about Heidegger? What about philosophy and non-philosophy after Heidegger, taking this phrase to mean, at least initially, according to Heidegger? What about philosophy and non-philosophy after Heidegger in other senses of this phrase? Is it readily apparent what the other senses are? Is it obvious what the locution 'after Heidegger' means? Can one simply assume that its senses remain intact, delimited by common sense or at least readily delimitable by a certain supplementary philosophical understanding? Can one assume such delimitation of sense despite the radical inversion, indeed the utter displacement, that philosophy as such – to say nothing of common sense – undergoes in and through Heidegger's work? What is the situation after the displacement of the conception of time that has held sway for more than two millennia? What is the situation with respect to the very 'after' by which the situation would be delimited? Do we today really know what 'after' means? Much less what it means to think after Heidegger, to think about philosophy and non-philosophy after Heidegger?

Do we even know indeed what it means to think according to Heidegger? How is one to listen to Heidegger so as then to be in a position to think in accord with what one has heard? Do we today really know what 'listening' means? Do we know what it means to be in accord with something heard?

What is the profundity of 'experience' into which one must enter? What is the inversion that one must undergo? What is the madness that one must risk? In other words, what is required in order to listen in the appropriate way to the echo of Heidegger, to the echo for which Heidegger's work has opened the space?

In *Being and Time* the relation between philosophy and non-philosophy prescribes the primary methodological structure. In this connection non-philosophy means pre-philosophy, the pre-ontological, which – however overlaid by the forgottenness of Being that becomes even more effective in the history of ontology – remains continuous with philosophy, essentially, structurally continuous. Indeed, the structure that guarantees the continuity is nothing less than that of Dasein itself, for Dasein *is*, pre-ontologically, the question of Being, the question definitive of ontology, of philosophy as such: 'But the question of Being is then nothing but the radicalization of an essential tendency of Being [*Seinstendenz*] which belongs to Dasein itself, the pre-ontological understanding of Being'.[9] To take up again the question of Being is to clear away the concealments in such a way as to make explicit Dasein's always already operative understanding of Being. Or, more precisely, it is to 'listen in on [*abzuhören*]' Dasein's own recovery of its understanding of Being; it is to interpret Dasein's own self-disclosure: 'Such interpretation takes part in this disclosure only in order existentially to raise to a conceptual level [*in den Begriff*] the phenomenal content of what has been disclosed'.[10]

Derrida has drawn special attention to this continuity, this unity, especially in the form it assumes in Heidegger's introductory discussion of the formal structure of the question of Being.[11] Here it becomes the unity joining questioner and questioned, the former taking up the question of Being by interrogating a being (Dasein) with which it is essentially continuous, in a

certain sense identical. That continuity, expressed in the
Heideggerian discourse by the 'we' – Derrida of course draws
the comparison with Hegel – is what guarantees the possibility
of the analysis of Dasein, of its being carried out phenomeno-
logically. On the other hand, whether Heidegger's reliance
upon this unity has the effect of placing the formal structure of
the question of Being – and ultimately the entire project of
fundamental ontology – within the horizon of metaphysics is
quite another matter. Any decision in this regard would require
an extended and careful analysis and one that takes account of
the full range of the analysis in the two published Divisions of
Being and Time. Here it must suffice merely to mention two
issues.

First of all, one ought to bear in mind that when *Being and
Time* was written – and quite explicitly a year afterwards in *The
Basic Problems of Phenomenology* – Heidegger regarded his project
as in a sense quite decisively placed within the horizon of
metaphysics, namely, as undertaking finally to fulfill 'the latent
goal and constant and more or less evident demand of the
whole development of Western philosophy.'[12] By carrying
through in the most radical way the same regress (from the
question of Being to the analysis of the 'subject') that has been
exercised throughout the history of philosophy, *Being and Time*
would bring metaphysics to the point of its fulfillment, would
move finally to that very center that would always have determined metaphysics. And yet, that way to the center would be,
as it were, precisely the way to the outermost limit of metaphysics, to the point at which a certain break would be made
with that determination of Being (oriented to production[13]) that
was the fruit of ancient ontology and its legacy to the entire
history of philosophy. All of this is merely to underline that in
Being and Time – to say nothing of the later texts, from which
virtually the entire contemporary discussion of the closure of
metaphysics is drawn – the relation which Heidegger explicitly
envisions between the project of fundamental ontology and the
history of metaphysics is, to say the least, quite complex.

Secondly, it is imperative to recognize that from the very
outset of *Being and Time*, Dasein's fundamental self-relation is
not considered simply as a matter of self-presence. More point-
edly, it is regarded not as a relation of Dasein to itself at all, to

itself as a presentable being, but rather as Dasein's relation to its Being, as its interrogative, disclosive comportment to its own Being. The functioning of the 'I' as a 'we' in the Heideggerian discourse does not therefore serve immediately to place that discourse within the horizon of the metaphysical privileging of presence. The question is whether and to what extent Dasein's self-relation, conceived as existence and no longer as simply the relation of one being to another being with which it is or becomes identical – whether and to what extent such a conception breaks with the privilege of presence.

In any case, the continuity between philosophy and non-philosophy is intact in *Being and Time*, and there is virtually no question of fixing a boundary between them, no question of a limit that would have to be transgressed in moving between them. The pre-philosophical is always already the philosophical to some degree.

On the other hand, in the later texts – the texts after 1930, forgoing for the moment any further discrimination – everything is in a sense different as regards philosophy and non-philosophy. The difference between philosophy and non-philosophy is no longer that between pre-ontological and onto-logical; indeed, one could say that the unity of the latter pair, the continuity between, as it were, common sense and meta-physics, is retained but only as one moment within the opposition to a kind of non-philosophy that was barely, if at all, in play in *Being and Time*. Now there is a boundary, a limit requiring transgression. Now the other of philosophy does not lie before philosophy, for the pre-philosophical is too thoroughly determined by philosophy, by the philosophical determination of Being as presence. Now the other of philosophy lies *after* philosophy. One must pass through philosophy on the way to this other, but not as one passes through the pre-ontological in the project of fundamental ontology. Now it is a matter of rupture, of transgression. Now it is a matter of the end of philosophy and the task of thinking.

The opening sentence of Heidegger's late text 'The End of Philosophy and the Task of Thinking' needs to be taken with utmost seriousness: 'The title names the attempt at a reflection that persists in questioning [*im Fragen verharrt*].'[14] It is not only a matter of recognizing the seriousness with which in this text Heidegger persists in questioning, for instance, in the sense of posing questions ever anew, seeking thus to avoid closing off interrogation; nor is it only a matter of reproducing such persistence as one reads Heidegger's text; but also it is a matter of letting this persistence remain itself open to interrogation, of not too facilely – or, rather, too seriously – assuming that it is obvious what it means to persist in questioning.

The opposition philosophy/non-philosophy, as well as the transition from the former to the latter, are expressed in the title of Heidegger's text; likewise in the two questions posed at the end of the opening section and adopted as headings for the two principal sections of the text:

1 To what extent has philosophy in the present age entered into its end?

2 What task is reserved for thinking at the end of philosophy? (E, p. 61/373)

The title and these two questions suggest a very simple schema: philosophy has recently come to an end or is now about to end; then, after the end of philosophy, something else is to begin, something called thinking. Presumably Heidegger's text is to fill out this schema by considering the manner in which philosophy has ended or is about to end and the character of the new beginning then to be made, of the task to which it will be addressed, the task of what is called thinking.

And yet, for Heidegger's attempt at a reflection to proceed in such a manner would be precisely *not* to persist in questioning. And so, rather than all-too-hastily detaching this schema from Heidegger's text in order then to employ it as a grid for reading that text, it would be more appropriate to begin by calling this all-too-obvious initial schema into question, preparing perhaps an eventual displacement of it. If one would persist in questioning, thus taking up in its proper element a text that professes such persistence, one ought, then, to question those questions that initially give every appearance of being utterly secure as questions, those questions that seem only to need answers.

What, then, is to be understood by end? What does it mean for something like philosophy to end? Does it mean simply termination? Is the end of philosophy simply the point at which

philosophy ceases to occur? But then, is not this very representation – of a point in history, in time, at which philosophy
ceases – itself thoroughly determined by philosophy? Are not
the very means by which the end of philosophy would thus be
understood drawn precisely from philosophy? Would one not
need to ask: Can philosophy understand its own end? Do its
means suffice for understanding their very limit? Or, does the
end of philosophy perhaps mean something else, for instance,
completion, fulfillment, perfection? In this case the end of philosophy might then turn out to be anything but its termination;
philosophy could, presumably, simply remain intact in its end,
persisting in its final state.

There are, then, these and other senses of end. All of them
have been determined by philosophy, in the course of that
history of philosophy that is now coming to its end. But then
what happens at the end of philosophy? What happens to these
various senses of end that have themselves been determined
by philosophy, within the network of basic philosophical
concepts? Do these senses simply remain intact at the end of
philosophy? Or, does that end not produce a certain displacement, an erosion, of the very senses of end?

What, then, about the opposition between philosophy and
thinking? What is the character of the opposition if, for instance,
philosophy could persist, even in its most perfect form, alongside thinking? Is the opposition, the otherness of thinking, such
as could be expressed within philosophy? Or is the articulation
of the 'non-' of non-philosophy already itself transgressive?

What, then, is to be understood by beginning? Is it simply
opposed to end? Is it simply temporal, i.e. in the present context
a time that follows the end of philosophy? Or is one to hear in
it an echo of ἀρχή, of origin? In that case the beginning, of
thinking would be not some time of commencement but rather
that by which, from which, thinking would originate, that
which would give thinking its task (*Aufgabe*), to which thinking
would be given up (*aufgegeben*), given over. Is this perhaps why
Heidegger names his attempt as he does: the end of philosophy
and the *task* of thinking? Is it also perhaps why the attempt
thus named must be one that persists in questioning?

The introductory section of Heidegger's text provides a
certain indication of just how that text persists in questioning.

The attempt named 'The End of Philosophy and the Task of Thinking' belongs to a larger context, a more comprehensive attempt, which is described thus: 'It is the attempt undertaken again and again ever since 1930 to shape the question of *Being and Time* in a more originary fashion [*die Fragestellung von* » *Sein und Zeit* « *anfänglicher zu gestalten*]' (E, p. 61/373). The attempt is – literally – to shape the *Fragestellung*, i.e. the way in which the question is posed, set up, deployed; and to do so in a way that is *anfänglicher*, more originary. To persist in questioning is to sustain this attempt to shape the *Fragestellung* more originarily, to deploy the question in a way that is more in accord with the origin.

What form does the more originary deployment assume? The introductory section of Heidegger's text gives a further indication: it is the attempt 'to subject the point of departure of *Being and Time* to an immanent critique,' that is, to pose to the deployment of the question as carried out in *Being and Time* 'the critical question.' In a sense of course the deployment of the question in *Being and Time* already poses the critical question, the question in which the fundamental turn of critique is constituted. In the case of Kantian critique – and one cannot but hear in this word an echo of Kant – it is a matter of an interrogative turn from objects to the conditions of the possibility of objects, of their appearing as objects. Since such conditions are to be found in the subject, Kantian critique assumes the form of a turn to the subject in the sense indicated by Kant's comparison of his project with the Copernican revolution. Within certain limits one can say that an analogous turn is carried out in *Being and Time*. There it is a matter of turning to that being that modern metaphysics called subject, of turning to what is now called Dasein, in order to uncover the operation of that understanding of Being, the genuine *a priori*, by which it becomes possible for beings to present themselves. That operation proves to be – in the very briefest formula – what is called disclosedness (*Erschlossenheit*), the operation in which is opened a space, a world, in which beings can present themselves. In this sense one could say that disclosedness is *die Sache des Denkens* in *Being and Time*, *die Sache* to which thinking turns, assuming that – though it can hardly be evident from this very schematic account – one can discern in *Being and Time* what later is called thinking.

The critical question is, then, the question of *die Sache*, the question of that to which philosophy, at least as critique in the broadest sense, would turn in its turn away from the presentation of beings. To shape the deployment of this question more originarily, to subject the critical question as deployed in *Being and Time* to an immanent critique can only mean, then, to carry through the critical question itself more radically, to engage in the question of *die Sache* more questioningly. What this requires is that in the turn to *die Sache* one set out of action the assumption that *die Sache* has as its locus that being that fundamental ontology calls Dasein, the assumption that *die Sache* is an operation of Dasein, even if the operation is constitutive of Dasein. What is required is that one no longer assumes, no longer resumes (even if more radically, even if most radically) that regress to the subject (in the broadest, not specifically modern sense) that is common to the entire history of metaphysics and that Heidegger recognized as such. What is required is that *die Sache* be allowed to become radically questionable, that the critical question become the question of the very site of *die Sache*: 'Thus it must become clear to what extent the *critical* question, of what *die Sache des Denkens* is, necessarily and continually belongs to thinking.' (E, p. 61/373). It is a matter of persisting in questioning *die Sache*, of letting its full questionableness come into play. To do so is to grant a certain distance between Dasein and *die Sache*, between – to mention only one such formulation – self-understanding and the understanding of Being. It is to begin to grant to *die Sache* a certain withdrawal.[15]

But what is it that makes a more originary shaping of the *Fragestellung* necessary? What is it that inscribes a distance between Dasein and *die Sache*? What is it that requires that *die Sache* be granted a certain withdrawal? How is it that one must persist in questioning? Why not rather do as common sense and metaphysics would prescribe: leave the question behind as quickly as possible for the sake of getting on to the answer? Why not – in a more properly metaphysical formulation – move on to a ground, even to a final ground in which questioning would reach its end?

Because questioning – metaphysical questioning – has

reached its end. It is precisely the end of metaphysics that generates the need for redeploying the question more originarily. It is the end of metaphysics that releases the distancing, the withdrawal, of *die Sache*, that disrupts the metaphysical drive to ground. It is in the wake of the end of metaphysics that one must persist in questioning.

For metaphysics is – in the very schematic conception to which Heidegger limits himself in this text – precisely the drive to ground, that is, the turn from beings back to their Being, which is taken to have the character of presence (*Anwesenheit*, παρουσία) or ground (ἀρχή): 'What characterizes metaphysical thinking, which investigates the ground for beings, is that such thinking, starting from what is present [*vom Anwesenden*], represents it in its presence [*Anwesenheit*] and thus exhibits it as grounded by its ground' (E, p. 62/374).

But what is meant by the end of metaphysics? Is it simply termination, as if the futility of the drive to ground had finally become apparent, vindication now a kind of utter positivism? Or is it final perfection, the fulfillment of the drive in a manner that would make any resumption superfluous? Heidegger insists that it is a matter neither of termination nor of perfection but rather of completion (*Vollendung*) in the sense of a certain kind of gathering, a certain kind of place of gathering: 'The end of philosophy is the place, that place in which the whole of philosophy's history is gathered into its most extreme possibility. End as completion means this gathering' (E, p. 63/375). The end of metaphysics is the gathering of the history of metaphysics into its most extreme possibility.

What happens, then, in the end of metaphysics? How is it announced concretely?

It is announced as the reversal, the inversion, of Platonism. Heidegger refers to the decisiveness of Plato's thinking: 'Metaphysics is Platonism' (E, p. 63/375). This decisiveness consists in the way that Platonism established the difference between beings and Being (ground, presence), the way in which it established the circuit, as it were, within which metaphysics turns. The end of metaphysics comes with Nietzsche's reversal of Platonism. In a text in which he reflects on Nietzsche as 'the last metaphysician,' Heidegger explains: 'But then what does it mean, "the end of metaphysics"? It means the historical moment in which *the essential possibilities* of metaphysics are exhausted. The last of these possibilities must be that form of metaphysics in which its essence is reversed'.[16] The end of metaphysics occurs as that form of metaphysics in which its essence is reversed, in which the difference that marks out its circuit is inverted. This form of metaphysics is the *last* possibility of metaphysics, the possibility with which it is exhausted, the possibility which withdraws all further possibilities, the extreme possibility.

And yet, in being gathered into its most extreme possibilities, metaphysics does not simply terminate. It does not simply give way to positivism, if for no other reason than that the inversion has the effect of displacing that very order of alleged positivity that would remain, opening within it a certain economy:

> The end of metaphysics that is to be thought here is but the beginning of metaphysics' 'resurrection' in altered forms; these forms leave to the proper, exhausted history of fundamental metaphysical positions the purely economic role of providing raw materials with which – once they are correspondingly transformed – the world of 'knowledge' is built 'anew.'[17]

Though its essential possibilities are exhausted, metaphysics in its end remains intact and continues to operate in a kind of compulsive repetition.

There is still another aspect: metaphysics not only continues in this purely repetitive way but also in another regard asserts itself still more forcefully: 'As a completion, an end is the gathering into the most extreme possibilities. We think in too limited a fashion as long as we expect only a development of new philosophies of the previous style' (E, p. 63/375). Heidegger refers to the relation of philosophy to science, to the way in which sciences develop within the field opened up by philosophy, finally separating themselves from philosophy. The end of philosophy occurs as the completion of such separation, that is, as the triumph of science and technology. One could say that metaphysics dissolves into science and technology, which are thus its outcome, its final possibility. And yet, it is a matter not merely of dissolution but also of completion. One would need, then, to ask: What is it about metaphysics that science and technology bring to completion? A detour through other texts – most notably, 'The Question concerning Technology' – would supply an answer: It is a matter of carrying to the extreme a certain concealment that belongs intrinsically to metaphysics. But one would need also to exercise a certain reticence, at least to wonder whether such an exposure would not require a certain transgression of the very limit it would establish. The question is whether one can delimit the end of philosophy without already having taken up the task of thinking. One must persist in questioning.

The first section of Heidegger's text, governed by the question of the end of metaphysics, concludes at the limit, concludes by announcing a certain operation of the limit: 'But is the end of philosophy in the sense of its evolving into the sciences also already the complete actualization of all the possibilities in which the thinking of philosophy was posited?' (E, p. 65/377). What can be meant by 'the thinking of philosophy'? What must be the character of the limit dividing philosophy from thinking if thinking also somehow belongs to philosophy? How can the other of philosophy, non-philosophy, belong also to philosophy? Heidegger continues:

> Or is there a *first* possibility for thinking apart from the *last* possibility which we characterized (the dissolution of philosophy in the technologized sciences), a possibility from which the thinking of philosophy would have to start, but which as philosophy it could nevertheless not experience and adopt? (E, p. 65/377)

It is by no means a matter of opposition and of transition between opposites, from philosophy to non-philosophy. Rather, it is a matter of a limit, of a 'first possibility' that would be the limit of philosophy, a limit whose operation would delimit philosophy such that philosophy, commencing only this side of the limit, could never experience the limit. Philosophy would always have been delimited by non-philosophy, and the transition from the end of philosophy to the task of thinking would be a transgression of this limit.

Everything depends on the transgression, on crossing the limit in the way called for by *die Sache*.

The limit of philosophy delimits the circuit in which metaphysics turns in its turning from beings as they present themselves to Being as the ground which makes such self-presentation possible, as the presence which lets beings come to presence. Transgression involves, first of all, asking what remains unthought in that turning. It involves regress to that which must be already, though concealedly, in play whenever such turning commences.

The second part of Heidegger's text is thus devoted largely to sketching this regress. It may be regarded as involving two stages. The first has as its point of departure the movement from the presentation of beings, their shining in such a way as to show themselves, to Being as that which, shining in and through them, makes it possible for them to present themselves as the beings they are. The regress itself – its first stage – is then expressed by Heidegger thus: 'Such shining [*Scheinen*] occurs necessarily in a brightness [*Helle*]. Only through brightness can what shines show itself, i.e., shine' (E, p. 71/383). Thus, the first stage of the regress is from the shining-showing of beings in their Being to that brightness, that light, which any such shining-showing requires. Echoes of Plato. The regress still short of the limit.

Then comes transgression:

But brightness in its turn rests in something open,
something free [*in einem Offenen, Freien*] which it might
illuminate here and there, now and then. Brightness plays
in the open and wars there with darkness. Wherever
something present [*ein Anwesendes*] encounters something
else present . . . , there openness already rules, the free
region is in play. (E, p. 71/383f.)

The regress, the transgression is to the openness, the free region; it is to what Heidegger calls *Lichtung*, clearing, which is to be rigorously distinguished from light. Indeed that distinction is the transgression: 'Light can stream into the clearing, into its openness, and let brightness play with darkness in it. But light never first creates the clearing. Rather, light presupposes the clearing' (E, p. 72/384).

What, then, is the non-philosophy to which the transgression would lead? What is thinking?

Thinking is *of the clearing*.

And yet, thinking is not *of* the clearing in the sense that intuition may be said to be *of* something that appears or in the sense that knowledge is *of* a being. Thinking is not *of* the clearing even in the sense that understanding can be *of* Being, say, as εἶδος. How, then, is thinking *of* the clearing?

At least two senses are readily distinguishable. The first pertains to the thinking *of philosophy*. Such thinking, which turns from beings to Being, is *of the clearing* in the sense that this turning must occur within the clearing. Yet, as a turning to Being as presence, the thinking of philosophy is incapable of thinking the clearing. The clearing is the unthought site of the thinking of philosophy, a site even unthinkable for the ~~thinking~~ of philosophy, for that turning whose very condition is that the site be concealed as such and, along with it, thinking's belongingness to that site.

The second sense pertains to thinking at the end of philosophy, to the thinking of non-philosophy. How is thinking *of* the clearing at the end of metaphysics? Does such thinking simply turn to the clearing? Does it turn to what remains unthought in metaphysics and thus turn away from metaphysics? Does it commence by turning once and for all away from metaphysics, away from the circuit of shining-showing by which metaphysics is comprised? Does it commence by turning decisively to the clearing, by installing itself unequivocally and irrevocably in an orientation to the clearing? Does thinking at the end of metaphysics *simply think* the clearing?

One cannot but be suspicious of the prospect of such a new immediacy. Even if non-philosophy could be impervious to philosophy in the end – that is, if it could go unchallenged by the sway of technology – still it would need to be, in a not undecisive way, mediated by the end of philosophy and thus would be held back from the freedom of which one might dream. Is it not to just such a need that the regress sketched in Heidegger's text attests? Is not that regress governed, to an essential degree, by philosophy? Not only in that philosophy, the circuit of the shining-showing of Being/beings, is the *terminus a quo* of the regress; but also in that, even in its finally transgressive stage, the regress remains structurally undifferentiated from a transcendental regress, a kind of imitation, more generally, of the metaphysical regress from beings to Being, a mimesis that would be carried out not in a pre-given sphere – tracing there certain lines already traced in another sphere, that of philosophy – but rather in a space that would first be opened up by the mimesis. Non-philosophy is not pre-given but only begins in imitation of philosophy.

Heidegger's text alludes to this involvement: 'For every attempt to get a look [*Einblick*] into the supposed task of thinking finds itself directed to a look back [*Rückblick*] into the whole of the history of philosophy' (E, p. 66/378). Thinking ahead into the clearing, the look into that to which thinking is to be given over, is also a thinking back toward philosophy, a look back into its history. Thinking at the end of metaphysics remains in the transition that one might otherwise mistake as the way to a new immediacy, beyond philosophy, simply non-philosophy. But there can be no simple non-philosophy, rather only a never-completed transition which would be such as to displace its very sense as something to be completed. Thinking at the end of metaphysics is a thinking at the limit of metaphysics.

Even at its end, when, as in death, it is gathered into its most extreme possibility, even when it is thus deprived of living speech – even if at the very moment of its most rigorous self-enclosure – philosophy still sounds, even if its words are no longer really its own. Even if a final madness leaves its voice dismembered, it continues to echo, to ring out into that open enclosure that Heidegger calls clearing.

Nonetheless, the mimetic opening of the clearing – the opening to non-philosophy – carries out a more originary deployment of the question. As in *Being and Time*, the movement is one beyond Being, that is, a movement toward that which makes possible the shining-showing of Being. In *Being and Time*, this 'beyond' – what Heidegger there calls the meaning of Being (*der Sinn vom Sein*) – is identified as temporality and its locus was taken to be Dasein.[18] In 'The End of Philosophy and the Task of Thinking' this identification is rescinded in favor of an identification of the 'beyond' of Being as the clearing. In the later text the question is, then, whether temporality, ecstatic time, is not to be regarded as possible only within the clearing:

Accordingly, we may suggest that the day will come when we will not shun the question whether the clearing, the free open, may not be that within which alone pure space and ecstatic time and everything present and absent in them have the place which gathers and shelters everything. (E, p. 72f./385)

Furthermore – and more assertorially – the 'beyond' is no longer taken to have its locus simply in Dasein, not even in the sense of constituting – as disclosedness, for instance – the very essence of Dasein. The 'beyond' is not a 'condition' within Dasein, something on the side of Dasein's understanding or thinking, that makes it possible for Dasein to understand or think Being. Rather, as clearing, the 'beyond' of Being precedes both thinking and Being in such a way as to make possible the very presence of thinking and Being to one another. The 'beyond' is to be thought 'as the clearing which first grants Being and thinking and their presencing to and for each other.' The clearing is to be thought as the place 'from which alone the possibility of the belonging together of Being and thinking, that is, presence and apprehending, can arise at all' (E, p. 75/387). If clearing first grants thinking, then thinking cannot be a representational activity of a subject that would take the clearing as the object of thinking. Thinking is not the subject of, but rather is subject to, the clearing – even in the case of a thinking that mimetically opens the clearing.

Yet, how is it that the opening to non-philosophy, even if a more originary deployment of the question, is such as to let the full questionableness of *die Sache* come into play? Is it not – apart from the complexity of its involvement with the echoes of philosophy – simply a regress to a more originary origin, to the clearing beyond Being and time, to the clearing that is a still more originary origin than Being or time? But in this case how is it that a previously unheard-of questionableness comes into play? How is it that the clearing is more questionable and that thinking, which is of the clearing, is thus required to persist in questioning?

In the regress to the clearing there sounds the echo not only of philosophy but also of another voice, one 'which still today, although unheard, speaks in the sciences into which philosophy dissolves' (E, p. 74/386f.), a voice which thus echoes in philosophy. The voice is itself responsive to something heard, something to which it responds mimetically. The voice is that of Parmenides' poem; what is heard and then said is the following:

> χρεὼ δὲ σε πάντα πυθέσθαι
> ἠμὲν Ἀληθείης εὐκυκλέος ἀτρεμὲς ἦτορ
> ἠδὲ βροτῶν δόξας, ταῖς οὐκ ἔνι πίστις ἀληθής.
> Fragment I, 28ff.

Heidegger's German translation:

> du sollst aber alles erfahren:
> sowohl der Unverborgenheit, der gutgerundeten,
>   nichtzitterndes Herz
> als auch der Sterblichen Dafürhalten, dem fehlt das
>   Vertrauenkönnen auf Unverborgenes. (E, p. 74)

Again the English translation already cited: 'It is necessary that you shall learn all things, as well the unshaken heart of well-rounded truth as the opinions of mortals in which there is no true belief.' Thus was the clearing, even if unthought by philosophy, named in the beginning of philosophy, named ἀλήθεια, named in a naming presented as a mimetic response to the words of the goddess, who is none other than ἀλήθεια itself.[19] Certainly not a naming in which a subject bestows a designation upon an object; rather, a naming in which one is subject to something heard from beyond Being, a voice which echoes silently from the open enclosure, opening that enclosure to the mimetic speech which, sounding forth into it, would name it.

But ἀλήθεια is not truth, Heidegger insists in 'The End of Philosophy and the Task of Thinking,' responding to Friedländer's criticism[20] and now distinguishing rigorously between ἀλήθεια as named in Parmenides' poem (Heidegger translates: Unverborgenheit – in English: unconcealment) and ἀλήθεια as ὀρθότης (correctness), now granting that even among the early Greeks the latter sense was dominant. The effect is to deny that there was ever any pure prevailing of ἀλήθεια as unconcealment, any speaking and thinking immediately open to it; rather, ἀλήθεια 'was experienced only as ὀρθότης' (E, p. 78/390). It is no more a matter of immediacy at the beginning than at the end of metaphysics.

But, then, ἀλήθεια is never simply present as such, and this is why the opening to it is not simply a regress to a more original origin but rather one in which the very determination of origin – as ground, i.e. presence, to be itself brought to presence in metaphysics – is eroded. What comes decisively into play in the opening to non-philosophy is concealment, even if itself persisting in its questionableness:

> Only what ἀλήθεια as clearing grants is experienced and thought, not what it is as such. This remains concealed. Does this happen by chance? Does it happen only as a consequence of the carelessness of human thinking? Or does it happen because self-concealing, concealment, λήθη, belongs to ἀλήθεια, not just as an addition, not as shadow to light, but rather as the heart of ἀλήθεια? (E, p. 78/390)

Such is the very medium of questionableness – that is, because concealment belongs to the clearing, the latter is so constituted as to be essentially questionable. It is thus that thinking, which is of the clearing, must persist in questioning.

Heidegger turns again to Parmenides at the end of a seminar held in Zähringen in September 1973. From the seminar only a protocol is available.[21] In the seminar Heidegger reads from a text written during the winter of 1972–3, a text devoted to a saying by Parmenides. Echoes within echoes.

Heidegger's turn to Parmenides, the turn back (*Rückkehr*) to the beginning, is, he says, a roundabout way that is necessary for the turn into (*Einkehr*) the experience of the clearing. He continues: 'The turn back takes place in the *echo* of Parmenides. It takes place as that listening that opens itself to the word of Parmenides from out of our present-day era, from out of the epoch of the dispensation of Being as *Ge-stell*' (S, p. 132). Not only does Heidegger repeat, at a very critical juncture of the seminar, that what is said occurs in 'the echo of Parmenides' (S, p. 134), but also he forestalls mistaking such discourse as mere appropriation of what Parmenides said. He is concerned not only with seeing how a certain matter 'has shown itself for

Parmenides' (S, p. 133) but even with hearing it 'with a Greek ear' (S, p. 135).

The theme of the text that Heidegger reads in the seminar is: the heart of ἀλήθεια. He begins by citing from 'The End of Philosophy and the Task of Thinking' the passage (cited above) in which the question is raised whether concealment is the heart of ἀλήθεια. Then he comments: 'What is said here is not so; Parmenides says no such thing' (S, p. 133). Thus the question is to be reopened: What is to be heard in Parmenides' saying about the heart of ἀλήθεια, about ἀληθείης εὐκυκλέος ἀτρεμὲς ἦτορ? It is to this question that the text read in the seminar is addressed. That text is itself primarily a reading of a series of Parmenides' sayings.

Heidegger establishes, first, that in Parmenides' saying that ἀλήθεια is εὐκυκλέος one is to hear – instead of the usual rendering 'well-rounded' – the well-encompassing, the appropriately encircling [das Wohlumfangende, schicklich Umkreisende] (S, p. 134). But what, then, of the ἀτρεμὲς ἦτορ, the unshaken, unwavering heart that would thus be appropriately encircled by well-encompassing ἀλήθεια?

Heidegger cites from Fragment 6:

ἔστι γὰρ εἶναι

and translates:

Ist nämlich Sein.

It is this unheard, unheard-of, scandalous saying (dieses unerhörte Wort) – that Being is – that marks 'exactly how far from familiar thinking Parmenides' extraordinary way is' (S, p. 135); it is what Heidegger insists must be heard 'with a Greek ear.' Heidegger continues: 'The name for what is addressed in this matter sounds thus [lautet]: τὸ ἐόν, which is neither a being nor simply Being, but rather τὸ ἐόν' (S, p. 135). Then he adds, in direct apposition to τὸ ἐόν: 'Anwesend: Anwesen selbst.'

What is to be heard in these words, these echoes within echoes? What is to be heard if one listens to them from out of the orientation given by 'The End of Philosophy and the Task of Thinking'?

The 'unwavering heart' to which Parmenides' unerhörtes Wort is addressed is not a being. Nor, Heidegger says, is it simply

Being (*noch lediglich das sein*). And yet, in a sense it is Being; it is, as he says, '*Anwesen selbst*,' or, still more explicitly, '*Anwesenheit selbst*.' It is presence, i.e. Being, not simply but rather as coming to presence. For coming to presence is precisely what presence, i.e. Being, simply does not do, does not do simply. Rather, in common sense, for example, it merely shines unobtrusively through beings in such a way that these beings themselves shine so as to show themselves, to come to presence. Metaphysics would of course invert common sense and direct itself to Being; yet, in turning merely within the circuit of Being/ beings, it cannot but turn Being into a being in the very process of bringing it to presence. What is at issue in the remote sayings of Parmenides is another coming to presence: Being would come to presence in being set back within the clearing, that is, in being appropriately encircled by ἀλήθεια.

But, then, ἀλήθεια too must be thought in the direction of τὸ ἐόν: ''Αλήθεια is not an empty openness, nor an unmoving chasm. It is to be thought as the disclosure [*Entbergen*] which appropriately encircles the ἐόν' (S, p. 136). He adds: 'This, presence itself coming to presence, permeates [*durchstimmt*] the encircling unconcealment which appropriately discloses it' (S, p. 137). The clearing is not simply a 'beyond' of Being; it is not the promise of a new immediacy at the end of philosophy. The clearing is, rather, the clearing *of* Being, of Being as τὸ ἐόν; that which the clearing encircles permeates it, sounds, resounds, echoes, throughout it.[22]

Non-philosophy does not, then, install itself beyond philosophy, in a 'beyond' of Being, but rather must endure being stationed at the *limit*. Indeed it crosses the limit, but not in a simple movement of transgression; rather in a movement simultaneously in both directions. It thinks what metaphysics would have thought, Being as Being, but does so only by crossing over to the clearing that encircles Being. And yet, it thinks the clearing only by returning to what is encircled, to what sounds throughout the open enclosure.

The limit at which non-philosophy would be stationed is a site where one hears several different echoes, those of philosophy, those from the beginning of philosophy, and those of one's own voice sounding back and forth into the clearing opened as the other of philosophy at the end of philosophy.

Chapter 3

SARTRE'S LAST PHILOSOPHICAL MANIFESTO

Peter Caws

As everyone knows, volume III is not the last volume of the *Idiot* (as I shall call the work in this paper). It is the last volume Sartre wrote, but he insisted that 'someone else could write the fourth on the basis of the three I have written'.[1] For that matter, the *Critique of Dialectical Reason* is not its own last volume either, although Sartre does not seem to have suggested that anyone else could go on with *that* project. Also, in spite of any quantity of subsequently published notebooks, the promise of a moral sequel to *Being and Nothingness* remained unfulfilled, even though in a sense Simone de Beauvoir did what could be done about it, on an elementary level, in *The Ethics of Ambiguity*. All this is familiar enough; 'perhaps all of Sartre,' I have suggested elsewhere, 'will have to be inscribed under the motto: "to be continued." '[2] But my thesis today is that perhaps it won't.

The place of philosophy in Sartre's writing has also been the object of a lot of commentary, starting from his own observation that philosophical ideas grew of their own accord, as it were, like cancer, like a hernia, even while he was writing *non*-philosophical works,[3] and had to be acknowledged and dealt with in subsequent *philosophical* works. In this light the *Critique* appears as an unwanted part of the Flaubert project, surgically removed at an early stage and allowed to find its own way in the world. However the Flaubert project went on for many years, and by the time we reach volume III more philosophical material has accumulated. By now, though, Sartre hardly has the resources to project a separate book, and the result is a mixed growth which requires disentanglement. This process is rewarding; what volume III contains can be regarded, I think, as a closure of the Sartrian philosophical *oeuvre* more satisfactory than anything in the writings of the middle years could have led us to expect.

The earlier writings, on the other hand, do anticipate to some extent the character of this closure. We tend to think when possible of philosophical careers, Sartre's among them, in terms of development, from earlier positions to later ones, and it is easy enough to find justification for this. At least three fundamental changes are to be observed between the Sartre of the 1940s and the Sartre of the 1960s: from the originating and constitutive subject to the constituted subject, from absolute and unconditional freedom to a quasi-total bondage due to scarcity, and from the heroism of the free subject to the modesty of the subject as 'n'importe qui.' However these changes do not constitute an epistemological break between an earlier and a later Sartre but involve rather shifts in point of view entailed by altered circumstances, the availability of new information, the posing of new moral and ideological challenges. And underlying them remains, it seems to me, some of the 'unshakeable certainty' of the earliest years. This is what re-emerges at the end of the *Idiot*.

One of the ideological challenges that Sartre makes a heroic effort to meet is that of Marxism. The whole period of the *Critique* is devoted to this effort. But the *Critique* ends at an impasse: can there be a contemporary historical totalization, from within the class struggle, on the part of an involved agent, or is a historical totalization possible only after the fact, and from without, on the part of a Third? This is the question that is answered, at the end of the first part of volume III, in favor of the second alternative. I shall come back to it at the end of this paper. I remark here however that it has to be answered in the negative because of a Marxist principle to which Sartre had always subscribed and to which he alludes at the beginning of *Search for a Method*.

Marx's claim to greatness lies in part in his stubborn insistence on the reinterpretation of abstract economic relations in concrete human terms, bringing the ideal constructions of the theory of the state or the market down to the real oppressions and deprivations inflicted and suffered by real capitalists or workers. This insistence finds a natural echo in Sartre; he has not learned it from Marx, but as he puts it *repeats* '*with* Marxism: there are only men and real relations between men.'⁴ (We would now be inclined to say 'men and women,' and Sartre would have no objection to that modification.) The point is that nothing happens in the social world that does not happen to individual human subjects. There are no agents or patients except individual men and women, each of whom is the subject of his or her own history, and in the end only individuals qualify to be 'subjects of history' at all.

But this follows from a more fundamental claim: only individuals qualify to be *subjects* at all. And with this we are back to the early Sartre, the existentialist, who never really gave up, at any point during his philosophical career, his original conviction that the whole theatre of human events is contained in the local and temporary separation of being-for-itself from being-in-itself that the force of nothingness makes possible. What does change is what might be called the egotistical component of the existentialist doctrine. From a concentration on the I and the Me in their heroic isolation Sartre comes to enlarge his attention to encompass a field of equivalent centers of subjectivity, each counting for as much as the others, any of whom I might be and with any of whom I may associate myself as a 'we.' One might, without straining either concept unduly, see in the Sartrian doctrine of 'n'importe qui' a form of Rawls's doctrine of the veil of ignorance – or vice versa – but that is not a point I wish to develop further here.

A view of the situation of the individual subject as a local and temporary flaw in being, the metaphysical equivalent of Valéry's poetic insight in 'Le cimitière marin,' is one of the fixed elements of Sartrian doctrine that re-emerges without essential modification in volume III of the *Idiot*. In the following passage, however, it is no longer a question merely of philosophical reflection on the part of Sartre, but of malediction on the part of Flaubert:

> Evil (*le Mal*) is this gnawing contradiction at the heart of being, this discovery in each being, when it devotes all its energies to persevering in its being, that it is only an illusory modulation of nothingness, and in general the vain denial of this truth anticipated in anger and the turbulence of the passions. (*IF* 3, pp. 21–2)⁵

The human condition was never amusing, to be sure. But this is one of the issues with respect to which volume III offers a perspective appropriate to the end of a philosophical career, a kind of reflective closure. For Flaubert after all is not Sartre, and this angry and turbulent indignation is not the philosophical last word on the subject.

Flaubert was a neurotic whose relation to the world was out of balance. In discussing the interdependence of objective events and our subjective perception of them Sartre remarks:

It will be said that we all go through this and that is true: to perceive is to *situate* oneself; there is therefore in any case a dialectic of interiorization and exteriorization. But what counts here is proportion: given that part of the object reveals itself as it is, while revealing what we are (that is our relation to it, our anchorage [in it]), one can hope, as the outcome of a long effort, to arrive at that reciprocity of position (the object defining us to the same extent as we define the object) which is the truth of the human [condition]. In Gustave's case subjectivity consumes the objective and leaves it just enough exteriority for it to transmit its inductive power to the fantasms that have digested it. His whole effort is to desituate himself. [Added in footnote: That is to destroy or hide the relation of reciprocity.] (*IF* 3, p. 12)

So the 'illusory modulation of nothingness' can have its solidity after all, a 'human truth' arrived at 'after a long effort.' That is of course no promise of permanence, but while it lasts the reciprocal process of subjectification-and-objectification is constitutive by its very dynamism. What I find impressive in this passage is precisely the phrase 'au terme d'un long effort' – Sartre can manage this eventual balance of subjectivity and objectivity, he seems to suggest, Flaubert can't; or, each of us can manage it to the extent that our neurosis doesn't prevent it. We have therefore in volume III a kind of test of normal or non-neurotic subjectivity, a sense of what it is like to balance existence against being, albeit for the limited span of a human life, that rounds out, it seems to me, a Sartrian doctrine that begins with the upsurge of the 'by-itself' as early as the first work on the imagination.

This is at the very beginning of volume III (we have in fact reached p. 22), and it is clear that space will not allow me to deal in such detail with all the issues on which Sartre has provided, in that work, a tacit or explicit response to questions left open by his earlier writings. I must save the end of this paper for the question of history, and will now merely sketch in a few intermediate points. These will be connected, in one way or another, with the doctrine of the objective Spirit, or spirit of the age. The situation of the individual involves relations not only to particular objects, the local facticity encountered in perception, but to the whole world of the practico-inert, as history has generated it up to the present of that individual. 'The objective Spirit – in a specific society, at a given epoch – is nothing but Culture as practico-inert' (*IF* 3, p. 44). What does this really involve? Obviously the practico-inert includes monuments, technology, and so on, but its main manifestation is language.

Now it is a fact insufficiently stressed by philosophers that nobody, now, ever learns a language without at the same time learning many things that are said in it by those from whom it is learned. Language is never free of ideology. Primitive thought, passed on in the context of practical life from generation to generation, could avoid this trap because such thought:

> must exist in act and as a part of an act or it does not exist at all. In other words it is born in work and disappears with work. Quite to the contrary systems of value and ideology, when they are verbalized, reside in the mind or at least in memory because language is matter and their elaboration has given them material inertia. Written words are stones. To learn them, to interiorize their assemblages, is to introduce into oneself a mineralized thought which will subsist in us in virtue of its very minerality unless some material work, exercised on it from without, comes along to relieve us of it. (*IF* 3, p. 47)

This 'material work from without' is of course precisely what other writers have named *deconstruction*. And Sartre cites, as a key example of this deconstructive criticism exercised on the practico-inert as given, culture as received, the raising of class consciousness: 'class consciousness appears only as the outcome of a theoretico-practical effort aimed at dissolving as far as it can the ideology in thought' (*IF* 3, p. 46).

This ideology is purely structural:

> By ideology, to be sure, we must not understand a philosophical system, a rigorous construction – even on the basis of false premises – and not even a vague and loose ensemble whose contents however would be common to all the individuals of a class. In fact it is a matter of a group of relations between terms defined only by their reciprocal oppositions or by a 'differential' which determines each by the others in that its only essence resides in its difference from such and such another term, and simultaneously from all the others, differentiation as the reciprocal determination of the couple appearing as a form (a formal duality) against a background constituted by a totality of differentials such that each can be differentiated from the others only in affirming itself as constituted by its difference from the coupled form that detaches itself from the ensemble. It is a matter, as we see, of a false totality, a non-substantial one, of matrices and operators, with no concrete individuation of the Whole nor of the paired relations. It is, if you like, less a thought than an abstract model of thoughts – these when produced able to be absolutely random [*quelconque*], as long as their skeleton and vertebrae are differential relations which engender the terms at the level of the model. Which means first of all that these thoughts can be indefinite in number and vary from one member of a class to another and even, according to the moment, in the same individual. (*IF* 3, p. 222)

It is this variability at the individual level of what other theorists tend to regard as general and objective that confers Sartre's mark on the analysis. And with his customary sure touch he puts his finger, in volume III, on what most dramatically ministers to that variability, by developing at length in a practical and political context a theme that in recent years has been most dominantly visible in a literary one: the theme of *reading*.

If they are to enter into the circuit of history, individuals have to transcend their local situation by interiorizing, through reading, elements of class culture or even world culture. Is there such a thing as world culture *apart* from its distributive objectification in the practico-inert? The objective spirit exists 'only by the activity of men and, more precisely, that of *individuals*' (*IF* 3, p. 50), each of whom, in his study, in the classroom, in the library, totalizes his own reading in his own way. There is, says Sartre in one of his lapses on the subject, a sense – which 'it would be too long to explain here' – in which 'despite this apparent atomization, the conjunction ceaselessly realizes an exhaustive totalization but without a totalizer' (*ibid.*). Too long indeed: just such a totalization without a totalizer was said to be the status of history at the end of the *Critique*; it didn't work there and it doesn't work here. Reading as the key to the totalization of culture, says Sartre, cannot be restored

> in its plenitude. In fact the syntheses of recomposition operate at once according to objective rules (structures of language, explicit or implicit intentions of the author, judgments about him on the part of other authors already read, etc.) *and* according to the idiosyncratic habits, of a singular interiorization (dreaming, resonances, bad faith, ideological interests, etc.). It follows from this that the work, understood by an individuality already formed, that is (at least to some extent) closed, is never altogether taken for what it is: reading illuminates it by the historical context and by the cultural resources of the reader (which precisely pigeonhole the latter at one or another social level) and it serves at the same time as a pretext for each reader to re-live his own history and perhaps the primal scene. No matter: under this subjective camouflage the skeletal structure of imperatives remains, which guides the reading thoughts as much as and more than the dreaming (and purely factual) complacency of the reader can guide them. (*IF* 3, p. 55)

Clearly Sartre still feels the need of a determining drive for history, and it looks as if this 'skeletal structure of imperatives' is to do the driving – but in what direction? For even if a totalization through reading were possible it would be thwarted anew by the appearance of new works:

As the ensemble of works published every day far

transcends the individual possibility of totalizing written culture, this perpetual addition of new material has the effect of preventing the totalization from closing on itself and turning into a calm totality: this is what will be called the life of the objective Spirit, a material detotalization that interiorizes itself in the demand to be totalized and that contradicts this dream in stone. . . . The objective Spirit of an epoch is at once the sum total of the works published at the time in question and the multiplicity of totalizations effected by contemporary readers. (*IF* 3, pp. 56–7)

A multiplicity of totalizations: this finally is the mature image of history in volume III of the *Idiot*. By the time we get to what Flaubert is doing in 1857 the abstract totality of French cultural and historical life has been re-personalized in a single neurotic reader-writer whose life is to be 'oracular,' that is to reflect in a privileged way the life of his epoch. Flaubert is elected by literature; he is 'a martyr, his evils are necessary and his life exemplary'; a 'strange reciprocity unites in [him] the singular and the collective' (*IF* 3, p. 40). He is in other words a paradigm case of the universal singular. I have dealt elsewhere[6] with the extraordinary images that Sartre evokes to render plausible the almost mystical parallel he wishes to establish between Flaubert and the July Monarchy, or in the second part of volume III the Second Empire. Flaubert is Sartre's last-ditch attempt to arrive at a totalized history – no longer now world history but merely the history of an epoch.

'We must admit that the finitude of an individual or micro-organic temporalization *can* embody the finitude of a macro-scopic temperalization, that is the finitude of a *historical period*' (*IF* 3, p. 435). The emphasis on 'can' here gives the impression of Sartre's trying to reassure himself, and one can understand that need, since when he is talking about history as such rather than about Flaubert's embodiment of it he faces squarely enough the daunting complexity of the project:

The truth is, in fact, that History, this ongoing totalization, detotalizes itself unceasingly in and by the very movement of totalization, because even if one were to assign it a single subject for centuries (the bourgeoisie since Etienne Marcel, the proletariat since the Commune, etc.), this subject would itself be *broken*, broken up into generations each of which has for its past the future of the preceding one – even though they all meet in this *common place*: the present – and interprets the present that has been made for it as a rejected future (even though it is accepted, because it is accepted as other). In other words Humanity *is not* and corresponds diachronically to no concept; what exists is an infinite series whose principle is recurrence, defined precisely by these terms: man is the son of man. For this reason history is perpetually finished, that is to say composed of broken-off sequences each of which is the *divergent* continuation (not mechanically but dialectically) of the preceding one and also its transcendence towards *the same* and *different* ends (which assumes that it is at once *distorted* and *conserved*). (*IF* 3, pp. 436–7)

The structure of history is now 'recursive' (*récurrentielle*), and this allows us to understand 'its continuity and the discontinuity of the sequences it totalizes' (*IF* 3, p. 440). *It* totalizes: again how exactly? Sartre does not revert to the larger question of history, but remains with the reciprocal relation that may subsist between an epoch and an individual, and between the birth and death of the latter. 'The absolute finitude of historical agents' (*ibid.*) – this seems to me to be an absolute limitation to the possibility of history in a global sense. There is a motor for history all right, but there is no reason to expect that what it produces will be intelligible. History is driven by the mutual contradictions of the lives that compose an epoch (no longer, it is to be noted, by *class* contradictions): 'the epoch *makes itself* as the totalization of a society in opposing itself to itself through thousands of particular incarnations which struggle among themselves in order to survive on the basis of infrastructural transformations' (*IF*, 3, p. 443).

Ontologically speaking, that seems to be about it: a lot of infrastructural transformations, but no objectively coherent historical superstructure except when an oracular individual comes along to embody and express it. And this seems right: that is the best that history can be, in so far as it is distinguished from the merely physical totality of its aggregate embodiment in the in-itself, the retrospective description of which would be the nearest we could get to totalized totalization if only we could find a neutral language in which to carry it out – which of course we can't.

I must admit that this situation leaves me in no discomfort at all. It is a relief to find, after the Marxist detour through the *Critique* (a characterization that is in no way intended to belittle that very great work), that Sartre's novelistic sense of the distributive actuality of the human world comes in the end to curb his historicist fantasies, and it is striking to notice the similarity of the conclusions of volume III of the *Idiot* to the preoccupations he was working out in the *Cahiers pour une morale* long before he set forth on this detour. If I call volume III the last philosophical manifesto it is in part because I think that the authentic Sartre, with his astonishingly detailed imagination, his cosmic ambition tempered by a redeeming self-irony, his mastery as a prose writer (if not as literary critic) and yet his almost hapless vulnerability to the intrusion of philosophy into his writing, even when he means to be attending to something else – all this *shows* itself at its old strength, if I may say so, in this last major publication. What follows in the bibliography is still enlightening, at least until the last distorted interviews when the parasites have taken over. But volume III is, or perhaps I should say contains (for the whole of Sartre's *Flaubert* cries out for a surgical reduction to make of it the purely philosophical work it potentially is), a fitting closure to an extraordinary philosophical corpus, no longer to be continued.

Post-script

Since this essay was written the second volume of *Critique de la Raison dialectique* has been published.[7] Among the posthumous works it is clearly the most significant supplement to the Sartrian corpus, and will afford material for a new round of scholarship. But it is not a *continuation* of the corpus: in spite of the inevitable temptation to think of works as recent when they have only just been published it is important to remember that *CRD* 2 is *not* a recent work – in fact it dates mainly from 1958, with a few notes from 1961–2. It represents the last valiant (and as usual massive) flounderings of a line of thought Sartre eventually, and for good reason, abandoned.

In *CRD* 2 Sartre is still flying under Marxist colors, and he is still struggling with the difficulty he got himself into at the end of the first volume (*CRD* 1). So the subtitle of the work is '*L'intelligibilité de l'histoire*,' the intelligibility of history. Now there are two main second-order questions that any intelligible project of history must be prepared to answer: *Whose* history? And intelligible *to whom*? Hegel's intellectual descendants (and this includes most continental philosophers, the Marxists among them) usually seem to have in the backs of their minds two plausible but in the end preposterous answers to these questions. History is not in the first instance anyone's history in particular, it is History, world-historical History, in Hegel of Spirit, in Marx of the material development of the species as embodied in the working class. And it is intelligible to itself (or in later Marxist-Leninist dogma to the Party).

Of course a kind of world history, limited to technological and cultural developments in the European mainstream and bringing in the Third World in reaction to these developments, by way of colonialization and liberation, can be recounted in Marxist terms, and I have no wish to belittle Marxist histori-ography or the contributions it has made to the discipline. But Sartre always saw things too clearly to accept either of the easy answers offered in the preceding paragraph, and kept trying to reconcile his desire for historical intelligibility with his old conviction, dealt with in the earlier part of this article, that only individual agents count in the actual making of history. The trick is to find an agent or class of agents who understand *fully* what they are doing *at the time* in the light of a *cumulative and all-inclusive* historical totalization. If anyone could do this then there would be a basis for talking about history as a whole and attributing a direction to it.

In *CRD* 2 Sartre approaches this task, over which he had provisionally thrown up his hands in the final pages of *CRD* 1, in terms of some case studies: boxing, and the early history of the Soviet Union. Boxing, because it is a microcosm of struggle; the Soviet Union, because it is a 'directorial' (or sometimes 'dictatorial') society in which history has a kind of *a priori* intelligibility. In both cases, however, he is as it were making it easy for himself, because in boxing the particular struggle (a given fight between given opponents at a given point in the series of fights leading to a championship, for instance) is surrounded by and included in a ramified system which specifies its intelligibility in advance whatever its outcome, and because in the Soviet Union there is in principle (and often in effect) no struggle – history is one-sided and thus to some degree at least protected from the contingencies that play havoc with its intelligibility in other contexts.

Sartre however goes about the theoretical work that accompanies his analysis of these cases with his customary originality and brilliance. The main category he introduces for this purpose is that of *totalisation d'enveloppement* (best rendered perhaps as 'encircling totalization,' by analogy with the military expression *manoeuvre d'enveloppement* or 'encircling maneuver'). However he slips sometimes into the expression *totalité d'enveloppement* ('encircling totality') – that is, his editors would like to think of it as a slip, though I propose to take it as significant. At one significant point, where Sartre says 'What exactly is it that we have called *encircling totality?*' an editorial note says 'Or rather "totalization" ' – as if the notions were interchangeable. But of course they aren't. That there exists some totality at every moment is a banal truism, at least in non-relativistic contexts (i.e. contexts whose dimensions and velocities are such as to require no corrections due to the theory of relativity, which accounts for all human activities in the history of the universe so far except for one or two highly technical and expensive experiments in physics), whether anyone is in a position to grasp this totality by an act of totalization is however highly problematic. And of course this is just the issue in question, an issue resolved for some limited epochs in the *later* Sartre, as we have seen, by the designation of some lives as 'oracular' – a resolution unsatisfactory enough, to be sure, but one that he is unable to resolve in *CRD* 2.

The temptation to slide from the impossible challenge to transcend one's own situation altogether (which is what totalization at any level above the local, momentary, and provisional requires) into an affirmation of an independent transcendence, is understandable enough. Sartre rejects it whenever the question comes up explicitly, insisting, much to his credit it seems to me, that totalization is something that can only be attempted from within and only by individuals, who 'as practical organisms are totalizing projects' (*CRD* 2, p. 274). What they can aim for is what he calls *la compréhension dialectique*. 'Dialectical understanding' seems too thin an equivalent for this; what *compréhension* means, says Sartre, is 'praxis itself in so far as it is *accompanied* by the situated observer' (*CRD* 2, p. 378). Something like 'dialectical grasp' might do, suggesting as it does a hold on things that is both practical and intellectual.

Here again an old problem surfaces, the problem of the Third alongside the two principals in any social encounter: is the observer who accompanies the praxis identical with the agent or is it someone else? The odd thing is that by the time Sartre gets to the dialectical grasp of events – which occurs in a late and perhaps independent section of the text partly titled *avène-ment de l'histoire*, the advent of history (as if at last we were about to get to the real thing) – all thought of encircling totaliz-ation seems to have been left behind, and we are once again on the familiar territory of the individual existential agent confronted with his own local facticity.

I do not doubt that it was because he always found himself executing this cycle, and because it always ended there, that Sartre abandoned the attempt to claim intelligibility for history, and with it the project of *CRD* 2 itself. It is true that the editors, by the provision of an index of main ideas at the end, suggest a kind of conceptual completeness for the project. There is for example an entry for 'diachronic sense of history,' defined as 'an axial direction by reference to which any possible deviation, now and in the infinite future of interiority, could be defined (and corrected)'; but when we look at the place in the text where these words occur we discover that Sartre has just said 'It remains of course to note that the existence of a diachronic sense of History is not even implied by the preceding consider-ations,' and that he goes on to say, 'We will return to this problem which demands instruments of thought we have not yet forged for ourselves' (*CRD* 2, p. 346).

He does return to the question, in some fairly well-developed notes on 'progress' given in an appendix. Here Sartre is working valiantly the last veins of a dwindling lode; the apparatus is as usual impressive, the yield for the purposes at hand disap-pointing. To put it in another way, this is rich Sartrian material (for us) but poor Marxist material (for Sartre). The case he finally chooses to exemplify the notion of progress is – incongruously enough, given the nature of the problem (but unsurprisingly given Sartre's known tendencies) – individual and cultural rather than collective and economic; it is the work of Verdi (*CRD* 2, p. 423), who thus joins Baudelaire, Genet, Tintoretto, and the others, and anticipates Flaubert, as an incarnation of sense. But that is of course what individual human subjects have always been. The point I wish finally to underline here is that *they and their lives and works are its only incarnations*; that is why History is not a candidate, though limited segments of it may be.

At the end of the notes on progress there is some enormously interesting and provocative material on science and on scarcity (the latter having loomed in the background ever since the beginning of *CRD* 1). These might have been the key concepts of a quite different, non-Marxian and non-dialectical, treatment of something like a direction of world history as measured by changes in possible individual histories under changes in possible conditions of knowledge and of purposive action. I think this is a pointer worth following. Sartre himself, in spite of some hints, does not follow it; instead he turns back – with the results we know, whose appreciation had been the topic of my article – to the culminating work on Flaubert.

Chapter 4

LACAN AND NON-PHILOSOPHY

William J. Richardson

Jacques Lacan is first, last and always a psychoanalyst. When he theorizes about his practice as an analyst, he weaves his speculations out of a general culture that is kaleidoscopic, and this has led him to dip into the waters of the philosophical tradition more often and more deeply than any other interpreter of Freud. Philosophers have the right, then, to probe the implications of these allusions according to the criteria of their own discipline, as a recent spate of books and articles suggest they are already doing,[1] provided that they respect Lacan's own explicitly *non*-philosophic intention. It is the purpose of the present reflection to engage in just such a philosophical enterprise.

Probably the most tantalizing philosophical allusion is a famous remark of 1953: 'of all the undertakings that have been proposed in this century, that of the psychoanalyst is perhaps the loftiest, because the undertaking of the psychoanalyst acts in our time as the mediator between the man of care <man according to Heidegger> and the subject of absolute knowledge <man according to Hegel>.'[2] Since then, Lacan has been seen to have a special affinity with these two thinkers, and several attempts have been made to explicate this affinity.[3]

But a close examination of Lacan's texts over the years indicates that his philosophical scope is even broader than this, for they are sprinkled with references that stretch from the pre-Socratics to Paul Ricoeur. And yet, since the early 1960s one can notice a gradual distancing of himself from philosophical discourse. In 1964, he acknowledged an earlier debt to Heidegger, in particular, but claimed that the latter's influence had served no more than a 'propaedeutic' purpose,[4] and by

1972 the alienation from all philosophy was clear. 'Mathematical formalism is our goal, our idea,'[5] to such an extent that he was thenceforth highly resolved that his teaching 'never make recourse to any substance or refer to any being, and <that it> rupture with anything at all that might be called philosophy'.[6] In fact, philosophy was no more than a variation of the 'discourse of the master'[7] – the very inverse of what he conceived to be the structure of psychoanalytic discourse, which was his own unique concern. This is what I am calling his 'non-philosophy.'

The gradual transition in Lacan's thinking about the relation between psychoanalysis and philosophy could well be a study of its own. My purpose here, however, is not to trace this development in detail but rather to examine it at its point of arrival – or at least of halt – in the Seminar XX: *Encore* (1972–3).[8] There he addresses the problem of philosophy more explicitly than anywhere else, specifically in terms of the problem of 'being,' which he considers to be the task of philosophy to examine. My purpose is to limit attention to this particular work in order to clarify, at least in this text, what he means by 'being,' what he understands by 'philosophy,' and how he attempts to 'rupture' with it. My hope is to understand better the terms of the challenge his conception of psychoanalysis presents to philosophers. To give some order to this reflection, I propose to begin by considering what Lacan means by the 'discourse of the master' after first sketching his conception of four fundamental modes of discourse in general. I shall then outline his understanding of the 'discourse of the psychoanalyst,' indicating subsequently the critique of philosophy to which it gives rise, and conclude by suggesting the beginnings, at least, of a philosophical response to such a critique.

1 The four discourses

So philosophical discourse is but a variation of the 'discourse of the master.' The terminology is first formalized in Seminar (XVII): *L'envers de la psychanalyse* (1969–70), where Lacan elaborated his conception of four fundamental structures of discourse. 'Discourse,' here, refers to a mode of human relatedness (*lien social*) mediated by speech: 'I designate <the social bond> by the term discourse because there is no other way to designate it once one realizes that the social bond is established only by being rooted in the manner in which language is situated and impressed . . . in the being that speaks'.[9]

We are familiar with the structuralist conception of language since Saussure.[10] Language is a system of signs, each sign composed of a signifying component ('signifier') and a signified component ('signified'), the relationship between them being arbitrary. Saussure suggests this by placing a bar between the two, as if they formed an arithmetic fraction ($\frac{Sd}{Sr}$). For Lacan, this arbitrariness is such that a signifier does not relate to any given signified but rather to other signifiers in a continual flow of signifiers under which any possible meaning slides. For him, then, the bar suggests rather a barrier to any one-to-one correspondence between signifier and signified. Hence, the well-known formula:

> We can say that it is in the chain of signifiers that the meaning 'insists' but that none of its elements 'consists' in the signification of which it is at the moment capable. We are forced, then, to accept the notion of an incessant sliding of the signified under the signifier.[11]

What, then, does the individual signifier refer to? Not to a given signified but rather to the speaking subject itself, which it thereby, in Lacan's terminology, 'represents' – and this in relation to (an)other signifier(s) in the signifying chain. Lacan designates the subject by S, but then places a bar through it ($). This is to suggest that the subject is divided as subject of speech, it is both subject that articulates (*sujet de l'énonciation*) and subject that is articulated (*sujet de l'énoncé*). For Lacan, the subject that truly articulates is the unconscious, i.e. the unconscious as subject, which he refers to as the 'subject of the unconscious.'

The bar between signifier and signified may be taken to suggest also a twofold relationship of another kind: relation to the signifying chain on the one hand and, on the other, to the object that polarizes desire through the mediation of phantasms giving representation to reality in the form of images. This object is what Freud referred to as the 'always already lost' object that may be thought of as the idyllic union with the mother that actually never was but which the subject none the less presumes that it had and seeks indefatigably to retrieve. It is experienced often enough under the guise of 'partial objects,' and Lacan refers to it simply as *objet a*.[12]

Reduced to bare essentials, then, any discourse consists of the relation between a subject and the object polarizing its desire (object α) as this relation is filtered through the complexities of the signifying chain. Transposed into symbols, the discourse consists of four elements: S_1 (the signifier as such); S_2 (all other members of the signifying chain $<S_2, S_3, S_4 \ldots$ etc.$>$ that are summed up as S_2 and constitute a body of at least partly unconscious knowledge $<savoir>$); the divided subject ($\$$); and the object polarizing desire in the subject (object α). As each of these four elements assumes the place of privilege in discourse and the other three elements arrange themselves accordingly, four fundamentally different modes of discourse emerge that Lacan designates as follows: discourse of the master, university discourse (*discours universitaire*), discourse of the hysteric and discourse of the psychoanalyst. Each discourse has its own algebraic matrix, schematizing (always differently) the varying relationships of the four elements. The four matrices are transpositions of each other, and taken in the ensemble they permit one to discern a pattern of uniformly shifting relationships among them that apparently governs the whole.[13]

To be sure, these four modes rarely exist in pure form. In the concrete they are often a blend of several modes, with one or other prevailing and characterizing the whole. In their schematized form, they serve the purposes of analysis and exposition only. I propose to consider them only in so far as they help explain how Lacan conceives the nature of philosophy, and limit attention to the first and last of the four.

2 Discourse of the master

In the discourse of the master a certain mastery, i.e. control or power, is manifest. We can see it operative, for example, in medical discourse.[14] As the patient reveals his symptoms, the doctor transposes them into signifiers that can be integrated into a wider signifying system that characterizes his expertise (S_2). It is by reason of this body of knowledge that the doctor can diagnose the illness and treat it appropriately, a genuine exercise of power. Of prime importance here is the signifying chain itself (S_1–S_2) as a corpus of knowledge.

What is not important in this context – and this is significant to note – is the subjectivity ($) of the doctor. For that matter, no account is taken of the subjectivity of the patient either. The object α that ultimately motivates desire in both is ignored as well. That the subject may be divided, then, is completely disregarded, and the only object of interest is the object of the research in question, e.g. the diagnosis. Lacan schematizes all this by placing the $ and its object α in a subordinate position thus:

$$\frac{S_1}{\$} \qquad \frac{S_2}{\alpha}$$

In underlining the primacy of the signifying chain as such, together with the power ('mastery') that S_2 as a body of knowledge implies, I do not mean to suggest that the body of knowledge is fixed and static or that control is ever complete. On the contrary, this body of knowledge may be continually expanding, as it does, for example, in medical research. But the coherence of this body of knowledge gives it a kind of wholeness (however provisional) that offers promise of eventual totalizability, if only as an ideal. Such is the discourse of medicine and of scientific discourse generally. Analogously, such, too, in Lacan's view, is the discourse of philosophy.

But why call it a discourse precisely of the 'master'? 'Master' connotes 'slave' at one time and 'disciple' at another. To the best of my knowledge, this terminology began to emerge in Seminar VII, *The Ethics of Psychoanalysis* (1959–60) where Lacan spoke of an 'ethics of the master.' There he referred in the first place to the ethics of Aristotle, designed, as he sees it, for the master-class in the City, i.e. the 'free' citizens as opposed to the slaves. Such an ethics obviously had its political correlate, even for Aristotle (as appears in the *Politics*), and therefore carried intimations of (political) power. More significant than that, however, is the fact that it had a deep metaphysical base in Aristotle's conception of final causality, according to which (in the grossest terms) every being seeks that which is a good (i.e.

an end) for it, and the general movement of all beings toward their good culminates around a Supreme Good which is the ultimate end of all (*Nicomachean Ethics*, Book I). Lacan describes an ethics of that kind as an 'economy' or 'system of goods' (*service des biens*) and characterizes it as the 'ethics of the master.' Here 'master' means not simply 'ruler,' as this term would be understood in the Greek City State, but anyone who exercises power by possessing, or controlling, or manipulating goods.

But such an ethics is not limited to Aristotle and to the tradition that followed him. It may be found under many guises, and in Hegel it emerges in terms of the dialectic between master and slave. In Seminar XVII (1969–70), Lacan alludes to the political ramifications, but in terms of the signifying chain itself, he remarks (according to students' notes): 'In the discourse of the master, the fiction of the signifier S_1 is that upon which rests the existence of the master. The field proper to the slave is the body of knowledge that is S_2' (November 26, 1969).[15] I take this to mean that the master signifier (S_1) in discourse is the dominant signifier in terms of which the rest of the signifying chain (S_2) is reorganized into the body of knowledge (*savoir*), and even the *savoir-faire*, of the slave (see Clavreul, 'L'enjeu de la psychanalyse'). If 'master' connotes 'disciple' as well as 'slave,' the power exercised by master over disciple will be that of knowledge itself. Likewise, it is in these terms that we must think of the discourse of science and philosophy.

3 Discourse of the psychoanalyst

The discourse of psychoanalysis is the very reverse of all this. Why? Precisely because it does not prescind from the subjectivity of its participants but rather engages this subjectivity in all its unique concreteness. We recall the nature of the subject[16]: it is strictly a subject of speech. 'According to the psychoanalytic discourse, there is an animal that finds itself speaking, and the result is that by inhabiting the signifying <chain> it is a subject of the <chain>'.[17] The subject is an effect of the signifiers that represent it, sliding (*glisse*) from one to another along the signifying chain (*XX*, p. 48). The chain is in effect the articulating subject, speaking with a knowledge (*savoir*) of which the subject who says 'I' is unconscious. 'I speak without knowing it. I speak with my body, and this without knowing it. I always say more than I know, then. That is how I arrive at the meaning of the word *subject* in psychoanalytic discourse. That which speaks without knowing it makes me *I*, subject of the verb' (*XX*, p. 108), subject that is transitory (*ponctuel*) and evanescent – always elsewhere (*ailleurs*) – precisely because it is subject only by reason of a signifier and for another signifier (*XX*, p. 130).

The subject emerges, as we know, when it is inserted into the signifying system of the symbolic order (the order of language) as soon as it begins actively to speak. It is the moment when the fullness of imaginary union with the mother is lost forever, only to be pursued unceasingly as the impossible dream. The lost fullness to be regained becomes the polarizing and motivating factor of the want-to-be that is the subject's desire. In that sense for Lacan it is the 'cause' of desire. *This* is the object α. That is why 'the reciprocity between the subject and object α is total' (*XX*, p. 114). The fact that this object is to be pursued by gliding from signifier to signifier along the signifying chain constitutes the division of the subject: 'For every being that speaks, the cause of its desire, in terms of structure, is strictly equivalent to the folding, i.e. to what I have called the division, of the subject' (*XX*, p. 114).

The task of psychoanalytic discourse, then, is to follow the flow of the signifying chain (S_1–S_2), not for its own sake but in order to discern the course of desire in its quest for object α. By tracing the vagaries of this object as it appears in and through the flight of phantasms, the analysis discerns the course of desire as one traces the flight of an airplane by following blips on a radar screen.[18] Lacan symbolizes this procedure by the formula:

$$α\text{–}\$,$$

suggesting thereby how the phantasm, through which object α appears, plays not an accidental but a structural role in the emergence of desire in the subject.

What of the other elements in the formula of discourse? The body of constituted knowledge (S_2), so decisive in the discourse of the master, is here completely subordinate to the functioning of the object α as it floats through the phantasms that represent it and in Lacan's schematized version located beneath it. At the same time, the focus on this object as it slowly discloses desire enables the master signifier that has dominated the signifying chain, hitherto proper to the subject, to emerge. Schematically, S_1 will be placed under $. The entire schema of the discourse of the analyst, then, appears as follows:

$$\frac{\alpha}{S_2} \to \frac{\$}{S_1}$$

If we compare the two schemata representing the discourse of the master and the discourse of the analyst, it is perfectly obvious that one is the reverse of the other. What characterizes the discourse of the master is the primacy of the signifier over the divided subject, involving somehow or another the exercise of power and an expanding body of knowledge. What characterizes the discourse of psychoanalysis is the primacy of the subject – the inconstant evanescent subject – in futile quest for the irretrievable object that 'causes' its desire. Since philosophy is allegedly a mode of the discourse of the master, it will be for Lacan the inverse of psychoanalytic discourse. Let us see this in more detail and draw what inferences we can.

4 Lacan's critique of philosophy

To begin with, the proper object of philosophy, according to Lacan, is 'being,' where 'being' is always a being – Aristotle's *on*: that-which-is (*XX*, p. 33). Hence, philosophy for Lacan is at best the 'metaphysics' ('ontology') of the tradition, and, indeed, in so far as this is accessible to *conscious* thought. As Assoun puts it, philosophical knowledge is inevitably *conscientialiste*[19] – 'being' conceived in this fashion is always, in good Aristotelian fashion, concrete, individual, substantial (*XX*, p. 107), corporeal (*XX*, pp. 127 8). It is of such beings as these that the 'world' is made up as their totality, so that the 'world' is essentially an ontological (*XX*, p. 33) or cosmological (*XX*, p. 43) concept that is no more than a conceptual correlate of the conscious subject (*XX*, p. 115). In these terms, being(s) would be in one way or another prior (at least logically/ontologically, if not temporally) to language and speech, which would in turn be thought of as somehow correlative with that being which is specifically human.

For Lacan, this metaphysical view of things and all that it implies must, as far as psychoanalysis is concerned, be reversed. For him, what is primordial in specifically human experience is not being but language and speech. In 1972 he has simply drawn the logical consequences of what he said in the first 'Discourse at Rome' (1953):

> The psychoanalytic experience has rediscovered in man the imperative of the Word as the law that has formed him in its image. It manipulates the poetic function of language to give to his desire its symbolic mediation. . . . It is in the gift of speech that all the reality of its effects resides; for it is by way of this gift that all reality has come to man and it is by his continued act that he maintains it. (*E*, p. 106)

The Word (i.e. language), then, is in its own order ultimate. '<This> is what I mean when I say that no metalanguage can be spoken, or, more aphoristically, that there is no Other of the Other'.[20]

There simply *is* no being anterior to the speech that articulates it: 'There is no pre-discursive reality. Every reality is founded in and defined by a discourse' (*XX*, p. 33). Again: 'There is not the least pre-discursive reality, for the good reason that what makes for collectivity, and what I have called men, women and children, has no meaning in the sense of a pre-discursive reality. Men, women and children are only signifiers' (*XX*, p. 34). For the 'collectivity' is in effect the 'social bond' mediated by language/speech – such is the very nature of discourse.

Hence, 'it is evident that nothing is except in the measure that it (*ça*) is said that it (*ça*) is' (*XX*, p. 126).[21] What, then, of 'being'? 'We only suppose it for certain words – individual, for example, or substance. For me it is only the fact of <being> said (*un fait de dit*)' (*XX*, p. 107). That is why 'the symbolic is not identified with being – far from it – but subsists as the ex-sistence of saying' (*ex-sistence du dire*) (*XX*, p. 108).

This does not mean, of course, that one can think of language/speech as separate from being: 'it is certain that something said can be <said> only about being' (*il n'y a du dit que de l'être*) (*XX*, p. 92). The point is that being is a function of speech. It was

128

the mark of the old ontologies to so emphasize the copula 'is' as to isolate it as a signifier (*XX*, p. 33). It is as if one could say 'man is,' for example, without saying what he is, and much of what was said about being was based precisely on this kind of abstraction (*XX*, p. 16). It is worth noting, perhaps, that in making these remarks Lacan ignores completely the classical distinction between the copulative and the existential sense of 'is.' As far as he is concerned, we are dealing merely with signifiers, and instead of talking about being as what-is (*c'est-ce-que-c'est*), we could simply refer to it, say, as 'wottiz' (*seskecé*) (*XX*, p. 33). The only difference: 'is' was given special weight in a particular kind of discourse (the discourse of the master), of which philosophy was always a function. Apart from that discourse, 'is' makes no claims to any ontological status. What is clear for Lacan, then, is the primacy of language/speech over being: 'Being – if you want me to use this term at any cost – . . . is the being of signification' (*XX*, p. 67), and human being, as speaker (*XX*, p. 114) is no more than the one who brings signification to pass (*fait signifier*) (*XX*, p. 42).

Given Lacan's anti-metaphysical stance, we are not surprised at his radical rejection of Aristotelian metaphysics and, by implication, any kind of ethics that might rest upon it as a base. For example, he affects utter bafflement before the famous text with which Aristotle opens the *Nicomachean Ethics*, Book I: 'Every art and every inquiry, and similarly every action and pursuit, is thought to aim at some good; and for this reason the good has rightly been declared to be that at which all things aim' (1094a). He intimates that the difficulty it has given so many commentators over the years may derive from the fact that the text might be simply unthinkable in itself (*XX*, p. 50), presumably because it supposes the entire Aristotelian machinery of final causality set up in pre-discursive being.

In particular, Lacan finds difficulty with the notion of good implied here, i.e. some congruity between a being and what it seeks (i.e. what attracts it) and what, when attained, offers that being, at least provisionally, some satisfaction. We are familiar with how in the *Ethics* Aristotle develops this line of thought into the conception of a Supreme Good for humans which consists in *eudaimonia* ('happiness'), however this be understood. Lacan will have none of it (*XX*, p. 55) and rejects the entire metaphysical apparatus of formal and final causality. When speaking of Aristotle's famous definition of 'essence' (*to ti en einai*), he translates it literally enough as 'that which would be produced if it came to be, <or> briefly, what was to be' but then dismisses it as 'being on order, what was about to be if you had understood what I am ordering <from> you' (*XX*, p. 33). Clearly, metaphysical essence is reduced here to a function of speech.

Lacan is bemused by the fact that Aristotle's conception of teleology permits him to conceive of a hierarchy of beings, each pursuing its appropriate end (i.e. good) in relation to some supreme being: 'each one of the beings that are in the world can only be oriented toward the supreme being by confounding its own proper good with that same <good> that radiates from the supreme being' (*XX*, p. 78), and this implies a kind of knowing (*XX*, p. 81), not only on the part of the being in question but on the part of the supreme being conceived as 'the place whence (*d'où*) the good of all the others is known' (*XX*, p. 101). Whether or not this is a fair presentation of Aristotle need not concern us. What is useful to note is that Lacan's total rejection of the notion of 'good,' with its obvious implications for an eventual ethics, is founded on his rejection of the metaphysics of final causality, i.e. more generally, Aristotle's concept of being.

How Lacan's own 'ethics of the subject' might be articulated is too complicated a problem to be addressed here. For now it must suffice, by way of example, to see how he transposes certain traditional metaphysical problems into his own panlinguistic context. To begin with some simple straightforward definitions (a rarity in Lacan): 'contingent' is that which 'ceases to not be inscribed (*s'écrire*)'; 'necessary' is that which 'does not cease to be inscribed'; 'impossible' is that which does not cease to not be inscribed (*XX*, pp. 86–7). This terminology does not play a very significant role in Lacan's argument, but it is symptomatic of his style.

The transposition of metaphysical concepts into linguistic terminology appears more clearly if we consider how Lacan deals here with the problem of the existence of God. God is reduced to a function of the Other of language:

The Other, the Other as locus of truth, is the only place, though an irreducible one, that we can give to the term 'divine being,' i.e., God – to call it by its name. God is properly the place where, if I may be permitted the word-play, god – the sayer – the saying <*le dieu – le dieur – le dire*> is produced. (*XX*, p. 44)

We can understand, then, how he can look back on 'The Agency of the Letter' (1956), when he was still elaborating the notion of the symbolic order in terms of the Other as the locus of speech, and see it not simply as a way of laicizing 'but of exorcising the good old God' (*XX*, p. 65) of metaphysics.

With God thus disposed of, Lacan has little trouble dealing with the origin of the universe. After discussing (*XX*, p. 40) the theology of Richard of St Victor who had, in good mediaeval fashion, distinguished between 'being from itself' and 'being from another,' Lacan continues:

The signifier . . . is 'from itself.' Isn't it clear to you that it participates . . . in that nothing in which the creationist idea tells us that something completely original was made *out of nothing.* . . . <*Genesis*> does not recount anything other than creation . . . from nothing else but signifiers. (*XX*, p. 41).

Finally, we can understand in these terms Lacan's antipathy to the notion of 'world':

<The> world, conceived as a whole, with what this word comports . . . remains . . . a view, a look, an imaginary grasp. . . . Is there not in analytic discourse warrant to lead us to the position that all subsistence, all persistence of the world as such ought to be abandoned? (*XX*, p. 43) . . . <For> the world is symmetrical with the subject. The world . . . is the equivalent, the mirror image, of thought. That is why as far as knowledge is concerned there was nothing but phantasm<s> up to the advent of the most modern science. (*XX*, p. 115)

Clearly, then, the 'world' for Lacan is purely 'ontic' – a totality of beings that is a correlate of the thinking subject, 'knowledge' of which is a kind of vision that he considers to be on the level of the phantasm, i.e. purely imaginary. To be sure, this last point does not cohere very well with one made earlier: 'Thank God, Aristotle was intelligent enough to isolate in the agent intellect what is at stake in the symbolic function' (*XX*, p. 102), suggesting that Aristotle and his mediaeval followers, in analyzing the process of knowledge, did indeed take account of what for Lacan is the symbolic order, i.e. something more than the phantasm, long before 'the advent of the most modern science.' But at this point, why be churlish? What Lacan wants to say is clear: 'What is produced in the articulation of this new discourse that emerges as the discourse of analysis is that the starting point is the function of the signifier' (*XX*, p. 43).

All this adds up to saying that Lacan's rejection of philosophy is a direct consequence of his thesis about the primacy of language over (metaphysical) being. 'In a general way, language proves to be a field much richer in resource than simply one in which, over the course of time, the philosophic discourse has been inscribed' (*XX*, p. 33). And if (metaphysical) being is the proper object of philosophy, we can understand why he wants to 'rupture' with it in theorizing about the discourse of psychoanalysis. But why does he insist so strongly on identifying philosophy, i.e. metaphysics, with the discourse of the master?

In *Encore* he does not tell us, but the fact is very clear. 'Every dimension of being is produced in the current of the discourse of the master' (*XX*, p. 33) and he takes advantage of a homophonic play on words, impossible to translate in English, between *maître* and *m'être* (*XX*, p. 40), between *maitrise* and *m'êtrise* (*XX*, p. 53). For want of better evidence, I think we can surmise this much: metaphysics, by reason of its abstraction, partakes of the same generality and disregard of unique subjectivity as the discourse of the master (*XVII*, p. 18); by reason of its pretension to articulate truth, it aspires to an analogous power.[22]

5 An initial response

What is one to think about all this? To begin with, it is fair to note that Lacan is not the first to call our attention to the limits of metaphysical thinking. The critiques of Heidegger and Derrida in particular have gone well beyond Lacan's own haphazard treatment of it, and the residue has become part and parcel of the 'post-modern' debate. Lacan's comments add only his own particular voice to an already familiar chorus.

The comments have their significance, however, and must be taken seriously. In addressing psychoanalysis, philosophers must take account of their own *conscientialiste* prejudices and acknowledge the specific originality of Freud's discovery of the *un*conscious, together with all the anomalies it imposes upon them by the discourse of psychoanalysis as Lacan has schematized it. The irreducible difference between the philosophic and the psychoanalytic discourse must be respected. If one allows that philosophy's concern is with being, one must also recognize that the concern of psychoanalysis is with lack-of-being (*manque-à-être*) and even un-being (*désêtre*).[23] No easy conflation of the two is possible.

This said, does philosophical reflection have no place at all in the psychoanalytic enterprise? Granted that the exercise of psychoanalysis deals with the uniquely singular concrete situation, the theory of it includes suppositions and hypotheses about the structure of the human being who speaks that are as universal as human being itself. Such structures concern, for example: the nature of language/speech, of the evanescent subject, of desire and its cause, of knowledge (especially scientific), of Lacan's own brand of mathematical formalism, of the kind of truth (or half-truth) that is possible through the process. One cannot expect that psychoanalysis as such raises and settles such questions – they are philosophical issues warranting philosophical scrutiny. The scrutiny would perform a service, one would think, for the psychoanalytic discourse itself, since this is based operationally on a presupposed resolution of them. At any rate, their relevance to the psychoanalytic discourse renders questionable any attempt to 'rupture' completely with philosophy.

But all this leaves unquestioned Lacan's conception of being as identical with that of the metaphysical tradition. This is just what has been challenged in the contemporary philosophical debate, however, especially since the contribution of Heidegger, whose relevance, at least as propaedeutic to his own thought, Lacan allows. It is a commonplace now to say that Heidegger's entire effort in raising the Being-question was to found or to ground – or, after those metaphors failed, to overcome – metaphysics by meditating Being (*Sein*) in its difference from being (*Seiendes*) as the what-is (*on*) of Artistotle. How this develops in Heidegger into a meditation on Being as a process of self-concealing revealment, whether as the *A-letheia, Logos,* or *Physis* of the pre-Socratics, cannot be followed here.[24] Let it suffice to recall that in meditating on Being in terms of the *Logos* of Heraclitus (Fragment 50) (an essay that Lacan translated personally for his students in 1956[25]), Heidegger explored the notion of *Logos*/Being as aboriginal language, more primordial than being as Lacan conceives it. How this might cohere with Lacan's adage that there is 'no Other of the Other' has been examined elsewhere.[26]

More pertinent here, perhaps, is to call attention to Lacan's frequent reference to Parmenides in *Encore* and compare it with Heidegger's treatment of the same material. More than once Lacan alludes to the celebrated gnome (Frag. 5): *to gar auto noein estin te kai einai* (often translated in the tradition: 'being and thinking are the same'). For Lacan, this indicates merely 'the reciprocity between *nous* and the world, between that which thinks and that which is thought' (*XX*, p. 116, cf. p. 103). For Lacan, what is thought here is simply being in the metaphysical sense, and the reciprocity between being and thinking would be the foundation of both science and philosophy in the ancient world. 'But Parmenides was wrong and Heraclitus right' when he said (Fragment 93): *oute legei oute kryptei alla semainei*[27]: '<the Lord> neither speaks out, nor conceals . . . but gives a sign' (*XX*, p. 103). Presumably Lacan takes *semainei* to mean not just 'gives a sign' but 'constitutes the symbolic order,' the order of language. His preference for Heraclitus over Parmenides in this case would be another way of reaffirming the primacy of language over <metaphysical> being.

Heidegger's understanding of these two thinkers and the relation between them is completely other. For him, *einai* in the Parmenides text is not at all the being of metaphysics but corresponds to *physis* in the pre-Socratic tradition: emerging, abiding presence[28] that 'loves to hide itself' (Heraclitus, Fragment 123) (*IM*, p. 114). In this it coincides with the original meaning of *logos*: a 'gathered together coming-to-presence' (*IM*, pp. 130–3). In other words, *einai*, according to Heidegger, refers to Being in the sense of self-concealing revealment: *a-letheia* (*IM*, pp. 170–1). As such, it coincides with *logos* in the sense of aboriginal language,[29] hence, is more primordial than the being of the metaphysical tradition.

As for the human correspondent in this process (*noein*), this is not to be understood as a being that thinks in any intellectualized sense but simply as one who responds to the self-concealing revealment of Being in the sense of *physis/logos*, i.e. as aboriginal language. And what the traditional reading translated as 'same' (*auto*), Heidegger understands in the sense not of 'identical' but of 'correlative.' In other words, Heidegger takes the Parmenidean text to mean that Being-as-aboriginal language and the human being that speaks (*l'être parlant*) are correlative with one another.

If we follow Heidegger's reading, then, the Parmenidean text does not so much offer us the pattern for metaphysical and scientific thinking in the ancient world (Lacan) as the paradigm for all thought whatever. It is the formula for the hermeneutic circle as such. Eventually Heidegger suggests that it may be discerned in all great thinkers (e.g. Kant and Hegel <*EGT*, pp. 149, 45>), and never more graphically, perhaps, than in the *esse est percipi* ('to be is to be perceived') of Berkeley. In this perspective, we have a way to situate the criticism that has been made of Lacan's claim for the primacy of language over being as no more than an idealism of the signifier after the manner of Berkeley. When all is said and done, what is at stake is the hermeneutic circle itself. And there is Lacan, *bon gré mal gré*, right in the middle of it.

None of this is intended to flatten the differences between Heidegger and Lacan. Let it serve to say that long after Heidegger has served his propaedeutic purpose, his thinking may still be able to throw light on some of the philosophical darkness that abounds in the presuppositions of Lacan's own discourse. If so, that would be a service, indeed. It might become a paradigm case for the effort to think through in philosophical terms the nature of the unconscious in human being that psychoanalytic discourse now makes accessible and philosophers no longer may ignore.

Chapter 5

FOUCAULT AND THE TRANSGRESSION OF LIMITS

Tony O'Connor

Over the years the thought of Michel Foucault has come in for considerable criticism. It has been claimed that it does not qualify as philosophy because it abandons the principle of universal reason, and that at best it qualifies as an extreme relativism, or at worst is to be identified as iconoclastic and anarchic. The virulence of the criticism directed against him reminds one of Bréhier's criticism of Merleau-Ponty's lecture, 'The Primacy of Perception and its Philosophical Consequences', to the effect that philosophy is not a matter of engagement in the world, but consists precisely in following a route directly contrary to this engagement.[1]

It is now well, and properly, recognized that Merleau-Ponty's lecture, and *Phenomenology of Perception* from which it was derived, make a very important contribution to the question of the status of philosophy in relation to its non-philosophical sources and goals.[2] As Silverman has made clear, Merleau-Ponty's discussion in *Phenomenology of Perception* of the 'non-philosophical' experience of spatiality, motility, freedom, etc., does not by any means deny or annihilate philosophy, but rather seeks to inquire behind accepted philosophical conventions and procedures in order to discover a renewed understanding of its sources and character.[3] 'Non-philosophy', for Merleau-Ponty, is philosophy rendered complex and experiential, which opens its links not only to lived experience, but also to the disciplines that describe, or seek to explain, that experience, namely, anthropology, psychoanalysis, political theory, history, etc.[4]

The difference between Bréhier and Merleau-Ponty, however, exemplifies a greater difference, or dispute, within philosophy itself. Bréhier can be seen to represent an old, time-honored view which holds that, despite difficulties and disputes, philosophy is a certain kind of discipline that is abstract and universalist, and, as such, must be clearly differentiated from other disciplines, and, certainly, from lived experience. Merleau-Ponty, on the other hand, represents more a modernist view, which, while holding some views in common with the older tradition, yet seeks to respond more to the situation of crisis in which modern philosophy, particularly continental European philosophy since Hegel, finds itself.

In this paper I will argue that both Foucault's thought, and the criticism of it, must be approached in the context of this general question of the crisis of philosophy. From this perspective, Foucault's work, and despite the many and trenchant criticisms of it, can be seen to be not different, at least in general intention, from that of many of the major thinkers in the continental European tradition, inasmuch as he faces squarely the problem of the character of philosophy itself by pursuing the question of the conditions of possibility that permit particular forms of knowledge to exist. Thus, he describes 'archaeology' as the determination of the historical *a priori* for the appearance of ideas, sciences, philosophies, etc.[5] Likewise, his notion of the 'episteme' is identified as the complete set of relations that link at any particular time the discursive practices that give rise to formalized systems, and that, in turn, permits the appreciation of the sets of constraints and limitations that may be imposed on discourse at a given time.[6]

It is interesting to discover that most of the serious objections against his work share the presupposition that philosophy must rest on secure foundations if it is to survive and flourish. From such a perspective, Foucault's examination of transgressive language is seen inevitably as a major threat, challenging as it does the traditional assumption that reason subordinates experience in an orderly fashion, and because he tries to determine the limits of philosophy as abstractionist and universalist endeavor.

Here Merleau-Ponty may be of assistance once more in getting the conflict between Foucault and his critics into perspective. In Chapter 1 of *Phenomenology of Perception*, in the course of a discussion of the character of sensation, Merleau-Ponty reflects on our experience of color, or our use of color terms. When, for example, we identify something as red, we have neither a pure impression nor sensation whereby the color is somehow communicated to us, nor do we possess a mental concept which we simply apply in all cases.[7] The actual situation of color-identification is more complex than this:

> This red patch which I see on the carpet is red only in virtue of a shadow which lies across it, its quality is apparent only in relation to the play of light upon it, and hence as an element in a spatial configuration. Moreover the colour can be said to be there only if it occupies an area of a certain size, too small an area not being describable in these terms. Finally this red would literally not be the same if it were not the 'woolly red' of a carpet.[8]

In this description Merleau-Ponty indicates, without spelling it out in detail, that the perception of color involves chromatic perception, or chromatic effect, and cannot simply be explained in terms of the pigmentation of substances in the environment. Recently, Eco has listed some of the major features of chromatic perception, which includes items such as the character of the surface or surfaces observed, light, contrast between objects, previous knowledge, etc.[9] Implicit in this discussion is the view that there is no single use of color-terms that is appropriate in each and every case. Eco makes this clear when he introduces the question of how to interpret color-terms discovered in ancient texts. The problem arises for the contemporary interpreter when he is faced with linguistic terms for colors, but does not know what chromatic effects these words refer to.[10] Eco takes for example a discussion of the nature of color-terms, particularly the term 'red' which occurs in Aulus Gellius: *Noctes Acticae* (Book II, Chapter 26).[11] Here the interlocutors, Fronto, a poet and grammarian, and Favorinus, a philosopher, identify the many color-terms for 'red,' as well as their many linguistic associations. As the discussion grows more complicated they find that the term *flavus*, which has associations with the river Tiber, the hair of Dido, and olive leaves, can be used to designate both red and green objects. This raises a major difficulty for them: what is the difference between 'red' and 'green'? What is the status of the general term 'red' (*rufus*) if many of the specific identifications of red appear to be derived not from it but from other terms? How can a single term identify both red and green?[12]

As observed above, this discussion indicates that color-terms have no essential feature or quality that can be discovered in every proper use of the term. Rather, a term is to be identified on the basis of similarities and differences, which are determined in terms of their particular and appropriate contexts. The question immediately arises, however, as to the appropriate criteria of use for the particular term. One possibly fruitful suggestion might be that interlocutors should select as clear an instance as possible, and then proceed by saying that this and similar instances should count in a particular way. But immediately the further question arises as to the basis on which the supposed clear instance is to be selected. Is it to be convention, the authority of one of the speakers, or something else?

When this particular problem is generalized it becomes evident that serious questions need to be raised about the matter of language in general, and also about the foundations on which our identifications and explanations rest. If, with Foucault, we conclude that there is no single foundation, source, origin, or center on which the edifice of language and explanation rests, then we have a radicalized vision both of our use of particular words and of language in general, with all its implications for philosophy, scholarship, etc. In this regard, the opening paragraph of the preface to *The Order of Things* makes interesting reading:

> This book first arose out of a passage in Borges, out of the
> laughter that shattered, as I read the passage, all the
> familiar landmarks of my thought – *our* thought, the
> thought that bears the stamp of our age and our geography
> – breaking up all the ordered surfaces and all the planes
> with which we are accustomed to tame the wild profusion
> of existing things, and continuing long afterwards to disturb
> and threaten with collapse our age-old distinction between
> the Same and the Other. This passage quotes a 'certain
> Chinese encyclopaedia' in which it is written that 'animals
> are divided into: (a) belonging to the Emperor, (b)
> embalmed, (c) tame, (d) sucking pigs, (e) sirens, (f)
> fabulous, (g) stray dogs, (h) included in the present

classification, (i) frenzied, (j) innumerable, (k) drawn with a very fine camelhair brush, (l) *et cetera*, (m) having just broken the water pitcher, (n) that from a long way off look like flies.'[13]

Foucault argues that, despite possible appearances to the contrary, each of the categories can be assigned a precise meaning and demonstrable content, even though some of them involve fantastic entities. Precisely because the categories have been differentiated, we are presented with the possibility of identifying the items appropriate to that category alone without interfering with the other categories. A major difficulty arises, however, when the question is raised of how the categories relate to each other to form a single whole: 'The animals "(i) frenzied, (j) innumerable, (k) drawn with a very fine camelhair brush" – where could they ever meet?'[14]

Foucault answers his own question directly: they can meet only in 'the non-place of language',[15] which, in turn, can spread these categories before us 'only in an unthinkable space'.[16] In other words, the world is linguistic through and through, in as much as language conditions both the world we see and the items in that world. Importantly, however, Foucault claims that Borges has ruled out the possibility of identifying what is common to all the categories. Borges, by introducing incongruous categories, 'does away with the site, the mute ground, upon which it is possible for entities to be juxtaposed.'[17] Any ground, or field of identity, that might be identified as somehow sustaining all of Borges's categories will be too wide not to be unstable.

This has major consequences for philosophy, Foucault argues, which can no longer offer 'utopias', in the sense of theories that claim to identify and define some 'common locus' beneath discourses. In the place of utopias the philosopher finds 'heterotopias', which shatter or tangle common names, 'dissolve our myths and sterilize the lyricism of our sentences.'[18] The establishment of this claim involves Foucault in a double task. Negatively, he must show that philosophical claims and theories based on some supposed common ground, feature or quality, simply do not work. Positively, he must show that his question about the conditions of the possibility of knowledge can be dealt with plausibly while rejecting universalist notions such as 'universal objectivity or rationality', the 'growing perfection' of history, etc., and acknowledging discontinuities, differences, diverse forms of knowledge that do not reduce to a single source.

Although Foucault pursued this task appropriately by means of detailed regional enquiries into specific forms of discourse – madness, the prison, the clinic, sexuality, etc. – enquiries that are well documented in the considerable secondary literature on Foucault, yet rather than offer a detailed account of these, I will pursue the critical point regarding the validity of his general enterprise. This is particularly important given the volume of negative criticism, some of it undoubtedly justified, not only of his specific analyses, but of his entire undertaking.

In identifying his undertaking as archaeological and epistemic, Foucault seeks to identify and evaluate the regularities and irregularities that constitute particular networks of discourses, or epistemes. Epistemes are linguistic or cultural features of the world, and are governed by certain 'regularities' such as principles, ideals, codes, methodologies, etc. These regularities determine the conditions of possibility of the discourse in question by determining not only what must be included in it but also what must be excluded from it. For example:

(a) During the Renaissance the question of the character of the relations between things was pursued in terms of linkage by resemblance. Interpretation became the central issue for this episteme, in so far as the task was that of discovering what words stood for, or of identifying the essence of the object designated by the word.

(b) During the Classical Age the central philosophical problem concerned the character of thought, which was taken to be the model for all language. This led to attempts to establish an ideal language whose elements related to essences in a direct way. Knowledge was considered in terms of representation, and was to be related to a universal science of measurement and order.

(c) In the Modern Age things were understood temporally according to their history, or, more generally, in terms of an origin that was taken to be both the essence of their being and yet fundamentally other than them. A major consequence of this episteme was the emergence of the notion of 'man' as both an object of knowledge and as a knowing subject.

These epistemes, according to Foucault, reveal both a structural regularity, and the impossibility of defining a common bond directly uniting all three. This is inevitable, he claims, given the character of the episteme, which does not establish universal or necessary features linking all discourses. An episteme, rather, is a 'space' of knowledge in which order occurs. Hence the epistemes of succeeding ages are discontinuous, often the results of abrupt ruptures in knowledge rather than successive stages of continuous progression. For example, in the modern episteme the meaning of the term 'man' cannot be designated simply as the human species, or as any particular member of it. Rather, 'man' is a technical term for an identity separated from itself by a distance which, on the one hand, is interior to and constitutive of it, and on the other hand, a repetition which posits identity as a datum, but in the form of a distance.[19] Hand in hand with the notion of 'man' has emerged the notion of 'continuous history,' which operates in the mode of a promise, such that everything that has eluded man hitherto may one day be restored to him: 'that one day the subject – in the form of historical consciousness – will once again be able to appropriate, to bring back under his sway, all those things that are kept at a distance by difference, and find in them what might be called his abode.'[20]

Thus Foucault argues, that in so far as the term 'man' is properly a function of the modern episteme, then it did not exist for classical thought. Although the term occurred in the writings of classical thinkers, yet he claims that it is important to bear in mind that for classical thought the person for whom a representation exists, and who represents himself within this representation, links together all the interacting threads in the form of a table. However, he himself is never to be found in that table: 'Before the end of the eighteenth century, *man* did not exist.'[21] Man, rather, is a modern construct, as a being who, when he thinks, reveals himself to himself as one who is in an irreducible anteriority: 'a living being, an instrument of production, a vehicle for words which exist before him.'[22]

Foucault has been accused of adopting an overly relativist stand, and of a certain unsureness in his overall position.[23] Merquior criticizes him for introducing epistemic distinctions that are too broad and rigid, and which lead him to neglect factors such as the presence of transepistemic streams of thought, breakdowns within a particular episteme as when a theory may be misunderstood in its own time, and the possibility of intraepistemic breaks.[24] Burgelin had already indicated the 'dubious assumption' on Foucault's part that people living at the same time are intellectual contemporaries.[25]

On the first charge it must be readily admitted that his position is a relativist one in so far as he denies that there is some absolute criterion which determines our philosophic judgments. On the second charge, Philip argues that in claiming that truth is what counts as true within a discourse, Foucault is equivocal about whether he is saying that truth is always relative to discourse, or that truth has political as well as epistemological status.[26] This particular criticism can be used to bring what appears to be an even stronger objection against him, namely, that it is possible to accept his claim that the complex modes of human expression do not reveal any static or well-defined origin, but yet claim that this is not simply the result of the modern episteme as Foucault thinks. Rather, the manner in which man is historical and rational is such that human endeavor must make rationality the *telos* of mankind. Hence the history of thought merely preserves this rationality and teleology, and indicates the need consistently to return to this foundation, and so to avoid the relativist charge.

This is the thrust of Merquior's more forceful criticism, in which Foucault is castigated for his lack of concern for the 'truth of knowledge':

what the archaeologist, as distinct from the epistemologist, does is merely to ascertain some historical conditions of possibility of a number of knowledge forms, in total disregard of the latter's 'growing perfection' – in other words, of their increase in truth rationally assessed. We may therefore say that Foucault's analysis does not care about the *story* of science – the tale of its progress of testable, objective knowledge.[27]

Foucault is accused of abandoning the principle of universal reason, making universalism the mask of mere dogmatism, and thereby spelling the end of philosophy.[28] Universal truth is only another name for power disguised as the criterion of all knowledge.[29] It would seem, therefore, that the best that one can say of Foucault's position is that it is subjectivist and arbitrary. At worst, it is, as Rose describes it, iconoclastic and arbitrary: 'Foucault is opposed to merely turning the table (of law) which opens up the space of the court-room – on the judge. He recommends that we smash it, and he is sanguine that the end of the law, the *finis*, can be executed.'[30]

In reply to the foregoing criticisms it may be admitted readily that Merquior's claim that Foucault introduces overly rigid distinctions between epistemes has a certain validity. This is particularly the case with regard to *The Order of Things*. However, a number of points must be made in Foucault's favour. Firstly, the term 'episteme' is absent from the works after *The Order of Things*, to be replaced by terms such as the 'apparatus,' the 'archive,' 'genealogy,' etc. It is as if, on Merquior's terms, Foucault recognized that his treatment of epistemes in *The Order of Things* was not pluralistic enough to allow for the heterotopias mentioned in the preface to the book.

Secondly, critics who claim that Foucault fails to account for continuity among epistemes, may themselves be open to a counter-objection that they fail to appreciate the character of discourse and the task of theory. Human discourse is not a matter of translation, whether of processes or operations, of phenomena that occur outside it. Neither is it reducible to the statements of any particular speaker or theorist, or community of speech. It is, rather, a more objective, or anonymous, field, whose configuration defines the statements that any set of speaking subjects might make.[31] This means that the critical task is not an abstractionist one of moving from various empirical statements about the world to their grounding in some explanatory structure which transcends them. On the contrary, the statement must be grasped in the exact specificity of its occurrence. This, Foucault argues, permits the identification of its conditions of existence, its limits, and its links with other connecting statements. Most importantly, it allows for the determination of the kinds of statement excluded by it.

Further, Foucault's stress on the non-abstractionist character of critique, or theory construction, and on the importance of individual statements, does not confine him to a pre-philosophical realm of particularity or common sense. His position allows also for the determination of connections between statements, objects, concepts, thematic choices, etc. These connections, or regularities, he describes as 'discursive formations'.[32] Discursive formations as well as individual statements can be described in their uniqueness if the specific rules which determine their elements can be established: 'if there really is a unity, it does not lie in the visible, horizontal coherence of the statements formed; it resides well anterior to their formation, in the system that makes possible and governs their formation.'[33]

The question arises, however, of how on Foucault's position it is possible to determine the accuracy of any particular investigation. Foucault's reply is that accuracy is to be determined in terms of the consistency of the investigation with the guiding episteme. For example, he maintains that phenomenology in its various manifestations involves an empirical description of actual experience, and an ontology of the unthought that automatically short-circuits the primacy of the 'I think'.[34] Examples to support this claim can readily be found. In Husserl, for example, the various components of consciousness are interconnected in such a way that we have an experience as of one fully-fledged object. Hence all there is to the existence of an object corresponds to components in the act.[35] Likewise, in Merleau-Ponty's later philosophy we find a similar position, though expressed in more ontological terms. *L'être sauvage* founds perception but is never itself an object of perception. The characteristic of perception is that it occurs on the basis of a representation of this *perception sauvage*. It is the invisible in the visible.[36] The point here is that phenomenological analysis is governed by various presuppositions and procedures that permit some statements to be made but not others, that allow for the ordering of the statements, and their identification as true or false, as well as the construction of a classification system for them.

If one allows even a modified version of Foucault's major claim, namely, that there are major breaks between epistemes, even if it now be admitted that these are not necessarily absolute, then Foucault is correct in claiming that the fundamental concepts of one may not be formulated in terms of the other. Hence statements made within one episteme may not correspond with those made in another. Any statement referring to madness or reason within the Renaissance episteme, for example, will have a different meaning from a similar-looking statement in the modern episteme.

What many of Foucault's critics fail to recognize, however, is that despite his stress on the incommensurability of epistemes, there is also a sense in which his position is not a relativist one. In acknowledging that there is a sociological dimension to theory construction and change, Foucault stresses the fact that members of a society are involved in a social situation that quite independently of them has certain features. Members of the society can maintain these features, or work to change them. Allowing that the preferences of individuals and groups will be conditioned by dominant epistemes, then, any action that may be taken to change a situation will have consequences that depend on the objective character of the situation, and may differ considerably from the intentions of the actor.[37] Foucault makes this clear especially in his account of the social uses of power from the public spectacles of the seventeenth and eighteenth centuries to the pervasive disciplinary networks of modern society. He argues in *Discipline and Punish* that individuals in society are confronted with objective situations, plus a range of raw materials and methods for coping with them.[38] These Foucault identifies as features of disciplinary practice that link knowledge and power, and which are available for the continuation of a particular situation as well as possibly contributing to its change.

Thus Foucault argues that there is more to philosophy than mere theories expressed in logical propositions. There is also its sociopolitical aspect. Philosophic knowledge is gained by means of a complex social endeavor, and derives from the activities of specialists and non-specialists alike, as well as from common beliefs and traditional practices. Philosophic theories occur within particular epistemes, provide standards – often conflicting ones – that are used in the evaluation of historical situations. Likewise, as part of a complex historical situation a philosophic theory cannot escape the political realm.

Foucault is insistent that knowledge and power imply one another: 'there is no power relation without the correlative constitution of a field of knowledge, nor any knowledge that does not presuppose and constitute at the same time power relations.'[39] This power/knowledge relation is linked, in turn, to the will to truth, which functions like other systems of exclusion, and rests on institutional supports: 'it is both reinforced and renewed by whole strata of practices such as pedagogy, of course, and the system of books, publishing and libraries; learned societies in the past, and laboratories now.'[40] Hence, 'discourse is controlled, selected, organized, and distributed according to a number of procedures whose role is to ward off its powers and dangers, to master the unpredictable event.'[41]

Merquior, following Habermas, argues against this that the critique of culture only makes sense if we preserve a standard of truth capable of telling theory from ideology, and knowledge from mystification.[42] He argues that ultimately Foucault's endeavor is caught on the horns of an epistemological dilemma: if Foucault's claims are true, then all knowledge is suspect in its pretence to objectivity, but in that case, how can the theory itself vouch for its truth?[43]

Foucault may respond to this objection by arguing that his negative claim, that there is no universalist and linear discipline called 'philosophy', is balanced by the positive claim that each area of knowledge operates on the basis of particular sets of regularities which determine its aims, methods, and results. Consequently, any particular knowledge area must be judged not in terms of some universal principles or truth, but by investigating its aims and results in terms of its particular episteme. From the beginning Foucault's work has raised a serious problem about the universalist claims of reason. Undoubtedly, we commonly accept that human behaviour is rational, and that the behavior of any particular person is rational, if it approximates to certain norms and processes which are accepted as appropriate. These will include items like consistency of behavior, intelligence, judiciousness, deliberateness, etc. But as Freud and others have shown convincingly, the behavior of the disturbed person can and does conform in many respects to the supposed norms of rationality. On the other hand, the behavior of 'rational' persons often includes supposedly extra-rational elements.

Merquior's dilemma arises primarily because his notion of truth rests upon a foundation which presupposes some epistemological purity. For example, he claims that if Foucault's demonstration of the truth of his analytics of power does not reduce to the mere pragmatism of the struggle, 'then at least one "pure" truth claim exists.'[44]

Presuppositions such as Merquior's can only be eliminated by turning the entire question round, as Foucault does. This will involve a transition from the continuity to the discontinuity of knowledge, and to its non-normative or variational mechanisms. This transition cannot be described simply as the rejection of knowledge and a return to the random or the arbitrary. Neither can it be seen merely as a change from one theory to another. As a plea for theoretical/practical complexity, rather, it argues against the dangers of homogenizing all the unique forms of historicity, and of reducing to the authority of a single model all the various thresholds that a discursive practice may cross.[45]

In 'The Order of Discourse', Foucault's inaugural address at the Collège de France, Foucault puts the matter very succinctly. Philosophy has consistently tried to evade the reality of discourse as a material event. For example, he claims that the major contemporary European philosophical theories tend to be centrist in orientation, in that they draw 'all phenomena around a single centre – a principle, a meaning, a spirit, a worldview, an overall shape.'[46] Thus phenomenology gives priority to the observing subject, 'which attributes a constituent role to an act which places its own point of view at the origin of all historicity – which, in short, leads to a transcendental consciousness.'[47] Likewise the structuralist notion of langue operates as a finite body of rules that authorizes an infinite number of performances but which avoids the diachronic issue: 'how is it that one particular statement appeared rather than another?'[48] Hermeneutics, in turn, operates on a principle which 'makes it possible to think the dispersion of history in the form of the same . . . (and) enables us to isolate the new against a background of permanence, and to transfer its merit to originality, to genius, and to the decisions proper to individuals.'[49]

Foucault, in claiming that philosophy must be seen as a social practice, holds that as such it will involve various philosophical claims or theories formulated according to different techniques or rules of procedure. While the thoughts and actions of individual thinkers are of paramount importance, as Deleuze attests when he indicates that the major theoretical conversion developed by Foucault is the indignity of speaking for others,[50] yet, as theorist, Foucault is no mere subjectivist. On the contrary, his repeated rejections of subjectivism, notably in his critique of phenomenology, goes hand in hand with his acknowledgment of the social relations and practices by means of which individuals become subject to power. Gordon makes this clear: 'it is already one of the prime effects of power that certain bodies, certain gestures, certain discourses, certain desires, come to be identified as individuals. The individual which power has constituted is at the same time its vehicle.'[51] This situation ensures that there will always be a gap between theory/practice on the one hand, and what it purports to describe or explain, on the other. The consequences of theory/ practice will never be totally determinable by its initiators, because they will also be influenced by elements of the social situation, and typically will be different from what the individual intended.[52]

Although the foregoing is sufficient to protect Foucault from the charge of complete subjectivism, yet perhaps a form of an earlier objection returns if the point is made that even if one grants that the history of thought has occurred in conformity with his account, yet this does not explain why it has occurred. A Foucauldian response to this charge, however, would be to the effect that things happen because of the various ways in which individuals and groups respond to the dominant codes, rules, etc. What Foucault cannot explain, however, is what specific things will occur.

Certain consequences follow from this for the change or development of philosophic theories. Because of the complexity of any realistic situation within philosophy, and the unpredictability of the future as far as the development of a theory is concerned, philosophers need not be constrained by the rules of any particular theory. Furthermore, no one theory absolutely determines what will follow after it, or which subsequent theory must be chosen in preference to another. This does not return Foucault to a subjectivist or anarchistic position. While it does recognize and allow that any particular theorist may follow out his own whims and fancies, yet, more importantly, it stresses that the construction of a theory or the development of a discipline will very likely involve random factors, unexplained elements, etc., but that these and other elements of the theory or discipline will tend to be constrained, though not absolutely, by the already established codes and practices operative in the discipline.[53]

On Foucault's position, while it will not be possible to provide a quantitative measure of how a line of thought/practice will develop, yet it will be possible to make qualitative comparisons. Furthermore, Foucault's account possesses long-term value precisely because it does not predict only one, or a few, lines of development, but allows for many possibilities. For example, psychiatry in its emergence involved 'infinitesimal surveillances, permanent controls, extremely meticulous orderings of space, indeterminate medical or psychological examinations.'[54] Change, or 'development' in psychiatry, however, involved the introduction of new techniques, the notion of normalization and its concomitant controls, etc.[55]

In conclusion, the major features of Foucault's enterprise may be summarized as follows. There is no timeless or universal view of philosophy and philosophic method which can establish truth in a neutral and objective manner. Any particular criterion of truth can only function as part of a certain episteme, which means that it will always involve a political or ideological dimension. Foucault is not confined to a position where he is forced to assert that any view is absolutely as good as any other. On the contrary, criticism of an established philosophical position, or the development of a new one, will involve a study of its aims, the degree to which its aims have been attained or are attainable, plus an account of the forces or factors which have influenced its development, or that will be likely to do so. To the degree that this occurs it becomes possible to make a more comprehensive judgment, but always within the constraints of a dominant episteme, on the particular claim, in terms of the desirability of its aims, the extent to which its methods enable the aims to be achieved, as well as the interests that it serves.

Thus, if situations are to be changed in a controlled way, whether this involves the development of some branch of knowledge, or some aspect of society, or both, this will be best achieved by means of a grasp of the situation, and a mastery of the means available for changing it.

Lest it be considered that this overly neutralizes Foucault's position, let me stress that in practice the situation of change will be rather turbulent. Conflicts and tensions will tend to be features of change, as the new theories and practices work to establish their own spaces and institutions. Those who hold power will tend not to be anxious to relinquish it, even when apparently more 'objective' claims suggest that they do so. There are no ideal situations.

Chapter 6

DELEUZE ON A DESERTED ISLAND

Alphonso Lingis

Lewis Carroll, Kafka, Zola, Beckett, Artaud, Schreber, D. H. Lawrence, Michel Tournier – Deleuze's writings have explored these materials as much as they have those of scientists such as Freud, Monod, Lévi-Strauss, and of philosophers such as Hume, Bergson, and Nietzsche. Fiction is not for him, as for phenomenologists, a procedure by which the invariant essence of mind, of things, of cultural formations, and of the world gets adequately intuited and definitively formulated. Literature for him is neither a narrative material to which philosophical hermeneutics supplies a master-narrative, nor a material which philosophy works over to generalize, critically appraise, or deconstruct. In Deleuze the critique of the *image of thought*, thought as an image or a representation, is also a critique of the philosophical practice of representation, of the major thought that would function as representative of, that would speak for, speak the truth of, every minor, babbling, stuttering, or immigrant discourse. Deleuze seeks to practice a *thought* prior to the formulation of the philosophy which makes the different an object of representation by relating the encountered with a conceived identity, a judged analogy, an imagined opposition, a perceived likeness. His non-universalist, non-university discursive practice would be provoked by regional, minor, minority practices of discourse in which an unrepresentable sensible, sensation without sense, is set forth. Provoked by the shock of the encounter, it would then not proceed to interpret it, to re-cognize its meaning, but to practice a mechanic's analysis – see how it works.

Deleuze's text devoted to Michel Tournier's novel *Friday*,[1] a this-time libidinal retelling of the story of Robinson Crusoe, is illuminating for what light, what problematization his kind of thinking yields on the experiences that 'comic adventure story' sets forth, for the provocation this analysis gives to Deleuze and Guattari's elaborated philosophy of libido in *Anti-Oedipus*, and for the fidelity and the infidelity it exhibits to Deleuze's concept of what philosophy, what thought is.

Robinson Crusoe is twenty-two years old, has a wife and two children. He has, then, been 'triangulated,' has achieved the *telos* of reproductive sexuality that the Oedipus structuration is the instrument for. Now he enlists as a seaman on the *Virginia*; he sets out to go far, far from the objectives of his English world, far, too, libidinally beyond paternal and reproductive sexuality. The book, Deleuze says, is the tale of the adventures not so much of Robinson as of the island of hope, Speranza, that will take him to a remote, exotic, ultimate sexuality which is not a return to the origins, to infancy. It is the narrative of a libido that *encounters*, beyond the recognized law and the recognizable meaning, the sensation without sense of the free elements, light that does not elucidate or clarify, wind-intoned musicality without a text, sun that fecundates an inhuman progeny in an orphan libido.

The primary-process libido, whose positions were charted by Melanie Klein, and whose mechanisms were illuminated by microbiology, functions as the model for the schizophrenic peregrinations of post capitalist culture *Anti-Oedipus* prophesizes. Michel Tournier's book does not illustrate this kind of libidinal destiny: what is recounted there is not a return, on the far edge of imperialist culture, of the primary process infancy. It tells of a triangulated Oedipal and reproductive sexuality that then goes further, toward an unbound, free, elemental sensibility in a time that is no longer teleological.

Certainly Deleuze's own initiative in writing a text on Tournier's novel is to recast Robinson's adventures into the structure of *perversion*. Does he not then *interpret* the *events* of Tournier's narrative in terms of the master-narrative supplied by Lacanian psychoanalysis? *Anti-Oedipus* will do a mechanic's analysis on the Lacanian machinery, showing how it works to recode the libidinal connections univocally from the world to the carceral space of the nuclear family, the asylum, and the psychoanalyst's couch. But here Deleuze takes as clinically established a *perverse structure*, where the cause of desire is detached from its objects, the different sexes are replaced by an androgynous population of doubles, the other engenders his own metaphor, an other of the other, and the perverse one himself is desubjectivized. One can hastily object that Deleuze is doing a psychoanalytic hermeneutics of this tale, as though it were a case-study to be interpreted. Deleuze answers that the imagination of existence on a deserted island is perversion; that perversion is existence without the master-category of the other. The other, not as an empirically encountered individual, but as a category, as the system of possible perspectives maintained about the actual, transforms every pattern from a plenum that mesmerizes the solitary gaze into an objective. Existence without the master-category of the other is then deviation with respect to objectives. Inevitably a detachment from the world of objects and objectives, it is entry into the purely surface spectacle of fiction. That Tournier's book is a work of fiction and not a case-study is then no obstacle to the psychoanalytic interpretation; the fiction here is the royal road to the essence, not, as for phenomenology, because the imaginary variation isolates the subsistent essence which is the reality, but because perversion is always produced as enacting a fictive existence. Fiction is being a Robinson Crusoe on a deserted island; fiction is a perversion, as perversion is fictive existence. Literary criticism objects to the philosophical naivety that draws on the discursive practices of psychoanalytic diagnosis to recast in terms of the master-narrative of psychotherapeutic practice the tale of Tournier, which is not a report of lived experience, but a fictive recasting in libidinal terms of the fictive adventures Daniel Defoe cast in terms of the master-narrative of Victorian imperialism. ('Have you ever seen a schizophrenic?' 'Have you ever been in an asylum?' the psychoanalysts asked Deleuze and Guattari when *Anti-Oedipus* was published.) But here the objection would only confirm Deleuze's thesis, that perversion is existence that never encounters the other, the really possible, but only the metaphor of the other.

We rather want to object to Deleuze not the objections of literary criticism, but the objection Tournier's own internal interpretation of his novel formulates. The work presents itself not as a fictive elaboration of a prior work of fiction, itself elaborated out of Victorian ideology rather than out of experience – but rather as a spiritual biography. Its genre is pages from a journal, and pages of a narrative voice filling in between those pages.

> For some time now I have occupied myself with an operation which consisted in successively tearing from myself one after another all my attributes – I do say all of them – like the successive layers of an onion. In doing so, I constitute far from myself an individual named Crusoe, first name Robinson, who is six feet tall, etc. I see him live and evolve in an island without profiting from his fortunes nor suffering from his mishaps. Who – *I*?. The question is far from being an idle one; it is not even insoluble. For if it is not *him*, then it is *Speranza*. There is from now on a floating *I* that sometimes lands on the man, sometimes on the island, and makes of me sometimes the one and sometimes the other.[2]

The journal pages and the pages filling in are then not pages of interpretation but of autobiography. An autobiography of a floating 'I' which is sometimes that of a Robinson Crusoe as far from the writer of those pages as from their reader, and sometimes that of Speranza, the deserted island, deserted also of the I of the writer. These pages, which the literary critic takes to be the recasting in the libidinal master-narrative of the twentieth century of the fictive autobiography of Daniel Defoe, itself but an instantiation of the master-narrative of Victorian imperialism, do not in fact become telling by inducing another interpretation, the Lacanian-Deleuzian, and now our own, 'interpreting' Deleuze on Tournier. How do they work? They induce other 'I's,' the readers, to come undergo the spiritual metamorphoses for which the book is a guide, to transform themselves into floating loci of consciousness over Speranza, over an earth deserted of civilization, interpretation, texts. The signs with which this adventure tale is inscribed are themselves the surface simulacra which induce the displacement into this 'I' on the part of the readers.

Deleuze published his text on Tournier as an appendix to his *Logique du sens*; in the body of that book he elaborated an analysis of the essentially *surface existence* (or rather subsistence, insistence) *of meaning*, which is capable of capturing the subject and leading it down ever-surface prolongations. The text on Tournier, however, discovers an *elemental surface*, that of the free elements – unbound, not univocally referential of objectives. Deleuze shows in Tournier's novel the collapse of the category of the other, the other as category and as possible obstinately passing for real. This other, locus of the possible obstinately passing for real, is the metaphorical relay that makes every surface pattern a metaphor for an object-objective; the language that circulates over the terra firma structured by the *a priori of the other* is a language destined to interpretation and interpretation of interpretation. But in the measure that the category of the other dissipates from the island, another island, the elemental island emerges, bringing to birth another Robinson, an elemental Robinson, and another other arrives, an elemental other to guide him with *elemental signs*.

The currency of metaphors

Existence on a deserted island, Deleuze shows, reveals how the category of the other works. Robinson discovers that the others are not a contingent multitude of factual substances, their apparitions contingent events, but a system of actualized poss-ibles. When I look at the face and the position of another, I see him as standing there where I might be standing; his body is put there as a variant of, a signifier for, a metaphor for, my body. In addition, his body is a signifier for what he faces: his color and his contours do not hold my look on themselves; they refer me to the frightening or alluring configuration of something I do not see. The possible configurations organized on the margin of my field of consciousness are materialized, fixed in actuality by the actual visible, audible, and tangible figure of the other. This system of possibles cushions the impact of reality; without it the real abruptly turns up before my eyes to assault me like a blow struck from the invisible. Without the others, Robinson finds nakedness unendurable, all things assaulting his surfaces of exposure without warning, as so many maliciousnesses. Language is a medium of communication with the others in their function as materializations of the possible; language, signalling sensory patterns as loci for multiple figures of the possible, designates them by metaphor; a deep well is designated as a quality of thought and an emotion.

What this system of possibles makes one take as actual, a crust formed over the elemental zone of one's contact sensibility, is a field of *objects-objectives*. An object is a momentary sensory pattern to which the marginal presence of the others affixes a depth of subsistent possibilities. The object stands upright and holds upright the powers with which one takes hold of it. The one who exists in a land populated with others is a 'framework of habits, responses, reflexes, preoccupations, dreams, associations' – a stabilized and erect figure of power. Without the others, the upright posture collapses. Robinson 'knew now that man resembles a person injured in a street riot, who can only stay upright while the crowd packed densely around him continues to prop him up' (F, p. 40).

It is the others too that constitute one as a mobile light-source that circulates among objects. Without them there is not first a theater of objects into which one watches oneself enter; there is only a moving zone of light in which patterns shine with their own phosphorescence. 'He is conscious of himself only in the stir of myrtle leaves with the sun's rays breaking through, he knows himself only in the white crest of a wave running up the yellow sand' (F, p. 93). This phosphorescence in the sensory elements is extracted out of them and shut up in itself as a separate entity, one's subjectivity, by the dense-packed crowd of the others, prone to riot, that tramples the sensory expanses under one's feet. But all that is deposited in this subject that now forms is taken from the objects.

> The light becomes the eye and as such no longer exists: it is simply the stimulation of the retina. The smell becomes the nostril – and the world declares itself odorless. The song of the wind in the trees is disavowed: it was nothing but a quivering of the timpani. . . . The subject is the disqualified object. My eye is the corpse of light and color. My nose is all that remains of odors when their unreality has been demonstrated. My hand refutes the thing it holds. (F, p. 95)

The crystallization of the subject is thus produced by an exile of the properties of the objects which the others had interposed over the original dimension of phosphorescent elemental reality. But this dis-qualification, this alienation of qualities from objects, Tournier affirms to have a purpose – it does not only exhibit the resistance of a material to a power that seeks to bury itself in it; it expresses the drive of the *other island*, the elemental island, to emerge. The object-structure that had formed in its elements, now reformed into a subject-structure, is repelled from the body of the elemental island. 'A knot of contradiction, a center of discord, it has been eliminated from the body of the island, rejected, repudiated. . . . The world seeks its own reason and in doing so casts off that irrelevance, the subject' (*F*, p. 94).

The other, incarnate figure of the possible, of the future, transforms the sensibility of the subject now made of the qualities of which the objects are divested – the subject now exiled from the elements in which it was immersed – into *desire*. Desire, craving for the unseen, the untouched, the inapprehended, is necessarily desire for the other, whose carnal body signals as a stand-in for, a substitute for, the possible, the future. What I, detached subject, crave is presented imperatively to me by the expression of the other. The other's figure is a materialized variant of my own; it is myself as possible obstinately passing for my actual body. To desire is thus to desire the other, that expression of the possible, and it is to desire what the other desires. The craving of desire arises inasmuch as my sensibility is mesmerized by the finalities he apprehends. The sensibility now turns to *goods* – not just the sensory patterns immediately in contact with me, not just additional patterns added to my patterns, to make up three-dimensional solids. Goods are constituted as exchangeable, objects the others possess but which in principle I can acquire by alienating my powers for theirs. Goods as the other possesses them and as I desire them are not extensions of sensory sustenance that content the others; they are poles that galvanize his expressive body, objectives that can be taken from him. All the objects I *desire* are so made into objectives by the others. Objects are sensory reality reduced to *currency*, wealth, or money. The desire that bears on alterity in the others is a desire for wealth. Money is desired not for its intrinsic sensuous properties, but for the relationship it makes possible with others. Gold, Marx explained, is chosen as the standard of measure precisely because it is the substance with the least use-value. It is too soft to serve in the making of implements, and although one's sensibility enjoys its glowing brilliance, it is too rare to serve as the primary substance of sensuous immersion. By evaluating all goods in monetary terms, one abstracts from objects all their sensuous qualities by which they cloy to the concrete sensibility, and one abstracts from them the use-value by which they now serve one practical agent in his particular field of operations; one converts all substance, all sustenance, into currency.

Robinson, who found himself cast by the winds and the sea upon an Island of Desolation, sets out to reconstruct the island of Speranza – hope for the civilization he had lost. The luxuriant life of the Island of Desolation had sustained his life as well; there was no utilitarian motive to subject it to cultivation. For Freud, the basic acquisitions of civilization – the building of shelters, the taming of fire, the fashioning of tools – did not, could not, originate out of utilitarian pressures. It is true that the human mutant is a particularly vulnerable species of animal, but this species became naked and muscularly weak as a result of living indoors, warmed by fire, his implements freeing his own muscles to atrophy. For Freud it was our unseasonal libido and not our utilitarian needs that contrived shelters of branches and moss as a substitute for the womb with which our nostalgic sensuality retains a bond, that invented tools which prolong and enhance our orifices and our couplings, that gather about it in homosexual competition with one another and with nature. What motivated Robinson's project for civilization on a deserted island was indeed libidinal, and in a contradictory way. On the one hand, the absence of others to sustain upright his subjective posture had led him to discover that the subject-structure, instrument for the dis-qualification of objects, is a reject cast off from the elemental earth. He conceives the project of becoming again nothing but 'the stir of myrtle leaves with the sun's rays breaking through, the white crest of a wave running up the yellow sand' – by subjective initiative.

> This prickly formula gives me a somber satisfaction. It shows me the rough and narrow road to salvation, at least to a kind of salvation – that of a fruitful and harmonious

island, flawlessly cultivated and administered, strong in the harmony of all its attributes, steadily pursuing its course without me, because it is so close to me that even to look at it is to make it too much myself, so that I must shrink to become that intimate phosphorescence which causes each thing to be known while no one is the knower, each one to be aware while no one has awareness. . . . Oh, subtle and pure equilibrium so fragile and so precious! (F, p. 95)

Yet this project to extinguish his separate subjectivity, that which exists in the longing to flee Speranza, by submerging it into the substance of Speranza, can only transform all life on Speranza into wealth, into currency, that is, into a materialized libidinal demand for the others. Robinson does not evolve his cultivating presence in the substance of Speranza out of the fragile and precious equilibrium he caught sight of and its own exigencies; rather he unloads everything from the wreckage of the *Virginia*, which had been richly equipped to sustain a whole community of men at sea and whose stores had been filled with luxuries it was transporting. Robinson builds on Speranza a shelter he will never sleep, cook, or wash himself in – a 'museum of civilization.' He puts into his armory and his warehouses all the tools taken from the *Virginia* which he will never use – he has no need of guns to kill the animals on Speranza, for its most bold bucks can be slaughtered with a blow with any branch, and he will till and harvest with his hands and with shells, sticks, and flails. The fire he tames will serve not for warmth, but to signal others.

The clepsydra he devises is the *a priori* form of the desubjectivization and subtle and pure equilibrium he now pursues with the island. If the others as a category constitutive of the field of objective-objectives, what Deleuze calls the other as an *a priori*, which precedes and makes possible the encounter with any empirical other, is the possible and the future affixed to every present, then the experience of a world inhabited by others is the experience of a time in which each present jostles on the heels of another time. The category of the other functions then as a time-structure of 'days, hours, minutes being leaned on by the ones to follow.' The clepsydra will then maintain the category of the other on the island in which, paradoxically, Robinson seeks to desubjectivize himself.

Henceforth, whether I am waking or sleeping, writing, or cooking a meal, my time is marked by this regular ticking, positive, unanswerable, measurable and precise. . . . I demand, I insist, that everything around me shall henceforth be measured, tested, certified, mathematical, and rational. One of my tasks must be to make a full survey of the island, its distances, and its contours, and incorporate all these details in an accurate surveyor's map. I would like every plant to be labeled, every bird to be ringed, every animal to be branded. I shall not be content until this opaque and impenetrable place, filled with secret ferments and malignant stirrings, has been transformed into a rational structure, visible and intelligible to its very depths! (*F*, p. 66)

The total intelligibility Robinson desires is that brought to sensory patterns by the total set of the others when they from all sides detach him from the sensory absorption in opaque sensory substance and fix his attention on the signs their bodies diagram. He wants an island become transparent, each of whose animals, vegetables, and minerals having been resituated and defined by its place in the universal table of goods maintained by the bodies of the others.

His labor then is not a husbandry that has as its purpose to ensure his own physical survival, but a metallurgy laboring to smelt the opaque ferments of the island into gold coins.

Money spiritualizes all that it touches by endowing it with a quality that is both rational (measurable) and universal, since property reckoned in terms of money is accessible to all men. . . . The venal man suppresses his murderous and antisocial instincts – honour, self-pride, patriotism, political ambition, religious fanaticism, racialism – in favor of his need to cooperate with others his love of fruitful exchanges, his sense of human solidarity. (*F*, p. 61)

The transition, Burridge explained[3] from a society based on the exchange of goods and services, a society then governed by the rigorous obligation incumbent on the receiver to give goods of equivalent use-value in return, into a society where the giving of goods and services can be repaid immediately with the useless substance of gold coins, is a transition to a society in which nonreciprocity, love, that is, unreciprocated service, becomes for the first time possible.

If then the years of Robinson's immersion in the island as its cultivating energy makes of it not an abundance destined for consumption – which is always solitary, isolating – but wealth spiritualized in the love of fruitful exchanges in which love, liberated, circulates, why then will Robinson's response to the Araucanian society that one day makes contact with his island be one of armed repulsion and murder? It is that the museum of civilization, that construction of metaphors made with wealth, currency, was from the first undermined by the emergence of the *other island*, the *elemental*. And under the I that wrote its accounts *another Robinson* was being born.

The elemental

When the others were gone – the crew of the *Virginia* driven into the storms, the Araucanians driven off by Robinson's firearms, Robinson discovers – through the progressive disintegration first of the pressure of possibilities around his own field of experience, then of language, of the double-meanings and metaphors in language, and finally through the violent destruction, by Friday's unintentional detonation of his gunpowder stores, of the whole museum of civilization Robinson had constructed – not Mas a Tierra, another island of the Juan Fernández archipelago, but a *phantasmal* island, as Deleuze identified it, made of doubles without resemblance, rising into surfaces to receive him – or rather to produce his double.

From the first the bounteous Island of Desolation, which offers its nourishment to him without any thought or initiative on his part, invites him. For days, for weeks, for months, delivered to *terra firma*, he is immobilized in passive contemplation of the 'vast gently heaving expanse of the ocean, green-tinged and glittering.' The huge cedar, tutelary genius of the island, brings him up to the air and skies and light. He resolved to keep fire going permanently.

The mire, zone of indistinction of waters and earth, two

elements of death, draws him voluptuously. The plenum of the mire is not that of infantile escapism – after the practical failure of his project of building the bark *Escape* – that inability to endure discord, difference, opposition, and the master-opposition of life and death which Nietzsche denounced in the ecstasy into mildness of Jesus and of every redeemer-type. It is rather the place of a present in which everything he had escaped from is rediscovered and possessed 'more observantly, more intelligently, and more sensually than was possible in the turmoil of the present' (*F*, p. 41). The mire, incestuous union of seas and earth, reunites Robinson with his sister. But Lucy, come to him on a phantom ship, does not disembark as another figure of the possible. She appears to him in the free elements 'suspended in the blue gaps between the motionless foliage' signalling to Robinson only as the sign of definitive departure of every possible.

Then, in the measure that the opaque substance of secret ferments and malignant stirrings has been transmuted into a crust of transparent metaphors, of currency, 'visible and intelligible to its very depths,' *another depth* beyond the nonvisibility of darkness, beckons to him imperatively with an invisible sign. Robinson follows, down into the cave at the summit, womb-hollow of the rock-core of the island. He is seeking that recess in cathedrals, in sacred constructions, from which can be heard the least whispers in the apside, choir, sanctuary, or nave. In this opaque and impenetrable hollow Robinson finds another transparency and visibility of the plants he had labeled, the birds he had ringed, the animals he had branded.

> Seated with his back to the rocky wall, his eyes wide open in the darkness, he saw the white unfolding of the sea on all the shores of the island, the benevolent sway of palm leaves stirred by the wind, the red flash of a hummingbird against a green sky. He smelled the moist freshness of the sand uncovered by the ebb, and watched a hermit crab as it took the air at the doorway of its shell. A black-headed gull slowed down suddenly in its flight to swoop down upon a small creature half-hidden in the red seaweed, gleaming brown in the drag of the undertow. (*F*, p. 99)

From this nerve center Robinson descends to the darkest recess, the womb. It is by a movement of systole and diastole to the core, the inner substance of the earth, that the surface life proliferates. He discovers the maternal substance of *terra firma*, the flawless, dry tenderness, the unfailing, undemonstrative solicitude he had known in childhood in his mother, strong high-souled, but deeply reserved and not given to a display of sentiment.

It would be quite wrong here to treat these words as metaphorical transfer – to begin now to make the novel an allegory, and the philosophical encounter with it a hermeneutical enterprise of translating its metaphors into the master-narrative of those Deleuze identifies as 'universal, university, intellectuals.' It is on the crust of objects laid over the elemental that the other is a figure of the possible obstinately passing for real, his objects currency, and his signs metaphors. On the island deserted of others, Robinson's perception is mesmerized by the immediate blows of the actual. The language he maintains in the museum of his diary loses all metaphoricity; he can no longer understand a deep well as a profound thought and a deep emotion. He has maintained the category or the *a priori* of the other with the clepsydra, whose waterdrop minutes are each jostled by the pressure of the next. But the clepsydra can only maintain the form of the presence of others – a category maintained in suspense in the absence of the others, a form suspended over the absence of its matter. Beneath the crust of currency and metaphors, while the clepsydra is stopped, Robinson has descended to a sphere where experience is without the conditions of possibility for metaphor. Here his libido no longer steps on, leans in passing on, terrestrial substances on the way to the womb of his human mother and of his own child, substances that would metaphorically transfer his energies toward that objective. More radically, his libido no longer has an object, an objective – that structure that it can have only by being the *desire of the other*. Robinson has no idea what he desires, what objects he seeks; his libido is a drive that is a cause that has no object, as Deleuze formulates it, a driving force without a representation of the directing force in consciousness, as Nietzsche, Deleuze explained, would have put it. 'Previously . . . I sought to console myself with visions of a house, *the* house in which I would end my days, built out of massive blocks of granite resting on unshakable foundations. I no longer indulge in that house. I no longer need it' (*F*, p. 107).

A libido that is no longer shifted metaphorically from object to object beneath object, which no longer finds the pole of its craving in the object another's craving designates, a libido that rests on its terrestrial cause, while there so close to death that the least shift of attention is enough to make it slip over into death (*F*, p. 105) – this libido none the less finds in its cause a specific energy to grow and to multiply. This movement of libido is not impelled by metaphorical transference toward ever more sublime detours from the original libidinal object-objective. With no object, it rests on its terrestrial nature and is the bearer of its terrestrial causality over ever more dispersed surfaces.

> It seems to me that a feeling such as love is better measured, if it can be measured at all, by the extent of its surface than by the degree of its depth. For if I measure my love for a woman by the fact that I love indiscriminately her hands, her eyes, her carriage, the clothes she wears, the commonplace things she merely touches, the place where she dwells, the sea in which she bathes. . . . All this, it seems to me, is decidedly on the surface! Whereas a lesser love aims directly – in depth – at sex and leaves all the rest in a shadowy background. (*F*, p. 67)

Thus it is a terrestrial libido intensifying or augmenting that brings Robinson out from the cave to the surfaces of Speranza. His libido intensifies in becoming superficial, but it does so circulating on the surfaces the causality of the core. 'Robinson reflected that there might be trees on the island, which, like the orchids with the hymenoptera, might be disposed to make use of himself for the transference of their pollen' (*F*, p. 115). The surfaces are no longer profiles of objects-objectives, no longer cross-sections opening up a depth, but themselves surface causes of a libido without objects. 'He felt as never before that he was lying on Speranza as though on a living being, that the island's body was beneath him. . . . His sex burrowed like a plowshare into the earth, and overflowed in immense compassion for all created things' (*F*, p. 119).

In the absence of the others, Robinson's libido is no longer structured as desire, insatiable desire for objects ever-distanced by the others. But the absence of the others from him and his absence from them – his death from among them, which marks him here – now fills his thought with understanding of the unrecognizable sensuality. 'All those who know me, all without exception, believe me dead. My own belief in my existence is opposed to that unanimous belief. No matter what I do, I cannot prevent that picture of Robinson's dead body from existing in all their minds' (F, p. 123). This death in their, and consequently in his own, mind reveals the dying in all libido. Reproductive sexuality which transfers life from the old to the new is evacuation and sacrifice; it is the 'living presence, ominous and mortal, of the species in the essence of the individual' (F, p. 124).

> Under the influence of darkness, warmth, and languor the enemy revives, unsheathes his sword, and diminishes the man, makes of him a lover, plunges him into a brief ecstasy, then closes his eyes – and the lover, couched on earth, lost in the rapture of forgetfulness and renunciation of self, sinks into that little death which is sleep. . . . Earth irresistibly draws the enclasped lovers with joined lips, cradling them after their embrace in the happy slumber of sensual delight. But earth also harbors the dead, sucks their blood and devours their flesh, that these orphans be restored to the cosmos from which for the length of a lifetime they were parted. Love and death, two aspects of the defeat of the individual, turn with a common impulse to the earth. Both are of their nature earthly. . . . Deprived of that fruitful byway which a woman's body affords, I must turn directly to the earth which will be my last resting place. What happened in the pink coomb? I dug my grave with my sex and died the transient death that we call pleasure. (F, p. 125)

Our sexuality is what the ancients called the vegetative system in our bodies – not organs by which our bodies are self-moving, animate, animal, but glands, sap, seed. 'He buried his face in the grass roots, breathing open-mouthed a long, hot breath. And the earth responded, filling his nostrils with the heavy scent of dead grass and the ripening of seed, and of sap rising in new shoots' (F, p. 120). Our sexuality, conceived as causality and not as objectifying desire, is terrestrial. It is that by which we belong to the vegetative abundance of the earth.

This immediate embrace of the earth gives birth to mandrakes, those plants whose roots lead the mind by meta-phorizing transfer to the body of a child. It is the sole magical incident in this otherwise rigorously naturalist novel. But we readers are also required to read this magical causality as naturalist and not allegorical. Robinson's first libidinal immer-sion in the elemental surfaces of Speranza was productive, cultured and cultivating; here it is reproductive. He remembers the explanations of the old naturalist Samuel Gloaming, who, before Deleuze, had taught him that reproduction is not representation of the identical, but repetition of difference. The reproductive causality which is libido is not a mechanism for the representation of the same individual in the form of an eternal genus. Reproductivity in the individual is the ominous and mortal force that sacrifices that individual to something else. The reproductive libido as causality is the vegetative life in the individual's body, which itself is produced by the earth's need to produce the superabundance and unending mutations of vegetative life so that something would survive 'were the earth to be frozen to a block of ice, or burned by the sun to a desert of stone' (F, p. 123).

The elemental sign

The Araucanians return, those people whose civilization is formulated by the female seer who rules according to the law stated in the Gospel of St Matthew: 'If thy right hand offend thee, cut it out and cast it from thee.' Her entranced finger points to a half-caste fifteen-year-old boy to be cast off. Robinson, deciding in accordance with his own imperative to save his Mosaic, patriarchal civilization, aims his pistol at the fleeing victim, but the dog Tenn struggles in Robinson's grip, Robinson misses his aim, and kills one of the pursuers instead. Thus, unintentionally, he saves Friday's life.

The venal civilization – that which 'suppresses murderous and anti-social instincts,' that exchanges goods not with recipro-cated goods of equivalent use-value but with useless currency and thus liberates love – had in fact met the others for whom it is wholly the materialized desire with 'self-pride, patriotism, political ambition, religious fanaticism, racialism.' Robinson immediately inserts Friday into his metallurgical enterprise; he teaches him English, teaches him to plow and sow and reap, to thresh and winnow, grind and cook. He sets him to work milking the goats, making cheese, collecting turtles' eggs and soft-boiling them, digging ditches, tending the fishponds, trapping vermin, calking the canoe, mending his garments, and polishing his boots, forcing him:

> to listen devoutly to words such as *sin, salvation, hell-fire, damnation, Mammon, and apocalypse* . . . . He paid Friday. He paid him a wage of a half-sovereign a month. Friday could spend the money on . . . trifles brought from the *Virginia*, or simply on buying himself a half-day's repose . . . which he spent in the hammock he had made for himself. (*F*, p. 141)

Robinson will one day see on Friday's face not a mirror of the total intelligibility of the transparent island, but fear of the unintelligible and the demented – materialized for Friday on Robinson's face.

That night Robinson goes to make love with Speranza in the coomb of the mandrakes, and in his absence the water of the clepsydra stops. Friday reverts in his nature, his libidinous, vegetative causality. Robinson finds him first in the magnolia tree, transformed into a vine, then in the mandrakes that extend Friday's reproductive libido across the surfaces of Speranza.

Friday will finally totally destroy the museum of civilization Robinson had built, destroy all his irrigated rice-fields, his granaries, disperse all his domesticated animals – as inadvertently, unintentionally as Robinson himself had unintentionally saved Friday's life from the matriarchal New-Testament civilization that had encroached on his island. But Friday's hand will save Robinson's life the night the great cedar, the tutelary genius of Robinson's island, turned its roots too into the air, like the willows Friday had planted. 'He would never again let go the hand that reached down to save him on the night the tree fell' (*F*, p. 181). Friday's hand will lead him to the summit of the araucaria tree.

Robinson and Friday form now not a society, figures of the

possible which stabilize the elemental patterns into objects-objectives, each for the other a desire for another desire of other objects, a system for the circulation of currency and love – but a brotherhood, an elemental association of two effects of vegetative sexuality, their hands clasped like vines. They are *doubles* – *phantasms*, Deleuze says, of the free elements rising over the elemental depths, from which each has freed himself in consigning his possible life to the death that embraced the other. Their association will not engender a civilization produced as the cultural prolongation of the family, understood as the reproductive libidinal drive by which the individual reproduces himself in a genus in which the same is re-presented. They form now not a homosexual couple, but, in Klossowski's and also Deleuze's terminology, a *perversion*. For, Klossowski had noted, history shows that homosexuality can, just as heterosexuality, institutionalize itself as the medium in which the genus is affirmed as the re-presentation across the dispersion of time and space of the same. Such would be 'normal' sexuality, that is, the individual as the locus of the reinstatement of the norm. Homosexuality, where each seeks in the other a figure of sex the same as himself, is as normal as the heterosexuality where two individuals seek in reproduction a re-presentation of individuals of the same species as themselves. Klossowski had defined perversion as a sexuality in which the genus, the representation of the same, is destroyed in the individual – where reproductive libido is the causality whose repetition is the engenderment of the different. The kind of fraternity which Robinson and Friday now form is the association formed by a perverse libido – *libidinal* if Samuel Gloaming is right to say that sexuality is the sacrifice of the individual for another, for their association is based on the fact that each has put himself in the place where death had gaped open to take the other – *perverse* in the sense that each sees in the other not the representation of the same, but the repetition of the different.

Thus in the measure that Robinson becomes now as naked, as copper-colored, as beardless as Friday, their phantasmal bodies are each for the other the more strange 'Two days ago,' Robinson notes in his diary, he came up to me while I lay dozing on the beach. He stood for some moments gazing at me, a dark, slender figure outlined against the brilliant sky. Then he knelt down beside me and began to examine me with an extraordinary intentness. His fingers wandered over my face, patted my cheeks, followed the curve of my chin, tested the flexibility of my nose. He made me raise my arms above my head, and bending over my body he explored it inch by inch like an anatomist preparing to dissect a corpse. He seemed to have forgotten that I lived and breathed, that thoughts might enter my head, that I might grow impatient. (F, p. 208)

After the death of Tenn, who had maintained the smile of benevolence, of understanding, of reciprocal confirmation of the project of constituting objects-objectives in elemental and savage nature, Robinson does not find and does not seek Friday's face as the locus of the smile of complicity. Instead he discovers the utter strangeness of eyes without the ray of searching, desiring, demanding looks, searching for objects, for objectives.

And it was now that he became aware of something pure and sensitive gleaming amid the unsightly, mishandled flesh. He noted Friday's eye, beneath its long, curved lashes, seeing how the wonderfully smooth and limpid ball was incessantly wiped clean and refreshed by the beating of the lid. He noted the constant widening and shrinking of the pupil, in response to the scarcely perceptible variations of light, as it regulated the message to be transmitted to the retina. Within the transparency of the iris was contained a tiny, intricate pattern like feathers of glass, a cultivated rose, infinitely precious and delicate, (F, p. 172)

Within the clasped hands of their vegetative brotherhood, Friday will be for Robinson a sign and a guide for Robinson's ultimate voyage: from every earth, every *terra firma*, from the summit of the araucaria tree, realizing the tree's own dream 'struggling under full sail to break away from its mooring,' realizing the evolutionary destiny of the vegetative life to become freely-mobile, to exist in the winds, the musicality, the sun.

Now in watching the figure of Friday, he does not see a possible which refers to and contributes to the object their desire makes of the elemental; Friday rather teaches him that the most perfect arrows are not made for hunting, for capturing life, but for flying forever into the skies.

The great buck Andoar had recreated a social order of command and subordination among the goats after Robinson's pens and stockades had been destroyed. Friday laboriously transforms Andoar into a windborn dancer and an aeolian harp, which Robinson hears 'not a melody to pluck at the heart with its form and rhythm, but a single note, infinite in its harmonies, which took possession of the soul, a chord composed of count-less elements in whose sustained power there was something fateful and implacable that held the listener spellbound' (F, p. 198). And Robinson understands that Andoar is an elemental sign of his own destiny under the hands and harsh knife of Friday.

But Robinson can learn these signs leading him irrevocably beyond all the metaphors with which on *terra firma* individuals represent the same to and for one another, because he has libidinously put himself in the place of the death that rose to take Friday. Rushing up the cliff where Andoar's fall had thrown Friday, Robinson discovers that his fear of heights is in fact the mortal attraction of the earth, which from the cliffsides looking down he sees as a harbor of death, scattered with rocky gravestones.

He realized that vertigo is nothing but terrestrial magnetism acting upon the spirit of man, who is a creature of earth. The soul yearns for that foothold of clay or granite, slate or silica, whose distance at once terrifies and attracts, since it harbors the peace of death. It is not the emptiness of space that induces vertigo, but the enticing fullness of the earthly depths. With his face now turned to the sky, Robinson felt that something stronger than the insidious appeal of those scattered gravestones might be found in the summons to flight of two albatross, companionly soaring amid the pink-tinted clouds. (F, p. 189)

There is then not a social economy in which the signs diagrammed on the figures of each signal metaphorically because each is for the other a possible obstinately passing for real, a desire for the other which is a desire for the objects-objectives of the other. There is a brotherhood in which the one makes himself the double of the other by casting himself into the locus of death which circumvents the other. It is because Friday has cast himself into the death that waits under the figure of Andoar that, even engaged in mortal combat with him, he becomes his phantasmal brother, his double. And it is because Robinson rushes into the mortal attraction of the cliff that he is reborn as the double, the phantasmal brother, of Friday, and that the sign Friday makes of Andoar doubles into a sign for Robinson.

For Deleuze thought constructs an image of thought, but it must exist thereafter in a spasm to break free from the image thought is for itself; it must encounter the sensible without sense, the unrecognized sensible. Deleuze's philosophical toolbox, containing the concepts of the *a priori* category of the other and the orphan libido, repetition that engenders difference, surface effects that are not metaphors but phantasmal doubles of one another, perversion outside the reproduction of the genus, prove their effectiveness in showing how a construction of fiction such as Michel Tournier's novel *Friday* works. But how has this study worked on Deleuze's own subsequent philosophizing? There are two things to be noted: his next book, *Anti-Oedipus*, will show how the Freud-Lacan Oedipus master-narrative works to recode the libidinal processes that resist the capitalist axiomatics upon the territory of family, asylum, psychoanalytic couch. When we go back then from *Anti-Oedipus* to the study of Tournier's *Friday* Deleuze published in *Logique du sens*, we can see the finally privative meaning he assigned to the concept perversion, and with it to non-philosophy – perversion, and fiction, as the lack of the category of the other – would have to be reworked, conceived as a positive production and not exhibited as a deviation taken from norms. On the other hand, by comparison with *Logique du sens*, *Anti-Oedipus* does show a strange impoverishment. For there Deleuze and Guattari reduce the functioning of sense in the libido to the model of a code in a machine. What for us is the most striking concept at work in Tournier's novel and in Deleuze's study of it – the concept of *elemental sign* – we are distressed to find no longer at work in Deleuze's later philosophy.

Chapter 7

THE ADVENTURES OF THE NARRATIVE: LYOTARD AND THE PASSAGE OF THE PHANTASM

Stephen H. Watson

I

In the 1961 special edition of *Les Temps Modernes* published after Merleau-Ponty's death, Jean Hyppolite began his contribution stating:

> What we owe to Merleau-Ponty is much more considerable than we believe. His work has become for us like those familiar paths (*passages*) that one no longer sees because they are always there and implied in our regard. The general themes of *The Structure of Behavior* and the *Phenomenology of Perception* are now the presuppositions of our research.[1]

Like the other claims accompanying this text, it now seems remote, its assertion in fact becoming increasingly controversial as the decade continued. As one now looks back one finds again and again such proper names as Cavaillès, Bachelard, and even Hyppolite himself[2] invoked to claim that the 'new' generation had chosen *against* the path of phenomenology and the philosophy of consciousness and *for* a philosophy of the concept, *against* the metaphysics of homogeneity, of unity and totality, and the subject and *for* heterogeneity, discontinuity, and a certain de-subjectivization which accompanied the ensuing dispersion. Still, there is perhaps no French thinker for whom the ambiguity of this itinerary remained more explicit than Jean-François Lyotard. And, in this regard, his works, in opening up the specificity of their own problematic, perhaps also most penetratingly deal with the failure of phenomenology and the difficulty that accompanied the passage of its *Überwindung*.[3]

Lyotard's first book, *La phénoménologie* (1954), openly attested to the commitment of French thought to Merleau-Ponty's understanding of phenomenology, one which in many respects was already cognizant of the latter's failure. By means of a strict, presuppositionless, and indubitable method founded on the intuition of essences, phenomenology was to constitute a science in which the realm of lived experience would be brought to adequation before the gaze of reflection. Moreover, Husserlian phenomenology was not simply a reflective enquiry, it was equally a critical tribunal. It was, that is, a transcendental account of this experience, the disclosure of an *a priori*, the originary level from which all true knowledge would proceed. And there was in this respect a strange complicity – and dissymmetry – between phenomenological 'description' and transcendental argumentation within its procedure. Husserl claimed both that reflective adequacy to the lived is 'an eidetic insight' and that the denial of this assertion involved 'a counter-sense', since without it no knowledge whatsoever could be had.[4] And he needed both claims, as well as their hinge, to make the strictness, the absoluteness of phenomenological reason viable.

Phenomenological *Evidenz* was not, after all, a matter of demonstration, but of exhibition (*Aufklärung*) and verification (*Bewahrung*). And the strictness which might adhere to transcendental proof, the strictness of demonstrability, was unavailable within the vicissitudes of verification.[5] On the contrary, the extension *in indefinitum* of verification could find the requisite strictness and closure only in failure, in refutation, that is, in 'cancellation.'[6] While the consequences of such a logic of verification escaped Husserl during his most transcendental moments, this inevitability ultimately struck home in a manner which was ineluctable, as he ultimately realized in a passage from *Formal and Transcendental Logic*, one which Lyotard did not fail to note in his account. 'Even an ostensibly apodictic evidence can become disclosed as deception . . .'[7]

In order to save the appearances, the infinite teleology of consciousness was invoked, a 'way of the cross of corrections', as Husserl put it.[8] Already in the *Investigations* he had characterized phenomenological experience as an *Erweiterung*, an extension beyond the given precisely motivated by it. Heidegger would accordingly speak of a transcendence.[9] But, what was at stake, in any case, involved a problematic of ideality and transcendental ideas, an ideality, that is, posited on an evidence which of necessity fell short. The bound character of the evidence remained inadequate to the unbound ideality which was infinitely to be reiterated within the idea of logic. Hence the Husserlian – and phenomen-ological – *Hexenkreis*:

> What if each and every truth, whether it be the everyday truth of practical life or the truth of even the most highly developed sciences conceivably, remains involved in *relativities* by virtue of its essence, and referrable to *'regulative ideas'* as its norms? What if, even when we get down to the primitive phenomenological bases (*Urgrunden*) problems of relative and absolute truth are still with us, and as problems of the highest dignity, *problems of ideas and evidence of ideas*?[10]

Merleau-Ponty's own version of phenomenology gave up the Cartesian commitments to apodicticity, to full self-possession, and coincidence, invoking again the teleology of consciousness in conjunction with Kant's third *Critique* and the problem of a *passage* between the sensible and the intelligible – now under the aegis of what Merleau-Ponty called the styles of *'sensorialite'*.[11] Even here, none the less, he followed (or at least viewed himself as following) Husserl's own expansion and its concerns with the problem of motivation, passivity, 'passive synthesis,' and, 'a logos of the aesthetic world.'[12]

Phenomenology thus became an articulation of an inexhaustible semantic reserve, the condition for the possibility of idealization and ideality – but one which could never fully be recuperated. On the contrary, this ideality itself, Merleau-Ponty claimed, again following Kant, arises only out of finitude, one which 'requires the field of ideality to become acquainted with and to prevail over its facticity.'[13] The philosopher's task then involved a Sisyphean attempt to say the unsaid, to present the unpresentable, to retrieve that nascence which is the origin of all truth, and thus, to describe even what he called the 'flesh' of ideas, the philosopher's lament for a 'lost secret' which Sartre would charge characterized Merleau-Ponty's existence in general.[14] And, Lyotard confirmed the search in his early book. There is, he claimed, a 'combat of language against itself in order to attain the origin.' Still, that this combat is 'the undoing of philosophy, of the logos is certain, since the origin described, is no longer the origin as described.'[15] It involved precisely the denial that language could be self-sufficient. And, if it was the recognition that the sign could not by rights simply precede the signified, it, too, was the recognition of the failure to *solve* the question of origins which had haunted the philosopher's text. Lyotard himself would reinvoke it as the denial of the tenability, or at least the 'closure' of deconstruction itself in *Discours Figure*, a book bent precisely on distending the non-linguistic figure from the ravages of the text.[16]

None the less, Merleau-Ponty never simply discarded the strange complicity in the bond between the transcendental and the phenomenological, even if it had been made equivocal. In the final analysis he denied too fast perhaps that the *écart* between the sensible and the intelligible was an abyss, as it had been for Descartes or Kant,[17] a move which risked, as many commentators (including Lyotard) have noted, simply substituting Schelling for Kant.[18] While, that is, Merleau-Ponty recognized the *hazard* implied by the 'teleology of consciousness', he disregarded it for the sake of the semantic reserve whose continual verification might delay its simple appearance.

Such a move, however, inevitably itself suffered from a certain 'transcendental illusion.' The invocation of the chiasm between the sensible and the intelligible increasingly detailed in the later works, whereby the visible and the invisible procured *homoisis* still by a kind of simple regulation and hyperdialectic[19] – one by which the ideal was to be seen as the invisible of the visible and vice versa – became perhaps Merleau-Ponty's most metaphysical, and, perhaps equally, most explicit, moment, substituting a matrix for a presumption. By means of it, notwithstanding all that escapes within the abyss of the *in indefinitum*, he was able, still, to attach the scepter of 'absolute knowledge'[20] to what had been transformed from dispersion to 'dehiscence', without regard for what that metaphorics itself ultimately implied.[21]

II

Granted all that had been attached to passivity, to passive genesis and to receptivity, Merleau-Ponty's work was never free then from that possibility by which 'phenomenal-ization' instituted a certain re-move of origins. He denied perhaps too strongly what Jacques Lacan termed in his own *Les Temps Modernes* article on Merleau-Ponty, the possibility of a 'fatal deviation' which disrupted the 'process of a direct relation of the body to the body.'[22] The possibility of such a re-move would require that all that phenomenology had consigned to the pre-predicative, the latent, the horizontal, and the gestural extensions of consciousness might not be recuperable, might not be reducible to the unity of an 'experience'[23] and the simple gaze of a subject, and hence, the difference which intervenes between the reflective and the unreflective might not be surmounted. In this sense the synthesis underlying presentation would be one between elements that were heterogeneous, one which would always be that of the same and the other. Thereby, all that for the rationality of phenomenological consciousness had remained merely implicit and available still to *Aufklärung* became in principle un-conscious, its phenomenon instead a phantasm within the scene of re-presentation in which the subject would be 'desubjectivized . . . in the syntax itself of the sequence in question,' as Laplanche and Pontalis were to conclude.[24]

The latter had once claimed in relation to Merleau-Ponty's account of the unconscious that 'a philosophy of perception does not have to refute Freudianism'.[25] None the less, it could ignore it *only* at its own risk – and *only* by calling its claims to link transcendentality and sensoriality, the bond of Being and logos, into question. And, there was undeniably a sense in which Merleau-Ponty glossed over this risk without truly facing it. In the 1955 lecture course outline on 'The Problem of Passivity,' for example, he claims:

> Freud's contribution is not to have revealed another reality
> beneath appearances, but that the analysis of given
> behavior always discovers several layers of signification,
> each with its own truth, and that the plurality of possible
> interpretations is the discursive explanation of a mixed life

in which every choice always has several meanings, it being impossible to say which of them is the only true one.[26]

Pontalis' interpretative charity doubtless remained too restrained. The fact is that Freud did see precisely 'another' reality in such appearances, not just another 'side' latently present, but one in principle unavailable. Moreover, it cannot follow, as Merleau-Ponty seems to have thought, along with virtually all hermeneutics since Chladenius in adopting the model of optics and perspectivism, that the polysemia introduced remained homogenous.[27] If it is not possible to say which of a plurality of interpretations is uniquely true, it does not follow that they are all partially true and reintegratable into a totality. Rather, the problem that this eventuality invokes is a conflict which places the appearances at risk *tout court*, a function of another scene which escapes and of which 'it has no idea,' regulated, differentiated, deferred, or otherwise.

Lyotard's *Discours Figure* showed – not without a certain nostalgia and romanticism its author was to relent[28] – the trajectory of these effects. In a sense, committed still to Merleau-Ponty's search for the 'underground' that all phenomenology continually mined and ultimately undermined, it did so now in open refusal of the illusion of transcendentalism: in the recognition that the conditions for the possibility of these 'origins' were at the same time precisely their remove from the text, the re-move of the phantasm from the speculative *Begriff* and the Husserlian *theatrum philosophicum*. This silence is rather the silence of another order, another frame of reference, of a 'view' which cannot be retrieved or subsumed, of a phantasm which cannot simply be structured like a language, i.e. 'substituted' or represented (either 'from above' or 'from below').[29] This 'silence' instead involves a figure, and a 'figuration,' a 'scoring of the primary process' which ruptures the unity of the text, all systematic closure, and the economy of all economimesis.[30] If Lyotard's commitments to the work of Freud would later seem somewhat inflated, his strategy in any case here was clear. Under an annunciation that was, as he put it elsewhere, 'very far from Husserl', and finally cognizant of all that escapes in his failure, it was time to realize that 'there is a rhetoric of scientific discourse.'[31] And consequently, 'the moment has come to interrupt theoretical terror.'[32]

III

The middle work of Lyotard (as with others of the same period) effects a transformation that must be seen to arise from this unencompassable sequence, addressing with a certain inevitability that he would later describe as 'purgatorical,'[33] a lacuna in theoretical assertion and the classical denials of its risk.

The theoretical text is a model, something to imitate, which itself has a model to imitate, its set of axioms; and this set has its own, properly formalist model. And rather than seek to show that the closure of models is impossible (Gödel's Proof) and there is always a primary opacity, of the symbol, of ordinary language, one would do better to identify this *pointing back to the same (renvoi au même)* as an apparatus of the passions (*dispositif passionnel*), neither more or less than the *pointing back to the origin* with which hermeneutics would like to contrast it. Both here and there it is semiotic; the opposition bears only on the relation between signs. Let us rather comprehend the model according to its force. This force reveals itself by its expansion through mimesis. The mannequin (*mannekijn* = little man) presents *collection* models. It vehiculates the jubilation of repeating the same, pleasure obtained through serial reproduction.[34]

The theoretical *topos* and its genre thus become committed to the specific machinations of the pleasure of iteration. Hence, reiteration of the same (verification, *Bewahrung*) became simply a matter of paralysis, an instrument now only for fixation and the dispersal of intensities.[35] And hence its failure, the false closure implied in any attempt to enframe the real. Classical accounts of science thus became science-fiction. After Bachelard, who first saw the problem of the creativity, transformation, and the sur-reality of science, Lyotard claimed, even science itself must be seen as experimental in an artistic sense, a fictive event within the libidinal economy and the play of invention. The phantasm and its narrative, *theoria*, are always already an effect.[36] Hence the necessity of a change in scene, beyond even the dream or the nostalgia for the lost origin. And consequently, granted the loss, indeed the fiction, of *adequatio*, theoretical practices can no longer strive to trace out their origin in hope of ultimate fulfillment, but must lose rather the delusion of identity itself.

> We say we are incapable of guaranteeing the link between our words, our gestures, our looks, and the sweeping movements of the drives. Hence no clarity: sometimes it works, sometimes not. What you ask of us, theoreticians, is that we constitute ourselves as identities, and responsible ones. Now if there is one thing we are sure of, it is that this operation of exclusion is a sham, that the glows are not produced by anybody and do not belong to anybody, that they are effects and not causes.[37]

What was to ensue was a kind of Dionysian revel, an affirmation beyond all theory and all concepts, a *Leistung* now not of *Evidenz*, but of the intensities which escaped its grasp, without hope and without care, an intensification which, it was claimed, exceeded the surfaces of the organic stases (biological or political) in a form of 'permanent revolution.'[38] Still, if Lyotard in this respect traded upon what Deleuze, too, had already described as 'the exhaustion of representation,' in the recognition that the identity characterizing the world of immemoriality and resemblance suffered from an insufficiency in the relative being which founds it – and that the *écart* of intensity then escaped all mnemonics[39] – it may not be the case that all is simply dissolved thereby. If, that is, Lyotard denied what he later would call, 'the reduction of truth to evidence'[40] for the sake of the 'theater' of intensities, it did not mean that he simply thereby denied 'truth.' If he reinvoked both the mimetic function and the Dionysian dance, a play of mask upon mask, it was not simply to the exclusion, let alone the exchange of *apophainestai* and what showed itself within its articulation.

In this regard there is a sense in which even the Dionysian dance of intensities and 'the theatrics of the faceless masks' which *Économie libidinale* evoked in its attack against the *stasis* of theoretical mimetics was not without its own exhibition, 'a metamorphic of *sonorous* intensities, *musica figure*,'[41] and, thus a *mimeisthai*, which (like the etymology of the word itself) was more primitive than '*mimesis.*' Consequently, this affirmation, like the dance itself, a revelation anterior to *theoria*, was not simply a decision for intensity over intention, nor had the 'phenomenon' simply been made epiphenomenal. The tracing of the phantasm and the ensuing refusal to subsume or negate the libidinal trace was not simply the substitution of a scene which took place elsewhere, the simple substitution of sign for signified, as the Lacanian transformation implied. Rather it was itself the event of a distortion, a rebus, and a primal figuring.[42] And, time and again in the early 1970s, Lyotard marked the event in which the artist *dis-plays* this figuration as insurpassable:

> Art is the locus of this double reversal where the space of dispossession that all phantasm encloses and upon which it is reclosed as on the lack of signifier from which it proceeds, returns to offer itself, from the outset, to that profound figure in order for it to therein inscribe its traces. . . . Trace bearing trace, a representation which is itself representing. This implies a desire desired, not in order to say it, to theorize it, but in order to see it.[43]

It would then literally be an *a pocalypsis*, an unveiling of what is hidden, as he affirmatively quoted André Green,[44] one whose purpose, as he also said 'is neither *knowledge*, nor *beauty* but *truth*.'[45]

IV

None the less, if there is a sense too in which even this reading of intensification appeared too weak for the *coda* of *Économie libidinale*, which hoped in the end 'to destroy the belief in truth under all its forms ("Is a dance true?"),'[46] the failure did not perhaps lie so much in its *ex-stasis*, as its own dream, perhaps its own delusion, and perhaps, too, its own terror, the credo that intensity or intensification, as the will to will and perhaps even 'experimentation,' might in the end account for or reveal everything. The failure involved the totalization which the reduction to intensities required. And, even the *Leistung* of intensification itself underwent a certain exhaustion in this respect. If desire 'bore witness' to desire, 'not in order to say it,' it still did not follow that all saying could be reduced to desire, nor art to the economics of 'desublimation' and ultimately the *ars vitae* to pleasure (or its opposite). In this respect, as Lyotard later would see, it becomes necessary in the order of ideas to choose 'Kant over Freud,'[47] an absence and an invisible over presence and determinacy, and an effect and in this regard the aesthetics of rupture, discontinuity, and the sublime over the metaphysics of the beautiful and its remainder. There was a sense in which, if Lyotard had already seen that the 'notion' of 'libidinal economy' was an 'idea'[48] which suffered from the risk of ideas, forcing one to 'think without criteria of falsification,' and 'deprived of all security,' it remained the case that his 'hypothesis' found 'surety' by a route that was perhaps entirely classical – in the self-certainty of the agent, a certain *affection* of the self by self. And as such it encountered the risk and perhaps the naiveté which have threatened all philosophies of the will.[49]

The libidinal reduction could neither differentiate nor acknowledge an 'affirmation' that was as much provoked and in the end even 'summoned' as 'effected.' As early as 1970 Lyotard's 'Jewish Oedipus' already traced the unveiling of an invisibility, a dis-possession of the phantasm, a *Faktum* which could not be reduced *either* to an experience or a libidinal mechanism. It invoked then, equally, a choice of Kant *and* Levinas over Nietzsche, provoked by an event which was more 'heard' than seen. 'In Hebraic ethics representation is forbidden, the eye closes, the ear opens.'[50] And it was the impossibility of marking this saying which hears from assertion, the impossibility to account for its own provocation, that blinded the experiment of *Économie libidinale* before an event, an idea, even a 'phantasm' which interrupted all desire and all economy, one whose origin as well as intensification precisely marked, instead, to speak Kantian, an 'abyss.'

This is not to say that the experimental transgression simply became exchanged for a renewal of theory. If anything, the failure of the libidinal reduction was not its 'being false,' so much as its contrary, precisely its commitment to the 'terror' of theory, the genre of the *non-fingo*.[51] This failure involved a refusal to take the heteromorphy and the labyrinth of language seriously: the claim that the indeterminacy of the epistemic could be regulated by an economic reduction, a simple *mise en scène*. The recognition of this heteromorphy and the crisis of narratives it entails was first openly analyzed in the *Post-Modern Condition* from the standpoint of a sociology of knowledge.[52] None the less Lyotard speaks perhaps most directly to the failure of his middle works in *Just Gaming* (1979).

This failure occurred first and foremost on the *topos* of *economie libidinale* itself, the energetics of the political, and specifically its inability to account for the latter's failure, that is the event, the *factum*, of injustice. As Lyotard put it, citing Dufrenne:

> It is not true that one can do an aesthetic politics. It is not true that the search for intensities or for things of that type can ground politics, because there is the problem of injustice . . . Aesthetic judgment allows the discrimination of that which pleases from that which does not please. With justice, we have to do, of necessity, with the regulation of something else.[53]

It became necessary to question, ultimately, whether the problem of injustice could arise within a philosophy of the will, a philosophy of intensities, in which 'differences can be found only by means of ratios and velocities, with the idea that by putting syntheses into play one will modify or one will transform the whole.'[54] Again, such transformations could only find their validity within a certain metaphysics. An intensification modelled on the over-determination of the death instinct might account for the 'desire' for rupture (or its lack), but it could not account for that which intervenes within this leveling. The attempt of French post-Nietzschean thought to deduce qualitative difference from quantitative difference, from 'intensities,' from 'an impersonal transcendental field'[55] would seem in this regard inextricably metaphysical – as perhaps Lyotard ultimately saw. And in this light it would no longer be possible to make the assertion which Deleuze had claimed was identical with Nietzsche's doctrine of the will to power, that 'what is first in thought is the will.'[56] As *Just Gaming* then relented, not without a certain reluctance, 'Any philosophy of the will . . . is a monistic philosophy.'[57] And thus, the attempt remained in the end reductive, assertive, and once again, perhaps, the terror of theory. As Lyotard came to realize in *Le différend* with regard to the concept 'force,' the account presupposed that 'intensity' and 'will' meant just one thing, could be captured and parsed by one narrative, *and* that all things could be reduced to, could be referred to by means of this narrative instance, in the belief that this instantiation did not indicate a heterogeneous narrative field, and, thereby, a problematic of difference that was irreducible.[58]

Accordingly, the *experimenta crucis* of this interruption within the sphere of the political were specifically marked by the splittings in the 'genre' of the prescriptive. Prescriptives regarding injustice depended neither upon a knowledge nor an assertion for their necessity (for their force, as Austin would say), but instead upon a 'yes older than spontaneity,' as Lyotard's 1970 tract already had seen.[59] And, this 'passivity' which Lyotard had dismissed in *Discours Figure* in a discussion of Levinas as an 'ethical lure'[60] became central to his concerns in *Just Gaming*, though not without an equally central transformation. The Levinasian account of the prescriptive still remained theoretical, inscribed by means of the truth predicate, when it was precisely his claim that the ethical breaks with theory and the speculative.[61] Levinas' claim that the ethical was based upon an evidence *more true* than the theoretical risked simply substituting a new truth for an old one.

V

The 'lure' of the ethical was in this sense precisely illusory – as Lyotard had seen in 1970. But what he did not see perhaps was that, quite apart from the question of its truth value, the illusion remained, again to speak Kantian, an idea which was precisely 'inextricable.'[62] As such, it marked a 'discourse' which was not subsumable beneath a speculative *Begriff* or its ground. It involved instead an inextricability which marked another discourse, not the former's fulfillment, but a *différend* which could neither be deduced nor induced, one fixed of itself, as Kant claimed of the ethical imperative, – in short, 'an obligation that comes,' as Lyotard put it, invoking Levinas once more.[63] And consequently, simply pronouncing the prescriptive 'true' did not aid but hid its difference, a difference which is as ineffable within the discourse of the speculative as was the figural event to which he ascribed a similar difference in the late 1960s – that of the silence of the beautiful as *'explosive fixe.'*[64] But equally it hid the fundamental agonistics of the ethical – and the good – and the 'implosion' of the 'ought.'

If the prescriptive signified not the innovation of a narrative of ethical action which was absolute and objective, but rather the limits of the speculative, it did so, however, not without risk. It marked a shattering of the quest for unity, of unified silence, or absolute knowledge, where harmony, *metaphysica rationalis*, the dream whereby rational or theoretical perfection, completeness and determinateness, might be had. And it is just in this regard that Lyotard claims his task – like so many others in contemporary French thought – faced 'the dangerous undertaking that is the *Dialectic* in the first *Critique*,'[65] that point at which the critical tribunal pronounced that what was in question was not an ultimate foundation but an abyss, not a speculative concept, but an idea, a *focus imaginarius* that no experience could present.[66] Precisely thereby, the *Dialectic* itself confronted the risk by which critique became in fact 'narratology,' the function of rational extensions and regulative ideas, syntheses whose ex-stasis could not be reduced to immanence. And hence, Lyotard claims, there arises the necessity of thinking beyond the abysses of 'the grand narratives' and 'the metalanguages' of Western architectonics, and beyond even the nostalgia of the lost origin which characterizes 'modern' romanticism.

> That is what the postmodern world is all about. Most people have lost the nostalgia for the lost narrative. It in no way follows that they are reduced to barbarity. What saves them from it is their knowledge that legitimation can only spring from their own linguistic practice and communicative interaction.[67]

Still, without the grand narratives or, in any case, without our ability to make the Ideas of Western culture immanent (i.e. demonstrably absolute), legitimation does not come to an end, if it does become local and decentralized, opening up, even at the level of imperatives, the confrontation of a 'rational' agonistics: 'in contradiction to what Kant thought this Idea is not for us today, an Idea of totality.'[68] Rather the agonistics is precisely one in which the invocation of ideas *cannot* rest on the presumption of totality: 'If you asked me why I am on that side, I think that I would answer that I do not have an answer to the question "Why?" and that this is of the order of transcendence. That is, here I feel a prescription to oppose a given thing, and I think it is a just one'.[69] While the content of such appeals is always of a matter of transcendence – an 'infinity,' Lyotard allowed – 'transcendence,' apart from the truth predicate, always remains 'empty', of the order of the singular, *doxa*, and its provocation, and thus, ultimately undecidable. Here, 'reasoning comes to an end,' as Wittgenstein said. And it is precisely in this respect that Lyotard's recent work willingly paired Kant and Wittgenstein. If Kant allowed for the heterogeneity of our rational practices, Wittgenstein more directly faced the problem of their grounds, without recourse to the logical facts, to the 'examples' of science, or the masks of common sense, and a 'universality' which is always at best wagered: 'You must bear in mind that the language game is so to speak something unpredictable. I mean: it is not grounded: neither rational nor irrational. It is there – like our life.'[70]

None the less, 'this occurrence before signification,' this '*Es steht da*,' as unavoidable as it is ungroundable – hinged between the *quaestio facti* and *quaestio juris* – is a 'problem' which remains. It is the question of 'passivity' for Lyotard, the question of what 'provokes,'[71] and thereby of rational interest, a 'resistance' which intervenes[72] – the question, hence of what 'surprises' in its incommensurability,[73] of what cannot be subsumed or grounded but instead 'provokes thought into reflection,' as Kant put it.[74] But that meant that it could not be reduced philosophically or metaphysically, that this *Ereignis* could not even be grasped within the classical ontological narratives:

No one knows what 'language' being understands, which it speaks, or to which it can be referred. No one even knows whether there is only one being or many, and whether there is only one language of being or many. The arrogance of the philosophical Treatise, implicit in its form, is saying at least. 'There is one single Being.'[75]

Hence, 'one never knows what *Ereignis* is.'[76] This event involves rather an abyss which no 'pre-ontological comprehension' might reconquer, forcing instead an interpretation whose articulation would need to take place beyond hope of immanence and determinateness, and perhaps as well beyond the masks of totalities which were deferred. Even if the 'ideas' in question were, as they had been by Husserl, modelled upon the homogeneous grids of Reimannian multiplicity, they still could not be reassembled into a harmony that could be made definite[77] and could not be elements of a deductive-nomological unity, or an analytics, but were instead, as Deleuze quite rightly saw, 'varieties of multiplicity' itself, 'differences' without hope of homogeneous resolution.[78] And, as such, in a retrieval which perhaps assists in unleashing its potential – having, that is, come to grips with the problem of heterogeneity within theoretical practices – they inevitably recalled for Lyotard the site of Kant's third *Kritik* and the problem of 'reflective judgment.'[79]

VI

The abyss in question could not be brought to determinateness, reduced to a unity, or to a simple identificatory synthesis. The 'judgment' which ensued in Kant's third *Kritik*, was in a sense a 'judgment' only in name, an articulation, a *di-judicare*, which was as much passive as active, a synthesis as much disjunctive as identificatory, as much art as rule, as much an elevation as a subsumption; one whose 'unity' would come about only by a kind of difference, variety, and discord between the faculties and their discourses, and one, hence, divided interminably between confirmation and conflict, extension and limit.[80] As such, against the unities of rational subsumption, this judgment itself would be more akin to the sublime than the beautiful. The former 'concept' seemed to Kant, 'not nearly so important or rich in consequences as the concept of the beautiful,' since it is spurred on not by unity and harmony – as judgment itself – but forced to come to grips with the possibility of chaos, disorder, and desolation,[81] all predicates of heterogeneity and what is hostile to the speculative,[82] and the presentation of what cannot be presented ultimately even within the limits of social consensus.[83] As such it was already the blinking recognition that there was a kind of 'ludicrous immodesty of decreeing . . . that there can only be a legitimate perspective from our nook'[84]

– both in the belief that ultimate or univocal legitimation could be provided *and* that such legitimation could be 'ours.' Instead, and precisely by a 'recognition which opened up a new perspective,' Kant saw with respect to the agon of Cosmological Ideas, 'that as many ideas are introduced . . . as there are differences in the conditions (in the synthesis of appearances).'[85] Moreover, the recognition of the heterogeneity of the syntheses in question forced the admission that, with this 'solution,' 'the quarrel has not ended' and that the litigation was in fact 'impossible to decide' – which is not to say that it could be reduced to mere silence, if it had been placed interminably at risk. And it was an ironical outcome for a science, a tract, a narrative, and perhaps even a tradition, which had proceeded under the protocol that 'it has to guarantee, as following from principles, the completeness and certainty of the structure in all its parts.'[86]

The business of reflective judgment in its wake was precisely to articulate the 'transition' or 'passage' (*Uebergänge*)[87] undergone within this resulting synthesis, a 'judgment otherwise' than simply subsumptive, and thus a step beyond, or perhaps despite, metaphysics, the tracing of a narrative passage and its provocation – between the phenomenon and its other. And there was a sense in which, as has been seen – if not from the beginning, then in its eclipse – this *'dispositif de passage'*[88] as Lyotard puts it, was itself the site of the phenomen-ological, a play of evidence and idea in the dispossession of the phantasm which all 'phenomenology' had believed could be overcome and subsumed beneath the gaze of cognition and presentation. But instead this passage marked the fracture of the *tabula rasa* – in Kant's term, the 'plane of re-presentation' – delivering it over to what exceeds it, its 'horizon.'[89] Accordingly, it could no longer be a question of a simple judgment or justificatory retrieval and *Be-wahrung*, but instead a denial and an indeterminacy before the unpresentable, an 'extension' and an 'elevation' which marked for Kant the sublime, but equally the inevitable illusions of the dialectical – a passage, that is, now not between elements in reiteration but ones which involved the incommensurable and the unfulfilled, the 'unattainable' and the 'inadequate.'

Thus, instead of the undisturbed ex-pression of the same, it was a question of a passage beyond and, for Lyotard, a certain para-phrase within the philosopher's text.[90] Literally in this respect, a matter of *paraphrasis* and *paragraphein*, of adjoining another clause and, thereby, of deregulating the *lexis* of econo-mimesis, admitting its tort, and hence a *différend* which no discourse might encompass.[91] If it were from the outset a problem of synthesis, and the faculty of synthesis, and even, as Kant put it, a 'figurative synthesis,'[92] it was equally the recognition that this figuration was ultimately the figuration of an abyss, one which ultimately transcended the possibility of the experience of *knowledge* in its institution. And, as such, it rested upon a paradox and an illusion which was, to use the subjunctive of the Kantian lexicon, doubly 'inextricable': As if it could be done/As if it could not.

Chapter 8

THE ORIGIN AND END OF PHILOSOPHY

John Llewelyn

> L'anneau de cette réflexion
> Ne se fermera peut-être pas.
> Du moins ne reviendra-t-il pas
> Où on l'attendait, à son origine,
> Avant d'y avoir laissé,
> S'y affectant, s'y infectant,
> Quelque venin fort peu philosophique:
> Ébauche ainsi d'un serpent, parmi l'arbre,
> Tirant sa langue à double fil,
> De qui le venin quoique vil
> Laisse loin la sage ciguë!

I

Let us not be in too great a hurry to break into the broken circle of Derrida's reflections. Let us approach it at a tangent. Since we are to be attempting to understand as far as is possible something so unfamiliar that it appears to defy traditional modes of philosophical understanding, let us begin with something familiar; the bridge of which Heidegger[1] and Valéry write or the one you cross every day, the table on which philosophers have been writing since Plato, words and the printed page.

Presence in the page proofs is no proof that a word will survive when the printed book finally comes back to its author. But there is an incompleteness that affects every book, however carefully composed and composited, the incompleteness that leads Valéry to compare a word with a plank that will enable us to cross a ditch only if we do not loiter (C 29, pp. 58–9; O II, p. 237).[2] Valéry's plank may be compared in turn with Eddington's, and with Eddington's table: 'The plank has no solidity of substance. To step on it is like stepping on a swarm of flies. . . . My scientific table is mostly emptiness.'[3] He refers to the scientific table as table no. 2. Of course 'There is a familiar table parallel to the scientific table.' The familiar table is his table no. 1. Table no. 1 is solid and substantial. It supports my writing paper. This reliability is explicable, Eddington tells us, by the at least statistically predictable behavior of the fundamental particles that constitute table no. 2. The raw materials to which the modern physicist has recourse in reporting the laws of this 'foreign territory' are electrons, quanta, potentials, Hamiltonian functions, etc., 'and he is nowadays scrupulously careful to guard these from contamination by conceptions borrowed from the other world'! Yet Eddington says that it is not only table no. 1 that supports his writing paper. Table no. 2 does so also, and it does so because of the electrons that 'keep on hitting the underside'. 'But,' asks Susan Stebbing, 'if electrons, belonging to world no. 2, are to be scrupulously guarded from contamination by world no. 1, how can it make sense to say that they "keep on hitting the underside" of a sheet of paper that, indubitably, is part of the familiar furniture of the earth?'[4] As she goes on to remark, it is Eddington himself who is introducing contamination. This is a little hard on Eddington in that it is of the younger physicists that he is speaking when he mentions conceptual purism, and he concedes that he himself has difficulty disinfecting his thought. Still, he is confident that for the physicist this separation of the concepts of physics from everyday concepts can be achieved. Although scientific research begins with the familiar world and returns to it, the physicist as physicist is a traveller in foreign parts. It is for the philosopher to deal with the question how the concepts of the familiar and those of the unfamiliar territories are related. It is presumably as a philosopher therefore that Eddington is speaking when he says of the scientific table that it is a duplicate of the familiar one, speaking not as do Newton's 'vulgar People' who indulge in tabletalk without realizing that they are talking nonsense, but talking nonsense knowingly, because only nonsense will make sense to the uninitiated. Thus Newton begs our indulgence when he speaks 'grossly' and 'not properly' of light and rays as though they were coloured and of the sound

of a bell as anything other than 'a trembling Motion'.[5] Likewise
Eddington:

> When I think of an electron there rises to my mind a hard,
> red, tiny ball; the proton similarly is neutral grey. Of
> course the colour is absurd – perhaps not more absurd than
> the rest of the conception – but I am incorrigible. I can
> well understand that the younger minds are finding these
> pictures too concrete and are striving to construct the
> world out of Hamiltonian functions and symbols so far
> removed from human preconception that they do not even
> obey the laws of orthodox arithmetic.

This amounts to the concession that he is talking figuratively
when he says that a table is part of the subject matter of modern
physics. Nor therefore must he be taken literally, as Stebbing
takes him, when, on her reading, he employs the word 'man'
to describe what is left supposing 'we eliminated all the unfilled
space in a man's body and collected his protons and electrons
into one mass', whether the residue be a mere speck or whether
we are as generous as is the speaker in Valéry's *L'Idée fixe* who
says, 'It appears that if one eliminates the inter- and intra-
atomic voids, the entire substance of a man can be contained
in a matchbox' (*O* II, p. 243). That the noun in Eddington's
phrase 'scientific plank' is not intended literally is evident from
his acknowledgment that the picture conjured up by the familiar
sense of the word 'plank' is too concrete for strictly scientific
purposes. So long as this is acknowledged, it is more than a
little harsh to say, as Stebbing does, that 'Nothing but confusion
can result if, in one and the same sentence, we mix up language
used appropriately for the furniture of earth and our daily deal-
ings with it with language used for the purposes of philosophical and scientific discussion.' Not only does this comment
assume that the terms she is willing to accept as part of the
scientific language – either, electron, quantum, potential, etc. –
are uncontaminated, an assumption Eddington also makes. It
is false that nothing but confusion can result. Something else
that can result is an advance to a new scientific hypothesis.
However, what has been said so far is not a preface to another
discussion of the function of the figurative in conceptual
revision. The aim of this first section is to recall a paradigm case

of appeal to a paradigm case purporting to fix the distinction between the literal, real, and proper, on the one hand, and the figurative, the imitation, and the improper, on the other. Here again is Stebbing's classic statement:

> The plank appears *solid* in that sense of the word 'solid' in which the plank is, in fact solid. It is of the utmost importance to press the question: If the plank appears to be *solid*, but is really *non-solid*, what does 'solid' mean? The pairs of words, 'solid' – 'empty', 'solid' – 'hollow', 'solid' – 'porous', belong to the vocabulary of common-sense language; in the case of each pair, if one of the two is without sense, so is the other.

Similarly, 'The opposition between a *real* object and an *imitation* of a real object is clear', and 'there could not be a *misuse*, nor a *figurative* use, unless there were some correct and literal usages'.

In what follows, certain texts of Derrida's, and texts that he cites, will be cited which suggest not that these oppositions are not for normal non-philosophical purposes clear and fixed, but that a traditional philosophical understanding of that clarity calls for questioning, that the fixedness of the oppositions may, in an extended sense of the word, be fixed, and that philosophers at least may be prone to accept a far too simple understanding of understanding, of the opposition between the normal and the extended sense of a word, and of the opposition between philosophy and the non-philosophical. Other writers have challenged this traditional philosophical conception of clarity and distinctness, and Derrida has challenged it in more than one way. There is room here to treat of only one of those ways.

II

In *Qual Quelle* Derrida cites passages from Valéry to show that the latter resists what he takes to be the Freudian theory of the interpretation of dreams because it is a theory of interpretation: a hermeneutic and a semantic theory. 'My theories of the dream are completely opposed to those of the day. They are completely "formal", while the latter are completely significative' (C 17, p. 766). But it is possible to take a low view of a semantic theory of dreams without taking a low view of a semantic theory of waking consciousness. And there are passages in the *Cahiers* where Valéry contrasts the fluidity of dreams with the solidity of the world of our waking life. This poses a problem for anyone who wishes to recount dreams or to theorize about them. 'One is seeking to apply the mechanics of solids to a world *in which things do not endure*' (C 8, pp. 504–5). So, as Valéry notes, there is something paradoxical about any attempt to put dreams into words. There is something paradoxical also, however, in the fact that although this first paradox arises because we are trying to apply to what is transitive words fitted for what endures, words themselves are wanting in the kind of solidity that is attributed to them by many philosophers, indeed by 'every philosophy' according to the entry in the *Cahiers* referred to in our opening section.

The role of language is essential, but it is transitive – that is to say, one cannot dwell on it.

That is why so many philosophical propositions and pseudo-definitions continue to be disputed.

Only mathematics can allow itself to remain in language, having the audacity to render language *creative – by convention*.

If philosophers consented to accept this condition and *to regard as mere products of conventions* the verbal abuses or verbal inventions they take advantage of, we could accept their metaphysics. Which amounts to treating their trade as an art or poetic fiction – which concocts abstractions. Every philosophy passes from the clear to the obscure, from the univocal to the equivocal by separating words from *real needs* and expedient and *instantaneous* applications. One should never linger on a word; fulfilling perfectly a real role, it has no other function to perform and yields nothing other than what is conferred upon it by immediate and transitive use. (C 29, pp. 58–9)

More specifically, the utility of a word does not depend on the existence of a meaning posited beneath or behind it like a source from which could flow more than one thinks when the word is before one's mind (C 2, p. 91; 4, p. 926). Here is a very Nietzschean entry that merits quotation at length not only because it identifies unmistakably the philosophy of meaning and truth that Valéry rejects, but also because it reintroduces the question of the relation between sense and sensibility that was mentioned in our first section and is taken up by Derrida, as we shall find in our last.

> The ancient Philosophers came in various ways to treat everything sensible as appearance; but in general they posited behind such apparitions a certain hidden reality – *Ideas* or *Laws* or *Being* – which was protected from the relativity of sensible knowledge. But the necessity for these verbal objects (if there is any) is only formal. And they have this failing: they borrow from the ordinary reality of appearances the reality they deny that they have. That is to say then that the following odd substitution is made: the force or the feeling of power and compellingness of sensations is borrowed from the sensible, transferred to essences and entities and given independence, while that which provides and entails it is repudiated as illusion. (C 12, p. 47)

It is not the semantic theories only of ancient philosophers and modern psychoanalysts that Valéry rejects. He rejects any 'Fido' – Fido account on the grounds that words do not have meaning in isolation. He replaces this kind of account with one that takes as its model the game of chess (C 23, p. 686). The meaning of a word is analogous to a *move* in a game of chess. 'The meaning of a word obtains only in each particular employment of it' (C 2, p. 261). Just as Wittgenstein hopes that the expression 'language game' may help us not to forget that games are *played*, so Valéry emphasizes that a word has meaning only in the context of an actual 'transitive' operation. When he calls his theory of meaning formalist this is what he means. It is functionalist in the sense that, as Wittgenstein says, the meaning of a word is the job it performs on the particular occasion on which it is employed. So Valéry's account, like Wittgenstein's, differs from that of Saussure in an important respect, although all three draw the analogy with the game of chess in order to counter the notion that words have meaning in isolation. Saussure is mainly interested in launching a science of *langue* seen as a system in abstraction from particular acts of *parole*. Valéry and

Wittgenstein consider it vital to retain contact with actual or imagined cases of use.

But performance is an exercise of competence. Competence is an aspect of what Valéry calls 'implex'. Implex covers the subjunctivity implicit in one's ability to indicate something, the depresence inseparable from presence, the distant in the instant, the resource that prevents the source from being an origin, the unpunctuality of the point of philosophy, preventing philosophy both in going ahead of it and in forestalling its arrival at itself. It is the *variété* that is Valéry's rewriting of *Vérité* and explains why he writes in the piece from volume III of *Variété* entitled *Léonard et les philosophes*: 'Intellectual effort can no longer be regarded as converging upon a spiritual limit, upon *Truth*' (*O* I, p. 1240). It assembles a bewildering diversity of functions for which 'memory' is as good a word as Valéry can find in common parlance, provided this be understood not as a repository of historical facts, but as disposition and the capacity to vary our response according to variations in circumstances (*C* 22, p. 109; 5, pp. 55–6). Skill and 'schema of all possible movements' (*C* 3, p. 265), implex is Valéry's retrieval of Kant's *Urteilskraft* and Aristotle's *phronesis* and *dynamis*. As contingency and counterfactual possibility, implex is the retention-protention of the Now whose implications for Husserlian phenomenology Derrida unravels in *La Voix et le phénomène* and whose complications in the texts of Valéry he announces in describing implex, so far as it can be described, as 'mathematical exponentiality of the value of presence, of everything the value of presence supports, that is of everything – that *is*' (*M*, p. 303 [p. 360]). Implex is the eventuality of the event, the *Enteignis* of *Ereignis*. 'This value of contingency, eventuality, describes what is at stake in the concept. The implex, a nonpresence, nonconsciousness, an alterity folded over in the *sourdre* of the source.' Here Derrida, ventriloquist and mimic at the same time, is glossing Valéry's observation that 'One must go back to the *source* – which is not the *origin*. The *origin*, in all, is *imaginary*. The *source* is the fact within which the imaginary is proposed: water wells up there. Beneath, I do not know what takes place' (*C* 23, p. 592). I do not know what takes place there because I am made deaf (*sourd*) to what takes place there, supposing there is something that takes place there, supposing there is a place there, supposing there is a there supposed – made deaf to it by the noise of the surging (*sourdre*) of the water, unable to hear (*entendre*) or understand (*entendre*). No simple location. Instead, a *da* as complex as the implex. Indeed the implex and the source are co-implicates. This is why the source is not a simple origin. Implex is capacity incapable of being present to itself and oneself. ' "Thinking" (in the sense of *mental work*) is therefore *re-thinking*' (C 26, p. 173). '*Recurrence*, repetition – an essential fact. Property of the *present*' (C 15, p. 134). The RE of representation is essential to presentation, externally constitutive of it, Derrida would say. At least where consciousness is consciousness of meaning or ideas, where there is ideality. As soon as there is *eidos*, whether this be understood as Form or Idea or concept or schema or image or impression or sense. Whether it be understood as form or content. As soon as there is presence. The presentation of the *eidos* is a depresentation. For the *eidos* is intrinsically extrinsic not only because it is a universal and therefore imports the necessary possibility of another context, but because other contexts are not entirely predictable and because the context is constitutive of the text, constitutive of meaning.

Or, Derrida asks, do what Valéry calls timbre and style escape this law? On the face of it, this might seem to be so. For timbre, on Valéry's account, is what is unique to an author's voice, expressing his haecceity, as does the style of the writing the author leaves behind when he retires from the scene. His irrepeatable fingerprint. We shall discover in the final section of our discussion that Derrida distinguishes two repetitions, in order to show that they cannot be separated. Our question here and his question there is how to mark this distinction; how to distinguish the timbre of Derrida's voice from that of Hegel, and how to distinguish their styles. If the repetition intrinsic to the ideality of form and content is liable to becoming interiorized and *aufgehoben* into infinite self-consciousness, what about timbre and style? If there are timbre and style as Valéry defines them – and Derrida warns us that he himself may have reasons for not granting the hypothesis – do they resist self-consciousness? The answer that Derrida extracts from Valéry is that they do. The timbre of my voice and the style of my writing cannot be present to me. They cannot then be present to themselves.

They are unrecognizable by me. Their presence is a presence only for the other. Along this path there is no fulfillment of the desire for self-coincidence. The other is not one's own other, but an other that infects auto-affection with hetero-affection, spontaneity with passivity. Since, however, Derrida, does not set out along this path, does not embrace the hypotheses of timbre and style as uniquely identifying *je ne sais quoi* and argues elsewhere that no mark is inimitable, he must find some other way to defeat the thought of an event uncontaminated by eventuality. He finds another way in Valéry.

Finds? This question is already the question of originality and the source. It arises everywhere in the texts of philosophy and non-philosophy and in Derrida's readings of them. It can be a relatively superficial question, as when similarities and dissimilarities between the writings of Valéry and Eddington, Valéry and Saussure, Valéry and Freud, Valéry and Nietzsche lead us to ask who read whom and when, the kind of question we ask on an author's birthday, as Derrida puts it (*M*, p. 300 [p. 356]). Although Eddington's *Space, Time and Gravitation* was in Valéry's library, did he read *The Nature of the Physical World*? Since it was only late in his career that Valéry read Saussure, was the chess analogy suggested to him in his reading of Poincaré's *La Valeur de la science*? These questions cause no more serious qualms than that of Shakespeare's indebtedness to Plutarch. They are put in place by Valéry's remark that 'The desire for originality is the father of all borrowings/all imitations/. Nothing more original, nothing more *oneself* than nourishing oneself on others – But they must be digested. The lion is made of assimilated sheep' (*C* 6, p. 137, to which is appended: 'Originalité' – Désirer être SOI. Désirer d'être neuf. Mais *soi* et *neuf* font . . . Dix.'). Less easily dealt with is that feeling we have, of vertigo alternating with relief, when it seems that there is nothing new under the sun, the feeling we get when we begin to believe that Whitehead was right when he said that all philosophy goes back to Aristotle or Plato, but then go on to be struck by how much in Plato and Socrates goes back to the pre-Socratics and beyond them to the Orient. Is what Valéry capitalizes as the ORIENT DE L'ESPRIT the fountainhead of philosophy (*O* II, p. 1042)? And would that source be an origin? One could not pursue these questions profitably unless one first distinguished the question of the origin from the question of the beginning. Derrida does not pursue the question of beginning in so far as that would be a question of etiology or etymology. He suspects our common notions of influence and cause, not to mention that of the common root. I suspect that he would not consider it entirely irrelevant to pause for thought, if not to linger, on the etymologies of 'find' and 'invent,' and their common root in the concept of *invenire*. There are some indications that he would endorse the Valérian dictum that 'One invents only what invents itself and wants to be invented' or at least the product issuing from a crossing of that with a similar dictum about finding. These indications include the above-mentioned reasons for his unwillingness to endorse the Valérian postulation of timbre and style, one of these reasons being a difficulty over a facile notion of authorship, authenticity, and event (*evenire*, *Ereignis*) which fails to recognize the complexity of the question as to who, in Derrida's monodialogue with Valéry, for example, is teacher and who is taught. In any reading and writing, do we have a proper idea as to who is master of what and of whom, of who is seigneur – or Monseigneur (*M*, p. 297 [p. 353]), who enseigneur, who signer? In any dialogue, it is as though it is the ear that speaks, as though one needs to invoke Valéry's monstrous notion of a *Bouchoreille*, especially in the dialogue of the soul with itself; and when one's discourse draws its nourishment from oneself, this notion may call to be supplemented by the notion of otobiography (*OA*, pp. 11–56).

As we were about to observe, Derrida credits Valéry with recognizing 'the paradoxical law . . . that formality, far from simply being opposed to it, *simultaneously* produces and destroys the naturalist, "originarist" illusion' (*M*, p. 292 [p. 347]). The only approach to this law is by way of case histories and textual analysis. Before considering briefly two cases that Valéry and Derrida work through together, we should take note that the law in question *intervenes* between the poles of classical philosophical oppositions. It has to do with an essential complicity between the terms, a 'structural' complicity, as Derrida sometimes says, leaving it for us to decide whether the inverted commas are scare quotes or not and whether quotation marks of some sort should be used when the paleonym

(')essence(') is employed to identify the nature of the unnatural law according to which the classical binary contrasts self-deconstruct. The complicities whose construction and deconstruction this law dictates must be distinguished from confusions arising from an identifiable simple equivocation in one or both of the terms. In the latter case we should have on our hands a contingent complicity removable by disambiguation, a 'verbal dispute' of the kind Hume dissolves in the third Appendix of the *Enquiry Concerning the Principles of Morals* by pointing out that justice or property can be both natural and artificial because 'natural' may be opposed either to what is miraculous or to what involves social convention. The risk of mistaking a merely semantic confusion for an arche-syntactic complicity would be high if in the case of Valéry's promotion of formalism as opposed to semanticism we lost sight of the difference between his functionalist formalism and the Platonic theory of Forms. This risk is perhaps in Derrida's mind when he follows the statement reproduced at the beginning of this paragraph by saying: 'Here we might elaborate the motif of a critique of formalist illusion which would complicate what is often considered to be Valéry's formalism somewhat.' We must also distinguish functionalist formalism, under which Valéry would subsume language quite generally, including everyday speech, and mathematical formalism whose purity and precision is best exemplified, he suggests, by the graph. What he says of this recalls what Eddington says of the language of modern physics and its basic technical terms as contrasted with the terms of everyday speech:

> The *graph* has a continuity of movement that cannot be
> rendered in speech, and it is superior to speech in
> immediacy and precision. Doubtless it was speech that
> commanded the method to exist; doubtless it is now
> speech that assigns a meaning to it and interprets it; but it
> is no longer by speech that the act of mental possession
> is consummated. One sees taking shape little by little a kind
> of ideography of the represented [*figurées*] relations
> between qualities and quantities, a language that has for
> grammar a body of preliminary conventions (scales, axes,
> grids, etc.). (*O* I, pp. 1266–7)[6]

Now it may be that Valéry's *graphique* could be coopted to

introduce us to Derrida's *graphique*, the graphic that supplements logic and takes us beyond semiology to grammatology. Alan Bass thinks so, presumably, when he gives 'graphic' as the translation for Valéry's *graphique*. Certainly, Derrida and Valéry are together at least in stressing script and spatiality, and the difference they introduce into the time of speech. But according to Derrida they thereby introduce discontinuity, *écart*, whereas Valéry's 'conventional' graph is said to have a 'continuity' and determinacy of which natural language is said to be incapable. Leaving aside the question whether the names for Valéry's conventions are as threatened by natural contamination as the vocabulary of Eddingtonian physics (for it is the marks on the graph paper that count), is Valéry's artificial language any purer of naturalism than the technical terms which philosophical writing hopes will furnish more solid planks to bridge the gaps that the words of natural and figurative (*figurée*) speech cannot always be relied on to do? Complicity between Valéry and Derrida there may well be, but that must extend far enough to entail that not only the philosophers whom Valéry attacks but also their assailant are subject to the paradoxical law that Derrida says Valéry recognizes. That this is so is perhaps what Derrida intends to communicate by citing Valéry's assertions that the lines of the graph are 'traced by the things themselves' and succeed in 'making the laws of science visible to the eyes.' (We need have no qualms over attributing intentions to Derrida or anyone else. He has no such qualms himself. What he does have qualms over is a certain philosophical construal of what it is to intend.) If that is Derrida's intention, it is not intended as a criticism. If the unnatural law in question prescribes a structural necessity, one could hardly expect Valéry – or Derrida – to escape it. Valéry, on Derrida's account, is as anxious as any of the philosophers he judges to get back *zu den Sachen selbst*, while being acutely conscious of the ocular and auditory tropes whose employment to describe presence with the things themselves defers that very presence, deprivileges 'the very element of our thought in so far as it is caught up in the language of metaphysics' (*M*, p. 16 [p. 17]). Therefore 'Presence is a determination and effect within a system which is no longer that of presence but that of differance'. Philosophy appears to be subordinated to non-philosophy because metaphysics is postponed by metaphor. But the predicament is more complex than that, as we shall discover if we look more closely at the philosopher's employment of metaphor.

III

Philosophy, says Novalis, has always been the desire to be at home everywhere. The philosopher, Derrida adds, has always tried to satisfy this nostalgia by hearing himself speak. Now Valéry, in Derrida's opinion, appreciated this 'better than Husserl, and better than Hegel, who nevertheless had described phonic vibration as the element of temporality, of subjectivity, of interiorization, and of idealization in general, along with everything which thereby systematically lets itself be carried along in the circle of speculative dialectics' (*M*, p. 287 [p. 341]). So we are in good hands with Valéry to lead us through this labyrinth, a labyrinth that is also a maze of speculative mirrors through which we are lured in the hope of seeing ourselves as we really are, at the source of the light by which we see ourselves.

But the source which would be a *point d'eau*, a point where water comes to light, is at the same time a *point d'eau*, a point where water is lacking. *Point d'eau* is an incalculable syntagm, unsublimatable in the circulation of speculative dialectics, impredicable in the predicate calculus and unpropoundable in propositional logic. Because in the *point d'eau* water's life-giving birth rhymes with water's absolute dearth. Its jet is a throw towards death, the death of the author. Furthermore, how can we understand this image of the source that returns again and again throughout Valéry's work unless we comprehend the literal meaning of origin, *origo*, orient? On the other hand, how do we understand this literal meaning of origin in general except via the relay of metaphor? The proper, literal meaning only pretends to be proper, '*se donne comme sens propre*'.

> Proper meaning derives from derivation. The proper meaning or the primal meaning (of the word *source*, for example) is no longer simply the source, but the deported effect of a turn of speech, a return or detour. It is secondary

in relation to that to which it seems to give birth, measuring
a separation and a departure from it. The source itself is
the effect of that (for) whose origin it passes. One no longer
has the right to assimilate, as I have just pretended to do,
the proper meaning and the primal meaning. That the
proper is not the primal is what Valéry gives us to read.
(*M*, p. 280 [p. 333])

That is to say, the only way we shall find the source itself will
be by losing it. The things themselves to which philosophy
dreams of getting back will turn out to be no more than tropes.
'Philosophy is reduced to a logic and to a rhetoric or poetics'
(*C*, 8, p. 911). The philosopher 'borrows metaphor from us
[poets] and, by means of splendid images which we might
well envy, he draws on all nature for the expression of his
profoundest thought.' 'All nature' is *phusis*, emergence into
light, the source 'in all', as Derrida says, of whatever light the
philosopher casts upon nature, including himself, the transcendental I which Kant distinguishes from the empirical I, the
transcendental phenomenological consciousness that Husserl
says is parallel to and covered by the purely psychological (*SP*,
p. 11 [p. 10]), the pure universal I that Valéry distinguishes
from the person and has no relation with a face, 'n'a pas de
rapport avec un visage' (*C* 8, p. 104; *O* I, p. 1229). The pure I
is neither the eye that sees nor what the eye sees. Yet Valéry
is constrained to say that it is like a glance. The invisible I is
figured through the visible eye of the face (*figure*), hidden by
what shows it forth, doubly hidden when Narcissus sees
himself mirrored in the water of the source. 'Glance of the
figure, figure of the glance, the source is always divided' (*M*,
p. 285 [p. 340]). Like the serpent's tongue.

The source itself cannot present itself to sight. Can it perhaps
hear itself speak? Once again derivation is derived. The *causa
sui* turns out to be a causeless effect. 'In the return of the phonic
circle, the source appears as such only at the moment, which
is no longer a moment, the barely second second, of the instant
emission in which the origin yields itself to receive what it
produces' (*M*, p. 288 [p. 342]). The phonic circuit is interrupted.
In biting its own tail the serpent poisons itself. The pure I
becomes impure as soon as its indestructible desire to hear itself

speak is fulfilled and frustrated because it can hear itself speak
only when its voice has become the voice of its ear. (The source
has *become*. Another incalculable syntagm.) I find myself consti-
tutionally incapable of finding myself. I wait for myself forever
in my own queue. I am here, *da*, but I am simultaneously *fort*,
elsewhere (*C* 10, p. 407; *O* II, p. 885; *CP*, p. 214). Two moments
of myself at one moment, a sending-receiving feedback. 'What
comes to "mind" – to the lips – modifies you yourself in return.
What you have just emitted, emits toward you, and what you
have produced fecundates you. In saying something without
having foreseen it, you see it like a foreign fact, an *origin* –
something you had not known. You were delayed in relation
to yourself' (*C* 12, p. 24; *C* 6, p. 195).

It is important to note that this description of the auto-hetero-
affection that takes place in the monodialogue of the soul with
itself is in principle indistinguishable from and inevitably
modelled on the description of uttered communication with
another. But the communication between the silent inner
communication and the public communication is incommuni-
cable. Like the identity of Eddington's table no. 1 and table
no. 2, which are the same thing although we cannot answer
literally the question, 'Namely what?,' like the difference
Husserl posits between transcendental and purely psychological
consciousness, a difference for which 'All names are lacking,'
there is here a 'supplementary nothing' that gives us pause
(Valéry delights in the etymological connection he supposes
between *pausa* and *positum*), an unpresentable chiasmus that
'passe donc l'entendement', exceeds hearing and understanding, perception and conception, exceeds the Concept.
Exceeds philosophy, unless the philosopher, recognizing that
non-philosophy is the constitutive outside of philosophy, recognizes that he must borrow metaphors, like the metaphors that
Derrida borrows from Hegel, Husserl, Heidegger and Valéry to
track to its source the illusion that the sourcepoint (*Quellpunkt*
writes Husserl in section 13 and Part II of the *Phenomenology
of Internal Time Consciousness*) is primal, and to recite that the
birthpangs (*Qual Quelle* writes Derrida, rewriting Hegel
rewriting what Boehme writes in *Aurora*) of the unquenchable
desire for the living present (*WD*, p. 194 [p. 291]) are in undecidable complicity with the pain of passing beyond being to

death. Death, which is metaphor quite literally, if the literal may be no more than a metaphor that is dead, if that hypothesis makes sense.

IV

It is beginning to look as though the beginning of so-called first philosophy is philosophy's end, as though non-philosophy is, in Kant's words, 'the death of all philosophy' (*TA*, p. 463 [p. 57]), a death than which nothing would be more natural: extrinsic, yet intrinsic; beyond philosophy's grave, yet at its centre of gravity.

But there are two deaths in the case of 'la mort *de* la philosophie' (*M*, p. 271 [p. 323]), a double degeneration, de-generation, corresponding to the duplicity of the genitivity of 'of,' of *de*: a recto death no. 1 and a verso death no. 2. Since if we have seen reason to concede to Derrida that metaphor and non-philosophy lie beyond philosophy and are to metaphysics a metametaphysics – a metametataphysics, we might say, in memory of Aristotle, Eddington, and Anatole France (*M*, p. 212 [p. 252]), we must now ask whether we should not also agree that philosophy, 'simultaneously life and death' (*WD*, p. 194 [pp. 291–2]), incorporates non-philosophy in so far as by non-philosophy we understand the metaphorical. For what do we understand by the metaphorical, in so far as we understand it at all? In understanding the nature of the metaphorical we grasp an idea or form a concept, namely the idea or concept of an expression not used in its literal or proper sense. It therefore belongs to the same system as the literal and the proper. It remains a metaphysical concept (*M*, p. 219 [p. 261]). As Susan Stebbing says, the opposition of the literal or proper that gives 'metaphorical' what meaning it has assumes we understand the meaning of propriety, understand what propriety means literally and properly. But how can we understand properly what metaphor is, how can we have a philosophical understanding of metaphor, if the idea we are to grasp is 'itself' not itself, because the very idea of idea – from *eidō*, to see – is metaphorical? 'Philosophy, as a theory of metaphor, will first have been a metaphor of theory' – from *theōriō*, to look (*M*, p. 254 [p. 303])? Or can the distinctness of the opposition be salvaged by saying that the so-called primary metaphors on which philosophy depends, idea, concept, intuition, conscious- ness, etc., are dead metaphors? Can we preserve philosophy by saying that the concept of idea and the idea of concept originally referred to concrete operations of states like grasping with the hands or seeing with the eye thanks to the natural light of the sun, then came to be employed metaphorically of intellectual functions and capacities, and finally came to lose even that metaphorical force, as Hegel, for example, says (*M*, p. 225 [p. 268])? Can we say with Nietzsche and Anatole France's Polyphilos that the basic terms of philosophy may be compared to coins whose relief has been so worn down that they have lost their cash value as coins of the realm, have 'gone West', become the currency of the universe of philosophical discourse where they wear their nudity like the Emperor wears his new clothes?

This contrast between living and worn-out metaphors might suffice to keep alive in daily use the opposition between what we call the literal and the metaphorical. It would not suffice to permit a purely philosophical account of that opposition, because that account would be dependent on the non-philo- sophical, on the metaphor of wear. We should still lack a meta- phorology. We should have in our hands no more than effects of literality and metaphor.

> This extra metaphor, remaining outside the field that it allows to be circumscribed, extracts or abstracts itself from this field, thus subtracting itself as a metaphor less. By virtue of what we might entitle, for reasons of economy, tropic supplementarity, since the extra turn of speech becomes the missing turn of speech, the taxonomy or history of philosophical metaphors will never make a profit. (*M*, p. 220 [p. 261])

The disappearance of metaphor (*plus de métaphore*) becomes the supplementary metaphor (*plus de métaphore*). The reduction of relief promises to compensate the bearer with relief, *Aufhebung*, into pure philosophy, thought thinking itself, but the pure philosophical thought is not forthcoming. *La métaphysique – relève de la philosophie*. Philosophy sublates and interiorizes non- philosophy, but philosophy is 'itself' non-philosophical. Its *for intérieur*, the source of its authority, is *fors*, transported outside itself: meta-phor; but, because accidentality is of its essence, the phor or vehicle is also in the *for*, the tenor or so-called theme. So the time of the thesis is unpunctual, deferred, out of joint. The position is de-posed, the locus displaced. The very instruments with which philosophy is to divide the chicken at its joints are divided against themselves. Hence, when Aristotle set up as the rule of philosophy absolute distinctness of sense (*M*, p. 248 [p. 295]), he was inviting the charge that he was infringing that other rule of his, 'to look for precision in each class of things just so far as the nature of the subject admits' (*Nic. Ethics* 1094b, 25). He was overlooking the possibility that philosophy and logic are no more than functions or effects of 'an unheard of *graphic*' that is 'an inscription of the relations between the philosophical and the non-philosophical', and that these relations are undecidable (*WD*, pp. 110–11 [p. 163]). Philosophy gets carried away by metaphor and metaphor 'gets carried away with itself, cannot be what it is except in erasing itself, indefinitely constructing its destruction' (*M*, p. 268 [p. 320]).

This suicide may be conceived, on the one hand, as the death suffered at their own hands by the philosophical figures of the *Phenomenology of Spirit* and the *Lectures on the History of Philosophy* where their passing away is a passing upward into an anamnetic recollection of a truth that saves them for an ultimate atonement of thought infinitely thinking itself. Or, secondly, it may be the death in this alleged infinite self-presence, the death of the Concept, of Philosophy, 'the death of a philosophy which does not see itself die and is no longer to be refound within philosophy'; the strewn ashes of truth: strewth.

Corresponding to these homonymous deaths are two homonymous repetitions and two *glas*. Repetition no. 1 is that of the sameness of the *eidos* and the Idea, of identity and resemblance. Even family resemblance belongs here with Platonic and Hegelian life-sustaining economic return surely, if we can say what Derrida, paraphrasing Du Marsais, says of the metaphor of the borrowed dwelling:

> it is a metaphor of metaphor; an expropriation, a being-outside-one's-own residence, but still in a dwelling,

outside its own residence but still in a residence in which
one comes back to oneself, recognizes oneself, reassembles
oneself or resembles oneself, outside oneself in oneself. This
is the philosophical metaphor as a detour within (or in
sight of) reappropriation, parousia, the self-presence of the
idea in its own light. The metaphorical trajectory from the
Platonic *eidos* to the Hegelian Idea. (*M*, p. 353 [p. 302])

Repetition no. 1 is the repetition of typicality, essence, meaning,
truth, consciousness, phenomenology, philosophy. Repetition
no. 2 is the repetition of the typographical lapsus, of the accident when 'the words come apart', when 'bits and pieces of
sentences are separated', when 'the presence of what is gets
lost' (*D*, pp. 168–9 [pp. 195–6]); the repetition of unconsciousness, non-truth and non-philosophy. It is the *glas* of the death
knell's trembling motion, while repetition no. 1 is *glas* as living
voice, *répétition vivante* (*G*, p. 89 [p. 107]). Derrida tells us that
his title *La Voix et le phénomène* becomes in Slovene *Glas in
phenomen*. An audio-visual Anglo-Slovene scanning of this
teaches the lesson that repetition no. 1 and repetition no. 2 are
not parallels; they are related chiasmically, as are the two deaths
and the two *glas*. *Glas* no. 1 as *viva voce* is in the phenomenon
which according to post-Platonic phenomenology presents itself
to consciousness as intimately as the voice that hears itself
speak; so it already involves an intermixing of metaphors that
Derrida marks with the image of the tympanum, which is, *entre
autres*, the ear drum and the usually triangular panel above a
doorway in which there is sometimes pierced a circular opening
called an *oculus* (*M*, p. xxii [p. XVII]). *Glas* no. 2 is not heard by
him for whom the bell tolls. (Did he overhear his death rattle,
his final glottal full stop?) Where *glas* no. 1 is timbre, phone,
and mnemic remembrance, *glas* no. 2 is style, graph, and the
forgetfulness that requires the hypomnetic *aide-mémoire*. Yet *glas*
no. 1 is where *glas* no. 2 'is,' as repetition no. 2 is a repetition
of repetition no. 1, the rehearsal of it that has differed and
deferred the première from time immemorial.

The first is always second. First philosophy is non-philosophy
or, since the 'non' here should not be taken to imply a parallelist
opposition, un- or *in*-philosophy, which is in philosophy, but
indecidably (*indécidablement*), because philosophy is not simply

in itself. Philosophy is exposed to the accidents of history no less than is the table on which it is written, whether this be the familiar solid and substantial piece of furniture of the earth on which Eddington composed the Gifford lectures he delivered at Edinburgh in a living tongue, the *pinax* and *tabula* of which his predecessors spoke in languages now dead, or the unearthly Paradigmatic Table Itself that is supposed never to become a paradigm case and is unutterable in any language, living, dead, or not yet born. And if philosophy is exposed to the accidents of history, so too is history. History is a history of accidents. Of necessity. Cruel necessity, Artaud would say (*M*, p. 194 [p. 291]). Beneath the syntactico-semantic law that is a principle of composition and classification, as its unoriginary and unprimal source, is an anasyntactic law of decomposition, like an inky-fingered *malin génie*, a printer's devil that deconstructs the typographical forms behind the compositor's back.[7] This law of the law of genre, genus, generation, family resemblance, kith, kin, kind, nature, essence, class, figure, form, and type makes distinct sense possible as theatrical function, staged performance, effect of a so-called 'primal' scene. But impossible and impositable except as *mise en scène*, because 'Beneath, I do not know what takes place.' I am stone-deaf to it. The table of the law of the law of genre is 'mostly emptiness'. This metalaw 'manages to do no more than transgress the figure of all possible representation. Which is difficult to conceive, as it is difficult to conceive anything at all beyond representation, but commits us perhaps to thinking altogether differently' (*S*, p. 326 [p. 30]). To thinking altogether differently the distinction between philosophy and non-philosophy.

Chapter 9

PHILOSOPHY AS THE HETERONOMOUS CENTER OF MODERN DISCOURSE: JÜRGEN HABERMAS

John McCumber

In the opening pages of his major work, *The Theory of Communicative Action*, Habermas writes that philosophy after Hegel surrendered not only its totality-claim – its pretension to yield substantive theories of nature and/or of transcendental subjectivity – but also its claim to foundationality: it can no longer hope to present, in any sense, the conceptual basis for such substantive theories. Elsewhere, he suggests that only two roles are left open for it: that of 'place-holder' and 'interpreter.'

As 'place-holder,' philosophy is fragmented into one element of scientific paradigm formation. It is typical, writes Habermas, for scientific 'research traditions' to start off with claims that are universal, and hence non-empirical (an instance is Mead's view that *all* human social identity is constructed through role-playing). Such 'philosophical thoughts' play an essential role in the constitution of new research paradigms: for a proposed research program can have no claim upon other researchers if it is grounded solely in the hunches, intuitions, or genius of a single individual. Being non-empirical, such 'philosophical thoughts' tend to be dismissed by scientists, and it is up to the philosopher to take them seriously: to examine how and to what extent their universality-claims might be justified.

Philosophy's other role is as 'interpreter,' in which it is the business of the philosopher to translate into ordinary language the specialized discourses that the modern age has produced, thereby mediating them with one another and with the 'lifeworld' of non-specialized human beings. But this, too, dissolves philosophy: its translations of specialized discourses are carried out with reference, not to some more general realm of meaning that it possesses for itself, but to the everyday 'life-world.' No specialists are required to interpret and articulate this. All 'discourse,' as we shall see, does so for Habermas, and philosophy can at most do it more reflectively.[1]

Habermas thus enters the contemporary constellation in which, as Merleau-Ponty puts it, we find philosophy, not as a distinct, unified discipline, but as a 'detached philosophy, which always reappears in disguise'.[2] Its Habermasian disguises are as universalistic elements in new research programmes and as the discursive articulation of the life-world.

But Habermas' position in this constellation is, I think, unstable: it rests upon the presupposition that his own paradigm – the theory of communicative action – is itself a typical scientific research program, containing a philosophical element (in the universalistic contention, as we shall see, that all human discourse makes certain validity-claims), but for the rest nonphilosophical.[3] I will argue that, on the contrary, Habermas' theory of communicative action is distinguished from other research paradigms by a particular sort of claim which I will call 'centrality,' and that this centrality makes it, in a certain ancient sense, philosophical through and through.

To argue this, we must begin by asking what a 'center' is. And to avoid mere stipulation, we must say that 'centers' are what they have always been. The 'always' here, as always in philosophy since the Greeks, means: since the Greeks.

The κέντρον was a goad or spike.[4] With the entry of mathematics into Greece one type of κέντρον was the leg of a compass, which could be jabbed down anywhere to begin the construction of a κύκλος, a circle. Eventually, the circle as a whole was viewed as derived from its center: the κέντρον was no longer established by the jab of the compass, but was a midpoint (a μέσον) which itself established the rest of the circle and whose own origin was arbitrary, unquestioned.[5]

When a circle rotates, its midpoint does not, and so is unchanging: this rendered the mathematical concept of the κέντρον exportable, via metaphor, into other types of discourse. Aristotle 'biologized' it, tracing the movements of animals to the leverage of their limbs against (relatively) unmoved movers at their centers.[6] Plotinus 'ontologized' it: centrality in his universe is assigned to the One, the unchanging source of all things.[7] And it was 'subjectivized' by Descartes, whose 'ego' was an Archimedean point of leverage capable of establishing itself anywhere by the self-reflection of the *cogito*, and then of generating from itself the totality of knowledge.[8]

Kant gave it practical significance: reason oriented the *thinker* as the midday sun, in the center of the sky, orients the sailor. It oriented the *actor* when his action originated – as it ought to at all times and places – from reason itself, autonomously legislating the categorical imperative.[9] And, finally, the 'mathematical' concept of a center as an unmoved, legislative source carried into Husserl's view of the ego as a 'well-defined central point of emanation' for meaning itself.[10]

In all these divagations, the 'centrality' of philosophy itself remained a fixed point. Aristotle was able to postulate the unmoved mover at the center of the body – a mover he had assuredly never seen – because of the general theory of causation developed in his metaphysics. For Plotinus, Kant, Descartes, and Husserl, philosophy was the discipline which revealed the center – however it was understood – and thus was foundational for all human discourse.

But the career of the center ended abruptly, on the threshold of the linguistic turn. As Merleau-Ponty notes, the problematic of consciousness was unable to cope with language, unable even to recognize it as a problem. The reason for this has to do with the fact that there is no single generative source for language, which is usually experienced as an interplay in which speakers reciprocally yield the stage, decentering themselves to engage one another. When language 'invaded the universal problematic,' writes Derrida, it became necessary to conceive of centers differently: not as present-beings with fixed loci but as 'a sort of non-locus in which an infinite number of sign-substitutions come into play.'[11] 'Infinite sign-substitutions' are precisely what philosophy, as rationally-warranted discourse, was traditionally designed to prevent. With this reconception of centers, any claim of philosophy to centrality among the discourses of man falls apart.

At least in the *mathematical* sense of 'center.' In the Greece of the Bronze Age we find another sort of sharp point or goad at the center of a κύκλος: here, the 'circle' formed of layered animal skins or bronze that formed the typical single-handled shield. Such a central spike was hardly the 'unmoved source' of the shield's movement, for it was wholly dependent on the arm which held the shield. It was also (paradoxically, if we take the term in its mathematical sense) dependent on the circumference: it was because the central spike was a μέσον, at the midpoint of the shield, that the shield's weight was equally balanced there and would not divert the impetus of any forward thrust. The center was a spike, rather than a mere boss, because at that point the defensive weapon could become offensive. The concentrated energy of the arm, augmented but not deflected by the balanced weight of the whole shield, could be used in close quarters to push at the enemy, goading him to stumble or retreat.[12]

The concept of a center which, far from 'grounding' the periphery, derives its status from balancing the forces of that periphery is explicated in Hegel's logic, where the *Zentrum* is constituted through the interactions of the other parts of an object. Its activity consists only in mediating these with one another, as if the sun were nothing more than the intersection of the gravitational pulls of all the planets.[13] Hegel surpasses the Bronze Age artisans, however: as *merely* such a mediator, the center can impart no additional thrust to what it mediates. An illustration of this occurs in the Preface to Hegel's *Philosophy of Right*: philosophy as a central discourse can only articulate the structures of the state. It cannot undertake to change, or even to criticize, what it comprehends.[14]

Habermas' thought exhibits, I will argue, a 'shieldlike' type of centrality. It seeks to take discourses which, left to themselves, are politically neutral or even defensive formations of a culture under threat (like Austinian speech act theory or Gadamerian hermeneutics)[15] and, by bringing them together, to give them an offensive, critical thrust. The theory of communicative action is to be 'central,' not in the sense that it generates other discourses, but to the contrary: in that they all come together in it. As determined by other sorts of discourse, the Habermasian center is heteronomous – but not in the inoffensive, Hegelian sense.

I Philosophy and non-philosophy in Habermas

In order to examine the universality-claims raised by new paradigms in the empirical sciences, philosophy needs an account of rationality in general. It thus aims at giving a formal (hence non-totalistic) and non-foundational account of reason (*TKH* I, pp. 15–24/1–7). The question immediately arises of whether reason *is* unified: of whether a single account of the formal conditions of something called 'rationality' is possible. Two levels on which this question arises for Habermas reveal three determinate forms of 'non-philosophy' significant for philosophy itself.

One such 'other' is the plurality of discourses present in the contemporary intellectual world. We may (after Max Weber) style this a new 'polytheism' with figures such as Marx, Durkheim, Mead, Freud, Piaget, and Weber himself, as deities. These thinkers have introduced paradigms for the study of man which, Habermas writes, remain today *gleichberechtigt*, on equal footing.[16] Their fundamental heterogeneity impeaches the unity of reason. To rescue philosophy requires reunifying them on a higher level, in a more general social theory which thereby legitimates itself as rational: 'the more freely it can take up, explain, criticize, and carry on the intentions of earlier theory traditions, the more impervious [any social theory] is to the danger that particular interests are being brought to bear unnoticed on its own theoretical perspectives.'[17]

This 'general social theory,' which for Habermas is his own theory of, communicative action, is then a second 'other' to philosophy. The passage cited reveals a tension in it. On the one hand, 'taking up,' 'criticizing,' and 'carrying on' are clear allusions to the three moments of Hegelian *Aufhebung*: preserving, destroying, and raising to a higher level. On this level, social theory is parasitic upon the diverse other paradigms which it integrates, operating as a sort of 'Hegelian' center. That is why the polytheistic discourses of the contemporary age are not legitimated by being sublated into general social theory, but the reverse: such theory achieves, through this process, assurance of its own generality and impartiality.

But in contrast to Hegel's apparently uncritical *Aufhebung* of the state into political philosophy,[18] we find Habermas claiming that general social theory is to retain a theoretical perspective independent of the paradigms it integrates. The 'criticism' Habermas refers to must then be something more than Hegelian 'destruction,' or mediation into a larger system. It must derive theoretical status independently of the discourses it takes up, in a further theory which establishes norms for the critique of other paradigms. This normative theory is then the formal theory of rationality to which we have seen Habermas relegate philosophy. Philosophy and general social theory – in particular, the theory of communicative action – stand in a relation of mutual dependence.

The need for a general social theory points to the third 'other' for philosophy, modern society itself. The various paradigms of social theory are for Habermas internally connected to the social contexts from which they arise, and in which they gain influence.[19] Those contexts themselves exhibit a Weberian form of 'polytheism' as a result of the process of modernization.

That process can be grasped, according to Habermas, as the disintegration of pre-modern 'rationality' into three distinct subtypes, each with its own patterns of argumentation and separate social sphere. The 'objectivating' rationality present in the sciences, geared to the production of technological means for the pursuit of various ends, has in the modern world been set off against 'moral-practical' rationality (socially embedded in the legal system and ethical norms of a society), and against 'aesthetic-practical' rationality (embedded primarily in the institutions of the art world).[20] These three systems in their separation constitute the 'signature of modernity,' and suffice to render the unity of reason historically counterfactual.

This means, first, that the theory of communicative action must be critical, not merely of paradigms in the social sciences, but of society itself.[21] It must provide a way to show that the 'grandiose exclusivities' in which modernity inscribes itself are occlusions of all that remains of philosophy's subject matter: of deeper, more inclusive structures of a unified, formal rationality.

In order to accomplish this, the theory of communicative action must include a detailed account of what modernity is and of how it has arisen: an account which is empirically-based and therefore sociological, but which interprets its data in the

light of its own underlying normative framework. It will ultimately argue that the process of modernization, separating the
forms of rationality from each other to the extent that just
one of them ('objectivating' or means/ends rationality) can be
developed at the expense of the others, is self-contradictory.[22]

Philosophy is thus for Habermas specified dialectically
through its others – through non-philosophies: through
modernity and the efforts of social theorists to grasp modernity.
Central to all this is the theory of communicative action, which
appropriates social theories in order to understand modernity,
and uses a philosophical account of rationality to criticize both.

Diogenes Laertius tells the story that Plato, after the death of
Socrates, burnt the tragedies which he had written and danced
before the flames crying 'Come out, Hephaestus, Plato has need
of thee.' The words echo those which, in the *Iliad*, summon
Hephaestus to make the shield of Achilles, the shield which
depicts all that is noble about the Argive way of life and thus
defends it. Plato's 'shield' – his *Republic* – is, however, more
than a conservative glorification of Athenian tradition. Centered
on the Theory of Forms, it argues that Athens must be radically
transformed if what is good in it is to be saved.[23]

So, I suggest, for Habermas and modernity. His general social
theory is to articulate and justify the achievements of the
modern era, and so to be a critical 'shield' for it.[24] But the shield
is not to be merely defensive: it must obtain, through its center,
an offensive critical thrust.

II The centrality of the theory of communicative action

Philosophy for Habermas requires one 'other' – a theory of
communicative rationality – in order to confront two other 'others'
which threaten it. In the absence of pretensions to foundational
authority, philosophy can dictate nothing to the competing
paradigms of social science. These must instead be put into a
mutual confrontation in which the claims of each are inspected
and, when disputes arise, the better argument prevails. This
calls for a 'theory of discourse' to show the formal conditions
of such argumentation, and thus for a theory of communicative
rationality.[25] And if the norms for rationality are to apply criti-

cally to modern society, they should not be generically different from society: views that 'rationality' is exclusively to be predicated of the isolated individual mind, for example, leave open the question of whether we can or should call societies 'rational.' Thus again, the normative deep structure of rationality is to be understood in communicative terms.

The concept around which Habermas develops his general social theory is thus one of *communicative* action. Any utterance made in a case of communicative action can be criticized from three points of view: with regard to its truth; to its social appropriateness; and to its 'truthfulness' as an expression of the speaker's mental state. If such criticism is actually made by a hearer of the utterance, the speaker must attempt to redeem it by establishing the particular claim challenged; the aim of such 'discourse' is to reach consensus with the challenging parties on the utterance's truth, appropriateness, or truthfulness.[26]

Habermas does not derive these validity-claims from some *a priori* domain such as logical space or transcendental subjectivity: his account of communicative action is a 'reconstruction' of the ways we actually use language in the modern 'lifeworld.'[27] Discourse, by contrast, has an ideal component, for it assumes that the interlocutors will be willing to reach consensus solely on the basis of the 'better argument.' The concept of communicative action enables philosophy to confront modernity as its other: each of the validity-claims raised together in communicative action corresponds to one of the components of rationality that modernity has separated from each other, and so in communicative action the unity of reason is still present. Through its discussion of the nature and forms of discourse, the theory of communicative action can articulate the structures and parameters of the kind of dialogical *Aufhebung* by which competing sociological paradigms can productively converge.

One way of justifying the theory of communicative action is then in terms of the kind of unification of the other social theories it achieves. Habermas' view of such unification at first appears to be the traditional notion of coherence. If theories as wholes were like the propositions of which they are built, they would be true or false. But Habermas does not think highly of that analogy. Theories of high generality cannot simply be tested against reality as many propositions can, and Habermas is left only with the rule of thumb that if two theories contradict one another, one or both must be suspect. The proper procedure in such a case is usually not to test each against reality, but to attempt to remove the contradiction via rational argumentation. The revisions required by this, however, must be mutual: no discourse, and certaintly not philosophy, is entitled to primary status as an 'unmoved mover' to which all others must conform. Habermas' picture is thus of a plurality of discourses, each adjusting itself to accommodate the rational insights of the others.[28]

This picture is incomplete. One respect in which theories for Habermas differ from propositions is that theories, like living organisms, develop over time. Habermas generally refers to such developing conceptual 'organisms' as *Forschungsrichtungen*, directions of research, or as 'learning processes'; each is a 'coherent argumentation developed around constant thematic cores' and leading to a 'cumulative production of knowledge.'[29] The theory of communicative action is central, not simply because it coheres with other discourses, but because they converge on it.

Sometimes they converge, so to speak, of themselves: all Habermas has to do is reveal the convergence.[30] At other times, apparently, it is up to him to bring theories which are not converging into a common universe of discourse.[31] In either case, while not a criterion of truth, 'the capacity to appropriate and work up the best traditions is certainly a sign of a social theory's capacity to connect with others [*Anschlußfähigkeit*] and strength of comprehension.'[32]

To participate in a common rational discourse means, however, to be open to criticism from the other participants; for such discourse, as a case of communicative action, allows one's own validity-claims to be challenged, examined, and abandoned if found wanting. Communicative action, in virtue of the criticizable validity-claims it raises, thus contains an intrinsic critical potential which enables the participants in a common discourse to 'penetrate a given context, to burst it open from within, and to transcend it.'[33] By providing a common universe of discourse for divergent paradigms in social theory, for example, the theory of communicative action unlocks their capacities for mutual and self-criticism; and this, we may take it, is for Habermas another indication of its merit.[34]

The above reference to *Anschlußfähigkeit* suggests a third way, in addition to convergence and the unlocking of critical potential, in which a social theory can be evaluated for Habermas: through its effects. The usefulness of a theory for further research 'can only be verified in its ramifications for research in the social sciences and philosophy,' and is not for its proponent to judge. But Habermas is aware that it matters to a theory whether other research directions can make use of it, and he devotes much of the closing section of *TKH* to a discussion of such possible ramifications.[35]

What makes Habermas' theory a 'good' one is therefore, in part, that other theories converge on it; have their 'offensive' critical potential unlocked by it; and ramify from it into subsequent research. Balanced at the midpoint of a number of circumferential discourses and imparting critical thrust to them, Habermas' theory of communicative action exhibits the kind of 'shieldlike centrality' we discussed earlier. It is 'central,' not like the mathematical center of a circle, but like Heidegger's conception of the '*Ort*,' or place – a word which originally, according to Heidegger, referred to the point of a spear:

> In it everything runs together. The *Ort* collects into itself the highest and the most extreme. That which gathers permeates and penetrates everything. The *Ort*, the gatherer, gathers in and preserves what it has gathered, not like an encapsulating shell but in such a way that it shines through and illuminates what it has gathered and thereby releases it into its own nature.[36]

Heideggerean 'illumination,' the disclosure of a thing in its own true nature, is not the same as the Habermasian unlocking of critical potential. Speech-act theory, for example, can exist independently of political critique, and to develop it as such critique is not to disclose its nature as speech-act theory. But Heidegger's *Ort*, though restricted to showing what things are rather than what they ought to be, is not uncritical in the same way as Hegel's *Zentrum*, in which everything also 'comes together.' For the *Ort* is not determined exclusively by what it gathers, but operates from out of a prelinguistic, inarticulate 'event' of Being, which provides dynamism to the spear (or shield).[37] And this suggests, for Habermas, two questions, which I would like to keep separate.

One is that of what, beyond the historically-conditioned problematic of philosophy and social theory, justifies the theory of communicative action: are other kinds of argument to be advanced for it? The other question concerns what we will see to be the theory's claim to set forth the formal structures of *all* rationality. This appears to be a claim, not for what we have called 'centrality,' but for universality in the traditional, philosophical sense. What justifies it? What, in fact, is its nature?

These questions have virtually governed the history of Habermas' reception, and have led to a welter of literature by Habermas and his critics.[38] My approach here will be, first, to reconstruct from *TKH* a further argument which seems to me the most sound way to supplement the argument from historical conditions given above. I will then measure what that argument can establish against the universality-claims Habermas actually makes, in order to reinterpret the nature of those claims. The result of that reinterpretation will be the view that Habermas' whole project deserves to be called 'philosophical.'

Communicative action for Habermas is embedded in a 'life-world,' which he defines by giving a dialogical twist to the Husserlian formulation: it is a 'reservoir of truisms or of unshaken convictions which the participants in communication use for cooperative processes of interpretation.'[39] In other words, any validity-claim presupposes various kinds of (generally) unquestioned background belief, and can be evaluated by explicating and examining items of this 'horizon.' Discourse is in part the articulation and scrutiny – the interpretation – of the life-world.

Communicative action is, indeed, relative not merely to a life-world, but specifically to the 'rationalized' type of life-world to be found in modern societies. As we have seen, it requires speaker and hearer to engage in discourse if challenged. Discourse begins by challenging one of the three claims made by the utterance, which it goes on to examine separately of the others. Because it thus separates one validity-claim from the rest, such discourse is characteristic of the modern world.[40]

The theory of communicative action is itself advanced discursively, as a set of theses to be challenged in open and rational debate: and so this relativity to the life-world must apply to it as well. Habermas makes the application when he says that any social theory which rests upon the theory of communicative action,

> In so far as it relates to structures of the life-world, must explicate a background knowledge which no one can control at will. The life-world is 'given,' to the theorist and to the layman, in the first instance as his own life-world. . . . Whether a life-world withdraws from or discloses itself to the researching gaze of the phenomenologist does not depend on the choice of a theoretical standpoint. No more than for any social scientist does the totality of background knowledge constitutive for the construction of the life-world stand at his disposition. . . . The context in which it arises does not remain external to the theory.[41]

In passages I have omitted from the above quote, Habermas makes the uncontroversial claim that the life-world is a necessary horizon for all communicative practice because it cannot, in its entirety, be put into question. We cannot become explicitly aware of all the background information that is relevant to our understanding of an utterance, or to our judgment of its validity. All such judgments are inescapably anchored in the life-world of the judgers, which in a sense becomes the final court of appeal for them:

> The life-world constitutes, in the situation of an action, a horizon we cannot get beyond. . . . For those belonging to a sociocultural life-world it is, strictly speaking, *senseless* to ask if the culture in whose light they come to understand themselves with respect to external nature, society, and internal nature empirically depends on something else.[42]

The life-world is thus the 'necessary' foundation of communicative rationality in the old Greek sense of 'ανανκή: not as what is logically deducible from self-evident premises or true in all possible worlds, but as what we must put up with. If we cannot challenge the totality of our life-world, we cannot globally challenge the structures which – like those of communicative action in the modern life-world – govern and define that totality. Those structures, in short, are indeed relative to a particular life-world; but it is *our* life-world, and there is nothing we can do about that. Being thus necessary, the life-world suffices as ground – to some degree unknown – for the theory of communicative action.

That theory, it now appears, is to be considered as an articulation of basic features of the life-world of modernity. As such, it is what Merleau-Ponty would call 'experience'; and as such, it gains a second sort of centrality: it is no longer merely central to the theoretical discourses of social science, but also mediates between them and the particular life-world which it articulates.[43] It is in being itself centered on the life-world that the theory of communicative action acquires a critical perspective independent of the social theories it unifies.

III   Universality and centrality in Habermas

We now have an answer to the first of our earlier questions. The theory of communicative action in general is 'justified,' not merely in virtue of the current state of social theory, but because the structures it treats are definitive for our life-world.

But the argument I have sketched can establish only centrality within and for the modern life-world, and Habermas wants more. Strongly universal validity-claims are for Habermas, as we have seen, typical of new paradigms in the social sciences. The theory of communicative action makes such claims when it asserts that all human discourse, to be rational, must claim truth, sincerity, and appropriateness. These claims are not for Habermas merely relative to the current state of social science, or even to the modern life-world. His clearest response to Weber's question of whether or not rationalization (with its concomitant, modernization) is a phenomenon restricted to the West is as follows: '[the three validity-claims of communicative action] form a system – however fraught with internal tensions – that did indeed first appear in the form of Occidental rationalism but that, beyond the peculiarity of this specific culture, lays a claim to a universal validity binding on all "civilised men." '[44]

223

This sort of universality-claim goes far beyond the centrality that the argument we have reconstructed seeks to establish. Does Habermas have yet other methods for establishing it? At the end of the Introduction to *TKH*, he distinguishes three possible strategies:

1 The account of validity-claims can be formulated out of speaker-intuitions, and then be empirically tested against as varied a sample of speakers as can be found. This can, at least, render the account 'plausible.'

2 We can try and show the empirical usefulness of the account in various fields.

3 We can examine critically the history of social theory, to see what problems are present in it and show those theories could be improved when supplemented by the concept of communicative rationality.[45]

The latter two strategies are, we have suggested, ways of arguing, not for the universality of the theory of communicative action, but for its centrality. The first way, as Habermas himself notes, can only serve to render the theory 'plausible.' So these strategies are unable to provide the truth of the universality claims Habermas wants to make.

But perhaps Habermas is not trying to *prove* these claims; perhaps they have a status other than that of theses advanced as definitely true. At the end of *TKH*, he refers to the 'strongly universalistic claim' of the theory of communicative action together with the merely 'hypothetical' status of those claims, a status which is only 'indirectly examinable.'[46] It seems that he is attempting, not to prove his universality-claims, but only to advance them for discussion. But why would he do this?

There are two answers. In the passage from the Introduction, the universality-claim is motivated by social science's claim to objectivity: 'we cannot expect objectivity in social/theoretical knowledge if the corresponding concepts of communicative action express a merely particular perspective on rationality, one interwoven with a particular cultural tradition.'[47]

This begs the question of whether social science's claims to objectivity are sustainable, which is certainly a major question. In the later passage, however, Habermas' motivation lies, not in the nature of social science, but in that of communicative action: 'the theory of communicative action aims at that moment of unconditionedness which is built into the conditions of consensus-formation by criticizable validity-claims – *as* claims these transcend all spatial and temporal, all provincial limitations of the context of the moment.'[48]

Because the theory of communicative action is itself advanced as a case of communicative action, it carries with it the kind of unconditional validity-claim that communicative action in general contains. But is the theory of communicative action itself merely an instance of communicative action?

In his more recent discussion of Derrida, Habermas suggests that philosophy requires such strong validity-claims if it is to be truly critical. It is easy to see why: critical or self-critical potential is for Habermas only unlocked through dialogue with others. What brings such dialogue about is the making of a validity-claim which transcends the location of the utterance: as Kant argued, an assertion which only claims validity for me (or us) here and now is not open to criticism by others.[49] Habermas is inviting, not merely the adherence of others to his new research paradigm, but their criticisms of it. Validity-claims whose purpose is thus to draw others into critical debate have to be provocative, not proven. To be provocative, they need to be only 'plausible'; and Habermas' strategies can show that they are, at least, that.

The justification for Habermas' strong universality-claims now appears to be pragmatic rather than theoretical. If such were the case, those claims would not be, in Austin's language, 'constative' speech acts. They would be made in order to achieve a 'perlocutionary' effect: to draw as many interlocutors as possible into the field of discussion. Their 'illocutionary' status would be similar to an invitation or summons.[50] This would be consonant with our suggestion of a centrality-claim for Habermas' theory, since the more partners he has in formulating and justifying that theory, the more 'central' it will be.

But if the point of making a universality-claim is to issue an invitation, why not simply issue one? Why take the risk – no small one, in the light of the Habermas literature – that one's universality-claims will be refuted?

The reference to Kant raises further questions, and I think offers a way out. For Kant, in general, three types of judgment claim validity beyond the situation of their utterance (and similar situations). One is the theoretical 'judgment of experience'; a second is the categorical imperative, and moral judgments founded exclusively on it. A third is reflective judgment, the paradigm of which is the aesthetic 'judgment of taste.'

In recent remarks on Richard J. Bernstein, Habermas seems to recognize only the first two of these. Bernstein's thought, in a much more explicit way, seeks to achieve the same sort of centrality as Habermas', but does so without being bound to the truth-value of universalistic claims. Critical dialogue is taken to be a kind of πρᾶξις, the nature of which is clarified and the centrality of which is established by bringing together models of discourse from divergent philosophical paradigms.[51]

Habermas construes Bernstein as offering a practical, as opposed to a theoretical, account of communicative reason: Bernstein 'locates the moment of unconditionedness built into the universalistic validity *claims* of our communicative practices in the horizon of *practical* reason . . . he refuses to regard the procedural unity of rationality within the historical and cultural multiplicity of standards of rationality as a question that is accessible to *theoretical* treatment.'[52]

It seems inadvisable to apply Kantian categories such as theoretical and practical reason to Bernstein, whose emphasis on the Aristotelian conception of φρόνησις is most un-Kantian in the ethical sphere.[53] Indeed, Bernstein's concept of dialogue has *aesthetic* affinities, rooted in Gadamer's hermeneutics; Bernstein traces it from those origins through its extension by Gadamer to literature itself, and then criticizes Gadamer for not continuing it into the practical sphere.[54]

Let us ask whether Habermas' universality-claims can be assimilated to the remaining type of Kantian judgment, the judgment of taste. As explicated in Kant's *Critique of Judgment*, this type of judgment indeed claims to be valid for everyone; but, for our purposes, the claim differs in three respects from those of the 'determining judgments' of theoretical and practical reason.[55]

1 Determining judgments start from a concept and subsume given particulars under that concept: reflective judgments do not begin with a concept, and in fact are for Kant the basic vehicle of concept *formation*. The universality-claim they make

is thus an imputation that anybody, if presented with *these* particulars, could go on to form *those* concepts.

2 Because the universality-claim of a reflective judgment refers to the 'presentation' of particulars, which for Kant always requires sensation, it claims validity only for all human beings – not, as with an a priori determining judgment, for all rational beings (some of whom may not have senses).

3 Because of its reference to sensation, this claim cannot be tested within the confines of an isolated 'monological' ego: aesthetic rationality is essentially dialogical.

Following a suggestion of Joel Whitebrook, we may say that these characteristics seem to be shared by Habermas' own theory of communicative action. That theory begins, not from a predetermined concept of communicative action or indeed from any conceptual 'foundation,' but from intuitive speaker-competences – 'presentations,' we may say, of the structures of interaction – which it then reconstructs via an 'explication of [that] concept.'[56] And, as we have seen, its claims are not advanced as proven truths, but as hypotheses to be dialogically examined.

Construing the universality-claims of the theory of communicative action as akin to the 'imputation' of assent made by a Kantian reflective judgment would yield precisely the status Habermas, at the end of *TKH*, wants for them. They would be 'strong' in that they would apply to everyone who can experience communicative action, i.e. to everyone who can live in a modern life-world – a class which, presumably, includes all humans. They would be advanced, not as a set of claims already proven, but dialogically, as a set of reasoned suggestions for the critical appraisal of all such persons. This would suffice for what we have called the 'pragmatic' purpose of those universality claims, but would not deprive them of their claim to rational validity.

IV Centrality and autonomy in Habermas

But for Habermas to view the theory of communicative action as explicated in quasi-Kantian reflective judgment would threaten his understanding of its rational character. For Kant, aesthetic arguments cannot be resolved because the concept of beauty cannot be objectively specified: to say that something is 'beautiful' is only to say that its sensory or imaginative presentation, in virtue of its harmonious form alone, gives me pleasure. Other reflective judgments, though they may issue in determinate concepts, begin without them; and in order for such a concept to be formulated, the original presentation from which it is to be worked up must be given as something harmonious in form – well-organized enough that it is possible to conceive of it as coming under a relatively small number of general laws.

But the perception of such harmony, as pre-conceptual, remains for Kant a matter of intuitive 'feel': though the adequacy of a subsequently-formulated concept to articulate it may be a matter for argument and debate, whether the original presentation itself is harmonious or not is a (subjective) given. Reflective judgment must therefore always begin afresh, so to speak, from the 'ground zero' of intuitive feel, and we cannot expect it to exhibit the kind of institutionalized, cumulative production of knowledge that characterizes the kind of rational investigation Habermas views as converging on his own thought.[57]

This presumably is why, though Habermas leaves space in his general account of rationalization complexes for a 'social/aesthetic' rationality, that space is filled, as Thomas McCarthy points out, not with examples of such rationality, but with an 'x.'[58] But McCarthy has shown that Habermas does not fully discharge the burden of proof he assumes with this claim, and that to do so would lead to inconsistencies with Habermas' treatment of Walter Benjamin.[59]

Why, then, does Habermas lean on this criterion of 'cumulative production of knowledge'? His argument maintains that such coherence is a necessary condition for rationality, and one motive for this is understandable. Contemporary cultural polytheism throws up demons as well as deities. We would not consider it a strong point for a social theory if it were able to accommodate the ravings of, say, a Charles Manson or a John Wilkes Booth; still less if subsequent luminaries, like Louis Farrakhan or Abu Nidal, should find it *Anschlußfähig*. The criterion of a 'coherent learning process' provides a way to filter these out, leaving only what we have seen Habermas refer to as 'the best traditions.'

But the use of this criterion poses difficulties other than the ones McCarthy mentions. For one thing, Habermas criticizes Horkheimer and Adorno for their 'completely affirmative attitude toward the art of the bourgeois epoch,' which delivered their critical theory over to the 'measure of the age.'[60] But his own reliance on discourses which have developed in academic and other institutionalized realms of modern society seems to reflect an attitude towards those institutions which is itself rather affirmative. It is possible that the discourses carried on in the academy are not simply communicative articulations of the structures of the modern life-world, but are also conditioned by such socially-influential factors as power and money. In relying on them, critical theory seems once again to be delivered over to the 'measure of the age,' i.e. of the modern world which has produced academies. This is, as Habermas notes, no objection to the 'systematic status' of his account of rationalization-complexes; but it does suggest, as McCarthy notes, that certain possibilities may be screened out.[61]

However that may be, Habermas' criterion of cumulative development of knowledge for rational discourse represents, I think, a last refuge of 'autonomy' in philosophy. For the communicative redemption of validity-claims which constitutes such rational discourses corresponds to Habermas' dialogical extrapolation of the kind of 'Kantian' ethic found on level six of Lawrence Kohlberg's hierarchy of moral development: the monadic, 'Kantian' individual, in opening out to dialogue, becomes an ego constituted through processes of communicative action. Similarly, then, for the discourses Habermas seeks to bring into dialogue, and which are accorded 'rational' status because they, too, are constituted through processes of communicative action.[62] Similarly as well, in Habermas' eyes, for the theory of communicative action itself: its 'heteronomous centrality' is nothing other than its dialogical autonomy.

It is then this residual concept of autonomy which seems to give Habermas' theory over to the measure of the academy; and the solution, I suggest, is not to abandon it, but to view it as an autonomy of the peripheries, not of the center. Habermas' critical theory, I suggest, is not like other discourses with which it seeks convergence: it is more than simply a dialogically-auton-omous statement and redemption of validity-claims. It does not merely describe the life-world theoretically, but arises out of it – from a set of specific disruptions in the life-world, which call it forth through the anguish they present.[63] The activity of thought which articulates that anguish – anguish which is the exact reverse of aesthetic pleasure at the presentation of a harmonious form – is not a 'theory' in Habermas' 'objectivating' sense.[64] It is what a Kantian might call a 'socio-reflective judg-ment,' to be distinguished from the rational redemption of validity-claims which ensues upon its formulation.

If the autonomous discourses of the social sciences constitute the 'periphery' of Habermas' shield, and the theory of communicative action is its center, then the anguish of the life-world is the dynamism of the arm which holds that shield, and which provides a critical thrust independent of those auton-omous discourses themselves.

We thus arrive at the picture of (dialogically) autonomous discourses finding their way to a center which is doubly heter-onomous: it 'takes its law' both from the discourses which converge upon it and from the stresses in the life-world which it articulates. With respect to the former, it exercises the power of inducing self- and mutual-critique into them, both among them and with itself. But its special critical perspective is unlocked only when it demands that those other discourses, in coming to the center, contribute to the articulation and, perhaps, to the eventual healing of the life-world.[65]

But whence the demand for healing? Why should we care that the life-world is under threat? If our particular life-world is only an ἀναγκαῖον, something we are stuck with, threats to it would not necessarily be bad; they may, indeed, have liberating potential. Why should the anguish of the life-world be Habermas', or our own? Why should it call forth a *critical* response in us?

To make another's anguish one's own, I suggest, is to adopt an attitude of love for that other. Habermas' critical shield is supported, in the last analysis, by a sort of love for the life-world: the *amor mundi* that is part of his inheritance from Hannah Arendt.[66] Recognizing the role of *amor mundi* in the theory of communicative action, Habermas' thought would give up all claims to autonomy – even of the dialogical kind – if not to centrality. It would rejoin the oldest meaning of 'philosophy': the attainment of wisdom (σοφία) through love (φιλία). Its critical perspective would be the demand of a life-world which has through love become philosophy, of a philosophy which has through love become experience.

Chapter 10

LEVINAS: PHILOSOPHY AND BEYOND

Robert Bernasconi

At the beginning of *Time and the Other*, a lecture series from 1947, Levinas proclaimed his intention to break with Parmenides, the father of philosophy. This act of parricide would be accomplished by confronting the thought of the One with 'a pluralism which does not fuse into unity.'[1] And by the end of the fourth and final lecture, Levinas judged himself in a position to say that 'the eleatic notion of being is surpassed' (*TA*, p. 88). The claim was made following descriptions of death, femininity, and fecundity. In the approach of death as an absolute inassimilable alterity, the subject is deprived of its mastery over itself and finds its solitude shattered (*TA*, pp. 62–3); the feminine is no longer to be conceived, as in Plato, on the model of the passivity of matter or as a complementary term in a pre-existing whole, but as an alterity which signals an insurmountable duality of beings (*TA*, p. 78); and in fecundity, there is a sense in which I am my child, not through sympathy but by virtue of my being (*TA*, p. 86). Death, sexuality, and fecundity introduce into existence a duality, an alterity which resists the ideal of fusion without succumbing to the model of straightforward exclusion. And this duality is not that of a reciprocal relation where the I identifies with the other and so is saved from its solitude. The Other is present only as a certain absence (*TA*, p. 89).[2]

These descriptions were taken up again and reworked in 1961 in *Totality and Infinity* and similar claims were made on their behalf. By recognizing the ultimate structure of being as split into the same and the other, 'we leave the philosophy of Parmenidean being.'[3] The immediate context was again provided by descriptions of the feminine and of fecundity, and these followed an account of the temporality of death. But although the break with Parmenides was understood as a break with the predominancy of ontology in Western philosophy, it did not amount to a break with philosophy as such.[4] Levinas drew a distinction between ontology as the philosophy of unity and of totality, on the one hand, and metaphysics as the aspiration to radical exteriority, on the other (*TI*, p. xvii/29). But to elucidate his sense of 'metaphysics,' Levinas found himself obliged to draw on the language of Western philosophy, borrowing both Plato's famous phrase from the *Republic*, the *epekeina tes ousias* or the beyond being, and the idea of infinity as found in Descartes. Not that Levinas thereby accepted a commitment to the ontologies of either Plato or Descartes. Rather, to take the latter as an example, Levinas adopts only Descartes' presentation of the idea of the infinite as a thought which I cannot think but which must be thought in me – the more in the less – and not the distinction between formal and objective reality which Descartes used in the Third Meditation to introduce it. And the fact that Descartes presents the *cogito* first is indicative of a relation in which the finite by its separation prepares for the infinite without being absorbed in it. But this is only the order of reasons and not the order of being. The *cogito* of Levinas's reading is not the ultimate basis of Descartes' philosophy; it finds in the infinite 'a point of view exterior to itself from which it can apprehend itself' and discover its finitude (*TI*, p. 186/210). In this way Levinas finds in Descartes the conceptual means for thinking the multiplicity occasioned by exteriority, that relation with alterity which he had already found – in different ways – in death, the feminine, and fecundity.

This notion of the infinite in the finite provides the basis for Levinas's attempt to find a way between transcendence and immanence. He turns aside from that version of the philosophy of transcendence which relies on mysticism at the expense of terrestrial existence, as much as from the philosophy of immanence which confines the source of meaning in this world, although perhaps postponing it to the end of history (*TI*, p. 23/52). That the infinite is in the finite means that the metaphysical relation is inscribed within the unfolding of terrestrial existence: 'This "beyond" the totality and objective experience is, however, not to be described in a purely negative fashion. It is reflected *within* the totality and history, *within* experience' (*TI*, p. xi/23). And yet if the descriptions of enjoyment, representation and dwelling in the second section of *Totality and Infinity* show the infinite within experience, Levinas is less explicit in that book as to how it might be found within history. History is condemned as blind to the human relation. 'When man truly approaches the Other he is uprooted from history' (*TI*, p. 23/ 52). This is applied not only to the Hegelian philosophy of history, but also to Heidegger's history of Being. Levinas accuses both histories of ignoring the Other. This, of course, does not deny that the relation with the other human being is a *theme* in their thinking, but neither Hegel's account of the master–slave relation, nor 'the neutral intersubjectivity' of Heidegger's *Mitsein* (*TI*, p. 39/68), manages to sustain the asymmetrical character of the separated I in the face of the Other who commands from a height. Levinas identifies this asymmetrical relation in favour of the Other as the ethical relation, the concrete relation of transcendence. Hence to break with Parmenides is, on Levinas's understanding, also to break with the philosophy of the Neuter as exemplified by Hegel's impersonal reason and Heidegger's Being. For all their differences, Hegel and Heidegger could both be characterized as having proclaimed a version of the end of philosophy (*TI*, p. 275/298). They may not have meant the same thing by that phrase, but so far as Levinas was concerned they both held to a philosophy of history whose basis lay in obedience to an impersonal force, whether it be Hegel's Concept or Heidegger's truth of Being.

But if this helps to explain why Levinas tended in *Totality and Infinity* to refer to history only negatively, it still needs to be explained why he did not construe his own break with the ontological tradition of philosophy as a break with philosophy as such. Having confined Heidegger to the so-called neutral philosophy of totality, Levinas might have been expected to announce that his own break with philosophy constituted the end of philosophy, an expectation which is fuelled by the tendency for the recent history of philosophy to be written as a series of such announcements, all of which have been premature according to each new thinker added to the chain. Hegel, Marx, Nietzsche, and Heidegger have all been construed in this manner and recent French philosophy is generally understood to be playing the same game. But Levinas, as we have seen, refuses the totalizing conception of history which announces the end of philosophy. And yet if metaphysics is juxtaposed with ontology, philosophy does not continue as metaphysics. Levinas understands metaphysics not so much as a way of doing philosophy as a way of transcendence. It is accomplished as service of the Other, so that metaphysical thought is 'attention to speech or welcome of the face, hospitality and not thematization' (*TI*, p. 276/299). Or again, 'our relation with the Metaphysical is an ethical behaviour and not a theology, not a thematization, be it a knowledge of analogy, of the attributes of God' (*TI*, p. 50/78). Metaphysics is neither a form of philosophy, nor is it dependent on philosophy. Already ethical, metaphysics does not seek a foundation for ethics in ontology. Rather, the ethical signification of the Other challenges the fundamental status of ontology.[5]

An essay written in 1958, 'Martin Buber and the Theory of Knowledge,' provides some indication of how Levinas understood the unique character of philosophy at that time. In that essay he posed the question, 'Is not *philosophari* essentially different from *vivere*?' Philosophy in this sense is always 'to one side,' independent and critical. It is to be understood as 'a rupture of our participation in totality.'[6] Levinas thus finds beneath the philosophical tradition of unifying and totalizing thought, another conception of philosophy which is characterized, to use a word from *Totality and Infinity*, by separation. Such separation was understood by Levinas to be necessary for transcendence in the appropriate sense and he had long complained that recent philosophy had, in its efforts to secure the spirituality of the subject, sacrificed the subject's substantiality.[7] The I had come to be dissolved by philosophers in what they called the 'situation,' just as they had dissolved the I in community, so doubly excluding the metaphysical relation with the other. The implication seemed to be that philosophy could take up the task of maintaining the separation necessary of transcendence. Another later essay on Buber also raised the question of the vocation of philosophy. Philosophy is the call not to be the victim of ideology, not to suffer the decisions and imperatives of society, culture, politics, or religion. In support of this conception Levinas cities the classic distinction between reason and opinion and associates it with the capacity to say 'I,' the ability to pronounce the *cogito*.[8] But any reader familiar with Levinas's work knows to suspect that such a question of philosophy will itself be questioned, just as, according to Levinas, Descartes allows the *cogito* to be put in question by the idea of the infinite.

Levinas certainly places a conception of critique at the center of *Totality and Infinity*, but it cannot be assimilated to the common conception of external criticism as a faultfinding. It is more closely related to the etymological sense observed by Heidegger, when he refers it to *krinein* in the sense of 'to separate' (*sondern*).[9] Critique in Levinas's sense 'calls into question the exercise of the same.' And this is brought about by the other. Levinas calls this questioning of 'my spontaneity by the presence of the Other' *ethics* (*TI*, p. 13/43). This conception of critique is not the same as that to which Levinas refers philosophy in his essays on Buber, where it is still the I or an impersonal reason who makes a critique of the other or of myself. In self-critique the self maintains its control when it questions itself. 'A philosophy of power, ontology is, as first philosophy which does not call into question the same, a philosophy of injustice' (*TI*, p. 17/46). One could say therefore that a whole conception of philosophy is also challenged when I am subjected to critique by the Other. The ethical relation, which is asymmetrical and irreversible, serves as the final court of appeal judging the justice of society and of philosophy.[10] Justice and philosophy believe in equality, be it equality before the law or before reason. The ethical relation, always in favour of the Other and so unequal, finds justice and reason wanting. But there is a passage from ethics to justice. The Other always refers to the Others. 'The third party looks at me in the eyes of the Other – language is justice' (*TI*, p. 188/213).

Levinas for the most part situates philosophy alongside society.[11] But does this ethical critique constitute another sense of philosophy? A later section of *Totality and Infinity* says as much. 'Critique or philosophy is the essence of knowing. But what is proper to knowing is not its possibility of going unto an object, a movement by which it is akin to other acts; its prerogative consists in being able to put itself in question, in penetrating beneath its own condition' (*TI*, p. 57/85). Such a philosophy is not primarily concerned with objective cognition, but rather it 'leads to the Other,' leads 'beyond the knowledge of the *cogito*' (*TI*, p. 58/85). It thus leads to the point where I am conscious of my own injustice. Philosophy in this sense puts in question the philosophy of injustice and can do so because it 'begins with conscience, to which the other is presented as the Other, and where the movement of thematization is inverted' (*TI*, p. 59/86). But can ethics be identified as first philosophy, as the title of a recent lecture by Levinas suggests,[12] without an ambiguity being introduced into ethics as both a relation and philosophy? Is there a sense in which metaphysics can be for Levinas not only service, but also philosophy?

In his influential essay 'Violence and Metaphysics', first published in 1964, Derrida examines Levinas's relation to philosophy. Derrida's opening sentences provide the framework for his reading of Levinas and place the latter within the context of the question of the so-called death of philosophy understood with reference not only to Hegel, Marx, Nietzsche, and Heidegger, but also to philosophy's opposition to non-philosophy as 'its past and its concern, its death and wellspring.'[13] This question, which can only be sustained 'in remembrance of philosophy' (*ED*, p. 119/80), becomes in the course of Derrida's essay the question of whether the challenge to the Greek foundations of philosophy could be called non-Greek (*ED*, p. 122/82), which in turn becomes the 'pre-logical', non-chronological question of whether we are first Jews or first Greeks (*ED*, p. 227/153). It is also the question of how 'a quite new' metaphysics of radical separation and exteriority can find its language in the traditional *logos* governed as it is by spatial dualisms like 'inside-outside' (*ED*, p. 132/88), and the question of how committing parricide on Parmenides could be accomplished except by feigning to be Greek or feigning to speak the Greek language (*ED*, p. 133/89). Then it appears as the question of 'whether history does not itself begin with this relationship to the other which Levinas places beyond history' (*ED*, p. 139/94), a question which is subsequently rephrased as the question of a possible history of 'departures from totality' (*ED*, p. 173/117). Furthermore, and without even beginning to exhaust this

237

remarkable essay, there is the question of whether there is any thought before language, which Derrida understands Levinas to have strenuously denied, very much to his disadvantage (*ED*, pp. 168–70/114–16). All of these questions will be touched on, however briefly, in what follows because, as Derrida is at great pains to insist, they are Levinas's own questions (*ED*, p. 125/84). And there is every indication that Levinas in his subsequent writing paid great attention to this essay. And yet it will also be necessary to ask whether Derrida did not too quickly assimilate Levinas's questioning of philosophy to a model derived from elsewhere, and in particular from Heidegger.

Derrida reads Levinas as equating metaphysics and critique. 'Metaphysics begins when theory criticizes itself as ontology, as the dogmatism and spontaneity of the same, and when it,[14] in departing from itself, lets itself be put into question by the other in the movement of ethics. Although in fact it is secondary, metaphysics as the critique of ontology is rightfully and philosophically primary' (*ED*, p. 143/96). Derrida refers here to the important section 'Metaphysics Precedes Ontology'. If Derrida appears to rewrite the relation between metaphysics and ontology in terms of the classic distinction between *de jure* and *de facto*, he complicates the reversal significantly when he suggests that the language adopted by philosophy already spoke the ethico-political of the city (*ED*, p. 145/97) and again when, following an analysis of Levinas's language and his relation to Heidegger he reverses it once more: 'Ethico-metaphysical transcendence therefore presupposes ontological transcendence' (*ED*, p. 208/141). Can one fail to suspect Derrida of already being on the way to a deconstruction of the hierarchy Levinas seeks to establish between metaphysics and ontology – even if in 1964 he had not yet introduced the word 'deconstruction'? But does Levinas simply establish a priority between metaphysics and ontology? Or is there a radical gulf, an abyss, between them which Derrida does not even suspect? Derrida understands Levinas's metaphysics as philosophy. But is metaphysics in Levinas philosophically prior? Is it not prior to philosophy? *Totality and Infinity* withholds an unambiguous answer to this question. Every indication one way is balanced by a hint in the other direction. Of course, it will be objected that even if metaphysics were prior to philosophy, any attempt to assert it would constitute a philosophical thesis and risk returning metaphysics to philosophy. It is perhaps for the same reason that Levinas refuses to characterize the metaphysics relation as either positive or negative (*TI*, p. 12/42). But if this is indeed the case, the precaution cannot be wholly successful, as Levinas knows full well. It requires more than a studious silence on certain topics to evade philosophy. The same problems surround the assertion of the primacy of ethics, which equally sounds like an ontological claim. Is there even a way by which metaphysics could be understood as radically different from philosophy?

I shall not pursue here the question of whether Derrida's essay is to be read as a critique (in the sense of faultfinding) or as a deconstruction.[15] But it should not go unnoticed that the necessity on which Derrida insists time and time again, 'the necessity of lodging oneself within traditional conceptuality in order to destroy it' (*ED*, p. 165/111), is not one which Derrida imposes on Levinas, but was already explicitly recognized by the latter. Derrida was well aware of this. At the end of 'Violence and Metaphysics' he quotes Levinas's statement that 'one could not possibly reject the Scriptures without knowing how to read them, nor say philology without philosophy, nor, if need be, arrest philosophical discourse without philosophizing.'[16] But Derrida gives to Levinas's statement a meaning other than that which Levinas would accept. He quotes alongside it – and in fundamental agreement with it – the Greek saying that 'if one has to philosophize, one has to philosophize; if one does not have to philosophize, one still has to philosophize (to say and think it). One always has to philosophize.'[17] In this context Derrida attempts to return Levinas's thinking to philosophy by identifying it as empiricism. To be sure, Derrida recalls – even if it will seem strange to some Anglo-American readers – that empiricism has 'always been determined by philosophy, from Plato to Husserl as *nonphilosophy*' (*ED*, p. 226/152). But Derrida insists that empiricism as a contestation of 'the resolution and coherence of the logos (philosophy) at its root' solicits the Greek *logos*. Empiricism is a name for the 'renunciation of the concept, of the a prioris and transcendental horizons of language.' It is, says Derrida, 'the *dream* of a purely *heterolog-*

ical thought, at its source. A *pure* thought of *pure* difference.' And he explains his use of the word 'dream' by reference to its naiveté on the question of relation between thought and language (*ED*, p. 224/151). 'Empiricism is thinking *by* metaphor without thinking the metaphor *as such*' (*ED*, p. 204/139). Derrida thus uses the title 'empiricism' to collect many of the themes of his essay, a move which is supported by two passages where Levinas embraces the word 'empiricism.'[18] Perhaps the most significant aspect of this discussion of empiricism for the reading of Levinas is Derrida's charge that the concept of experience has always been determined by the metaphysics of presence (*ED*, p. 225/152). Although Levinas had previously shown some reservations about the word (*TI*, p. xii/25), he would never again use it so freely.

I shall for the remainder of this essay pursue the question of the relation between philosophy and non-philosophy in Levinas's thinking by focusing on his response to Derrida's questioning. In addition to Levinas's brief essay on Derrida, 'All Otherwise', Levinas's response to Derrida is most clearly visible in three essays to be found in Levinas's 1982 collection *De Dieu qui vient à l'idée*: 'God and Philosophy', 'Ideology and Idealism', and 'The Thought of Being and the Question of the Other'. My discussion of these four essays will be supplemented by references to *Otherwise Than Being or Beyond Essence*, Levinas's most far-reaching book and one which shows the impact of 'Violence and Metaphysics' on his thinking, though rather less explicitly.[19]

Levinas begins the 1975 essay 'God and Philosophy' by requoting, although without reference to Derrida, the saying 'not to philosophize is still to philosophize.'[20] Near the end of the essay he italicizes his own denial: '*Not to philosophize would not be "to philosophize still,"* nor to succumb to opinions' (*DVI*, p. 126/GP, p. 143). What does he mean? The phrase 'not to succumb to opinions' is a reference to Plato's notion of *doxa* to which philosophy as *episteme* was originally opposed. Levinas is inviting us to conceive of a possibility which would be outside the opposition between philosophy and non-philosophy as traditionally conceived. He is attempting, one could say, to turn the tables on Derrida. He is inviting us, in implicit remembrance of Derrida's essay, to conceive what in a Derridian context might be called a deconstructed notion of philosophy, although it will prove not to be the concept of deconstruction itself. Why has it become important for Levinas to find a way of avoiding philosophy, a way beyond philosophy, and how does he arrive at it?

Under the title 'The Priority of Philosophical Discourse and Ontology', Levinas in the first section of 'God and Philosophy' would appear to equate philosophy and the thesis which states the priority of ontology. Whether or not one understands this as a revision of Levinas's earlier presentations, it is clear that the underlying question is not new to his work. Is not ontology based on a restriction of meaning? Is it not, despite its claims to ultimacy, only a derivative form of signification? Levinas observes, as Heidegger had done before him, that although philosophy has tended to conceive of God as a being, it has nevertheless failed to pose the question of the Being of this being. Levinas's characterization of Western philosophy as a 'destruction of transcendence' corresponds in this way to Heidegger's conception of the ontotheological character of philosophy. Rational theology is indicative of what is at stake here, because in its self-conception it has already submitted to the presumption that every discourse must justify itself before philosophy. It accepts philosophy as the arbiter of sense and the realm of being is accepted as the sole realm of meaningful thought. Hence Levinas now construes the question as that of whether there is another kind of meaning from that which is acknowledged by philosophy.

Such a non-philosophical source of meaning cannot be construed in terms of either faith or opinion, for these are simply the traditional alternatives to philosophy and as such already determined by it. They are not therefore genuine alternatives, but are defined with reference to philosophy and remain in its orbit.[21] Hence Levinas entertains the idea of 'a rational discourse which would be neither ontology nor faith' (*DVI*, p. 96/*GP*, p. 129). But what does it mean to characterize as 'rational', a discourse which seeks to situate itself beyond or outside philosophy? Can the word 'rational' here be construed without reference to the *logos* and the philosophical tradition which sustains the thought of that *logos*? And is not the task of bypassing philosophy and its classic alternatives inevitably only in the final analysis another form of opposition to it? More specifically, it might seem that Levinas attempts to show that philosophy is a conditioned form of discourse, in which case that which conditions it would amount to a source of meaning beyond philosophy in the required sense. And yet is not the precarious nature of such an enterprise apparent from the fact that it has recourse to the language of conditions characteristic of transcendental philosophy? Would not such an inquiry, even if successful, only extend the realm of philosophy, taking it back to a foundation which it had not previously suspected, rather than surpass philosophy as such? To pose such questions is perhaps to do no more than find a new application for the kind of questioning already found in 'Violence and Meta-physics', although that is not to say either that Derrida's essay does not extend beyond such questioning or that in writing the essay 'God and Philosophy' Levinas was unaware of their force. 'God and Philosophy' invokes such questioning precisely because it is – in my view – best read as Levinas's reply to Derrida's essay.

It is anyway in order to address such questions that Levinas in 'God and Philosophy' returns to the account of insomnia which he had first presented in 1947 in *Existence and Existents* and had taken up again in 1974 in *Otherwise Than Being* and an essay on Husserl entitled 'From Consciousness to Vigilance.'[22] Insomnia was understood by Levinas in the 1947 work to be the bare fact of the oppression of being held by Being. The vigilance of insomnia is not only a watching without anything to watch, without objects; it is anonymous, so that the ego is also swept away. The 'there is' (*il y a*) encompasses things and consciousness. 'There is no longer any outside or any inside' (*EE*, p. 110/65). Hence Levinas is able to say in 'God and Philosophy' that the vigilance of insomnia can be characterized neither as a modification of the intentionality of consciousness, nor as a simple negation of sleep. Insomnia cannot be referred to consciousness or its opposite. But, by contrast, intentionality can be traced back to insomnia, and sleep remains obedient to vigilance. 'Ever on the verge of awakening, sleep communicates with vigilance' (*DVI*, p. 98/GP, p. 129). In other words, consciousness and sleep together form an oppositional structure with reference to which insomnia is a 'meta-category,' which is reducible neither to consciousness nor sleep, but yet negates and informs them both. The prefix *meta* in 'meta-category' is presumably to be understood in the same sense that it bore when Levinas wrote of metaphysics, although here the provision, which was only implicit earlier, is clearly made: the *meta* becomes meaningful through insomnia and not by way of opposition. Insomnia therefore is presented by Levinas in such a way that it would – at least at first sight – appear to meet the formal demands of a thinking which thinks otherwise.

But this account is not without difficulties which become apparent as soon as we pose the question of how it is possible to say and to think this 'phenomenon' which, because it breaks with consciousness, cannot be a 'phenomenon' in the familiar sense. Levinas concedes this already in *Existence and Existents*, although without apparently offering any solution. 'Our affirmation of an anonymous vigilance goes beyond the *phenomena*, which already presupposes an ego, and thus eludes descriptive phenomenology' (*EE*, p. 112/66). *Otherwise Than Being* takes up this question by acknowledging the *il y a* as an absurdity which signifies, the surplus of nonsense over sense (*AQ*, p. 209/164). These phrases are only a form of affirmation rather than a solution to a problem, which cannot be entirely dismissed but which as a philosophical problem cannot be met with either without returning it to a realm from which it is excluded *ex hypothesi*. Both in *Otherwise Than Being* and in 'God and Philosophy', Levinas confirms the *il y a* as not ontological, but transcendent and – even more surprisingly – as ethical. So, for example, in 'God and Philosophy' the identity of insomnia is understood to be not that of the same, but of the other. For what keeps insomnia from sleep is that it is 'disturbed by the other.' Insomnia is thus found to bear the mark of alterity, like death, the feminine, and fecundity in *Time and the Other*. It has the ethical structure of 'a demand to which no obedience is equal,' the more in the less of infinity, 'dis-interestedness' in its literal sense.

The question of a non-philosophical meaning has become that of whether there is a discourse which signifies otherwise than by signifying a theme (*DVI*, p. 104/GP, p. 132). Levinas – perhaps recalling Derrida's remarks referred to above – is clear that such a discourse could not appeal to experience. Experience depends on philosophy and refers back to the *cogito*. And yet in his quest for another way of thinking and speaking, Levinas turns, as he had done in *Totality and Infinity*, to Descartes who, with 'the idea of the infinite put in us' breaks open the *cogito*. The structure of Descartes' text is, as it were, already a de-structuring (*DVI*, p. 110n./GP, p. 145n.12). 'The actuality of the *cogito* is thus interrupted by way of the Idea of Infinity' (*DVI*, p. 106/GP, p. 133). For the infinite is the more in the less, the surplus which I cannot think but which must be thought in me, as Descartes himself insists.

I would suggest that Levinas repeats his reading of Descartes from *Totality and Infinity* to show that it already bears the basis of a reply to some of Derrida's questions in 'Violence and Meta-physics,' even before they were asked. Levinas finds in the prefix of the word 'infinity' both a negation and an inclusion of the finite: 'as though – without wanting to play on words – the *in* of infinity were to signify both the *non* and the *in* (*dans*)' (*DVI*, p. 106/GP, p. 133). This serves as a response to Derrida's insistence in 'Violence and Metaphysics' that the 'infinitely other' could not be absolutely exterior to the same without ceasing to be other and thereby compromising the closed struc-ture of totality: 'How could there be a "play of the Same" if alterity itself was not already *in* the Same, with a meaning of inclusion already betrayed by the word in (*dans*)' (*ED*, p. 186/126–7)? Derrida in 'Violence and Metaphysics' tends to exag-gerate the dominance of the 'inside-outside' opposition in his reading Levinas and this question is a consequence of his doing so. The sense in which the ' "beyond" the totality and objective is . . . reflected *within* the totality and history, *within* experience' (*TI*, p. xi/23) is clearly marked in *Totality and Infinity* and indeed provides the key to the book. What Levinas does in 'God and Philosophy,' and elsewhere, is to show the double structure of inclusion and negation inscribed in the single word *infinite*. Inclusion in the sense of immanence and negation in the form of exteriority, for Descartes is explicit that the infinite is not arrived at by the simple negation of the finite. When operating separately each fail to mark a 'beyond.' But in the tension of their conjunction, a tension amounting almost to the absurdity of contradiction, the beyond is signified.

Descartes' observation that the idea of the infinite is 'in some way' earlier than the finite is exploited by Levinas in terms of his notion of the trace. The idea of the infinite signifies prior to presence and prior to origin, that is to say, an-archically (*DVI*, p. 107/GP, p. 134). Levinas constructs a chain which links presence, Being, consciousness, intentionality, the unity of apperception, transcendental subjectivity, thematization, and experience. Within this chain philosophy is not so much a knowledge of immanence as immanence itself. It has its extreme form in reminiscence where the past is understood only as a modification of the present and so open to recovery. The trace 'as a past that has never been present' has no place in this chain of philosophical concepts. 'It signifies with a signifyingness from the first older than its exhibition, not exhausting itself in exhibiting itself, not drawing its meaning from its manifestation, and thus breaking with the coincidence of being and appearance in which, for Western philosophy, meaning or rationality lie, breaking with synopsis' (*DVI*, p. 107/GP, p. 134). Levinas's formula 'older than its exhibition' recalls Heidegger's discussion of *Ereignis* as 'the oldest of the old in Western thought: that ancient something which conceals itself in *a-letheia*.'[23] This is not the occasion on which to pursue the question of how far that phrase of Heidegger's constitutes a *historical* reference. To do so would involve an investigation of what it means when Heidegger suggests that the concealment which belongs to metaphysics – the *lethe* in *a-letheia* – only emerges when the history of Being is at an end (*ED*, p. 44/41). There is already an obvious difference in the way that Heidegger engages in a careful – however controversial – reading of the various earliest Greek thinkers of which there is no hint in Levinas. Furthermore, the notion of trace in both thinkers is crucial here. If Derrida has accustomed us to the idea that the thinking of *trace* in Heidegger and Levinas can in some way be joined, even 'reassembled,' Levinas himself would certainly dispute it.[24] But it should not be forgotten that Derrida makes this point always with reference to *différance* as 'older than Being' (*M*, pp. 28/26 and 78/67). And this too is how Levinas conceives the trace: older than Being, than history, than thought.

Having passed from insomnia as a meta-category to the infinite as the beyond inscribed within a philosophical text, Levinas turns to the ethical significance of transcendence. This passage from transcendence to ethics, which Levinas sometimes seems to make light of – for example in his use of Plato's phrase 'the good beyond being' and Descartes' word 'the infinite' – proves decisive for the question of philosophy and its beyond. I shall return later to this transformation whereby 'a description that at the beginning knows only being and beyond being turns into ethical language' (*AQ*, p. 120n./193n.35). For the moment, what is most apparent is the extraordinary originality of the language Levinas uses to describe the ethical relation, both that drawn from *Totality and Infinity* – face, desire, impossibility – and terms like substitution, hostage, and glory from *Otherwise Than Being or Beyond Essence*. Original, that is, in respect of the philosophical tradition, although it is not without precedent in the Talmudic writings which Levinas had been studying since the Second World War. So, for example, when Levinas insists that my responsibility for the other human being extends even to responsibility for his or her responsibility, he has already found this in the Talmud.[25] But 'the impossibility of indifference in respect of the misfortunes and wants of the neighbour – impossible without default' (*DVI*, p. 116/GP, p. 138) is not established by textual authority. It is an 'empirical event,' albeit outside the order of representation or of transcendental apperception. My responsibility extends far beyond any obligations I might have freely contracted.

Such responsibility announces itself in the *me voici*. Levinas adopts it as his translation of *hineni*, the response made by the Lord's servant to the Lord.[26] Unfortunately 'here I am,' its English translation, fails to convey the accusative form of a subject who is always already under the accusation that he or she comes on the scene too late to meet his or her responsibilities – an accusation which is the ethical meaning of the trace (*DVI*, p. 117/GP, p. 138). The 'here I am' is the pronouncement of a 'new identity' (*DVI*, p. 120/GP, p. 140). It says my openness, my exposure without reserve to the other. It is 'sincerity' itself in a sense which Levinas explains as a 'saying without a said' (*le Dire sans Dit*). It is described by Levinas as a speaking so as to say nothing, as simple as 'hello', but at the same time 'the recognition of a debt' (*AQ*, p. 183/143). This saying without a said of sincerity is 'pre-original,' 'prior to all civilization' (*AQ*, p. 182n./198n.6). 'Saying as testimony precedes every Said'

(*DVI*, p. 122/GP, p. 141). It is found in the face of the Other, 'his being "without resources" which has to be heard like cries already addressed to God, although without being voiced or thematized' (*DVI*, 118/GP 139). Levinas is not proposing here an ordering of foundation which simply digs deeper into the foundations. If Levinas in one place describes his own enterprise as 'more ontological than ontology' (*DVI* 143), that 'more' must be understood as the excess of a trace which shows itself in contradiction and disorder or anarchy. In 'God and Philosophy' he is quite explicit that there is 'no question of the transcendental condition for some sort of ethical experience' because it is the break-up of the unity of transcendental apperception as the condition for all being and experience which is at issue (*DVI* 123/GP 141).

And yet are we not always too late for the 'saying without a said'? Is not all saying always in a context determined by a said? This objection gains its force by assimilating Levinas's saying without a said to the more familiar idea of a thought without language. And because Levinas introduces the saying and the said to address the difficulties of saying transcendence, they focus on the same issues which according to Derrida in 'Violence and Metaphysics' are most readily dealt with in terms of the distinction between thought and language. Is not the saying without a said introduced to do the same work as the thought before language which Derrida mourned the lack of in Levinas? And if so, how could we then separate this distinction which promises to take us beyond ontology from the ontological distinction? But the distinction between the saying and the said is so far from being assimilable to that between thought and language that it is even misleading to refer to the former as constituting a distinction at all, for the saying and the said are non-synchronizable. It cannot be said that Levinas introduced this way of addressing the problem of saying transcendence in response to what Derrida wrote in 'Violence and Metaphysics' because it was in certain respects already anticipated in *Totality and Infinity*.[27] So, for example, Levinas writes of the relation with the Other that 'the very utterance by which I state it and whose claim to truth, postulating a total reflection, refutes the unsurpassable character of the face to face relation, nonetheless confirms it by the very fact of stating this truth – of saying [*dire*] it to the Other' (*TI* 196/221). In other words, as a discourse *about* the face to face it belongs to the order of the said, but as addressed to the reader in his or her otherness it is a saying. The multiplicity is recreated in a new face-to-face relation. However, this reference of the discourse about ethics to a saying of ethics is not without its problems, because it might be objected that, if every saying ruptures the said and somehow brings it to transcendence, Levinas has not so much saved ethical discourse but all discourse, and it is formally indifferent whatever is said, be it ethics or any other theme said in a saying.[28] One cannot simply object that the ethical relation according to Levinas is not a theme, because that still leaves unexplained how his discourse is possible, even while granting that any explanation would as such amount to a submission to philosophy's insistence that all discourse be justified before it.

Does the language which testifies to the ethical interruption escape ontology? In 'God and Philosophy' Levinas insists that transcendence can be expressed in such 'ethical terms' as proximity, responsibility, hostage, gift, and so on. But is that supposed to mean that these 'meta-categories' have the same status as the ethical cry of revolt? How could they amount to a saying without a said? When in *Otherwise Than Being or Beyond Essence* Levinas takes up the question of his ethical language and suggests that it 'does not arise out of a special moral experience, independent of the description hitherto elaborated,' his remarks are open to misunderstanding. For although it is clear that he must insist that 'the ethical situation of responsibility is not comprehensible on the basis of ethics' (*AQ* 154/120), does not every attempt to comprehend that situation suffer the same difficulty? Even if one was prepared to acknowledge 'what Alphonse de Waelhens called non-philosophical experiences', would they not become contaminated as soon as they were forced into language? Can any discussion of responsibility, whatever precautions it takes with its language and however strenuously it divorces itself from principles and moral imperatives, maintain itself in independence from any and every specific ethics, as Levinas's obvious indebtedness to Judaic ethics shows?[29] And yet Levinas – as Derrida observed – does not have recourse to the claim that it remains outside language. Indeed, 'the tropes of ethical language are found to be adequate for certain structures of the description: for the sense of the approach in its contrast with knowing, the face in its contrast with phenomenon' (*AQ* 155/120). And yet perhaps we should be more ready to admire and follow the way Levinas shows his commitment to a higher 'value' than that of maintaining a philosophical language in its purity. Some philosophers seem to conceive their only task as that of keeping their hands clean – or rather their language pure. We must above all avoid imposing a purifying formalism on the attempt to say the ethical situation of responsibility, as if that attempt would be contaminated by contact with a concrete ethical situation or a concrete language. We do not need to recall Hegel's exposure in the *Phenomenology of Spirit* of judging consciousness's attempts to keep its hand clean. It is enough to think of Levinas's insistence in the context of a discussion of Buber that ethics lies not in the spiritual realm of friendship, but in a giving which necessarily has to handle the things of this world.[30]

Levinas's 'saying without a said' is not introduced to secure an empty formalism. It may be 'without words' but it is not 'with empty hands' (*DVI* 122/GP 141). To say this is not to open the way to preaching. It arises out of the proximity of the ethical relation and justice, a proximity on which Levinas has always insisted, and which gives rise to that between ethics and ontology. In *Otherwise Than Being*, for example, Levinas explicitly acknowledges that the very gravity of the questions that assail ethics require of it both that it assemble itself in being and that it call for philosophy. The philosopher, on this understanding, shows the beyond in saying and maintains the said in ambiguity (*AQ* 56/44). Levinas is familiar to the point of exasperation with the objection that his own discussion is a thematizing (*AQ* 198/155). He is clear that the beyond, the anarchical, the non-thematizable, can only be said by 'an abuse of language' (*AQ* 148n./196n.19), such as the unsaying of every saying. This unsaying is forced on saying by the latter's association with the said, and the unsaying must unsay itself in turn and so on without halt. There are no definitive formulae, but always only the recourse to an 'otherwise said' (*DVI* 141). It would seem that the so-called positive infinity of Descartes joins forces at this point with the so-called bad infinity of Hegel.

Even if no language is fully adequate to the task, it is the only task worthy of language. One might say with Eliot that:

> each venture
> Is a new beginning, a raid on the inarticulate
> With shabby equipment always deteriorating

'For us, there is only the trying. The rest is not our business.'[31] It is not simply that the language of *Totality and Infinity* proved not to be definitive and so gave way to the language of *Otherwise Than Being* (*DVI* 133). Rather, saying as a non-saying or unsaying allows no language of transcendence to be conceived as definitive. It is always only provisional. But that is not a deficiency.

This saying without a said, and further this saying which unsays itself, lie behind Levinas's claim towards the end of 'God and Philosophy' that not to philosophize is not to philosophize still. The implications of this sentence can best be clarified with reference to the essay 'Ideology and Idealism,' where Levinas is rather more expansive than elsewhere about the way he understands his thinking in relation to the broader currents of nineteenth- and twentieth-century thought.[32] Levinas acknowledges that the critique of ideology as it has been accomplished in the writings of Marx, Nietzsche, and Freud 'probably marks the end of traditional ethics and, in any case, overthrows the theory of duty and of value' (*DVI* 17/*MJE* 123). But Levinas understands this suspicion of ideology as a prophetic cry, 'a voice other than that which bears coherent discourse,' 'a cry denouncing a scandal to which Reason . . . would remain insensitive if there were not this cry.' Levinas is not at all disarmed by the fact that the first victim of this struggle against ideology inspired by ethics is ethics itself. Instead, he interprets it to deny the claim – and he quotes it again in its original form – that 'not to philosophize is still to philosophize.' 'The forcefulness of the break with ethics does not evidence a mere slackening of reason, but rather a questioning of the validity of *philosophizing*, which cannot lapse again into philosophy' (*DVI* 19/*MJE*, p. 124). Elsewhere Levinas says that 'It is necessary not to sleep; it is necessary to philosophize' (*DVI* 35). He means that philosophy is necessary in order to dispel illusions. And yet philosophy itself threatens to be one of the first casualties of the 'suspicion of reason' (*DVI* 136/*MJE* 124). And this suspicion has its source outside philosophy (*DVI*, p. 126/ *MJE* 143). Levinas briefly considers science and structuralism, but he comes to focus on the call for a better society, the rebellion against an unjust society. This 'idealism of disinterestedness,' unlike ethics and unlike philosophy, cannot be dismissed as ideological. And if the call itself is not new, it has taken on the new tonality of youth (*DVI* 26–7/*MJE* 130). Even if ethics is a victim of this rebellion, the rebellion itself is clearly ethical. Perhaps more clearly than elsewhere, the gap between philosophy and the cry of the ethical relation, can be recognized: 'The crisis of meaning, which is evident in the dissemination of verbal signs that the signified no longer dominates (for it would only be illusion and ideological deception), is opposed by the meaning that, spurning words, is prior to the "said," unchallengeable in the nudity of his face, in the proletarian destitution of the Other and in the offence he suffers' (*DVI* 32/*MJE* 135). But if Derridian dissemination is here opposed to the saying without a said, it is also the case that that dissemination can itself be shown to bear an ethical significance.

The last quotation, like many phrases in 'God and Philosophy' or *Otherwise Than Being*, can be recognized as a response to Derrida, but they do not address him directly, as 'Tout Autrement' does.[33] There Levinas admires the intellectual rigor of Derrida's *Speech and Phenomenon* and observes its effect in the way that after Derrida 'one surprises oneself by using familiar notions with a surplus of caution' (*NP* 82). Levinas likens the effect of Derrida's work generally to that of Kant's critical philosophy which similarly showed the naiveté, the unsuspecting dogmatism, at work in previous philosophy. And yet the implication is clear that to accept that there is a parallel between Kant and Derrida is to assimilate Derrida to the history of philosophy, so that his contribution would be simply another instance of the 'growing awareness of the difficulty of thinking,' a further moment in the continuity of philosophy (*NP* 81). The dogmatism that Derrida reveals – although it is surprising that Levinas does not also give Heidegger some of the credit – is that in favour of presence. Derrida 'liberates a system of signs, signifiers without signifieds, a language guided by no full sense'

(*NP* 84). So, if it is still possible to speak the verb to be, 'all is otherwise' (*NP* 85). And it is otherwise in Derrida. Levinas describes the 'reversal of the "limiting concept" into a *precondition* (*préalable*), of defect into source, of abyss into condition, of discourse into place, reversal of these very reversals into fate: the concepts purged of their ontic resonance, released from the alternative of truth and falsehood' (*NP* 82). And yet, as Levinas observes, 'the severe architecture of the deconstructive discourse' remains. He toys with the possibility of contesting Derrida's recourse to logocentric language, but rejects the temptation, although without failing to notice that Derrida himself has often used a similar argument in his polemics (*NP* 85). What Levinas does not say is that he himself was one of the first of those against which Derrida used the argument. Nor does Levinas admit that his own gesture of specifying a possible argument, only to decide not to pursue it, is equally typical of Derrida's discourse. The argument has already been made, even if one has withdrawn one's commitment to it.

At this point in 'Tout Autrement' Levinas calls in question the thinking which 'turns in the circle of being' and asks if ontology is indeed not 'without outlet' (*NP* 87). He observes that for the first time in the West it is possible to think 'the being of the creature,' a phrase he does not explain in this context but which we know from *Totality and Infinity* where a created being is a being which has 'its origin prior to its origin' (*TI* 57/85). 'To posit knowing as the very *existing* of the creature, as the tracing back beyond the condition to the other that founds, is to separate oneself from a whole philosophical tradition that sought the foundation of the self in the self, outside of heteronomous opinions' (*TI* 60/88). These difficult sounding phrases – such as 'its origin prior to its origin' – refer to the way an independent being ('an atheist!') which believes it supplies its own condition can have that condition shattered by virtue of the shame that it feels in the face of the Other who challenges its arbitrary freedom. Levinas, of course, recognizes that he has here passed from an examination of Derrida to an account of his own thinking. Acknowledging that Derrida would probably refuse this line of thought, Levinas renounces 'the ridiculous ambition of "improving" a true philosopher' and cuts short the essay (*NP* 89).

Fortunately the 1978 essay, 'The Thought of Being and the Question of the Other,' takes up the reading of Derrida once more. It is an important essay not only for clarifying Levinas's response to Derrida, but also for understanding how Levinas conceives the way the saying of the said takes place in the history of philosophy. The essay begins with the philosophical question of the meaning of meaning and proceeds quickly – no doubt in recollection of such essays as 'God and Philosophy' – to the recognition that situating meaning in appearance, truth, and the understanding of being is the answer of a specific philosophy. But is it the only answer? Is there another meaning than that recognized by this philosophy? That the question is itself a theoretical or ultimately philosophical one does not exclude the possibility that there is another order of meaning to which it is subordinated (*DVI* 173–4).[34] This is suggested by the crisis of philosophy which takes the form of an inability to satisfy its own criteria of meaning (*DVI* 178). Levinas says elsewhere, philosophy is permanently in crisis (*DVI* 270), but on this occasion he goes further and claims to hear the death-knell of the philosophy of Being in the triumphal and irresistible march of science. The universal communicability of science has done much to challenge the credibility of philosophical language, whose variety amounting frequently to contradiction, was, although Levinas does not say so, what inspired Hegel to present philosophy as a science. Strikingly, Levinas evokes the death-knell of philosophy to establish a context for his discussion of Derrida, just as Derrida set a similar context at the beginning of his presentation of Levinas fourteen years earlier. But, if Levinas gives any significance to the end of philosophy, it is not a philosophical significance, but an ethical one.

Derrida's *Speech and Phenomena* provides a reading of the first of Husserl's *Logical Investigations* which shows at work there a presupposition unsuspected by Husserl, a belief in the privilege of presence.[35] This belief is operative, for example, both in a conception of evidence which appeals to the presence of sense to a full primordial intuition and in the value accorded to the voice and to solitary discourse. Furthermore, Derrida takes this presupposition to be characteristic of Western philosophy generally, to which he also gives the name 'metaphysics,' though not of course in Levinas's sense. Derrida focuses on Husserl's distinction between indication (*Anzeichen*) and expression (*Ausdruck*). He remarks on the fact that meaning is always caught up in an indicative system and shows how Husserl represses this general structure of the sign in the search for a phenomenological situation where expression is no longer contaminated by indication. Or, as Levinas paraphrases Derrida's critique, the plenitude of presence is constantly postponed and 'simply indicated,' whereas in Husserl 'meaning' is referred exclusively to intuitive fullness (*DVI* 181). But for all his admiration of Derrida's text, Levinas is not without reservations. He observes that Derrida's so-called deconstruction of intuition remains faithful to the gnoseological signification of meaning. The notion of the perpetual postponement of presence still conceives metaphysics in its own terms, that is, with reference to presence (*DVI* 182). Does not Derrida, precisely by following Husserl so rigorously, reflect Husserl's own limitations in the very process of exhibiting them?

For my own part I would want to explain this with reference to the way *Speech and Phenomena* is – and perhaps for once the word is properly applied to one of Derrida's texts – a critique rather than a deconstruction. This is not to say that there cannot be elements of critique within a deconstruction, but they are always subordinated to the double reading of the text at issue. In *Speech and Phenomena*, by contrast, the double reading is not developed. In other words, a gesture is made towards outlining a double reading, but then the double reading is repressed in favour of critique. So, at the end of the first chapter, Derrida announces 'two possible readings': one according to which Husserl represses the structure of the sign in general; and the other where the failure to pose the question of the sign is understood as 'critical vigilance,' a proper caution in the face of the assumption that there is an essential unity to the sign (*VP*, pp. 24–5/23–4). Derrida observes these two motifs according to which phenomenology is, on the one hand, an adherence to classical ontology and, on the other hand, the reduction of naive ontology. But then he announces quite explicitly that he has chosen to concern himself with the former (*VP* 27/26), even though he has often instructed his readers – and this is already true for 'Violence and Metaphysics' – on the need to 'interlace the two motifs of deconstruction' which form so-called double reading: the continuous process of making explicit what is implicit in the founding concepts; the discontinuous and irruptive changing of terrain (M, p. 162/134–5).

Why did Derrida restrict himself to one limb of the double reading? Levinas does not pose this question because he is satisfied with his understanding of *Speech and Phenomena* as a critique. But he is not blind to the necessity which makes it impossible to limit the reading of Husserl to a critique, without that reading becoming one-sided and ultimately self-defeating. Levinas learned of this necessity not, it would seem, from Derrida but at the hands of Hegel to whom he credits the view that 'negation, while claiming to refuse being, is still, in its opposition, position on a terrain upon which it rests' (DVI 177). To make good what is lacking in Derrida's text, Levinas focuses on indication. Husserlian indication bears no intrinsic meaning and it is, as a conventional sign, impoverished from the ontological point of view. But Levinas asks whether the indicative sign does not rely on another source of meaning than that of formal association. The extrinsic character of the indication is that of a radical exteriority or difference which cannot be reduced to the manifestation of a content for thought. Instead of regarding indication as a diminished form of intuition, its intelligibility arises from transcendence. It is irreducible to intentionality conceived as adequation with a content. In Husserl's pure indication, 'the one evokes the other without any "hunger" for the other' (DVI 187). Indication cannot therefore be assimilated to consciousness of an object, but is rather affection or passivity: the traumatism of vigilance. In this way, Levinas finds in the postponement or *différance* of pure indication the suspicion of an incessant diachrony (DVI 184). This may not be the second reading of Husserl's text which Derrida only briefly sketches, but is it not the outline of a reading which could perform that role? Of course, construing Derrida as offering a critique of Husserl, Levinas does not conceive his task specifically as that of supplementing Derrida's text in this way. But Levinas's reading of Husserl is governed by the same necessity which produces what in the context of Derrida can be called a double reading or, in his own words, the weaving and interlacing of the two motifs of deconstruction (M 163/135).

Whatever judgment one passes on Levinas's proposed re-reading of Husserl, its significance for us lies in the way of reading the history of philosophy that it announces. Levinas in *Totality and Infinity* is clear in his identification of history and totality. He presents history in *Otherwise Than Being* similarly as 'a time that can be assembled in a present' (*AQ* 107/162). But if the former book already gave a special place to certain phrases of Plato and Descartes, the latter book explains why it meant to do so: it was a recognition of the trace of events on the margins of Western history carrying another signification (*AQ* 224–5/178). The essay 'The Thought of Being and the Question of the Other' takes this discussion a significant stage further. 'The philosophy which is transmitted to us has not failed to name the paradox of non-ontological meaning, even if it immediately returned to being as the ultimate foundation of the reason which it named' (*DVI* 184–5). Alongside the familiar names of Plato and Descartes, Levinas offers his most extended list to date of the occasions when 'under different terms, this relation of transcendence shows itself – even if it is in its purity only for an instant – in the philosophy of knowledge' (*DVI* 185). The list names the agent intellect in Aristotle, the elevation of theoretical reason into practical reason in Kant, the recognition of 'the other man' in Hegel, the renewal of duration in Bergson, and the sobriety of reason in Heidegger. Elsewhere other candidates for inclusion may be found, for example, the truth which challenges as announced in Augustine's *Confessions* (*DVI* 255). That which is beyond ontology is in this way found within the history of philosophy as ontology and in a way which puts this ontology and its denial of transcendence in question. The infinite within the finite, the other within history, the beyond within philosophy.

These references to other thinkers form a list which resembles that of Heidegger's words of Being or Derrida's chain of supplements. I cannot pursue the comparison on this occasion which would also require a consideration of the relation between these lists and the practice of double reading. It should also be noted that even if the saying of transcendence which Levinas finds in and alongside the history of ontology formally has the structure of a double reading – and so addresses the same questions which gives rise to Derrida's practice of double reading – it is not without significant differences. In Derrida, the second limb of a double reading is established by close textual observation of an apparently traditional kind, distinguished only by its readiness to follow the text at issue, even into what standard logic would recognize as contradiction. In Levinas, transcendence is said only as interruption of the ontological. 'Transcendence has to interrupt its own demonstration' (*DVI* 127/143). Its justification of enigma and contradiction is therefore less readily distinguished 'from arbitrariness and illusions' (*AQ* 120n./193n.35). But it can be founded not by resorting to the values recognized by ontology but with reference to the ethical significance of transcendence which goes beyond what the saying of transcendence, as it takes place within ontology, explicitly acknowledges. This concrete ethical significance was already sketched in 'God and Philosophy' and in *Otherwise Than Being*.

At the end of 'The thought of being and the question of the other', Levinas marks the double more explicitly: the one way, that of the evidence of knowledge where the identity of being is sought in its equality with appearance, and the other way, that of the patience of the infinite as an incessant disturbance of the same by the other, the diachrony of time which is concretely produced in my responsibility for the Other or in ethics (*DVI* 188). The acknowledgment of the double is not new in Levinas's writing. It might already be found in his understanding of the *in* of infinity as both negation and inclusion. Or again, in the non-synchronicity of the saying of the said. But the acknowledgment in *Totality and Infinity* that the prophetic word doubles all discourse has another, a further, meaning.[36] 'By essence the prophetic word responds to the epiphany of the face, doubles all discourse not as a discourse about moral themes, but as an irreducible movement of a discourse which by essence is aroused by the epiphany of the face inasmuch as it attests the presence of the third party, the whole of humanity, in the eyes that look at me' (*TI* 188/213). The prophetic word says both the ethical language of the face and the language of justice which belongs to society. It therefore says more than philosophy can say, for the saying without the said of the ethical call would seem always to be beyond it. It is only in the ethical relation and its cry of revolt that there is any escape from philosophy's insistence that all discourse must seek justification from it. But before the face of the Other, philosophy loses its place. Philosophy has to justify itself before ethics, before ethics has to justify itself before philosophy. And yet if philosophy, like justice, arises only 'when the third party enters' (*AQ* 200/157), this is because justice is also a problem for ethics.

Non-philosophy in Levinas's thinking is not determined by the end of philosophy, a notion of which he has long been suspicious because it seems to arise from a totalizing discourse.[37] And yet Levinas gives a special significance to the present crisis of philosophy, suggesting that the moment when philosophy comes to be suspected of being ideology 'is not just any moment' (*DVI* 126/*GP* 143). It does not mark an end, so much as serve as an interruption (*AQ* 24/20). This interruption of philosophy by an ethical cry which comes from outside it is, however, different from the interruption of ontological discourse which takes place by the saying of transcendence. Is it not this suspicion cast on philosophy, and on ethics as a philosophical discipline in particular, which makes possible Levinas's recognition of the ethical significance of the transcendence which is inscribed within the history of philosophy? Would not this differentiate the present crisis of philosophy from other interruptions of philosophy and establish its uniqueness as not just any moment? The so-called crisis of philosophy would then indeed not be a cause for distress (*DK* 64), for it would be the opening up within philosophy of a saying with another signification from that which belongs to philosophy and one whose source is beyond it.

Chapter 11

THE DEATHS OF ROLAND BARTHES[1]

Jacques Derrida

(translated by Pascale-Anne Brault and Michael Naas)

How does one reconcile this plural? With whom might it agree [*accorder*]?[2] And these questions must also be understood in terms of music. With a confident obedience, with a certain abandon that I feel here in it, the plural seems to follow an order, after the beginning of an inaudible sentence, like an interrupted silence. It follows an order and notice, it even obeys, it lets itself be dictated. It asks (for) itself. And as for myself, at the very moment I let myself order a plural for these deaths, I had to give myself over to the law of the name [the law of the number].[3] No objection could resist it, not even the modesty immediately following an uncompromising and punctual decision, a decision which takes place in the almost no time of a [camera's] click. Thus it will have been like this, uniquely, once and for all. And yet I can scarcely bear the apparition of a title in this place. The proper name would have sufficed, for it alone and by itself says death, all deaths in one. It even says death while the bearer of it is still living. While so many codes and rites work to take away this privilege, because it is so terrifying, the proper name alone and by itself forcefully declares the unique disappearance of the unique, I mean the singularity of an unqualifiable death (and this word 'unqualifiable' already resonates like a quotation from one of Roland Barthes' texts that I will reread later). Death inscribes itself right in the name, but it does so *in order to* immediately disperse itself there in order to insinuate a strange syntax – in the name of only one to answer to many.

•

I don't yet know, and in the end it doesn't matter, if I will be able to make it understood why I must leave these thoughts for Roland Barthes fragmentary, or why I value them for their incompleteness even more than for their fragmentation, more for their pronounced incompleteness, for their punctuated but open interruption, without even the authoritative edge of an aphorism. These small pebbles, thoughtfully placed, only one each time, on the edge of a name like the promise of return.

•

These thoughts are *for him*, for Roland Barthes, meaning that I think of him and about him, not only of or about his work. 'For him' also suggests that I would like to dedicate these thoughts to him, give them to him, and destine them for him. But they will no longer reach him, and this must be the starting point of my thought; they can no longer reach him or reach out to him, if ever they could have while he was still living. So where do they go? To whom and for whom? Only for him in me? In you? In us? It's not the same thing, it's done so many times, and as soon as he is in another the other is no longer the same, I mean the same as himself. And yet Barthes himself is no longer there. We must hold fast to this evidence, to its excessive clarity, and continually return to it as if it were the most simple, as if it were that alone which, while withdrawing into the impossible, still gives and allows for thought.

•

(No) more light, leaving something to be desired and to be thought.[4] To know or rather to accept that which leaves something to be desired, to love it from an invisible source of light. From where did the singular clarity of Barthes come? From where did it come to him, since he also had to receive it? Without simplifying anything, without doing violence to either the fold [*pli*] or the reserve, it always *emanated* from a certain point which yet was not a point, remaining invisible in its own way, a point which I cannot locate – and of which I would like, if not to speak, to give at least an idea of what it remains for me.

•

To keep [the other] alive within oneself: is this the best sign of fidelity? Uncertain whether I was in fact going to the most living, I just read two of his books that I had never read before. I thus secluded myself on this island as if to convince myself that nothing had stopped. And so I believed this, and each book told me what to think of this belief. I had, for quite different reasons, postponed reading these two books, the first and the last. First, *Writing Degree Zero*: I understood better its power and necessity beyond all that had previously turned me away from it, and it was not only because of the capital letters, the connotations, the rhetoric, and all the signs of an era which I had then thought I was *leaving* [*sortir*] and from which it seemed necessary to take [*sortir*] the writing. But in this book of 1953, as in those of Blanchot to which he often sends us, the movement which I awkwardly and mistakenly call the exit [*la sortie*] is underway. And second, *Camera Lucida*, whose time and tempo accompanied his death as no other book, I believe, has ever kept vigil over its author.

•

For a first and a last book, *Writing Degree Zero* and *Camera Lucida* are timely [*heureux*] titles. It is a dreadful and dreadfully unstable timeliness [*bonheur*], made up of chance and predestination. I like to think of Roland Barthes now, as I endure this sadness, that which is mine today and that which I always thought I felt in him, a sadness which was cheerful yet weary, desperate, lonely, refined, cultivated, epicurean, so incredulous in the end, always letting go without clinging, endless, fundamental, and yet disappointed with the essential. I like to think of him in spite of the sadness, as of someone who in fact never renounced any pleasures [*jouissance*] but instead treated himself to all of them. And if one may say, as families in mourning naively say, though I feel certain I can say it, he would have liked the thought. To put it differently, the image of the I of Barthes would have liked this thought, the image of the I of Barthes that Barthes inscribed in me, though neither he nor I are completely in it. I tell myself now that this image likes this thought in me, that it rejoices in it here and now, that it smiles at me. Since I've read *Camera Lucida*, Roland Barthes' mother, whom I never knew, smiles to me at this thought, as at everything she breathes life into and revives with pleasure. She smiles at him and thus in me, since, let's say, the Winter Garden Photograph, since the radiant invisibility of a look [*regard*] which he describes to us only as clear, so clear.

•

Thus for the first time I read the first and last Barthes, with the welcomed naïveté of a desire, *as if* to read the first and last without stopping, to read them back to back, as a single volume with which I would have secluded myself on an island. I was finally going to see and know everything. Life was going to continue (there was still so much to read) but perhaps a history was going to gather itself, a history related to itself, History having become Nature in this collection, *as if*. . . .

•

I just capitalized Nature and History. He used to do it almost all the time. He did it frequently in *Writing Degree Zero*, and from the very beginning. 'No one can without formalities pretend to insert his freedom as a writer into the resistant medium of language because, behind the latter, the whole of History stands unified and complete in the manner of a Natural Order.'5 And again in *Camera Lucida*:

> this couple who I know loved each other, I realize: it is love-as-treasure which is going to disappear forever; for once I am gone, no one will any longer be able to testify to this: nothing will remain but an indifferent Nature. This is a laceration so intense, so intolerable, that alone against his century, Michelet conceived of History as love's Protest.6

These capital letters which I myself used out of mimicry, he too played with, in order to mime and, already back then, to quote. They are quotation marks ('this is how you say') which, far from indicating an hypostatization, actually lift up and lighten, expressing disillusionment and incredulity. I don't think he believed in this opposition [Nature/History] (or in any others). He would use them only for a time. Further on, I would like to show that the concepts which seemed the most squarely opposed, or opposable, were put in play by him, the one *for* the other, in a metonymic composition. This lighthearted way of mobilizing [concepts] by playing them against each other [*déjouant*] could provoke a certain logic, while at the same time resisting it with the greatest force, with the greatest force of play.

•

As if: I read these two books *one after the other*, as if the negative of a type of language were finally going to appear and develop before my eyes, as if the pace, step, style, timbre, tone, and gestures of Roland Barthes – so many signatures obscurely familiar, already recognizable among all others – were all of a sudden going to yield me their secret, as one more secret hidden behind the others (and I call secret not only that which is intimate but that which is like a style: the inimitable); I read these two books as if the unique trait were all of a sudden going to appear in full light. And yet I was so grateful for what he said about the 'unary photograph,' which works naturally against itself as soon as it negates the 'poignant' in the 'studied,'[7] the *punctum* in the *studium*. I was dreaming: as if the point of singularity, even before becoming a line, though continuously asserting itself from the first book to that which in the last book was its interruption, were resisting in different ways, though resisting nonetheless, the mutations, upheavals or displacements of terrain, the diversity of objects, corpora and contexts. I was dreaming: as if the insistence of the invariable were finally going to be revealed to me as it is in itself – and in something like a detail. Yes, it was from a detail that I asked for the ecstasy of revelation, the instantaneous access to Roland Barthes (to him and him alone), a free and easy access requiring no labor. I was expecting this access to be provided by a detail, which would at once be very visible and very hidden (too obvious); I was not expecting this access to be provided by the great themes, subjects, theories, or strategies of writing which, for a quarter of a century, I thought I knew and could easily recognize throughout the various 'periods' of Roland Barthes (what he called 'phases' and 'genres' in *Roland Barthes by Roland Barthes*). I was searching *like him*, as him, and in the situation in which I write since his death, a certain mimicry is at once a duty (to take him into oneself, to identify oneself with him in order to let him speak, to make him present and faithfully to represent him) and the worst of temptations, the most indecent, the most murderous; it is the gift *and* the revocation of the gift, just try to choose. Like him, I was looking for the *freshness* [*fraicheur*] of a reading in relation to detail. His texts are familiar to me but I don't yet know them – this is my certainty – and this is true of all writing that matters to me. The word 'freshness' is his and it plays an essential role in the axiomatics of *Writing Degree Zero*. The interest in detail was also his. Benjamin saw in the analytic enlargement of the fragment or minute signifier a point of intersection between the era of psychoanalysis and the era of technical reproduction, as seen in cinematography, photography, etc. (Moving through, extending beyond, and exploiting the resources of phenomenological *as well as* structural analysis, Benjamin's essay and Barthes' last book could very well be the two most significant texts on the so-called question of the Referent in the technological age.) The word *punctum*, moreover, translates, in *Camera Lucida*, one meaning of the word 'detail': a point of singularity which punctures the surface of the reproduction – and even the production – of analogies, likenesses and codes. It pierces, strikes me, wounds me, bruises me, and, first of all, seems to look only at me. Its definition is that it addresses itself to me; it is the Referent which, through its own image, I can no longer suspend, while its 'presence' forever escapes me, having already receded into the past. (That is why the word 'Referent' could be a problem if it were not reformed by the context.) It addresses itself to me, this solitude which tears the fabric of the same, the networks and ruses of economy. But it is always the singularity of the other in so far as it comes to me without being directed towards me, without being present to me; and the other can even be 'me,' me having been or having had to be, me already dead in the future anterior and past anterior of my photograph. And, I will add, in my name as well. Although it seems, as always, slightly pronounced, this range of the dative or accusative which addresses to *me* or destines *me* the punctum, is, I think, essential to the category [of the punctum], at least as far as it is put into play in *Camera Lucida*. If we bring together two different aspects or exposures of the same concept, it indeed appears that the *punctum* points to *me* at the instant and place where I point to it; it is thus that the punctuated photograph points me. Even on its minute surface, the same point divides itself: this double punctuation disorganizes from the start both the unary and the desire that finds its order there. First exposure: 'it is this element which rises from the scene, shoots out of it like an arrow, and pierces me. A Latin word exists to designate this wound, this prick, this mark made by a pointed instrument: the word suits me all the better in that' (*CL*, p. 26). (This is the form of what I was looking for, of *what suits him* and is relevant only to him; as always, he claims he is looking for what comes *to him* and suits him, what agrees with him and fits him like a garment; and even if it is a readymade garment, and only in fashion for a certain time, it must conform itself to the inimitable *habitus* of a unique body; thus to choose these words, either new or very old, from the treasury of languages, as one picks out a garment, taking everything into account: the season, the fashion, the place, the fabric, the shade, the cut.)

> the word suits me all the better in that it also refers to the notion of punctuation, and because the photographs I am speaking of are in effect punctuated, sometimes even speckled with these sensitive points; precisely, these marks, these wounds are so many *points*. This second element which will disturb the *studium* I shall therefore call *punctum*; for *punctum* is also: sting, speck, cut, little hole – and also a cast of the dice. A photograph's *punctum* is that accident which pricks me (but also bruises me, is poignant to me). (*CL*, pp. 26–7)

This parenthesis does not enclose an incidental or secondary thought: as it often does, it lowers the voice – as in an *aside* – out of a sense of modesty. And elsewhere, twenty [thirteen] pages later, *another exposure*.

> Having thus reviewed the *docile interests* which certain photographs awaken in me, I deduced that the *studium*, in so far as it is not traversed, lashed, striped by a detail (*punctum*) which attracts or distresses me, engenders a very widespread type of photograph (the most widespread in the world), which we might call the *unary photograph*. (*CL*, p. 40)

•

His *manner*, the way in which he displays, plays with, and interprets the pair *studium/punctum*, while at the same time explaining what he is doing by giving us his *notes* – and a little later on we will hear the music. This manner is unmistakably his. He makes the opposition *studium/punctum* and the evident *versus* of the bar appear slowly and cautiously in a new context, a context in which, it seems, they had no chance of appearing before. He gives to them or he welcomes this chance. The interpretation can at first appear rather artificial, ingenuous, elegant perhaps, but specious, for example in the passage from the *point* to the *pointing me* to the *poignant*, but little by little it imposes its necessity without concealing the artifact under some invented nature. It demonstrates its rigor throughout the book, and this rigor mixes its productivity with its performative fecundity. He makes it *yield* the greatest amount of meaning, of descriptive or analytic power (phenomenological, structural, and even beyond). The rigorousness is never rigid. In fact, the supple [*le souple*] is a category which I believe to be indispensable to any description of Barthes' manners. The virtue of suppleness is practiced without the least trace of either labor or labor's effacement. He never did without it, whether it was in theorization, writing strategies, or social intercourse; and it can even be read in the graphics of his writing, which I read as the extreme refinement of the civility he locates, in *Camera Lucida* and while speaking of his mother, at the limits of and even beyond the moral. It is a suppleness which is *liée* [linked] and at the same time *déliée* [unlinked, flowing, shrewd], as one says of writing or of the mind. In the liaison as well as in the undoing of the liaison, it never excludes accuracy [*justesse*] or justice; it must have secretly served him, I imagine, even in the impossible choice. The conceptual rigor of an artefact remains supple and playful here, and it lasts the time of a book; it will be useful to others but it only suits perfectly the one who signs it, like an instrument that can't be lent to anyone, like the [unique] history of an instrument. For above all, and in the first place, this apparent opposition (*studium/punctum*) does not forbid but, on the contrary, facilitates a certain *composition* between the two concepts. What is to be understood by composition? Two things which compose together. First, separated by an insuperable limit, the two concepts exchange compromises;

they compose together, the one *with* the other, and we will later recognize in this a *metonymic* operation; the 'subtle beyond' of the *punctum*, the uncoded beyond, composes with the 'always coded' of the *studium* (*CL*, pp. 59, 51). It belongs to it without belonging to it and is unlocatable in it; it never inscribes itself in the homogeneous objectivity of the framed space but instead inhabits, or rather haunts it: 'it is an addition [*supplément*]: it is what I add to the photograph and *what is none the less already there*' (*CL*, p. 55). We are prey to the ghostly power of the supplement; it is this unlocatable site which gives rise to the specter.

> The *Spectator* is ourselves, all of us who glance through
> collections of photographs – in magazines and
> newspapers, in books, albums, archives. . . . And the
> person or thing photographed is the target, the referent,
> a kind of little simulacrum, any *eidolon* emitted by the object,
> which I should like to call the *Spectrum* of the photograph,
> because this word retains, through its root, a relation to
> 'spectacle' and adds to it that rather terrible thing which
> is there in every photograph: the return of the dead. (*CL*,
> p. 9)

As soon as it ceases to oppose the *studium*, while still retaining its heterogeneity, as soon as we can no longer distinguish between two places, contents or things, the *punctum* is not entirely subjugated to a concept, if by this one means a predicative, distinct, and opposable determination. This concept of a ghost is as scarcely perceptible in itself [*en personne*] as the ghost of a concept. Neither life nor death, it is the haunting of the one by the other. The *versus* of the conceptual opposition is as insubstantial as a camera's click. '*Life/Death*: the paradigm is reduced to a simple click, the one separating the initial pose from the final print' (*CL*, p. 92). Ghosts: the concept of the other in the same, the *punctum* in the *studium*, the dead other alive in me. This concept of the photograph *photographs* all conceptual oppositions, it traces a relationship of haunting which perhaps is constitutive of all logics.

•

I was thinking of a second meaning of *composition*. Thus, in the

ghostly opposition of the two concepts, in the pair S/P, *studium/
punctum*, the composition is also the music. One could open
here a long chapter: Barthes as musician. In a note, one would
(to begin) locate such an analogy between the two heterogeneous elements S and P. One can discretely suggest, with
the relation no longer a simple exclusion, with the punctual
supplement parasiting the haunted space of the *studium*, that
the *punctum* gives rhythm to the *studium*, that is, 'scans' it.

> The second element will break (or punctuate [*scander*: to
> scan]) the *studium*. This time it is not I who seek it out (as
> I invest the field of the *studium* with my sovereign
> consciousness), it is this element which rises from the
> scene, shoots out of it like an arrow, and pierces me. A
> Latin word exists . . . *punctum*. (*CL*, p. 26)

With the relationship to scansion already stressed, music
returns, from some other place, at the bottom of the same page.
Music, and more precisely, the composition: the analogy of the
classical sonata. As he often does, Barthes is in the process of
describing his train of thought, of giving us an account of what
he is doing while he is doing it (what I earlier called his notes).
He does so rhythmically, progressively, according to the tempo,
in the classical sense of tempo; he marks the various stages
(elsewhere he underlines in order to accentuate and, perhaps,
to play point against point, or point against study: '*at this point
in my investigation*') (*CL*, p. 55; italics omitted in translation). In
short, he is going to make it understood, with an ambiguous
gesture of modesty and defiance, that he will not treat the pair
of concepts S and P as essences coming from outside a text in
the process of being written, thereby lending themselves to
some vague philosophical significance. They only carry the
truth within an irreplaceable musical composition. They are
motifs. If one wishes to transpose them elsewhere, and it is
possible, useful, and even necessary, one must proceed analogi-
cally, though the operation will not be successful unless the
other opus, the other system of composition, itself carries these
motifs in a way just as original and irreplaceable. Hence:
'Having thus distinguished two themes in Photography (for in
general the photographs I liked were constructed in the manner

of a classical sonata), I could occupy myself with one after the other' (*CL*, p. 27).

•

It would be necessary to return to the 'scansion' of the *studium* by a *punctum* which is not opposed to it even though it remains completely other, a *punctum* which comes to stand in for it, link itself to it, and compose with it. I am thinking of a musical composition in counterpoint, of all the sophisticated forms of counterpoint and polyphony, of the fugue.

•

The Winter Garden Photograph: the invisible *punctum* of the book. It doesn't belong to the corpus of photographs he exhibits, to the series of examples he displays and analyzes. Yet it irradiates the entire book. A sort of radiant serenity comes from his mother's eyes, the clarity of which he describes but we never see. The radiance composes with the wound that signs the book, with an invisible *punctum*. *At this point*, he no longer speaks of light or photography, of anything to be seen, but of the voice of the other, the accompaniment, the song, the accord, the 'last music':

> Or again (for I am trying to express this truth) the Winter Garden Photograph was for me like the last music Schumann wrote before collapsing, that first *Gesang der Frühe* which accords with both my mother's being and my grief at her death; I could not express this accord except by an infinite series of adjectives. (*CL*, p. 70)

And elsewhere:

> in a sense I never 'spoke' to her, never 'discoursed' in her presence, for her; we supposed, without saying anything of the kind to each other, that the frivolous insignificance of language, the suspension of images must be the very space of love, its music. Ultimately I experienced her, strong as she had been, my inner Law, as my feminine child. (*CL*, p. 72; 'Law' is capitalized in original but not in Howard's translation)

•

269

For him, I would have wanted to avoid not evaluation (if it were possible or even desirable) but all that which insinuates itself into the most implicit evaluation in order to return to the coded (once again to the *studium*). For him I would have wanted, without succeeding at it, to write at the limit, as close to the limit as possible but also beyond the 'neutral,' 'colorless,' 'innocent' writing of which *Writing Degree Zero* shows at once the historical novelty and the infidelity. 'If the writing is really neutral . . . then Literature is vanquished. . . . Unfortunately, nothing is more fickle than a colourless writing; mechanical habits are developed in the very place where freedom existed, a network of set forms hem in more and more the pristine freshness of discourse' (*WDZ*, p. 78). It is not a question here of vanquishing literature but of preventing it from neatly and cleverly sealing up the singular and flawless wound (nothing is more unbearable or laughable than all the expressions of guilt in mourning, all its inevitable spectacles).

•

To write – to him, to present to the dead friend within oneself the gift of his innocence. For him, I would have wanted to avoid, and thus to spare him, the double wound of speaking of him, here and now, as one of the living *or* one of the dead. In both cases I disfigure, I wound, I sleep, or I kill. But whom? Him? No. Him in me? In us? In you? But what does this mean? That we remain among ourselves? This is true but still rather simple. Roland Barthes looks at us (inside of each of us, so each of us can then say that Barthes' thought, memory and friendship concern only us) and we do not do as we please with this look, although each of us has it at his own disposal, in his own way, according to his own place and history. It is within us but it is not ours; we do not have it available to us like a part or moment of our interiority. And that which looks at us may be indifferent, loving, dreadful, grateful, attentive, ironic, silent, bored, reserved, fervent, or smiling, a child or already close to death; in short, it can present in us all the signs of life or death which we draw from the circumscribed reserve of his texts or our memory.

•

I would have wanted to avoid neither the Novel nor the Photograph but something in both, which is neither life nor death but something he himself said before I did (and I will return to this – always the promise of return, a promise which no longer facilitates the composition). I will not succeed in avoiding this, precisely because this *point* always lets itself be reappropriated by the cloth which it tears toward the other, because the studied veil always mends its ways. But perhaps it would be better not to achieve this, not to succeed, and to prefer, in the end, the spectacle of inadequacy, failure, and especially here, truncation. (Is it not derisory, naïve, and downright childish to present oneself in front of the dead to ask for their forgiveness? Is there any meaning in this? Unless it is the origin of meaning itself? The origin of the scene you would make with the others who observe you and who also play off the dead? A thorough analysis of the 'childishness' in question would here be necessary but insufficient.)

•

Two infidelities, an impossible choice: on the one hand, not to say anything which concerns only oneself or one's own voice, to remain silent, or at the very least to let oneself be accompanied or preceded in counterpoint by the friend's voice. Thus, out of approbation, out of a zealous devotion or gratitude, to content oneself with just quoting, with just accompanying that which more or less directly belongs to the other, to let him speak, to efface oneself in front of and to follow his speech, and to do so right in front of him. But this excess of fidelity would end up saying and exchanging nothing. It returns to death. It points to death, sending death back to death. On the other hand, by avoiding all quotation, all identification, all rapprochement even, so that that which is addressed to or spoken of Roland Barthes really comes from the other, from the living friend, one risks making him disappear again, as if one could add more death to death and thus indecently pluralize it. It remains then to do and not to do both at once, to correct one infidelity by the other. From one death, the other: is this the uneasiness that ordered me to begin with a plural?

•

271

Already, and often, I know that I have written *for him* (I always say him, to write to him, to address him, to avoid him); well before these fragments. For him: but persistently I want to recall, for him, that today there is no respect, no living respect that is, no living attention paid to the other, to the only name hereafter of Roland Barthes, that doesn't have to expose itself without respite, without weakness, and without mercy to this evidence which is too transparent not to be immediately exceeded: Roland Barthes is the name of he who can no longer hear or bear it. And he [*il*; Roland Barthes] (not the name but the bearer of the name) will receive nothing of what I say here of him, for him, to him, beyond the name but still within it, as I pronounce his name which yet is no longer his. This living attention tears itself toward that which can no longer receive it; it precipitates toward the impossible. But if his name is no longer his, was it ever? I mean simply, uniquely?

•

The impossible sometimes, by chance, becomes possible: as in a utopia. This is in fact what he said before his death, though for him, of the Winter Garden Photograph. Beyond analogies, 'it achieved for me, utopically, *the impossible science of the unique being*' (CL, p. 71). He said this uniquely, turned toward his mother and not toward the Mother, but the poignant singularity does not refute the generality, it does not prevent it from having the force of law but only arrows it, marks, and signs it. Is there, then, in the first language, in the first mark, another possibility, another chance beyond the pain of this plural? And as for metonymy? And homonymy? Would it be possible to suffer from something else? Could we speak without them?

•

What we could playfully call the *mathesis singularis*, what is achieved for him 'utopically' in front of the Winter Garden Photograph, is impossible and yet takes place, utopically, metonymically, as soon as it marks, as soon as it writes, even 'before' language. Barthes speaks of utopia at least twice in *Camera Lucida*. Two times he speaks of it between his mother's death and his own – that is, in as much as he entrusts it to writing: 'Once she was dead I no longer had any reason to attune myself to the progress of the superior Life Force (the race, the species). My particularity could never again universalize itself (unless, utopically, by writing, whose project henceforth would become the unique goal of my life)' (*CL* p. 72).

•

When I say Roland Barthes it is certainly him whom I name, him beyond his name. But since he himself is now inaccessible to this appellation, since this nomination cannot become a vocation, address, or apostrophe (supposing that this possibility revoked today could ever have been pure), it is him in me that I name; through his name, it is toward him in me, in you, in us that I am drawn. What happens and what is said remains between us. The mourning began at this point. But when? Indeed, even before the unqualifiable event called death, interiority (of the other in me, in you, in us) had already begun its work. With the first nomination, it preceded death as another death would have done. The name alone makes possible the plurality of deaths. And even if the link between them were analogical, the analogy would be singular, without common measure with any other. Before death without analogy or relief [*relève*], before death without name or sentence, before that in front of which we have nothing to say and must remain silent, before that which he calls 'my total, undialectical death' (*CL*, p. 72), before the last death, the other movements of interiorization were at the same time more and less powerful, powerful *in a different way*, and, *in a different way*, more and less certain of themselves. More inasmuch as they were not yet disturbed or interrupted by the deathly silence of the other, the silence which always comes to remind us of the limits of a speaking interiority. Less inasmuch as the appearance, the initiative, the response, or the unforeseeable intrusion of the living other *also* recalls this limit. Living, Roland Barthes cannot be reduced to that which each or all of us can think, believe, know, and already recall of him. But once dead, might he be so reduced? No, but the chances of the illusion will be greater *and* lesser, different in any case.

'Unqualifiable' is another word I borrow from him. Even if I transpose and modify it, it remains marked by that which I read in *Camera Lucida*. 'Unqualifiable' there designated a way of life

– it was for a short time his, after his mother's death – a life which already resembled death, one death before the other, more than one [actually], a life which mimicked death in advance. This doesn't prevent it from having been an accidental and unforeseeable death, outside the realm of calculation. Perhaps this resemblance allows for the transposition of the unqualifiable in life into death. Thus:

> It is said that mourning, by its gradual labor, slowly erases pain; I could not, I cannot believe this; because for me, Time eliminates the emotion of loss (I do not weep), that is all. For the rest, everything has remained motionless. For what I have lost is not a Figure (the Mother), but a being; and not a being, but a *quality* (a soul): not the indispensable, but the irreplaceable. I could live without the Mother (as we all do, sooner or later); but what life remained would be absolutely and entirely *unqualifiable* (without quality). (CL, p. 75)

•

La chambre claire no doubt says more than *camera lucida*, the name of the apparatus anterior to photography which Barthes opposes to *camera obscura*. I can no longer not associate the word luminosity [*clarté*], wherever it appears, with what he says much earlier of his mother's face when she was a child, of 'the luminosity of her face' (CL, p. 69; Howard translates *clarté* as 'distinctness'). And he soon adds: 'the naive attitude of her hands, the place she had docilely taken without either showing or hiding herself.'

•

Without either showing or hiding herself. Not the Figure of the Mother but his mother. There should be no metonymy in this case; love protests against it ('I could live without the Mother').

•

Without either showing or hiding herself. This is what took place. She had already occupied her place 'docilely,' without initiating the slightest activity, according to most gentle passivity, and she neither shows nor hides herself. The possibility of this impossibility details and shatters all unity, and this is love; it disorganizes all discourses and studies, all theoretical systems and philosophies. They must decide between presence and absence, here and there, what reveals and what conceals itself. Here, there, the unique other, his mother, appears, that is to say, without appearing, because the other can only appear by disappearing. And his mother 'knew' how to do this so innocently, because it is the quality of a child's soul that he deciphers in her unpretentious pose, in her pose-without-pose. He says nothing more and underlines nothing.

•

He speaks, moreover, of the luminosity as the 'evidential power' of the Photograph (*CL*, p. 47). But this carries both presence and absence; it neither shows nor hides itself. In the passage on the *camera lucida* he quotes Blanchot:

the essence of the image is to be altogether outside, without intimacy, and yet more inaccessible and mysterious than the thought of the innermost being; without signification, yet summoning up the depth of any possible meaning; unrevealed yet manifest, having the absence-as-presence which constitutes the lure and fascination of the Sirens. (*CL*, p. 106)[8]

•

He insists, and rightly so, upon the adherence of the 'photographic referent': it doesn't relate to a present or to a real but, in a different way, to the other, and each time differently according to the type of 'image' (photographic or not. All differential precautions being taken, it will not be a reduction of what he says about the photograph specifically to find it pertinent elsewhere: I would even say everywhere. It is a matter of at once acknowledging the possibility of suspending the Referent (not the reference) wherever it is found, including in the photograph, and of suspending a naive conception of the Referent, one which is so often taken for granted.)

•

A brief and preliminary classification rooted in common sense:

there are, in the *time* that brings us back to texts and to their presumed, nameable, and authorized signatories, at least three possibilities. The 'author' can already be dead, in the usual sense of the word, at the moment we begin to read 'him,' indeed even when this reading orders us to write, as we say, about him, whether it be about his writings or about himself. These authors whom we never 'knew' while they were living, whom we never met or loved (or did not), make up by far the greatest number. This asymbiosis does not exclude a certain modality of the contemporaneous (and vice versa), for it too implies a degree of interiorization, an *a priori* mourning rich in possibility, a complete experience of absence which I cannot here describe in its original form. A second possibility is that the authors are living when we are reading them, indeed even when this reading orders us to write about them, etc. We can, knowing that they are alive, and this involves a bifurcation of the same possibility, know them or not, and once having met them, love them (or not, etc.). And the situation can change in this regard; we can meet them after having begun to read them (I have such a vivid memory of my first meeting with Barthes), and a thousand different relay systems can confirm the transition: photographs, correspondence, hearsay, tape recordings, [etc.]. And then there is a 'third' situation: at the death and after the death of those whom we also 'knew,' met, loved, etc. [. . .] Thus it has happened that I write about or in the wake of texts whose authors have been dead long before I read them (for example, Plato or John of Patmos) or whose authors are still living at the time I write, and this is apparently always the most risky. But what I thought impossible, indecent, and unjustifiable, what long ago and more or less discretely and resolutely I had promised myself never to do (out of a concern for rigor or fidelity if you will, and because it is in this case *too* serious), was to write *at the death*, not after, not long after the death *by returning* to it, but at the death, *on the occasion of the death*, at the commemorative gatherings and tributes, in the writings 'to the memory' of those who if still living would have been my friends, still present enough to me that some 'declaration,' indeed some analysis or 'study,' would seem at that moment completely intolerable.

– But what then? Silence? Is this not another wound, another insult?

– To whom?

– Yes, to whom and of what do we make a gift? What are we doing when we exchange these discourses? Over what are we keeping watch? Are we trying to negate death or retain it? Are we trying to put things in order, make amends, or settle our accounts? With the other? With the others outside and inside ourselves? How many voices intersect, observe, and correct each other, argue with each other, passionately embrace each other, or pass by each other in silence? Are we going to evaluate them and single out a final authority? Should we convince ourselves that the death never took place or that it is irreversible, that we are protected from a return of the dead? Or should we make the dead our ally ('the dead within me'), take him by our side, or even take him inside, to draw up secret contracts, to finish him off by exalting him, to reduce him in any case to that which can still be contained by a literary or rhetorical performance, a performance that highlights its own qualities according to stratagems whose analysis would be interminable, as are all the ruses of the individual or collective 'labor of mourning'? And this so-called 'labor' still remains and names a problem here. For if mourning labors, it does so only to dialectize death, to dialectize that which Roland Barthes *called* 'undialectical' ('I could do no more than await my total, undialectical death') (*CL*, p. 72).

•

A bit [*morceau*] of myself like a bit of the dead [*mort*]. To say 'the deaths,' is thus to dialectize them or, as I would want, the contrary (though we are here at a limit where to want is never enough)? Mourning and transference. In a discussion with Ristat about the 'practice of writing' and self-analysis I remember him saying: 'Self-analysis is not transferential, and it is there perhaps that the psychoanalysts would disagree.' Probably so. Perhaps there is still transference in self-analysis, particularly when it proceeds through writing and literature; but transference plays differently, it plays more – and the difference in the play is essential here. Considering the possibility of writing, we need another concept of transference (if there ever was one).

•

For what was earlier called 'at the death,' 'on the occasion of death': a whole series of typical solutions. The worst ones, or the worst one in each of them, are either base or derisory, and yet so common: still to maneuver, to speculate, to try to profit or derive some benefit, whether it be subtle or sublime, to draw from the dead a supplementary force that one directs toward the living in order to denounce or insult them more or less directly, to authorize and legitimate oneself, to raise oneself to the very heights where we presume death has placed the other beyond all suspicion. There are of course lesser offenses, but offenses nonetheless: to pay homage with an essay that treats the work or a part of the work bequeathed to us, to talk on a theme that we confidently believe would have interested the author who has passed away (whose tastes, curiosities, and project should, it seems, no longer surprise anyone). Such a treatment would both point out the debt and repay it; and one would tailor one's remarks according to the context. For example, in *Poétique*, to stress the essential role Barthes' works have played and will continue to play in the open field of literature and literary theory (it is legitimate, one has to do it, and I am doing it now). And then, why not, to engage in, as an exercise made possible and influenced by Barthes (an initiative which would find approval in us through the memory of him), the analysis of a genre or discursive code, the rules of a particular social arrangement, and to do so with his meticulousness and vigilance, which, as uncompromising as they were, still knew how to yield with a certain disenchanted compassion, a rather nonchalant elegance that would make him give up the fight (though I sometimes saw him get angry over a question of ethics or fidelity). But what genre? Well, for example, what in this century has come to replace the funeral oration. We could study the corpus of declarations in newspapers, on radio and television; we could analyze the recurrences, the rhetorical constraints, the political perspectives, the exploitations by individuals and groups, the pretexts for taking a stand, for threatening, intimidating, or reconciling. (I am thinking of the weekly newspaper which, upon Sartre's death, dared to put on trial those who deliberately, or simply because they were away, had said nothing or had said the wrong thing. Using their photographs to bring them to justice, the newspaper accused all of them in the title of still being afraid of Sartre.) In its classical form, the funeral oration had a good side, especially when it permitted one to call out directly to the dead, sometimes very informally [*tutoyer*]. This is of course a supplementary fiction, for it is always the dead in me, always the others standing around the coffin, whom I call out to; but because of its caricatured excess, the overstatement of this rhetoric pointed out that we could no longer remain among ourselves. The interactions of the living must be interrupted, the veil has to be torn toward the other, the other dead *in us* though other still, and the religious promises of an afterlife could indeed still grant this 'as if.'

•

The deaths of Roland Barthes: *his* deaths, these and those of his relatives, those deaths which must have inhabited him, situating places and solemn moments, orienting tombs in his interior space (his mother's death to end and probably even to begin with). *His* deaths, those he lived in the plural, those he must have linked together, trying in vain to 'dialectize' them before the 'total' and 'undialectical' death; those deaths which always form in our lives a terrifying and endless series. But how did he 'live' them? No answer is more impossible or forbidden than this one. But a certain movement had quickened in those last years; I could feel a sort of autobiographical acceleration, as if he were saying 'I am aware that I have little time left.' I must concern myself first with this thought of a death that begins, like thought and like death, in the memory of language. While still living, he wrote a death of Roland Barthes by himself. And finally *his* deaths, his texts about death, everything he wrote, with such insistence on displacement, on death, on the theme of Death if you will, if indeed there is such a theme. From the novel to the photograph, from *Writing Degree Zero* (1953) to *Camera Lucida* (1980), a certain thought about death set everything into motion, into transit really, a sort of traversal toward the beyond of all closed systems, all forms of knowledge, all the new positive sciences whose novelty always tempted the *Aufklärer* and discoverer in him, though only for a time, the time of a passage, the time of a contribution which, after him, would become indispensable. And yet he was already elsewhere, and he said so; he would speak openly about it with a calculated modesty, with a politeness that revealed a rigorous demand and an uncompromising ethic, like an idiosyncratic destiny naively assumed. In the beginning of *Camera Lucida* he speaks, and speaks to himself, of his 'discomfort' at always

> being a subject torn between two languages, one expressive, the other critical; and at the heart of this critical language, between several discourses, those of sociology, of semiology, and of psychoanalysis – but that, by ultimate dissatisfaction with all of them, I was bearing witness to the only sure thing that was in me (however naive it might be): a desperate resistance to any reductive system. For each time, having resorted to any such language to whatever degree, each time I felt it hardening and thereby tending to reduction and reprimand, I would gently leave it and seek elsewhere: I began to speak differently. (*CL*, p. 8)

The beyond of this crossing is no doubt the last outpost and the great enigma of the Referent, as it has been called for the last twenty years, and death is clearly not in this for nothing (it will be necessary to return to this in another tone). In any case, as early as *Writing Degree Zero*, all this passes through the novel: the beyond of literature as literature, literary 'modernity,' literature producing itself and producing its essence as its own disappearance, showing and hiding itself at the same time (Mallarmé, Blanchot . . .); and 'the Novel is a Death' (*WDZ*, p. 38).

> Modernism begins with the search for a Literature which is no longer possible. Thus we find, in the Novel too, this machinery directed towards both destruction and resurrection, and typical of the whole of modern art. . . . The Novel is a Death; it transforms life into destiny, a memory into a useful act, duration into an orientated and meaningful time. (*WDZ*, pp. 38–9)

And it is the modern possibility of the photograph (whether it be an art or a technique matters little here) which combines death and the referent in the same system. It wasn't for the first time, and this conjugation of death and the referent didn't have to wait for the Photograph to establish an essential relationship to reproductive technique, or to technique in general, but the immediate proof given by the photographic apparatus [*dispositif*] and by the structure of the *remains* it leaves behind are irreducible events, ineffaceably original. It is the failure, or at any rate the limit, of all that which, in language, literature and the other arts, seemed to permit grandiose theories on the general suspension of the Referent, or of that which was classified, by a sometimes ridiculous simplification, under that vast and vague category. By the time the *punctum* rends space, the reference and death are hand in hand in the photograph. But should we say reference or referent? Analytical precision must here be equal to the stakes, and the photograph puts this precision to the test: in the photograph, the referent is noticeably absent, suspendable, vanished into the unique past time of its event, but the reference to this referent, let us say the intentional movement of reference (since Barthes does in fact appeal to phenomenology in this book), also implies irreducibly the having-been of a unique and invariable referent. It implies the 'return of the dead' in the very structure of both its image and the phenomenon of its image. This doesn't happen in other types of images or discourses, or let's say in signs in general, at least not in the same way, the implication and form of the reference taking all sorts of different twists and turns. From the beginning of *Camera Lucida* the 'disorder' introduced by the photograph is largely attributed to the 'unique time' of its referent, a time which doesn't lend itself to reproduction or pluralization, and whose referential implication is inscribed as such in the very structure of the photogramme, regardless of either the number of its reproductions or the artifice of its composition. Hence 'this stubbornness of the Referent in always being there' (*CL*, p. 6). 'It is as if the Photograph always carries its referent with itself, both affected by the same amorous or funeral immobility. . . . In short, the referent adheres. And this singular adherence' (*CL*, pp. 5–6). Although it is no longer *there* (present, living, real, etc.), its *having-been-there* now part of the referential or intentional structure of my relationship to the photogramme, the return of the referent indeed takes the form of a haunting. This is a 'return of the dead,' whose spectral arrival in the very space of the photogramme well resembles an emission or emanation. Already a sort of hallucinating metonymy: it is something else, a bit come from the other (from the referent) which is found in me, in front of me but also in me like a bit of me (since the referential implication is also intentional and noematic; it belongs neither to the sensible body nor to the medium of the photogramme). Moreover, the 'target,' the 'referent,' the '*eidolon* emitted by the object,' the '*Spectrum*' (*CL*, p. 9), can be me, seen in a photograph of myself:

> I then experience a micro-version of death (of parenthesis): I am truly becoming a specter. The Photographer knows this very well, and himself fears (if only for commercial reasons) this death in which his gesture will embalm me. . . . I have become Total-Image, which is to say, Death in person. . . . Ultimately, what I am seeking in the photograph taken of me (the 'intention' according to which I look at it) is Death: Death is the *eidos* of that Photograph. (*CL*, pp. 14–15)

•

Carried by this relationship, drawn or lured by the pull and character of it (*Zug, Bezug*, etc.), by the reference to the spectral referent, Roland Barthes traversed periods, systems, modes, 'phases,' and 'genres'; he marked and punctuated the *studium* of each, passing *through* phenomenology, linguistics, literary mathesis, semiosis, structural analysis, etc. His first move was to recognize in each of them their necessity or richness, their critical value and light, in order to turn them against dogmatism.

•

I will not make an allegory out of it, and still less a metaphor, but I remember that it was *while traveling* that I spent the most time alone with Barthes. Sometimes head to head, I mean face to face (for example on the train from Paris to Lille or Paris to Bordeaux) and sometimes side by side, separated by an aisle (for example in the trip from Paris to New York to Baltimore in

1966). The times of our travels were no doubt different and yet the same, and it is necessary to bear with these two absolute certainties. Even if I wanted or was able to give an account [*récit*], to speak of what he was for me (the voice, the timbre, the forms of his attention and distraction, his polite way of either being or not being there, his face, hands, clothing, smile, and cigar, so many features that I name without describing, since it is here impossible), even if I tried to reproduce what took place, what place would be reserved for the reserve? What place for the long periods of silence, for the silences of discretion, for avoidances, for that which could be of no use, for that which was too well known, or for that which remained infinitely unknown to both of us? To go on speaking of this all alone, after the death of the other, to sketch out the least conjecture or risk the least interpretation: all this I experience as an endless insult or wound – and yet also a duty, a duty towards him. I will not carry this out however, at least not here and now. Always the promise of return.

•

How to believe a contemporary? It would be easy to show that the times of those who seem to belong to the same epoch, defined in terms of an historical frame or social horizon, etc., remain infinitely heterogeneous and, to tell the truth, completely unrelated to each other. One can be very sensitive to this, though sensitive at the same time, on another level, to a being-together which no difference or disagreement can threaten. This being-together is not spread out in any homogeneous way in our experience. There are knots, points of great condensation, places of high valuation, paths of decision or interpretation that are virtually unavoidable. It is there it seems that the law is produced. Being-together refers and recognizes itself there, even though it is not constituted there. Contrary to what is often thought, the individual 'subjects' who inhabit the most unavoidable zones are not authoritarian 'superegos,' they do not have any power at their disposal, assuming that Power can be at one's disposal. Like those for whom these zones become inescapable (and it is first a question of their history), they inhabit them; and, rather than ruling them, take from them a desire or an image. It is a certain way of dismantling authority,

283

a certain freedom in fact, an acknowledged relationship to their own finitude, which, by an ominous and rigorous paradox, confers on them additional authority, an influence, radiance, or presence which takes their ghost to the place where they are not and from which their ghost will never return; in short, it makes one ask, more or less openly: What does he or she think of this? Not that one is ready to prove someone right, *a priori* and in all cases, not that one awaits a verdict or believes in a lucidity without weakness, but even before looking for it, the image of an evaluation, look, or affect imposes itself upon us. It is difficult to know then who addresses this 'image' and to whom. I would like patiently and interminably to describe the trajectories of this address, especially when its reference passes through writing, when it then becomes so virtual, invisible, plural, divided, microscopic, mobile, infinitesimal, specular even (since the demand is often reciprocal and the trajectory easily lost), punctual, seemingly on the verge of negating itself [*dans le zéro*] even though its exercise is so powerful and so diverse.

•

Roland Barthes is the name of a friend whom, basically, in the depths of familiarity, I knew little, and of whom, it goes without saying, I haven't read everything, I mean reread, understood, etc. And my first response was most often certainly one of approval, solidarity, and gratitude. But not always it seems, and as insignificant as it may be, I must say this so as not to give in too much to the genre. He was, I mean he remains, one of those of whom I have constantly wondered, for almost twenty years now, in a more of less articulated way: What does he think of this? In the present, the past, the future, the conditional, etc.? Especially, why not say it, for who would be surprised by it, at the moment of writing. I even told him this in a letter long ago.

•

I return to the 'poignant,' to this pair of concepts, this opposition which is not an opposition, the ghost of this pair, *punctum/studium*. I return to this because the *punctum* seems to speak, to let Barthes himself speak the point of singularity, the traversal

284

of discourse toward the unique, the 'referent' as the irreplaceable other, the one who was and will no longer be, who returns
like that which will never come back, who marks the return of
the dead to the reproductive image. I return to this because
Roland Barthes is the name of that which points me, or points
to that which I am awkwardly trying to say here. I return to this
in order to show also how he himself treated and appropriately
signed this simulacrum of an opposition. He first highlighted
the absolute irreducibility of the *punctum*, the unicity of the
referential as we say (I appeal to this word so as not to have to
choose between reference and referent: what adheres in the
photograph is perhaps less the referent itself, in the effectiveness of its reality, than the implication in the reference of its
having-been-unique). The heterogeneity of the *punctum* is
rigorous, its originality suffers neither contamination nor
concession. And yet, in other places, at other times, Barthes
accedes to another descriptive demand, let's call it phenomenological since the book is presented *also* as a phenomenology.
He accedes to the requisite rhythm of the composition, a musical
composition which, to be more precise, I would call contrapuntal. It is indeed necessary for him to recognize, and this is
not a concession, that the *punctum* is not what it is. This absolute
other composes with the same, with its absolute other which is
thus not its opposite, with the locus of the same and of the
studium (it is the limit of the binary opposition and, undoubtably, of any structural analysis the *studium* itself can exploit). If
it is more or less than itself, dissymmetrical to everything
including itself, the *punctum* can invade the field of the *studium*,
although it technically doesn't belong to it. One will recall that
it is located outside all fields and codes. As the place of the
irreplaceable singularity and the unique referential, the *punctum*
irradiates and, what is most surprising, lends itself to
metonymy. As soon as it allows itself to be drawn into a system
of substitutions, it can invade everything, objects as well as
affects. This singularity which is nowhere *in* the field mobilizes
everything everywhere; it pluralizes itself. If the photograph
bespeaks the unique death, the death of the unique, this death
repeats itself immediately, as such, and is itself elsewhere. I
said that the *punctum* allows itself to be drawn into metonymy.
Actually, it induces it, and this is its *force*, or rather than its force

(since it exercises no actual constraint and exists completely in reserve), its *dynamis*, in other words, its power, potentiality, and even its dissimulation, its latency. Barthes marks this relationship between force (potential or reserved) and metonymy at certain intervals of the composition which I must here unjustly condense (p. 74). 'However lightning-like it may be, the *punctum* has, more or less potentially, a power of expansion. This power is often metonymic' (*CL*, p. 45). Further: 'I had just realized that however immediate and incisive it was, the *punctum* could accommodate a certain latency (but never any examination [*examen*: Howard translates *examen* as "scrutiny"])' (*CL*, p. 53). This metonymic power is essentially related to the supplementary structure of the *punctum* ('it is a supplement') and of the *studium* which receives from it all its movement, even if it must content itself, like the 'examination' with turning around the point.[9] From that moment on, the relationship between the two concepts is neither tautological nor oppositional, neither dialectical nor in any sense symmetrical; it is supplementary and musical (contrapuntal).

•

The metonymy of the *punctum*: scandalous as it may be, it allows us to speak, to speak of the unique, to speak of and to him. It yields the trait [*trait*: line, trace, feature, reference, draught, musical passage, etc.] that relates to the unique. The Winter Garden Photograph, which he neither shows nor hides, which he speaks, is the *punctum* of the entire book. The mark of this unique wound is nowhere visible as such, but its unlocatable clarity (that of *his* mother's eyes) irradiates the whole study. It makes of this book an irreplaceable event. And yet only a metonymic force can still assure a certain generality to the discourse and offer it to analysis by submitting its concepts to a quasi-instrumental employment. How else could we, without knowing her, be so deeply moved by what he said about *his* mother, who was not only the Mother, or a mother, but the only one she was and of whom such a photo was taken 'that day . . .'? How would this be poignant to us if a metonymic force, which yet cannot be mistaken for something that facilitates the movement of identification, were not at work? The alterity remains almost intact; it is the condition. I don't put myself in his place, I don't tend to replace his mother with mine. If I were to do this, I could only be moved by the alterity of the without-relation, the absolute unicity which the metonymic power recalls in me without effacing it. He is right to protest against the confusion between that which was his mother and the Figure of the Mother, but the metonymic power (one part for the whole or one name for another, etc.) will always come to inscribe both in this relation without relation.

•

The deaths of Roland Barthes: because of the rather improper brutality of this plural, one might think perhaps that I resisted the unique; I would have thus refused, denied, and tried to efface his death. As a sign of protection or protest, I would have in the same stroke accused and put his death on trial before a studied metonymy. Perhaps, but how do we speak otherwise and without taking the risk? Without pluralizing the unique or generalizing that which is held most irreplaceable in it, his own death? And didn't he himself speak right up until the very last moment of his death and, metonymically, of his deaths? And didn't he say what is essential (especially in *Roland Barthes by Roland Barthes*, a metonymic title and signature par excellence) about the indecidable vacillation between 'speaking and keeping silent'?[10] And one can still remain silent by speaking: 'The only "thought" I can have is that at the end of this first death, my own death is inscribed; between the two, nothing more than waiting; I have no other resources than this *irony*: to speak of the "nothing to say"?' (*CL*, p. 93). And just before: 'The horror is this: nothing to say about the death of one whom I love most, nothing to say about her photograph' (*CL*, pp. 92–3).

•

Friendship [*L'amitié*]: from the few pages at the end of the volume which bears this title, we have no right to take anything.[11] What linked Blanchot to Bataille was unique, and *Friendship* expresses this in an absolutely singular way. And yet the metonymic force of even the most poignant writing allows us to *read* these pages, which doesn't mean however to expose them outside their essential reserve. It lets us think that which it in fact never releases, never shows nor hides. Without being able to enter

into the absolute singularity of this relationship, without forgetting that only Blanchot could write this and that only of Bataille
could he be speaking, without understanding, or in any case
without knowing, we can think about that which is being
written here. We shouldn't be allowed to quote, but I take upon
myself [the responsibility for] the violence of the quotation,
especially one necessarily truncated.

> How to let oneself speak of this friend? Neither out of praise
> nor in the interest of some truth. The characteristics of his
> personality, the forms of his existence, the episodes of his
> life, even if in agreement with the investigation he himself
> felt responsibile for, even up to the point of being
> irresponsible: these don't belong to anyone. There are no
> witnesses. The closest to him only say what was closest to
> them; they do not speak of the distant [*le lointain*] that
> asserted itself in this proximity, and the distant ceases as
> soon as presence ceases. . . . We only seek to fill a void;
> we cannot stand the pain: the assertion of this void. . . .
> All that we say tends only to veil this unique assertion:
> that everything must efface itself and we can only remain
> faithful by watching over this movement which effaces
> itself, this movement to which something within us that
> rejects all memories already belongs. (*L'amitié*, p. 326)

•

In *Camera Lucida*, the value of *intensity* (*dynamis*, force, latency),
which I am now in the process of tracking down, leads to a
new contrapuntal equation, to a new metonymy of metonymy
itself, to the substitutive virtue of the *punctum*. This is Time.
For is not Time the ultimate resource for the substitution of
one absolute instance by another, for the replacement of the
irreplaceable, the replacement of this unique referent by another
which is yet another instant, completely other and yet the same?
Is not Time the form and punctual force of all metonymy *in its
last instance*? Here is a passage where the passage from one
death to another, from Lewis Payne's death to Roland Barthes',
seems to pass (between others if one dare say it) through the
Winter Garden Photograph. And on the theme of Time. It is,
in short, a terrifying syntax, from which I pluck out first a

singular accord, the transition between S and P: 'the photo is handsome, as is the boy' (*CL*, p. 96). And here is the passage from one death to the other:

> I now know that there exists another *punctum* (another 'stigmatum') than the 'detail.' This new *punctum*, which is no longer of form but of intensity, is Time, the lacerating emphasis of the *noeme* ('*that-has-been*'), its pure representation.
>
> In 1865, young Lewis Payne tried to assassinate Secretary of State W. H. Seward. Alexander Gardner photographed him in his cell, where he was waiting to be hanged. The photograph is handsome, as is the boy: that is the *studium*. But the *punctum* is: *he is going to die*. I read at the same time: *This will be* and *this has been*; I observe with horror an anterior future of which death is the stake. By giving me to the absolute past of the pose (aorist), the photograph tells me death in the future. What *pricks* me is the discovery of this equivalence. In front of the photograph of my mother as a child, I tell myself: she is going to die: I shudder, like Winnicott's psychotic patient, *over a catastrophe which has already occurred*. Whether or not the subject is already dead, every photograph is this catastrophe. (*CL*, p. 96)

And further on: 'It is because each photograph always contains this imperious sign of my future death that each one, however attached it seems to be to the excited world of the living, challenges each of us, one by one, outside of any generality (but not outside of any transcendence)' (*CL*, p. 97).

•

Time: the metonymy of the instantaneous, the possibility of the narrative [*récit*] magnetized by its own limit. The instantaneous in photography [*instantané*: the snapshot, the instamatic] would itself only be the most striking metonymy of an older instantaneity, its apparatus [*dispositif*] being part of the modern, technical age. This instantaneity is older, certainly, but is never foreign to the possibility of *techné* in general. By taking a thousand differential precautions, one must be able to speak of a *punctum* in all signs (and the repetition and iterability structures it already), in any discourse, whether it be literary or not.

Provided that we do not hold to some naive and 'realist' referentialism, the relation to some unique and irreplaceable referent *interests* us and animates our most sound and studied readings: what happened one time only, while dividing itself already, in order to take aim, in front of the lens of the *Phaedo* or *Finnegans Wake*, the *Discourse on Method* or Hegel's *Logic*, John's *Apocalypse* or *Coup de dés*. The photographic apparatus reminds us of this irreducible referential by means of a very powerful telescoping.

•

The metonymic force divides the referential line [*trait*], suspends the referent and leaves it to be desired, while still maintaining the reference. It is at work in the most loyal friendship; it plunges the destination into mourning while at the same time engaging it.

•

Friendship: between the two titles, that of the book and that of the final farewell [*envoi*] in italics, between the titles and the exergue ('quotations' of Bataille saying 'friendship' twice)[12] the exchange is still metonymic though the singularity doesn't lose any of its force, on the contrary.

> I know there are books. . . . The books themselves refer to
> an existence. This existence, because it is no longer a
> presence, starts to unfold in history, and in the worst of
> histories, literary history. . . . We want to publish
> 'everything,' to say 'everything'; as if there were only one
> exigency: that everything be said; as if the 'everything is
> said' were at last to permit us to put an end to [*arrêter*] dead
> speech. . . . As long as the one who is close to us exists,
> and with him, the thought in which he asserts himself, his
> thought opens up to us, though it is still preserved in this
> very relationship; and what preserves it is not only the
> mobility of life (that would be little) but something
> unforeseeable introduced into it by the strangeness of the
> end. . . . I also know that in his books George Bataille
> seems to be speaking of himself with an unconstrained
> freedom that should free us from all discretion – but which
> doesn't give us the right to put ourselves in his place, or

the power to speak in his absence. But is it certain that he is speaking about himself?. . . . We must renounce knowing those to whom something essential links us; I mean, we must greet them in the relation with the unknown, where they also greet us in our own estrangement. (*L'Amitié*, pp. 327–8)

•

From where does the desire to date these last lines come (the 14 or 15 of September, 1980?)[13] The date, and this is always a type of signature, accentuates the contingency or insignificance of the interruption. Like an accident and like death, it seems to be imposed from the outside, 'that day' (time and space are here in accord, the frameworks for a publication, etc.), but it no doubt also bespeaks another interruption. This interruption is neither more essential nor more interior, but announces itself in another register, as another thought of the same. . . .

•

Having returned from the depths of the somewhat insulary experience in which I had secluded myself with the two books, I look today only at the photographs in other books (especially in *Roland Barthes by Roland Barthes*) and in some newspapers; I can no longer tear myself away from the photographs and the handwriting. I don't know what I'm still looking for, but I'm looking for it in the direction of his body, in what he shows and says of it, in what he hides of it perhaps, like what he couldn't *see* in his writing? I am looking at the photographs without the least illusion, I believe, and without indulgence, for 'details,' for something that looks at me without seeing me, as I believe he says at the end of *Camera Lucida*. I try to imagine the gestures around what we believe to be the essential writing. How, for example, did he choose all these photographs of children and old people? How and when did he choose this back cover [*quatrième de couverture*] where Marpa speaks of his son's death?[14] And what about these white lines on the black background of the inside cover of *Roland Barthes par Roland Barthes*?[15]

•

Today somebody brought me a note (less than a letter, a single sentence) which had been destined for me but never given to me twenty-four years ago, almost to the day. On the eve of a journey, the note was to accompany the gift of a very singular book, a little book which even today I find unreadable. I know, or I think I know, why this gesture was interrupted. Actually, it was held back (and the little book was in fact itself placed inside another) as if to preserve the memory of the interruption itself. This memory, for reasons at once serious and playful, was indeed concerned with something I would be tempted to call the whole of my life. This note (which I thus received today on the eve of the *same* journey, I mean to the same places) was found by chance, long after the death of the one who destined it for me. Everything is very close to me, the form of the writing, of the signature, these very words. Another interruption makes all this as distant and unreadable as that little, insignificant *viaticum*; but in the interruption, the other, returning, addresses himself to me, in me, the other truly returning. . . . The paper retains its folds of these twenty-four years; I read the blue writing (more and more I am sensitive to the color of writing, or at any rate I am now more aware that I am sensitive to it) of someone who, speaking about death, had told me in a car one day, and I recall these words often: 'It will happen to me soon.' And it was true.

•

That was yesterday. Today, another strange coincidence: a friend sent me from the United States a photocopy of a text by Barthes that I have never read before (*Analyse textuelle d'un conte d'Edgar Poe*, 1973).[16] I will read it later. But while 'leafing' through it, I picked out this:

> Another scandal of enunciation is the reversal of the
> metaphor in the letter. It is indeed common to utter the
> sentence 'I am dead!'. . . [But] the transposition of the
> metaphor into the letter, *precisely for this metaphor*, is
> impossible: the utterance 'I am dead,' according to the letter
> [*selon la lettre*: literally] is foreclosed. . . . It is therefore a
> question, if you like, of a scandal of language . . . it is a
> question here of a performative utterance, but one which,
> certainly, neither Austin nor Benveniste had foreseen in

their analyses . . . the extraordinary [*inouïe*: unheard of] sentence 'I am dead' is by no means the incredible statement, but much more radically, the *impossible utterance*.

•

Would this impossible utterance 'I am dead' never have taken place? He is right when he says that 'according to the letter' it is 'foreclosed.' Yet one understands it, one hears its so-called 'literal' meaning, even if only legitimately to declare it impossible as a performative utterance. What did he think of at the moment he referred himself to this letter? Probably of at least this, that in the idea of death, all other predicates remaining problematic, this idea is analytically understood: there is an inability to utter, to speak, to say *I* in the present, etc. Yes, a punctual *I*, punctuating in the instant a reference to itself as to a unique referent, etc., this auto-affective reference which defines the heart of the living. To return from this point to metonymy, to the metonymic force of the *punctum*, without which there would undoubtably be no *punctum* as such. . . . At the heart of the sadness felt for the friend when he dies, there is perhaps this point: that after having been able to speak about a death so pluralized, and to say so often 'I am dead' metaphorically or metonymically, he was never able to say 'I am dead' to the letter. Had he done so, he would have again given in to metonymy. But metonymy is no mistake or falsehood; it doesn't speak untruths. And to the letter, there is perhaps no *punctum* as such. What makes all utterances possible but doesn't reduce suffering in the least is actually a source, the un-punctual, illimitable source of suffering. If I were to write *revenant à la lettre*, and if I were to try to translate it into another language. . . .[17] (all these questions are also questions of translation and transference).

•

I: the pronoun [*pronom*], or the first name [*prénom*], the borrowed name [*prête-nom*] of the one whom the *utterance* 'I am dead' can never reach, the literal utterance that is, and if it were possible, the non-metonymic *utterance*? This, even when the enunciation of it would be possible?

293

•

Wouldn't the enunciation of the 'I am dead,' which he says is impossible, fall into the province of that system which he elsewhere calls *utopic* – and which he also calls upon? And doesn't this utopia impose itself in the place, if one can still say this, where metonymy is already at work on the *I* in its relation to itself, the *I* when it refers to nothing else but the one who is *presently* speaking? There would be something like a sentence of the *I*, and the time of this elliptical sentence would leave room for metonymic substitution. In order to approach this concept of time, we would have to return here to that which implicitly links, in *Camera Lucida*, Time as a *punctum* to the metonymic force of the *punctum*. . . .

•

'What should I do?' In *Camera Lucida* he seems to approve of that which places 'civil value' above 'moral value' (*CL*, p. 67). In *Roland Barthes by Roland Barthes* he says that *morality* should be understood as 'the precise opposite of ethics (it is the thinking of the body in a state of language)' (*RB*, p. 145).

•

Between the possibility and the impossibility of the 'I am dead' there is the syntax of time and something like a category of imminence (that which points from the future and is on the verge of taking place). The imminence of death presents itself, it is always of the verge, while presenting itself, of presenting itself no longer, so that death then stands between the metonymic eloquence of the 'I am dead' and the instant when death ushers in absolute silence, allowing nothing more to be said (a point is all [*un point c'est tout*; and that's all there is to it]). This punctual singularity (I understand 'punctual' as an adjective but also as a type of verb, the enduring syntax of a sentence) irradiates the corpus from its place of imminence and breathes into it, especially into *Camera Lucida*, this 'air' which is more and more dense, more and more haunted and peopled with ghosts. Thus I use these words to speak of this: 'emanation,' 'ecstasis,' 'madness,' 'magic.'

•

It is inevitable [*fatal*], both just and unjust, that the most 'auto-biographical' books (those of the end, as I have heard said) begin with death by concealing all the other books. And what is more, they begin at death. If I were to give myself over to this movement, I would no longer leave this *Roland Barthes by Roland Barthes*, which, on the whole, I didn't know how to read. Between the photos and the graphics, all these texts I should have talked about, left alone, or come closer to. . . . But didn't I do this without realizing it in the preceding fragments? For example, at the precise moment, almost by chance, under the titles *His voice* ('inflection is the voice in so far as it is always past, silenced,' 'the voice is always *already* dead'), *Plural, differ- ence, conflict, What is a utopia for?, Forgeries* (*'I write classic'*), *The circle of fragments, The fragment as illusion, From the fragment to the journal, Pause: anamneses* ('The *biographeme* [. . .] is nothing but a factitious anamnesis: the one I lend to the author I love'.), *Limpness of important words* ('History' and 'Nature,' for example), *Passing bodies, Foreseeable discourse* (example: *Text of the Dead*: a litaneutical text, in which no word can be changed), *Relation to psychoanalysis, I like/I don't like* (one line before the end, I try to understand how he could have written '*I don't like . . .* fidelity.' I know that he also said he liked it and that he was able to make a gift of this word. I suppose – it's a matter of tone, mood, inflection, and a certain way of saying quickly but incisively *I like, I don't like* – that in this case he didn't like a certain pathos with which fidelity is so easily laden, and especially the word, for at the very moment the discourse on fidelity gets tired, it becomes drab, indifferent, stale, forbidding, unfaithful). *Choosing clothes, Later. . . .*

•

Contrapuntal theory or a procession of stigmata: a wound no doubt comes in (the) place of the point signed by singularity, in (the) place of its very instant (*stigmê*), of its point [*pointe*: sharp end, tip, etc.]. But *in (the) place of* this event, the place is left, because of the same wound, for the substitution that repeats itself there, retaining of the irreplaceable only a past desire.

•

I still cannot remember when I read or heard his name for the first time, and then how he became one for me. But anamnesis, even if it always breaks off too soon, promises itself each time to begin again: it remains to come.

NOTES

CHAPTER 1 MAURICE MERLEAU-PONTY: PHILOSOPHY AND NON-PHILOSOPHY SINCE HEGEL

1 Text of the 1961 course notes established by Claude Lefort. English translation by Hugh J. Silverman. Lefort has footnoted the many passages, sentences, and terms which Merleau-Ponty left in German with translations borrowed from the current French version of Heidegger's *Holzwege* by Wolfgang Brokmeier, and of Marx's writings in the Costes edition. By contrast, for purposes of clarity and brevity, my translations of the German are integrated into the body of the work. They are based on the English version in *Hegel's Concept of Experience* and in *Karl Marx: Early Writings* (New York, Vintage, 1975) by Rodney Livingstone and Gregor Benton. In consulting both the German text and the French translation, I have sometimes modified the rendering of passages in the aforementioned English translations. Also, when Merleau-Ponty gives his own translation of Nietzsche, Hegel, Heidegger, and Marx, I have found it necessary to provide the English reader with a formulation which comes closer to Merleau-Ponty's version than to the direct English rendering from the German. When a particularly significant French or German expression occurs, I have placed it in brackets after its English equivalent. Any notes for which this translator is responsible are followed by (HJS). Claude Lefort's notes are followed by (CL). Merleau-Ponty's own notes (and marginal notes) are followed by (M-P). Annotations by the translator have been restricted to those which will be useful for an adequate appreciation of the status, context, and content of the text. Any major interpolated additions to the text are indicated by an asterisk*. (HJS)

2 As we know from the Pseudo-Dionysius, negative theology is the view that God *is* only in terms of his absence. This is not the

seventeenth-century French 'hidden god,' studied by Lucien Gold-
mann in terms of Pascal and Racine. Rather it is the positing of
God in terms of all that He is not. God is not His creatures;
therefore, He must be other than what is created, etc. To bring
this negative theology around to negative philosophy, recall a
phrase used by Sartre in reference to the self: I am what I am not,
and I am not what I am. In negative theology, God is what He is
not, and He is not what He is. It has been argued by some, e.g.
Mikel Dufrenne, that Jacques Derrida's philosophy is a negative
theology. Derrida's conception of the 'trace' that appears in writing
(l'écriture) but which is the manifestation of a decentered subject
that can only be a differencing at the textual level did not receive
public expression until the late 1960s – after Merleau-Ponty's
death. But the notion of difference does send us back to a Heideggerian ontological difference (ontologische Differenz), which is, in a
sense, where Merleau-Ponty begins his elaboration of negative
philosophy. The return to a Hegelian philosophy of negation must
nevertheless pass through its Heideggerian 'double.' (HJS)

3 The Greek etymology for 'phenomenology' as logos of the phainomenon is taken here to mean the 'structure or logic of appearance.'
(HJS)

4 Dépasser and dépassement will be translated respectively as 'to
surpass' and 'surpassing.' It means going beyond, superseding,
or transcending and is the French equivalent for the celebrated
Hegelian Aufheben or Aufhebung. Although Walter Kaufmann
prefers 'sublimination' to force the link with Freud, it is not
employed here. (HJS)

5 Translated into English by Thomas Common as Joyful Wisdom
(New York, Ungar, 1960) and by Walter Kaufmann as The Gay
Science (New York, Vintage, 1974). (HJS) Merleau-Ponty translates
Nietzsche's text himself from the German edition: Die Fröhliche
Wissenschaft. (CL) The new edition appeared in 1887 and not 1886
as Merleau-Ponty indicates. Of the two English versions, only
Kaufmann's includes the 'Preface' to which Merleau-Ponty refers.
(HJS)

6 F. Nietzsche, Die Fröhliche Wissenschaft (Leipzig, Fritzsch, 1887),
p. 8. Hereafter cited as FW. This passage refers to those persons
who philosophize out of their riches and strengths. For these
persons, as opposed to those who need philosophy out of depri-
vation, 'it is merely a beautiful luxury – in the best cases, the
voluptuousness of a triumphant gratitude that eventually still has
to inscribe itself in cosmic letters on the heaven of concepts.'
Kaufmann translation, The Gay Science, pp. 33–4. Hereafter

abbreviated 'trans.' In order more closely to approximate the French translation which Merleau-Ponty offers, I have at times wandered afar from Kaufmann's rendering. This is the case for all of these passages from Nietzsche's Preface. (HJS)

7 In his first work, *The Birth of Tragedy* (1872), Nietzsche centered upon these two Greek gods (Apollo and Dionysus) as representatives of two psychological tendencies. The Apollonian was associated with illusion, dream, a rational reserve. The Dionysian was appropriately wild, drunken, frenzied passion. Thus the god of the Bacchinales, of wine and festival, was well represented. But according to Nietzsche, a new tendency arose in Greek thought, the basis of tragedy, a new Dionysian, evidencing the harnessing of passion, the fusion of the two forces – 'superficiality through profundity.' It is not entirely clear how Merleau-Ponty sees the relationship between these two. But we can assume that the Apollonian, through the significance of the dream, will be profound; and that the Dionysian, because of this Thracian god's recorded novelty to the Greek scene, because of the seemingly frivolous character of its presence, and because of its coming into being at certain times of the year, will be superficial.

Appearance and profundity in Hegel are not contraries, i.e. opposed to one another. As Merleau-Ponty explains in the next paragraph, the absolute can be achieved through the unification of appearance and profundity. Merleau-Ponty associates appearance with (Dionysian) superficiality but he wants to suggest that the superficial can become profound. Similarly, in Nietzsche, profundity should not be opposed to appearance in order for appearance (*phainomenon*) to be absolute – for phenomenological intuition (as in the Husserlian *Anschauung* and the Nietzschean Apollonian tendency) to reveal appearances. In Nietzsche, appearance becomes autonomous in the work of philosophy. (HJS)

8 See Part Two of this text for Merleau-Ponty's discussion of Marx on this issue. (HJS)

9 [marginal note] *Gott ist tot: das sagt alles andere, nur nicht: es gibt keinen Gott.* God is dead, which means everything, except: there is no god. (M-P)

10 In French, *conscience* can be either 'conscience' or 'consciousness.' The ambiguity is relevant here since *Er-innerung* (re-collection, re-memberance, re-minder) can be both a conscious activity and an aspect of moral awareness. (HJS)

11 Whenever words, sentences or passages, which Merleau-Ponty left in German, are included here in English, quotation marks are used to identify them as such. (HJS)

12 As presented by Dostoevsky's Raskolnikov (in *Crime and Punishment*) and Nietzsche's Zarathustra (in *Thus Spoke Zarathustra*). (HJS)

13 Heidegger's notion of *Zusammengehörigkeit* is appealed to here. (HJS)

14 *connaissance*, i.e. knowledge by acquaintance. Where Merleau-Ponty says *'savoir'*, i.e. knowledge by description (to continue Russell's terminology), the English 'knowledge' will be used without any indication. (HJS)

15 *dévoilement* – the French expression for Heidegger's *Unverborgenheit*, i.e. bringing out of concealment. Heidegger relates it to a conception of truth as ἀλήθεια – the revealing or appearing of what is. (HJS)

16 *connaissance*. This is the French equivalent of *Erkennen*, while *savoir* is to be associated with *Wissen*. (HJS)

17 Heidegger, *Holzwege* (Frankfurt-am-Main, Klostermann, 1950), p. 105. (M-P) This passage is from Hegel's 'Introduction' to the *Phenomenology of Mind*, cited by Heidegger in his essay 'Hegel's Begriff der Erfahrung,' pp. 105–92 in *Holzwege* (henceforth referred to as *Holz*). Issued separately in English as *Hegel's Concept of Experience*, trans. Harper & Row Publishers (New York, Harper & Row, 1970), it will be cited henceforth as 'trans.' The passages from Hegel are translated by Kenly Royce Dove, and although they are often given here, some divergence is made when Merleau-Ponty's understanding seems to differ. The clause cited occurs on p. 8 of 'trans.' (HJS)

18 This fear of being wrong is the error itself: *schon der Irrtum selbst ist*. (M-P)

19 [marginal note] *Sie setz . . . voraus . . . einen Unterschied unserer selbst von diesem Erkennen*. (M-P) [This distrust presupposes that there is a difference between ourselves and this knowledge.] [below] This attitude presupposes *dass das Erkennen, welches indem es ausser dem Absoluten, wohl ausser der Wahrheit ist, doch wahrhaft sei* (M-P) [that knowledge, which, while remaining outside the absolute and thus certainly also outside truth, is nevertheless true.] *Holz*, p. 107; trans., p. 10. (HJS)

20 [marginal note] To give priority to certainty, as Descartes does, is to give priority to a truth outside truth; – an 'other' truth: a confusing distinction, – we have a *Bedeutung* of the absolute, a *Bedeutung* of *Erkennen* which must be rendered equal. (M-P) [below] *Erkennen* is not to be placed outside the absolute because the absolute is not to be placed outside *Erkennen*: *alle diese Vorstellungen von einem Erkennen, das von Absoluten, und einem Absoluten das von dem Erkennen getrennt ist*. (M-P) [all these representations

of a knowledge separated from the absolute and of an absolute separated from knowledge. (CL)]

21 Descartes' universal doubt, formulated in the *Meditations*, is suggested here as the paradigm for affirmation of truth by negation of itself. The dualism created by distinguishing the denial from that which is denied does not place knowledge outside truth. On the contrary, knowledge is thereby included in truth because the denial is knowledge. (HJS)

22 'Semblance' is Dove's rendering, but *Schein* is also a 'shining forth.' (*Holz*, p. 108 (M-P); trans., p. 12) (HJS)

23 [We include and translate the text from which this quotation is taken] This presentation can be regarded as the pathway of natural consciousness striving towards true knowledge, or as the path of the soul making its way through the sequence of its own transformations as through waystations prescribed to it by its very nature. By purifying itself it may lift itself to the level of the mind and attain cognizance of what it is in itself through the completed experience of its own self. (CL) (*Holz*, p. 109; trans., p. 13). (HJS)

24 The central notion of the penultimate completed chapter in *The Visible and the Invisible*, ed. Claude Lefort, trans. Alphonso Lingis (Evanston, Northwestern University Press, 1968), which Merleau-Ponty was writing at the time of his death and hence while he was offering this course at the *Collège de France*. The chiasm is an intertwining of visible and invisible, seen and seeing, touched and touching. It is associated with an inside becoming outside, outside becoming inside, in short, a reversibility. The last working note (dated March, 1961) in *The Visible and the Invisible* (p. 275) reads: 'worked-over-matter-men = chiasm.' (HJS)

25 *Bildung* is both formation and education. Where consciousness works on the self, a process of learning occurs. Self-knowledge arises along with the realization of knowledge. (HJS)

26 Merleau-Ponty's orientation is to avoid the Sartrian negation of the for-itself. For Merleau-Ponty, the for-itself is not nothingness, but intimate interrelation with the in-itself through the body (in *Phenomenology of Perception*) and through 'visibility' (in *The Visible and the Invisible*). In Chapter 2 on 'Interrogation and Dialectic,' Merleau-Ponty takes up his critique of Sartre, indicating that perceptual faith cuts across the separation between the for-itself and the in-itself. (HJS)

27 This interpretation of Sartre's for-itself suggests that all consciousness must become eternally caught up in a Hegelian 'unhappy consciousness.' For Hegel, the unhappy consciousness is only a stage on the way to the absolute. The 'unhappiness' is due to an

unsatisfied desire for complete consciousness of self. In Sartre, consciousness is continually being frustrated by being thrown outside of itself, for consciousness can never achieve happiness or repose in itself. Thus, a Sartrian consciousness is denied the absolute. (HJS)

28 *mesurant*, which stands in opposition with *mesuré*. Literally, these would be measurer, or measuring, (*mesurant*) and measured (*mesuré*). The participle used as a substantive (here *mesurant*) is equivocal. I translate it as 'standard of measurement' (or just 'standard') to mean 'measurer,' but it could also be rendered as 'the act of measuring,' both of which are distinct from what is measured (*mesuré*): the measured. The opposition is parallel to de Saussure's conception of signifier (*significant*) and signified (*signifié*) in his *Course in General Linguistics*, trans. Wade Baskin (New York, McGraw-Hill, 1959). In his semiology, however, the nature of the opposition (as de Saussure calls it) or relation, is precisely the 'sign.' Merleau-Ponty, who taught a course on de Saussure at the *École Normale Supérièure* in 1948–9, would certainly be aware of this implication. See Merleau-Ponty, *Consciousness and the Acquisition of Language*, trans. Hugh J. Silverman (Evanston, Northwestern University Press, 1973) for a further discussion of the linguistic model. If the *mesurant* is the standard of measurement and the *mesuré* is what is being measured, then the relation may well be the measurement itself as a form of sign. (HJS)

29 The French text reads 'natural consciousness'. However, from the sense of the passage, Merleau-Ponty must have meant 'philosophical consciousness.' (HJS)

30 Merleau-Ponty follows the same paragraph divisions Heidegger indicates. (CL) Hegel's Introduction is divided by Heidegger into sixteen paragraphs. Merleau-Ponty has commented upon the first twelve. At this point he translates the last four paragraphs into French and comments on them in pairs. (HJS)

31 K. R. Dove's translation of Hegel has been followed here, except where Merleau-Ponty has selected a term or phrase which emphasizes a different interpretive direction. The German phraseology included in these passages is found parenthetically in Merleau-Ponty's French version and not in the Dove rendering. (HJS)

32 'Since consciousness provides itself with its own standard, the investigation will be a comparison of consciousness with its own self.' (*Holz*, p. 113; trans., p. 20) (M-P)

33 We might hypothesize that Merleau-Ponty is suggesting the relationship between nature and culture in Lévi-Strauss' work.

Nature achieves its form through social and cultural structures (kinship, myth, prohibitions) and the latter have their basis in nature. The point becomes particularly evident in the relationship between exchange and symbolic function within kinship systems, as Merleau-Ponty points out in 'From Mauss to Lévi-Strauss,' *Signs*, trans. Richard C. McCleary (Evanston, Northwestern University Press, 1964), pp. 114–25. (HJS)

34 *automovement*. As Piaget points out in his *Que sais-je?* volume entitled *Structuralism*, trans. Chaninah Maschler (New York, Harper & Row, 1970), one of the three key elements of a structure is its self-regulative aspect, along with wholeness and transformation. (HJS)

35 In a footnote to their translation of Heidegger's *Being and Time* (New York, Harper & Row, 1962), p. 377, J. Macquarrie and E. Robinson write:

> The root meaning of the word 'ectasis' (Greek ἔκσασις; German, '*Ekstase*') is 'standing outside.' Used generally in Greek for the 'removal' or 'displacement' of something, it came to be applied to states-of-mind which we would now call 'ecstatic.' Heidegger usually keeps the basic root-meaning in mind, but he also is keenly aware of its close connection with the root-meaning of the word 'existence.'

The relevant passage from *Being and Time* itself, p. 377, reads, 'Temporality is the primordial "outside-of-itself" in and for itself. We therefore call the phenomena of the future, the character of having been, and the Present, the "*ecstases*" of temporality.' (HJS)

36 *Sens* can be both sense (or meaning) and direction. Merleau-Ponty is concerned here that Husserl's notions of *noema* (*Sinn* or meaning (*sens*)-given in an intentional act) and *noesis* (*Sinngebung* or meaning (*sens*)-giving act) not be taken as unidirectional. It might be argued that Brentano understood intentionality, the directionality out of which an object is known, as unidirectional. The act always precedes what is to be known. In Husserl, the noetic–noematic correlates form a structure in which neither has precedence. The difficulty, however, arises in that Husserl conceives of intentionality as starting from a transcendental ego going out toward the thing in question (*die Sache*). Merleau-Ponty wants us to realize that experience, or even consciousness, also comes from the subject matter (the thing) as well as from the self. (HJS)

37 Intertwining is the translation for *l'entrelacs* employed by Alphonso Lingis in Chapter 4 of *The Visible and the Invisible*, 'The Intertwining – The Chiasm,' pp. 130–55. (HJS)

38 *avènement*. The term is associated with the coming of Christ, but also with Heidegger's notion of *das Ereignis*. *Er-eignis* is that which comes to be one's own (*eigen*) property. *Das Ereignis* is sometimes rendered as 'appropriation.' Thus here with Merleau-Ponty, we have not only the advent of knowledge, but even more so, the appropriation of knowledge. For an extended study of *das Ereignis* see Otto Pöggeler, 'Being as appropriation' in *Philosophy Today*, Vol. 19, No. 2/4 (Summer, 1975). The monograph originally appeared in German as '*Sein als Ereignis*' in 1959 (two years before Merleau-Ponty's course) and is translated by R. H. Grimm. Heidegger expanded his discussion of appropriation (or advent – as I translate *avènement* here), the year after Merleau-Ponty's death, in a lecture entitled *Time and Being*, trans. Joan Stambaugh (New York, Harper & Row, 1972). It was first published in France as the lead paper of a *Festschrift* for Jean Beaufret: *L'Endurance de la pensée* (Paris, Plon, 1968). In this text, Heidegger indicates the manner in which time is given and appropriated along with Being. (HJS)

39 As early as *Phenomenology of Perception* (1945) trans. Colin Smith (London, Routledge & Kegan Paul, 1962), Merleau-Ponty had developed his notion of the *déjà là*. For him intentionality is precisely the experience of what is already there. (HJS)

40 Merleau-Ponty's version of this sentence diverges significantly from Dove's translation. As indicated in note 31, I approximate the French text. (HJS)

41 Jean Hyppolite is the French translator of Hegel's *Phenomenology of Mind*. His important commentary on that work is now in English as *Genesis and Structure of Hegel's Phenomenology of Spirit* (1947), trans. S. Cherniak and J. Heckman (Evanston, Northwestern University Press, 1974). (HJS)

42 The colloquial translation of *aufheben* as 'canning' is relevant here in that Merleau-Ponty speaks of *dépassment* in relation to a process of conserving. That surpassing is also conserving is what occurs when fruit, for example, is taken out of its fresh state, preserved, and hence given a new form. See also note 5. (HJS)

43 *Umkehrung* is literally a 'turning around' or 'overturning' ('reversal,' 'inversion,' or 'conversion') of consciousness. (HJS)

44 The expression '*le chemin, s'il mène quelque part*' alludes to the French title of Heidegger's *Holzwege*, i.e. *Chemins qui ne mènent nulle part*, trans. W. Brokmeier (Paris, Gallimard, 1962). Literally it means 'Paths which Lead Nowhere.' The phrase 'the path, if it is going somewhere' is therefore presented with *Holzwege* in the background. As such, for philosophy, it is a conditional that is either counterfactual or rhetorical. We may also recall Merleau-

Ponty's own introduction to an anthology of major philosophers, *Les Philosophes célèbres*, which he entitled 'Partout et nulle part' and which he included in *Signs* (translated as 'Everywhere and Nowhere,' pp. 126–58). The path, about which Merleau-Ponty speaks in the text offered here, is between 'everywhere' and 'nowhere.' Hence it has a unitary direction, it is science and not philosophy, not the experience of consciousness. (HJS)

45 παρουσία, being present, presence. It is related to ουσία, being, essence. Heidegger defines them as παρουσία, *Präsenz*, presence; and as ουσία, *Seienheit*, mode of being, or state of being, something that is. They are the ontic analogies of the ontological *Anwesenheit* (Presence) and *Sein* (Being). See, for example, *Holz*, p. 122; trans., p. 34. (HJS)

46 In the Greek polis a certain form of self-understanding is established from tyranny through the court of the Areopagus and then in democratic government until ultimately it becomes part of the Macedonian and subsequently Roman empires. At each stage, a Gestalt arises, but it does not have full independent knowledge of itself. On the one hand, it is related to a previous form, on the other it is moving toward a new Gestalt. Similarly, in Christianity, the form established in Christ's own lifetime could not have had the knowledge within it of what it would be under the Apostles, Paul, Augustine, Anselm, Thomas Aquinas, and on. The appearing of the phenomenon in human history is an indication in human history of each stage in its development. Hence, at no moment is a particular *Gestalt* 'free.' (HJS)

47 *Erscheinung* is the appearance, whose root word is *Schein*, a shining forth. Hence the appearance makes itself separate from what appears. See note 22. (HJS)

48 [marginal note] cf. Goethe: *man geht nie weiter, als wenn man nicht mehr weiss wohin man geht.* – In being a full phenomenon, the absolute is fully absolute. (M-P). The passage from Goethe can be translated: one never goes further than when he no longer knows where he is going. (HJS)

49 Merleau-Ponty is proposing that from 'demonstration' (someone showing something) follows the neologism 'auto-monstration' (someone showing oneself or something showing itself). (HJS)

50 The reference is to Montaigne's pyrrhonist question: *Que sais-je?* (What do I know?). With Montaigne, particularly in his skeptical period (as distinct from his enthusiasm for epicureanism and stoicism), little, if any, knowledge of the various levels of the great chain of being could be acquired. Conviction could be based only

in skepticism and in fideism. See Merleau-Ponty's essay 'Reading Montaigne' in *Signs*, pp. 198–210. (HJS)

51 The crack (*fissure*) causes failure because it allows a support system to crumble, while the overhang (*porte à faux*) is where the support system has overextended itself causing the whole structure to fall. Merleau-Ponty's metaphors are designed to indicate two opposing cases in which consciousness could be viewed as inadequate. Since these two alternatives (consciousness as a hole in being and consciousness as overhanging outside itself) may be construed as consistent with Sartre's position, this may be a further critique of Sartre. (HJS)

52 The meaning of intentionality as bi-directionality, as an intentional arc which is reversible, is Merleau-Ponty's particular contribution. Of course, he is assisted by his understanding of the Hegelian dialectic as this bi-directionality. From the time of *Phenomenology of Perception*, Merleau-Ponty has emphasized the reversibility of conscious experience. In his view (a position that would be difficult to ascribe to Husserl), intentionality is both sparks flying up at us and our grasping of them.

53 Merleau-Ponty's association of the unreflected with 'perceptual faith' as against reflection is elaborated in the first chapter of *The Visible and the Invisible*, pp. 3–49, entitled 'Reflection and Interrogation.' (HJS)

54 [marginal note] This is a knowledge in which subject and object, savage consciousness and reflected consciousness reciprocate each other. Both fall within knowledge, which is therefore not our *Singebung*, itself. (M-P)

55 Lévi-Strauss' structural anthropology presupposes that criticism can be addressed both at the object of research and at study of the object. Attention given to only one or to the other: the collected facts or the research itself will not show that the true focus of interest should be the relation between the two. This relation is revealed in terms of structures: structures of kinship, myth, and totem. The resolution of the double critique is the concept of structure. See note 33. (HJS)

56 See note 35.

57 *négatité* corresponding to *entité*. *Negatité* is Sartre's term in *Being and Nothingness* for the implication of some element of negativity in human activity. This would include experiences such as the presence of absence. Merleau-Ponty considers *négatité* as a pole opposed to *entité* and essentially static, while negativity is the active component which mediates *qua* consciousness. (HJS)

58 Kierkegaard's conception of the 'becoming' of the human indi-

vidual (in *Concluding Unscientific Postscript*) is matched here with, for example, Abraham the Knight of Faith who must sacrifice his son Isaac at the request of God (in *Fear and Trembling*). Abraham must will the impossible. For him simply to affirm his faith to others would not be to establish it. Abraham must go beyond any objectification of his belief (the leap of faith). Since the Pharisees were the doctors of law, self-righteous in their strict observance of doctrine and ritual, Merleau-Ponty is suggesting, paradoxically, that Kierkegaard's affirmation that one cannot be a Christian when one claims to be a Christian is itself a Pharisaical law. For Kierkegaard to deny someone his Christianity on the basis of his assertion of faith is a kind of law which seems to be set down to hold in all cases. (HJS)

59 *Vieldeutigkeit* emphasizes the multiplicity of meanings. *Zweideutigkeit* (cited above in adjectival form), usually translated as ambiguity, also has the sense of multiple meanings given at once. (HJS)

60 [marginal note] what is essentially vision and not *Sinngebung*. (M-P)

61 The verb *begreifen*, which means 'to grasp' or 'to comprehend,' is the term which Merleau-Ponty has translated as '*saisir*.' He plays on the relationship between *begreifen* and *Begriff* (i.e. concept) in this sentence. (HJS)

62 [marginal note] the experience as *reine* [purely] *Zusehen*. Reciprocally in Marx

1 the dialectic of consciousness is illusory only as long as the principle of alienation remains (Lukács: *Funktion-Wandel*). Afterwards, dialectic is no longer a reflection of matter. – Capitalism is a phenomenology of concrete experience. –

2 Even before the revolution, no given force perfects Reason; human matter, the non-objective.

Lenin: one needs an oblique consciousness, the party (without which there would be trade-unionism) – Dialectic-*Erfahrung* is the philosophy of Marx just as it is that of Hegel. For both, there cannot be simple [assent?] to a mystique of experience. What is necessary is a *Begriff*, by which the experience of capitalism will be understood – or even by which the externalization, to the extent that it is necessary, will be recognized. Without this *Begriff*, consciousness (which is its own concept) might be misguided.

Certain Marxisms will give a major role to experience (i.e. the reabsorption of the State into society) or, conversely, they will make this *praxis* itself into the work of dictatorship. Hegel keeps it on the border. Precisely if truth is experience, it must not be a shocking experience; there ought to be [a mystery?], a philosophy (a logic).

Cf. para. 15 – Show that experience as progress towards truth requires an *Umkehrung* of *Bewusstsein* (that the thing becomes consciousness). But this means that science is not life. – There are two orders:

1 the idea itself of experience, as truth, controlling from outside experience (the very idea of the proletariat becoming the control of the Party over the proletariat); and

2 the very idea of phenomena, as carriers of truth, becoming extreme dogmatism.

– What is the solution? (M-P)

63 [marginal note] Recall the problem at hand:

1 Nothing can enter into [phenomenology] from the outside; it is 'open,' experience, and, therefore, nothing can get behind its back. –

2 Experience can be discontinuous, 'empirical,' erroneous, and blind. A *Zutat* of philosophy would therefore be necessary, something that goes behind the back of *Bewusstsein*. –

3 *Bewusstsein* is a surpassing of *Bewusstsein*, [whence] Logic (the solution given in the last paragraph). (M-P)

64 The date in which Hegel's *Phenomenology of Mind* was published. (HJS)

65 The Moscow Trials, which Koestler discussed in *Darkness at Noon*, and which serve as the focus for Merleau-Ponty's interpretation of Bukharin's 'defense' in *Humanism and Terror*, trans. John O'Neill (Boston, Beacon, 1969). (HJS)

66 The alienation which Hegel delineates in the master–slave relation, but which his successors argue he has eliminated in his formulation of the State, history, mind, etc. The collapsing, congealing, or eliminating occurs through synthesis. (HJS)

67 The object in the sense of that which stands against or alongside what is there. Consciousness, on the other hand, opposes itself to the *Gegenstand* or object. Consciousness separates itself from what is there. (HJS)

68 [marginal note] The ambiguity, a representational concept – *dieses Zweideutige ist das Form das Vorstellens* (Heidegger, *Holz*, p. 153; trans, p. 90), but the philosophy of *Vorstellen* tends to surpass itself as *Bewusstsein* achieves its reversal. (M-P)

69 ὄν ἤ ὄν – 'the other side' (*nach der anderer Seite*) (*Holz*, p. 144; trans., p. 73. M-P).

70 'Science of the Experience of Consciousness' [marginal note] the announced title for *The Phenomenology of Mind* and for which had

been substituted *Die Phänomenologie des Geistes*, then (1832), *Phänomenologie des Geistes*. (M-P)

71 *'gestaltet* itself.' For example, the master's search for recognition is objectivized and, in that way, surpassed. (M-P)

72 We do not even allow men the consciousness of what they do, their experience –; we overburden them with the weight of history. (M-P)

[At the bottom of the page underneath this footnote, separated by a dash, the following few lines summarize the subsequent development of thought. (CL)]

Hegel's solution (circularity – Hegelian 'equivocation' is more and more skeptic-dogmatic – the emptiness of absolute knowledge – reconciliation – what is the Hegelian absolute?)

The impossibility of this solution. Return to Hegelian dogmatism (The *Logic* – The *Encyclopedia*) – Phenomenology under a particular determination of consciousness leaves a place for metaphysics or logic which is the dialectic of Being –. As for his successors, Marx's critique must be placed aside, in that it does not see

1 that Hegel has seen the problem of the inverted world, and that his secret from experience *runs counter to* dogmatism;
2 that Marx himself with his philosophy of the object falls back into the dogmatism of absolute subjectivity.

The reason for this failure is that consciousness, subject–object, is a *philosophy of representation*, which necessarily ends up in ambiguity, that is, in skeptico-dogmatism, and hence the absence of philosophy–non-philosophy.

The solution will be that neither naked experience, nor recourse to another source (i.e. God before the creation as Hegel notes in the *Logic*) is decisive. Only representation is an alternative. *Unsere Zutat*, the contribution of philosophy, must be precisely the abstention of all contribution, 'it is the mute experience which must be brought to pure expression in its own sense.' We must understand that the Being of what is, the *Erscheinen* of the *Erscheinende*, the 'birth' of truth is not the movement to another *Seiende*. Certainly, phenomenology, affected by the mark of consciousness, does not suffice, but what is beyond does not lack subjectivity either. (M-P)

73 See note 36. (HJS)

74 Jean Hyppolite, *Genèse et structure de la Phénoménologie de l'Esprit de Hegel*, (Aubier, Montaigne, 1947), p. 567. *Genesis and Structure of Hegel's Phenomenology of Spirit*, trans. S. Cherniak and J. Heckman (Evanston, Northwestern University Press, 1974), p. 588. (M-P)

75 Hegel, *Phänomenologie des Geistes*, Werke III (Frankfurt, Suhrkamp,

1970), p. 20. *The Phenomenology of Spirit*, trans. A. V. Miller (Oxford, Clarendon Press, 1977), p. 10. (M-P)

76 What is to be surpassed here are the sequential, successive impressions that the empiricist, such as Locke and Hume, regard as our only mode of Experience. For Hegel, sense-certainty is not yet the absolute. (HJS)

77 Hegel, *Logik*, IV, p. 31. (M-P)

78 Hyppolite, *Genèse et Structure*, p. 566 (M-P); *Genesis and Structure*, p. 586. (HJS)

79 The movement of categories should include the Self, but it tacitly presupposes the concept. (M-P)

80 Hegel, *Phänomenologie*, p. 30. (M-P)

81 It is worthy of note that this statement by Heidegger comes near the end of 'Hegel's Concept of Experience,' which is followed (in *Holzwege*) by his essay 'Nietzsches Wort "Got ist Tot," ' *Holz*, pp. 193–247. (HJS)

82 Signification arises out of experience as the act or process of giving meaning to experience. 'Oldness' is associated here with that which is established, and with tradition, and with what is unself-consciousness. (HJS)

83 See note 58. (HJS)

84 [marginal note] the Hegelian absolute is the decay of a separate absolute, the death of God; this does not mean 'There is no God,' the end of all fetishizing. (M-P)

85 In French paper currency, the water-mark of Voltaire, for example, appears to be neither on one side nor on the other. One must hold the bill up to the light in order to see the image. Hence, Merleau-Ponty claims that the absolute is 'within' the movement of experience – like a water-mark. (HJS)

86 On at least two occasions, Merleau-Ponty made reference to the 'good ambiguity.' At the time of his candidacy to the *Collège de France*, i.e. between 1951 and 1952, he sent a text to Martial Gueroult which has come to be known as 'An Unpublished Text' trans. Arleen B. Dallery in *The Primacy of Perception*, ed. James M. Edie, (Evanston, Northwestern University Press, 1964), pp. 3–11. In the final paragraph, he writes:

> The study of perception could only teach us a 'bad ambiguity,'
> a mixture of finitude and universality, of interiority and
> exteriority. But there is a 'good ambiguity' in the phenomenon
> of expression, a spontaneity which accomplishes what
> appeared to be impossible when we observed only the separate
> elements, a spontaneity which gathers together the plurality

of monads, the past and the present, nature and culture into a single whole. (p. 11)

The second occasion is in his inaugural lecture to the *Collège de France*, given in 1952, entitled 'In Praise of Philosophy': *Éloge de la Philosophie* (Paris, Gallimard, 1953), pp. 10–11. The passage beings:

> The philosopher recognizes the *inseparability* of his taste for evidence and a sense of ambiguity. When he tries to keep himself out of ambiguity, it is called equivocation. With the greatest philosophers, it becomes a theme and contributes to the establishment of certainty instead of threatening it. We must therefore distinguish a bad ambiguity from a good one. Even those who have always wanted to create a fully positive philosophy have been philosophers only in that they have refused, in the same moment, the right to install themselves in absolute knowledge, and in that they have not taught this knowledge, but rather its becoming in us, not the absolute, but at the most, as Kierkegaard says, an *absolute relation* between it and us. (my trans)

Both the topic of an *absolute relation* between the absolute and us, and the polemic in favor of 'bad ambiguity' are again the focus, a decade later. (HJS)

87 The 'vertical' is the bi-directionality of the ambiguity: experience of knowledge and knowledge of experience. Experience is the vertical intentionality of the subject–object relation. Here it is given depth by the absolute. The absolute is the profundity (as Merleau-Ponty said of Nietzsche's Apollonian) and signification (also Dionysian appearance) arising out of experience. (HJS)

88 [marginal note] cf. Marx's claim 'I am not a Marxist.' What is needed is a self-critique of absolute knowledge, which is the only absolute, the only *Selbstbewusstsein*. An (external) knowledge of the absolute in the sense of *Bewusstsein* is, by definition, false. Marxist *praxis* is something like Kierkegaard's *decision*. (M-P) 'Kierkegaard's decision' could be either his 'attack upon Christendom' in order to assert what is truly Christian or his decision not to marry Regina because his ideal love for her could not be fulfilled. See also note 150. (HJS)

89 For Merleau-Ponty's stress upon utterance and the speaking subject in experience, see the 1949–50 *Consciousness and the Acquisition of Language*, and the posthumous *The Prose of the World*, trans. John O'Neill (Evanston, Northwestern University Press, 1973). The utterance can deny in content, but affirm by its very expression and *praxis*. (HJS)

90 The second part of 'Philosophy and Non-philosophy since Hegel' was published in a subsequent issue of *Textures*. A short statement repeats the information which Claude Lefort had already offered in the preceding issue (74, pp. 8–9) as part of his introduction. (HJS)

91 'A Contribution to the Critique of Hegel's Philosophy of Right,' and 'Economic and Philosophical Manuscripts' in Karl Marx, *Early Writings*, pp. 243–57, and pp. 280–400, respectively, trans. Rodney Livingstone and Gregor Benton (New York, Vintage, 1975). [Henceforth cited in the text as *EW*.] (HJS)

92 Note the 1839 Feuerbach article 'Towards a Critique of Hegelian Philosophy' in *The Fiery Brook: Selected Writings of Ludwig Feuerbach*, trans. Zawar Hanfi (New York, Anchor, 1972), pp. 53–96. (M-P)

93 Rendered alternatively as 'to settle accounts with our former philosophical conscience' in the Preface to *A Contribution to the Critique of Political Economy* in *EW*, p. 427. (HJS)

94 Literally, his own (*eigen*) movement (*Bewegung*). *Bewegung* is the term that Merleau-Ponty has rendered as '*passage*' in French, and which is translated into English as 'movement.' (HJS)

95 Hegel's project was for 'the world to become philosophy.' The task for Marx – and for Merleau-Ponty, as evidenced also by *The Visible and the Invisible* – is for 'philosophy to become the world.' This negation of philosophy as a realization of non-philosophy is more commonly characterized by Merleau-Ponty as 'philosophy becoming life.' In that way, he also reaffirms his debt to Bergson's vitalism. (HJS)

96 The references given refer to the *MEGA* (*Marx/Engels Gesamtausgabe*), I, vol. 1 (Frankfurt, 1927). (CL) The English version is 'A Contribution to the Critique of Hegel's Philosophy of Right. Introduction,' in *EW*, pp. 243–57. [Henceforth IntroCHPR] (HJS)

97 Note, for example, the treatment of Religion in the beginning of the 'Introduction.' (M-P)

98 Marx employs the French expression *à la hauteur des principes* in the German text. *MEGA*, pp. 613, 40–614, 22; IntroCHPR, p. 251. (HJS)

99 Charles Péguy (1873–1914), French poet and essayist, wrote *Clio, dialogue de l'histoire et de l'âme païenne* in 1909. Through Clio, the muse of history, he defends the mystical in his polemic against the modern spirit and the scientific view of history. (HJS)

100 *MEGA* I, 1, p. 63ff. (M-P). The thesis itself was entitled 'On the Difference between the Democritean and Epicurean Philosophy of Nature.' (HJS)

101 We have here a formula which without any further information

from Marx is not expressed according to his own goal. There is the world's becoming-philosophy which can be reduced to philosophy's becoming-world, that is, to its pure and simple destruction (and, without a doubt, also, philosophy's becoming-world which, in truth, is only the world's becoming philosophy, i.e. conservation of the system). Marx's goal is not to realize these two slogans as such. This would be a simple addition of illusions, with practice disguised behind theory and theory disguised behind practice. His goal would be to realize the chiasm of the two movements, the *two in one*. (M-P)

102 Cf. Hegel's analysis of 'the unhappy consciousness' in *Phenomenology of Spirit*. (M-P)

103 Read *MEGA*, p. 616; IntroCHPR, p. 252 (M-P). The passage indicated here occurs on p. 99 of the Costes edition: 'But Germany did not pass through the immediate stages of political emancipation at the same time as modern nations. . . . A radical revolution can only be the revolution of radical needs, but the preconditions and seed beds for such needs appear to be lacking.' (CL)

104 Read *MEGA*, p. 619; IntroCHPR, p. 156 (M-P).

105 Read *MEGA*, pp. 219–20; IntroCHPR, p. 256 (M-P). 'This is our answer . . . this dissolution of society as a particular class in the proletariat.' (CL)

106 *MEGA*, pp. 620, 35–621,10; IntroCHPR, p. 257: 'Just as philosophy finds its material weapons in the proletariat . . . the proletariat cannot transcend itself without the realization (*Verwirklichung*) of philosophy.' (CL)

107 See note 38. (HJS)

108 Merleau-Ponty's translation of this expression as 'mystery of existence,' rather than 'secret of its own existence,' recalls Gabriel Marcel's use of the phrase. One of Merleau-Ponty's earliest publications was a review of Marcel's book *Being and Having* in *La Vie Intellectuelle* (1936). (HJS)

109 The notes which follow occur in the margin at the end of the manuscript for the preceding lecture. Then there are new notes which again bear the April 24 date. (CL)

110 Same as note 106. (M-P)

111 Merleau-Ponty translates and comments upon the texts referred to here in the next lecture. (CL) *Economic and Philosophical Manuscripts* (1844) in *EW*, pp. 281–400. Henceforth cited as *EPM*. (HJS)

112 This text is in accord with the views of Feuerbach. Cf. *MEGA*, p. 152; *EPM*, p. 382. (M-P)

113 Merleau-Ponty translates from the German; therefore I have attempted (here and in subsequent passages from *EPM*) to render

an approximation to his French version in English. However, the reader will also note the similarity to the Benton translation indicated above. (HJS)

114 See note 123 on 'nowhere and everywhere.' (HJS)

115 It goes without saying that when the abstract thinker decides in favor of intuition, he sees nature abstractly. For the abstract thinker, nature lies enclosed in a hidden shape, and nature itself remains enigmatic, like the absolute Idea, and like a rational thing. When the abstract thinker gives birth to nature out of himself, it is, in truth, still only abstract nature. In adding to it the sense of a 'being-other of thought', real, intuitive nature is distinguished from the abstract thinker. Only nature as a rational thing has been born from him. Or even, to speak in human language, the abstract thinker discovers, from his intuition of the experience of nature, that those beings which he thought he was creating out of nothing, out of pure abstraction, in a divine dialectic (as the pure products of the labor of thought weaving into thought itself. without ever looking at reality) are nothing other than abstractions drawn from nature's determinations. For the abstract thinker, the whole of nature amounts only to a repetition of logical abstractions in a sensuous and external form. He analyzes nature and the abstractions again. His intuition of nature therefore is only a renewal of the abstraction from the intuition of nature, a conscious reenactment of the process by which he produced his abstraction. For example, time becomes the image of negativity referred back to itself. The future surpassed as being-there (*Dasein*) corresponds to the natural form of movement, surpassed as matter. Light is the natural form of reflection-in-itself. Body, such as the moon and the comets, is the natural form of opposition, which, according to the *Logic*, is the positive resting on itself, and the negative resting on itself. The earth is the natural form of the logical ground (*Grund*) – as the negative unity of the opposition, etc. In so far as it is appreciably distinct from its secret sense hidden within itself, separate and different from these abstractions, nature *qua* nature is nothing, a nothing confirming itself as nothing. Nature has no sense, or has only the sense of an externality that has to be surpassed. . . . Externality should not be understood here as self-externalizing sensuousness (*Sinnlichkeit*), accessible to light and to sensuous men. There is no externality except in the sense of alienation (*Entaüsserung*), in the sense of a flaw, a weakness which ought not to be. For that which is true is still the Idea. Nature is only

the form of its Being-other. *MEGA*, pp. 170–1; *EPM*, pp. 398–200. (M-P)

116 L. Feuerbach, 'Preliminary Theses on the Reform of Philosophy' (1842), in *The Fiery Brook*, trans. Z. Hanfi, p. 154. (HJS)
117 György Lukács, *Der junge Hegel und die Probleme der kapitalistischen Gesellschaft* (Zürich, Europa-Verlag AG, 1948), p. 708. (M-P)
118 [marginal note] Man has his sense, his being outside himself. The relation subject–object is born out of a pre-conscious relation with the outside. It is not a 'pure activity,' but an 'objective' heavy one. Cf. *MEGA*, p. 160; *EPM*, p. 389. (M-P)
119 [marginal note] And, at the same time, because he has this instinctual relation with things, he is 'other' for another man. – Intercorporality. – Chiasm: nature–sociality. Man produces and reproduces society. He is produced and reproduced by it, just as he produces objects and is produced by them. *MEGA*, pp. 115–16; *EPM*, pp. 349–50. (M-P)
120 [marginal note] '*Society* is the perfected unity in essence of man with nature, the realized naturalism of man and the realized humanism of nature' (*MEGA*, pp. 115–16; *EPM*, pp. 349–50). (M-P)
121 [marginal note] Everything that precedes was only a natural [peculiarity?], but because man is for himself, he is a generality, that is, he interiorizes his relations with the world and with the other, or he projects himself into them. He is the others and they are he. (M-P)
122 Lukács, *Der junge Hegel*, p. 708. (M-P)
123 *Ibid*, p. 686 (M-P)
124 Jean Hyppolite, *Logique et existence: Essai sur la logique de Hegel* (Paris, Presses Universitaires de France, 1952), p. 238. (M-P) [Henceforth cited in the text as *LE*].

CHAPTER 2   JOHN SALLIS: ECHOES: PHILOSOPHY AND NON-PHILOSOPHY AFTER HEIDEGGER

1 Ovid, *Metamorphoses*, III, lines 359–61. Translation cited is that of Rolfe Humphries (Bloomington, Indiana University Press, 1955).
2 *Ibid.*, III, lines 390–2.
3 *Ibid.*, III, lines 396–401.
4 Longus, *Daphnis and Chloe*, III, 23. Translation cited is that of George Thornley (London, William Heinemann, 1916).
5 Parmenides, I, lines 28–30. Translation cited is that of Leonardo Taran, *Parmenides* (Princeton, Princeton University Press, 1965), p. 9.

6 Plato, *Sophist*, p. 216 c-d. Translation cited is that of H. N. Fowler (London, William Heinemann, 1921).

7 G. W. F. Hegel, 'Einleitung. Über das Wesen der philosophischen Kritik überhaupt und ihr Verhältnis zum gegenwärtigen Zustand der Philosophie insbesondere,' *Jenaer Kritische Schriften*, eds Hartmut Buchner and Otto Pöggeler, *Gesammelte Werke* (Hamburg, Felix Meiner Verlag, 1968), IV, pp. 124f.

8 Maurice Merleau-Ponty, 'Philosophy and Non-Philosophy since Hegel,' trans. Hugh J. Silverman, *supra*, p. 46.

9 Martin Heidegger, *Sein und Zeit* (Tübingen, Max Niemeyer Verlag, 1960, 9th edition), p. 15.

10 *Ibid.*, p. 140.

11 Cf. Jacques Derrida, 'Les Fins de l'homme,' *Marges de la philosophie* (Paris, Les Éditions de Minuit, 1972), esp. pp. 147ff.

12 Martin Heidegger, *Die Grundprobleme der Phänomenologie* (Frankfurt a.M., Vittorio Klostermann, 1975), p. 106. English translation by Albert Hofstadter, *The Basic Problems of Phenomenology* (Bloomington, Indiana University Press, 1982), p. 75.

13 *Ibid.*, pp. 149ff. (Engl. pp. 106ff.).

14 Martin Heidegger, 'Das Ende der Philosophie und die Aufgabe des Denkens,' *Zur Sache des Denkens* (Tübingen, Max Niemeyer Verlag, 1969), p. 61. English translation by Joan Stambaugh: 'The End of Philosophy and the Task of Thinking,' in Martin Heidegger, *Basic Writings*, ed. D. F. Krell (New York, Harper & Row, 1977), p. 373. (Hereafter cited as E with page-numbers, first, of the German edition, second, of the English translation.)

15 These formulations and several others that cannot be systematically developed in the present context are dealt with more extensively in John Sallis, *Delimitations: Phenomenology and the End of Metaphysics* (Bloomington, Indiana University Press, 1986), esp. Part III.

16 Martin Heidegger, *Nietzsche* (Pfullingen, Günther Neske, 1961), vol. II, p. 201. English translation by Frank A. Cappuzzi: *Nietzsche*, vol. IV: Nihilism (San Francisco, Harper & Row, 1982), p. 148.

17 *Ibid.*

18 Matters would be more complex if one proceeded in terms of Heidegger's entire project as sketched in the introductory chapters rather than in terms of the two published Divisions. One would then need to distinguish between *Temporalität*, the meaning of Being as such, and *Zeitlichkeit*, the temporality of Dasein. But the published portion of *Being and Time* provides virtually no means for developing this distinction.

19 Cf. Martin Heidegger, *Parmenides* (Frankfurt a.M., Vittorio Klostermann, 1982), p. 6f.

20 An extended account of the exchange between Heidegger and Friedländer is given by Robert Bernasconi, *The Question of Language in Heidegger's History of Being* (Atlantic Highlands, Humanities Press, 1985), ch. 2. I have dealt with it, more briefly, in *Delimitations*, ch. 14.

21 Martin Heidegger, 'Seminar in Zäringen 1973,' in *Vier Seminare* (Frankfurt a.M., Vittorio Klostermann, 1977). Hereafter S.

I am grateful to Kenneth Maly for calling my attention to the importance of this text in a seminar that he conducted near ancient Elea during the 1985 session of the Collegium Phaenomenologicum.

22 Such a thrust in the direction opposite that established by the regress from Being to clearing is broached, though briefly, in the very passage of 'The End of Philosophy and the Task of Thinking' where the regress is first traced, indeed in the very sentence that bespeaks the transgression: 'But brightness in its turn rests in something open, something free, which it might illuminate here and there, now and then' (E, p. 71/383f.). This point is unfortunately obscured by an error in the English translation.

CHAPTER 3   PETER CAWS: SARTRE'S LAST PHILOSOPHICAL MANIFESTO

1 Jean-Paul Sartre, *Life/Situations: Essays Written and Spoken*, trans. Paul Auster and Lydia Davis (New York, Pantheon Books, 1977), p. 20.

2 Peter Caws, *Sartre* (London, Routledge & Kegan Paul (paperback edition with additional notes) 1984), p. 140.

3 Jean-Paul Sartre, *Between Existentialism and Marxism* (New York, Pantheon Books, 1974), p. 10.

4 Jean-Paul Sartre, *Search for a Method*, trans. Hazel E. Barnes (New York, Alfred A. Knopf, 1963), p. 76 (emphasis added).

5 Jean-Paul Sartre, *L'Idiot de la famille: Gustave Flaubert de 1821 à 1857* (Paris, NRF/Gallimard, 1972), vol. III. (Henceforth cited as *IF* 3; translations are my own.)

6 Peter Caws, 'Oracular Lives: Sartre and the Twentieth Century,' *Revue Internationale de Philosophie*, no. 152–3, 1985, pp. 176ff.

7 Jean-Paul Sartre, *Critique de la Raison dialectique*, tome II (inachevé): *L'Intelligibilité de l'histoire*, ed. Arlette Elkaim-Sartre (Paris, NRF/Gallimard, 1985). (Henceforth cited as *CRD* 2.)

CHAPTER 4   WILLIAM J. RICHARDSON: LACAN AND ANTI-PHILOSOPHY

1 See, for example, the work of: A. Juranville, *Lacan et la philosophie* (Paris, Presses Universitaires de France, 1984, henceforth cited as

LP); J. Dor, 'L'alienation philosophique de l'enjeu psychanalytique,' in *Esquisses Psychanalytiques* 5, 43–7, 1986; E. Ragland-Sullivan, *Jacques Lacan and the Philosophy of Psychoanalysis* (Chicago, University of Illinois Press, 1986).

2 J. Lacan, *Écrits: A Selection*, trans. A. Sheridan (New York, Norton, 1977), p. 105 (henceforth cited as *E*).

3 For example: see Casey-Woody, in J. Smith and W. Kerrigan, eds, *Interpreting Lacan*, (New Haven, Yale, 1983, henceforth cited as *IL*) with regard to Hegel; with regard to Heidegger, see W. Richardson, 'Psychoanalysis and the Being-question,' in *IL*, pp. 139–59.

4 J. Lacan, *The Four Fundamental Concepts of Psychoanalysis*, ed. J.-A. Miller, trans. A. Sheridan (New York, Norton, 1978), p. 18.

5 J. Lacan, *Le Seminaire: Livre XX. Encore*, (Paris, Editions du Seuil, 1972), p. 108 (henceforth cited as *XX*).

6 *XX*, p. 16. This and all the translations that follow are the author's own.

7 *Ibid.*, p. 40.

8 For the full scope of the problem, see *LP*.

9 J. Lacan, *Le Seminaire: Livre XVII, L'envers de la psychanalyse* (1969–70), unpublished manuscript, p. 51 (henceforth cited as *XVII*).

10 For a fuller exposition of Lacan's use of Saussurean linguistics, see, J. Muller and W. Richardson, *Lacan and Language. A Reader's Guide to the Écrits* (New York, International Universities Press, 1983), pp. 1–25.

11 *E*, pp. 153–4.

12 Translation problem: *Objet petit a* flows mellifluously off the Gallic tongue, but 'little o object' does less well in English. Besides being less melodious, it is less precise than the French. The *cognoscenti* tell us that it shouldn't be translated anyway, for as an algebraic sign it is a specimen of the 'mathematical formalism' that, as such, Lacan claims is 'capable of being transmitted integrally' (*E*, p. 108). Maybe so, but 'object little a,' for this Anglo-Saxon ear, doesn't work either. I propose to transpose it as the Greek α (*alpha*): because Greek letters are familiar in English as acceptable algebraic symbols; because *alpha* is the first letter of the Greek word *agalma*, which serves as a prime example of *objet a* in Lacan's Seminar VIII: *On Transference* (*Le Seminaire VIII: Le Transfer* (1960–1), unpublished manuscript); because, once explained, it sounds better and is more easily intelligible in spoken discourse.

13 The ensemble appears, for example, as follows (cf. 'Radiophonie,' *Scilicet* 2/3 1970, p. 99):

$$
\text{M} \qquad\qquad\qquad \text{U}
$$

$$
\frac{S_1}{\$} \rightarrow \frac{S_2}{\alpha} \qquad\qquad \frac{S_2}{S_1} \rightarrow \frac{\alpha}{\$}
$$

$$
\text{H} \qquad\qquad\qquad \text{A}
$$

$$
\frac{\$}{\alpha} \rightarrow \frac{S_1}{S_2} \qquad\qquad \frac{\alpha}{S_2} \rightarrow \frac{\$}{S_1}
$$

14 See, J. Clavreul, *L'Ordre medical* (Paris, Seuil, 1978). Clavreul's entire study is worthwhile, but pp. 159–72 in particular offer an illuminating summary of the four discourses. See also, M. Marini, *Jacques Lacan* (Paris, Pierre Belfond, 1986), pp. 70–4.

15 A full explanation of the analogy with Hegel would force one to ask whether the eventual reverse of roles between master and slave in the evolution of the Hegelian dialectic finds correlation in an eventual reversal between S_1 and S_2 in the discourse of the master, but Lacan does not go that far in Seminar XVII.

16 See, W. Richardson, 'Lacan and the Subject of Psychoanalysis,' in *IL*, pp. 51–74 (henceforth cited as LSP).

17 *XX*, p. 81.

18 Just as desire in the subject is articulated in metonymic fashion through the chain of signifiers in terms of the symbolic order, so, too, the object α, which 'causes' desire, is represented by a myriad of images (i.e. 'phantasms') that correlate with the signifying chain in terms of the imaginary order.

19 P. L. Assoun, *Freud, la philosophie et les philosophes* (Paris, Presses Universitaires de France, 1976) Chapter I, cited by Dor, p. 45.

20 J. Lacan, *Écrits* (Paris, Editions du Seuil, 1966), p. 31.

21 I am translating *parler* by 'to speak' and *'dire'* by 'to say.'

22 Within the limits of the present reflection, it is impossible to examine how, in the philosophic enterprise, both university discourse and the discourse of the hysteric intertwine with the discourse of the master in a kind of dialectic. Lacan treats the matter in Seminar XVII. See *LP*, pp. 353–8.

23 Muller orchestrates this theme in terms of the notion of 'gap' (see J. Muller, 'The Analogy of Gap in Lacan's *Écrits: A Selection*,' in *Psychohistory Review*, 8(3), pp. 38–45).

24 I have attempted to examine basic conceptions of Heidegger in terms of their possible relevance to Lacan elsewhere (LSP, and W. Richardson, 'Psychoanalysis and the God-question,' in *Thought*, 61 (March, 1986), pp. 68–83 (henceforth cited as 'PG').

25 J. Lacan, trans., 'Logos,' de M. Heidegger, *La Psychanalyse* 1, 1959, pp. 59–79.

26 'PG.'

27 G. S. Kirk and J. E. Raven, *The Presocratic Philosophers* (New York, Cambridge University Press, 1957), p. 211.
28 M. Heidegger, *Introduction to Metaphysics*, trans. R. Manheim (New Haven, Yale, 1959), pp. 14–15 (henceforth cited as *IM*).
29 M. Heidegger, *Early Greek Thinking*, trans. D. Krell and F. Capuzzi (New York, Harper & Row, 1975), pp. 207–9 (henceforth cited as *EGT*).

CHAPTER 5 TONY O'CONNOR: FOUCAULT AND THE TRANSGRESSION OF LIMITS

1 M. Merleau-Ponty, 'The Primacy of Perception and Its Philosophical Consequences', in: *The Primacy of Perception and Other Essays*, ed. James M. Edie (Evanston, Northwestern University Press, 1964), p. 28: 'I see your ideas as being better expressed in literature and painting than in philosophy. Your philosophy results in a novel' p. 30.
2 M. Merleau-Ponty, *Phenomenology of Perception*, trans. Colin Smith (London, Routledge & Kegan Paul, 1962).
3 H. Silverman, 'Re-Reading the Tradition with Merleau-Ponty', in *Telos* 29, Fall 1976, pp. 108–9. Also *Inscriptions*, ch. 8.
4 *Ibid.*
5 M. Foucault, *The Archaeology of Knowledge*, trans. A. M. Sheridan Smith (London, Tavistock, 1972), pp. 135–40.
6 *Ibid.*, pp. 191–2.
7 Merleau-Ponty, *Phenomenology of Perception*, pp. 3–12.
8 *Ibid.*, pp. 4–5.
9 U. Eco, 'How Culture Conditions the Colours We See,' in *On Signs*, ed. M. Blonsky (Oxford, Blackwell, 1985), p. 157.
10 *Ibid.*, p. 158.
11 *Ibid.*, p. 157. This is a Latin encyclopaedia of the second century ad.
12 *Ibid.*, p. 159.
13 M. Foucault, *The Order of Things*, (London, Tavistock, 1970), p. xv.
14 *Ibid.*, p. xvi.
15 *Ibid.*, p. xvii.
16 *Ibid.*
17 *Ibid.*
18 *Ibid.*, p. xviii.
19 *Ibid.*, p. 340.
20 Foucault, *The Archaeology of Knowledge*, p. 12.
21 Foucault, *The Order of Things*, p. 308.
22 *Ibid.*, p. 304.

23 M. Philip, 'Michel Foucault' in *The Return of Grand Theory in the Human Sciences*, ed. Q. Skinner (Cambridge, Cambridge University Press, 1985), p. 71.

24 G. Merquior, *Foucault* (London, Fontana, 1985), pp. 56–75.

25 P. Burgelin, 'L'archéologie du savoir,' in *Esprit*, 35, 1967, pp. 843–61.

26 M. Philip, p. 71.

27 Merquior, p. 71. Interestingly, it never occurs to Merquior to consider that what he calls 'the *story* of science' and 'the growing perfection' of knowledge forms, to be the story only according to one particular episteme or theoretical orientation. Rather it is simply assumed that the perfection story is settled without doubt, an assumption that is given added weight by quotations from historians, philosophers, and scientists who support this view. However, those thinkers like Popper, Kuhn, Feyerabend, Lakatos, etc., who hold a counter-view are not introduced into the debate, or their positions are summarily dismissed.

28 *Ibid.*, p. 148.

29 *Ibid.*, p. 149.

30 G. Rose, *Dialectic of Nihilism*, (Oxford, Blackwell, 1984), p. 171.

31 Foucault, *The Archaeology of Knowledge*, p. 122.

32 *Ibid.*, p. 38.

33 *Ibid.*, p. 72.

34 Foucault, 1970, *The Order of Things*, p. 326.

35 D. Føllesdal, 'Husserl and Heidegger on the Role of Actions in the Constitution of the World' in *Essays in Honour of Jaako Hintikka*, eds, E. Saarinen, R. Hilpinen, I. Niiniluoto, M. Provence Hintikka (Dordrecht, Reidel, 1979), p. 368.

36 J. Mepham, 'The Structuralist Sciences and Philosophy' in *Structuralism*, ed. D. Robey (Oxford, Clarendon Press, 1973), p. 129.

37 I have drawn on the work of A. F. Chalmers for this and subsequent formulations of Foucault's position. See, A. F. Chalmers, *What Is This Thing Called Science?* (Milton Keynes, Open University Press, 1982), pp. 125–33.

38 M. Foucault, *Discipline and Punish*, trans. Alan Sheridan (New York, Vintage Books, 1979).

39 *Ibid.*, p. 27.

40 M. Foucault, 'The Order of Discourse' in R. Young (ed.), *Untying the Text* (London, Routledge & Kegan Paul, 1981), p. 55.

41 *Ibid.*, p. 52.

42 Merquior, p. 148. See also J. Habermas, *Lectures on the Discourse of Modernity*, (Cambridge, Harvard University Press, 1985).

43 *Ibid.*, p. 147.

44 *Ibid.*
45 Foucault, *The Order of Things*, p. 189.
46 Foucault, *The Archaeology of Knowledge*, p. 10.
47 Foucault, *The Order of Things*, p. xiv.
48 Foucault, *The Archaeology of Knowledge*, pp. 21–7. See also F. Lentric-chia, *After the New Criticism* (London, Methuen, 1983), p. 193.
49 *Ibid.*, pp. 222–4.
50 M. Foucault and G. Deleuze, 'Intellectuals and Power', in *Language, Counter-Memory, Practice*, trans. Donald F. Bouchard and Sherry Simon (Ithaca, Cornell University Press, 1977), p. 209.
51 M. Foucault, *Power/Knowledge*, ed. C. Gordon (Brighton, Harvester Press, 1980), p. 98.
52 Chalmers, 1982, *op. cit.*, p. 121.
53 *Ibid.*, pp. 134–5.
54 M. Foucault, *The History of Sexuality*, vol. I, trans. Robert Hurley (Harmondsworth, Penguin, 1981), pp. 145–6.
55 *Ibid.*, p. 89.

CHAPTER 6   ALPHONSO LINGIS: DELEUZE ON A DESERTED ISLAND

1 Gilles Deleuze, *Logique du sens* (Paris, Minuit, 1969), 'Michel Tournier et le monde sans autrui,' pp. 350–72; Michel Tournier, *Friday*, trans. Norman Denny (New York, Pantheon, 1969).
2 Tournier, *Friday*, pp. 85 (henceforth cited as *F*).
3 K. Burridge, *Someone, No One: An Essay on Individuality* (Princeton, NJ, Princeton University Press, 1979), p. 96.

CHAPTER 7   STEPHEN H. WATSON: THE ADVENTURES OF THE NARRATIVE: LYOTARD AND THE PASSAGE OF THE PHANTASM

1 Jean Hyppolite, 'Existence et Dialectique dans la Philosophie de Merleau-Ponty,' *Les Temps Modernes*, no. 184–5, 1961, p. 228.
2 With regard to the importance of the work of Jean Cavaillès in this light see, for example: Michel Foucault, 'Introduction' to George Canguilhem, *On the Normal and Pathological*, trans. Caroly R. Fawcett (Dordrecht, Reidel, 1978), p. x; Michel Serres, *Hermès ou la communication* (Paris, Minuit, 1969), p. 67; Julia Kristeva, 'Du Sujet en Linguistique,' *Languages*, no. 24, December, 1971, p. 109; Jacques Derrida, *Edmund Husserl's Origin of Geometry: An Introduction*, trans. John P. Leavey (Stony Brook, Nicholas Hays, 1978), p. 142ff.: Jean-François Lyotard, *Économie libidinale* (Paris, Minuit, 1974), p. 300. (The last work will be abbreviated hereafter as *EL*.)

3 Jean-François Lyotard, *La phenomenologie* (Paris, Presses Universitaires de France, 1982). The first edition of this work was published in 1954. (This work will be abbreviated hereafter as *Ph*.)

4 Edmund Husserl, *Ideas Pertaining to a Pure Phenomenology and to a Phenomenological Philosophy*, trans. F. Kersten (The Hague, Martinus Nijhoff, 1982), p. 187.

5 Cp. *Ph*, p. 48. In this sense there is, to speak Kantian, a kind of transcendental illusion in phenomenology's attempt to bring about a harmonious resolution to what Foucault aptly called 'a transcendental-empirical doublet' in *The Order of Things* (New York, Pantheon, 1970), p. 318f. None the less the illusion was not one which could be readily surpassed. If it remained necessary to acknowledge what Lyotard, too, calls the 'duality' between the speculative and the evidential (*Ph*, p. 123), it remained likewise necessary to acknowledge the ineliminability of its 'richness,' as he likewise put it (*ibid.*), and hence the failure of its simple denial by a claim which would, again to speak Kantian, always imply more than it knows. Compare Lyotard's similar remarks in his recent book, *La différend* (Paris, Minuit, 1983), p. 23: 'It cannot be said that a hypothesis is verified, but only that until further notice it has not yet been falsified.' (This work will be referred to hereafter as *Dif*.)

6 While there is a certain rapprochement between Husserlian and Hegelian phenomenology, Lyotard acknowledged, that rapprochement finds a certain limit. From Husserl's standpoint, 'The recuperation of the totality of the real (in the Hegelian sense) appears as impossible' (*Ph*, p. 42). Rather, 'There is not, thus, an absolute truth, the common postulate of dogmatism and scepticism; truth is defined in becoming, as revision, correction and surpassing of itself' (*Ph*, p. 38).

7 Edmund Husserl, *Formal and Transcendental Logic*, trans. Dorion Cairns (The Hague, Martinus Nijhoff, 1978), p. 156. See Lyotard's discussion in *Ph*, pp. 38f.

8 Edmund Husserl, *Phenomenological Psychology*, trans. John Scanlon (The Hague, Martinus Nijhoff, 1977), p. 95.

9 Edmund Husserl, *Logical Investigations*, Vol. II, trans. J. N. Findlay (London, Routledge & Kegan Paul), pp. 784f. For further discussion of the issue see Jacques Taminiaux, 'Heidegger and Husserl's *Logical Investigations*: In Remembrance of Heidegger's Last Seminar,' in *Dialectic and Difference: Finitude in Modern Thought*, trans. R. Crease and J. Decker (Atlantic Highlands, NJ, Humanities, 1985).

10 Husserl, *Formal and Transcendental Logic*, p. 278.

11 Maurice Merleau-Ponty, *Phenomenology of Perception*, trans. Colin Smith (New York, Humanities, 1962), p. 241.

12 Husserl, *Formal and Transcendental Logic, op. cit.*, p. 257.

13 Merleau-Ponty, *Phenomenology of Perception*, p. 241.

14 Jean-Paul Sartre, 'Merleau-Ponty', in *Situations*, trans. Benita Eisler (New York, Fawcett Publications, 1965), pp. 157ff.

15 Lyotard, *Ph*, p. 43.

16 See Jean-François Lyotard, *Discours Figure* (Paris, Klincksieck, 1971). This work opens precisely as 'a defense of the eye' (p. 11) *vis à vis* the text and the interpretative act, a defense as well of a 'silence which is the contrary of discourse, a violence which is at the same time that of the beautiful' (p. 14). (This text will be referred to hereafter as *DF*.)

17 Maurice Merleau-Ponty, *The Visible and the Invisible*, trans. Alphonso Lingis (Evanston, Northwestern University Press, 1968), p. 185. For further discussion of this issue see my 'Abysses' in *Hermeneutics and Deconstruction*, ed. H. Silverman and D. Ihde (Albany, State University of New York Press, 1985).

18 See for example Xavier Tilliette, 'L'esthétique de Merleau-Ponty,' *Rivista di estetica*, vol. XIV, Jan., 1969, p. 108; Jean-François Lyotard, 'A la place de l'homme, l'expression,' *Esprit*, vol. 7, Juillet 1969, pp. 175f.

19 Merleau-Ponty, *The Visible and the Invisible*, p. 94.

20 Merleau-Ponty was still in fact able to appeal to an absolute both in the 'early works,' for example in the *Phenomenology of Perception, op. cit.*, p. 62, and the later works, as the lecture course published in this issue demonstrates, *supra*, pp. 9–83.

21 Merleau-Ponty, *The Visible and the Invisible, op. cit.*, pp. 117–18, 265.

22 Jacques Lacan, 'Merleau-Ponty,' *Les temps modernes*, no. 184–5, 1961, p. 249.

23 Cf. Jean-François Lyotard, *L'assassinat de l'expérience par la peinture, Monory* (Paris, Le Castor Astral, 1984), p. 7 – a rendering which is entirely consistent with Husserl's commitant of synthesis of identification to the horizon of time and verification to an extension *in indefinitum*:

> Experience is a modern figure. There is necessarily first of all a subject, the instance of an I, someone who speaks in the first person. There is necessarily a temporal disposition of the Augustinian type in *Confessions* XI (modern work that it is), in which the view of the past, the present and the future is always grasped from the standpoint of a present consciousness which is ungraspable. With these two axioms, one is able already to engender the essential form of experience: I am no more than what I already was, and I am no longer it. Life signifies the

death of what one is, and this death attests that life has a
meaning.

24 See Jean Laplanche and J-B Pontalis, 'Fantasme originaire, fantasme
des origines, origine du fantasme,' *Les temps modernes*, vol. 19, no.
215, 1964, p. 1868.

25 J-B Pontalis, 'Note sur le problème de l'inconscient chez Merleau-
Ponty,' *Les temps modernes*, no. 184–6, 1961, p. 295.

26 Maurice Merleau-Ponty, 'The Problem of Passivity,' in *Themes from
the Lectures*, trans. John O'Neill (Evanston, Northwestern University
Press, 1970), p. 50. Cf. Lyotard's similar affirmations in *Ph*,
pp. 68–70.

27 See Michel Serres, *Le système de Leibniz et ses modèles mathématiques*
(Paris, Presses Universitaires de France, 1968), vol. I, p. 168. On the
Lebnizian background of hermeneutics, likewise see Hans-Georg
Gadamer, *Truth and Method*, trans. Garrett Barden and John
Cumming (New York, Seabury Press, 1975), pp. 160f.

28 See Lyotard's comments in an interview with Georges Van Den
Abbeele published in *Diacritics*, Fall, 1984, p. 17, and *Dif*, p. 197.

29 See 'The Dream-Work does not Think,' trans. Mary Lydon, *Oxford
Literary Review*, 6, No. 1 (1983), p. 32 (a translation of *DF*, p. 270).

> Desire does not manipulate an intelligible text in order to
> disguise it. . . . We must presume a primordial situation where
> repression and the return of the repressed are born together.
> Here, precisely, for Laplanche and Pontalis, is the phantasm.
> Reverie, dream, phantasm are mixtures containing both
> viewing and reading matter. The dream work is not a
> language, it is the effect on language of the force exerted by the
> figural (as image or as form). This force breaks the law. It
> hinders hearing but makes us see; that is the ambivalence of
> censorship. But this composite makes us see. It is found not
> only in the order of the 'primal' phantasm itself: at once
> discourse and figure, a tongue lost in a hallucinatory
> scenography, the first violence.

30 See *DF*, p. 277.

31 See Jean-François Lyotard, 'Apathie dans la theorie,' in *Rudiments
paiens* (Paris, Union générale d'éditions, 10/18, 1977), p. 18.

32 *Ibid.*, p. 9.

33 See Jean-François Lyotard and Jean-Loup Thébaud, *Just Gaming*,
trans. Wlad Godzich (Minneapolis, University of Minnesota Press,
1985), p. 89. Hereafter cited as *JG*.

34 *EL*, p. 194. A partial translation of the last chapter of this text
appeared in 'For a Pseudo-Theory,' trans. Moshe Ron in *Yale French*

Studies, no. 52, 1976, a work which is not identical to *EL* but incorporates much of its text. When this 'mirroring' occurs the pagination of the English translation will be given in parenthesis: (118–19). For further discussion of Lyotard's view of hermeneutics, see *DF*, p. 13.

35 *Ibid.*, p. 295 (119).

36 *Ibid.*, p. 301. See Bachelard's discussion of 'an *experimental reason* susceptible of surrationally organizing the real as Tristan Tzara's *experimental dream* surrealistically organizes poetic freedom' in 'Le surrationalisme' (1936) in *L'engagement rationaliste* (Paris, Presses Universitaires de France, 1972), p. 8.

37 *EL*, p. 306 (125).

38 *EL*, p. 29.

39 See Gilles Deleuze, *Différence et répétition* (Paris, Presses Universitaires de France, 1972), p. 119.

40 *Dif*, p. 75.

41 See Jean-François Lyotard, 'Adorno as the Devil,' trans. Robert Hurley, *Telos*, 19, Spring, 1974, p. 133.

42 See *DF*, pp. 259ff.

43 Jean-François Lyotard, 'Jewish Oedipus' (1970), trans. Susan Hanson, *Genre*, 10, 1977, p. 397. Cp. also Lyotard's 'The Unconscious as *Mise-en-scène*,' trans. Joseph Maier in *Performance in Postmodern Culture*, ed. M. Benamou and C. Carmello (Madison, Coda Press, 1977), p. 98:

> Works must not be taken as symptoms symbolically expressing a concealed discourse, but as attempts to state perspectives of reality. Interpretation in turn must give way to description of devices. As for these descriptions, they are no less prescriptive in nature than works; they continue and eventually reroute the perspective creating potentialities these works contain.

44 *Ibid.*, p. 396

45 Jean-François Lyotard, 'The Psychoanalytical Approach', in *Main Trends in Aesthetics and the Sciences of Art*, ed. Mikel Dufrenne (London, Holmes & Meier, 1979), p. 143.

46 *EL*, p. 311.

47 Jean-François Lyotard, *La pittura del segreto nell'epoca postmoderna, Baruchella*, trans. Maurizio Ferraris (Milano, Giangiacomo Feltrinelli Editore, 1982), pp. 9f.

48 *EL*, p. 41.

49 See for example, *ibid.*, p. 43:

> We are sure, absolutely sure of what we say . . . and at the same time, in the same instant, completely deprived of all security; – sure magistarily sure of the points on which in the

moment we 'think,' the libido comes to intensity, because we are educated and refined in pleasure (*jouissance*) and pain enough to have acquired the flair of pyromaniacs.

50 Lyotard, 'Jewish Oedipus,' *op. cit.*, p. 402. Cf. *JG*, p. 71: 'There are language games in which the important thing is to listen.'

51 Jean-François Lyotard, 'Theory as Art: A Pragmatic Point of View,' trans. Robert Vollrath in *Image and Code* (Ann Arbor, University of Michigan Press, 1981), p. 76.

52 Jean-François Lyotard, *The Post-Modern Condition*, trans. Geoff Bennington and Brian Massumi (Minneapolis, University of Minnesota Press, 1984). I have further discussed this issue in my 'Jürgen Habermas and Jean-François Lyotard: Post-Modernism and the Crisis of Rationality,' *Philosophy and Social Criticism*, Fall, 1984, no. 2.

53 *JG*, p. 90. In 'On Theory: An Interview,' trans. Roger McKeon in *Driftworks* (New York, *Semiotext*(e), 1984), p. 31, Lyotard based the relation between theory and *praxis* under the rubrics of the *explosive fixe*. In describing the events leading up to the May 1968 political upheaval, Lyotard claims, 'what was taking place was a fulgurant junction, a flash of lightning between theory and practice – the most immediate practice and the most elaborated theory that we have known in the last forty years.' Only in *Dif* perhaps would the *dispositif de passage* demystify this event.

54 *Ibid.*

55 See Gilles Deleuze, *Logique du sens* (Paris, Minuit, 1969), p. 120. Deleuze himself attempted to make this turn on the heels of Sartre's ejection of the ego from the transcendental field of experience, without regard to the determinacy, the realism, and the metaphysics of Sartre's own phenomenological descriptions. See Jean-Paul Sartre, *The Transcendence of the Ego*, trans. Forrest Williams and Robert Kirkpatrick (New York, Farrar, Strauss & Giraux, 1971).

56 Deleuze, *Différence et répétition, op. cit.*, p. 258.

57 *JG*, p. 90. Still, it should be noted that *El* refused simply to reduce intensity and desire to the will, because 'desire cannot be assumed' and thus the 'voyage of intensities' occurs without identity. See *EL* p. 30. The former is just what *JG* denies, that the phenomenon of injustice requires 'a regulation of the will' (*JG*, p. 91), but one still that does not rest upon the presence of a subject, or a faculty (*Dif*, p. 96).

58 *Dif*, pp. 227, 228. Cp. *EL*, pp. 174f. But, what is true of the concept of force or of the will is equally true of both will and intention, of course. See *Dif*, p. 197.

59 'Jewish Oedipus,' p. 404.

60 *DF*, p. 23.

61 See Emmanuel Levinas, *Totality and Infinity*, trans. Alphonso Lingis (Pittsburgh, Duquesne University Press, 1969), p. 24.

62 *JG*, p. 75.

63 *Ibid.*, p. 69. See also 'Logique du Levinas,' in *Textes pour Emmanuel Levinas*, ed. F. Laruelle (Paris, Editions Jean-Michel Place, 1980).

64 Lyotard, *Discours figure*, p. 15.

65 *JG*, p. 80. See for example: Gilles Deleuze, *Kant's Critical Philosophy*, trans. Hugh Tomlinson and Barbara Habberjam (Minneapolis, University of Minnesota Press, 1984); Michel Foucault, *Introduction à l'anthropologie de Kant*, vol. I (Paris, University of Paris Faculty of Letters and Human Sciences, 1961). This text, Foucault's *Thèse complementaire* can be seen at the *Bibliothèque Sorbonne*. For further discussion of this work see my 'Kant and Foucault: on the Ends of Man,' *Tijdschrift Voor Filosofie*, vol. 47, no. 1, March, 1985. Likewise see Jacques Derrida, *Edmund Husserl's Origin of Geometry: An Introduction*, pp. 135ff.

66 *JG*, p. 88.

67 Lyotard, *The Post-Modern Condition*, p. 41. In *Positions* Jacques Derrida equally affirmed that 'there is no metalanguage,' adding immediately that he 'would say, rather, that there is nothing outside of the text.' See *Positions*, trans. Alan Bass (Chicago, University of Chicago Press, 1981), p. 111. Since *Discours Figure*'s appeal to the figural, to silence, to a violence which is at the same time that of the beautiful, Lyotard can be seen to have denied this strict reading of deconstruction in the recognition that 'one does not at all break with metaphysics in placing language everywhere, on the contrary, one accomplishes it' (p. 14). In this respect this denial has held, beyond the topic of *Discours Figure*, beyond the figural to libidinal economics, and later in retrieving the dimension of the unsaid within the domain of the ethical, the problem of injustice and the *différend*. Even so, all of this cannot be simply opposed to Derrida. In *Of Grammatology*, trans. Gayatri Spivak (Baltimore, Johns Hopkins University Press, 1976), the same text in which he originally claimed that there was 'nothing outside the text' (p. 158) he likewise was led to acknowledge that this position could not imply a simple reduction of the signified to the signifier:

> This does not by simple inversion, mean that the signifier is fundamental or primary. The 'primacy' or 'priority' of the signifier would be an expression untenable and absurd to formulate illogically within the very logic that it would legitimately destroy. The signifier will never by rights precede the signified, in which case it would no longer be a signifier

and the 'signifying' signifier would no longer have a possible signified. (p. 324n).

To perform this simple inversion would make, to use a phrase he has elsewhere in related matters, 'the ultra-transcendental text . . . so closely resemble the precritical text as to be indistinguishable from it' (p. 61). Nor for the same reason should Lyotard's own refusal to place language everywhere be seen as a return to the phenomenological 'pre-linguistic stratum.'

68 *JG*, p. 88.
69 *Ibid.*, p. 69.
70 Ludwig Wittgenstein, *On Certainty*, trans. Denis Paul and G. E. M. Anscombe (New York; Harper & Row, 1972), p. 73.
71 *JG*, p. 37.
72 *Ibid.*, p. 22.
73 *Ibid.*, p. 52.
74 Immanuel Kant, *Critique of Judgment*, trans. J. H. Bernard (New York, Hafner, 1968), p. 143.
75 Jean-François Lyotard, 'Philosophy and Painting in the Age of Their Experimentation: Contribution to an Idea of Postmodernity,' trans. D. Brewer, *Camera Obscura*, 12, 1984, p. 121.
76 *Dif*, p. 129. See also p. 200, 236.
77 See Husserl, *Formal and Transcendental Logic*, *op. cit.*, Chapter three.
78 Deleuze, *Différence et répétition*, *op. cit.*, p. 236. The point is likewise discussed in Michel Serres, *Hermès II: L'Interférence* (Paris, Minuit, 1972), pp. 45f. Similar criticisms of Husserl's position could be found as early as Cavaillès' 'On Logic and the Theory of Science,' trans. Theodore J. Kisiel in *Phenomenology and the Natural Sciences*, ed. J. Kockelmans and T. Kisiel (Evanston, Northwestern University Press, 1970), and Jean Ladrière, *Les limitations internes des formalismes* (Louvain, E. Nauwelaerts, 1957), pp. 405ff.
79 See *JG*, pp. 73ff, *Dif*, Notice Kant I, pp. 96ff, Notice Kant II, pp. 189ff.
80 See Deleuze, *Différence et répétition*, p. 190.
81 Immanuel Kant, *Critique of Judgment*, p. 84.
82 Immanuel Kant, *Critique of Pure Reason*, trans. Norman Kemp Smith (New York, Macmillan, 1973), p. 540(A465/B683).
83 '*Separation from all society* is regarded as sublime if it rests upon ideas that overlook all sensible interest.' *Critique of Judgment*, p. 116.
84 Friedrich Nietzsche, *The Joyful Wisdom*, trans. (London, Russell & Russell, 1964), p. 340.
85 *Ibid.*, pp. 445(A501/B529)ff.
86 *Ibid.*, p. 60(A13/B27)
87 Kant, *Critique of Judgment*, p. 12. See *Dif*, p. 190.

88 *Dif*, p. 100.
89 Kant, *Critique of Pure Reason*, p. 606 (A759/B787). Compare a similar remark in *JG*, p. 77. Likewise see Deleuze's discussion in his *Kant's Critical Philosophy*, p. 60: 'In fact, determining judgment and reflective judgment are not like two species of the same genus. Reflective judgment manifests and liberates a depth which remained hidden in the other. But the other was also a judgment only by virtue of this living depth.'
90 Kant, *Critique of Judgment*, p. 108.
91 *Dif*, p. 104.
92 Kant, *Critique of Pure Reason*, p. 164(B151).

CHAPTER 8   JOHN LLEWELYN: THE ORIGIN AND END OF PHILOSOPHY

1 Martin Heidegger, 'Building Dwelling Thinking', in D. F. Krell (ed.), *Martin Heidegger: Basic Writings* (London, Routledge & Kegan Paul, 1978), pp. 323–39.
2 The following abbreviations are used in the text:
   C   Paul Valéry, *Cahiers*, 29 volumes (Paris, Centre National de Recherche Scientifique, 1957–61).
  CP Jacques Derrida, *La Carte postale de Socrate à Freud et au-delà* (Paris, Flammarion, 1980).
   D Jacques Derrida, *Dissemination*, trans. Barbara Johnson (Chicago, University of Chicago Press, 1981); (London, Athlone Press, 1981); [*La Dissémination* (Paris, Éditions du Seuil, 1972)].
   G Jacques Derrida, *Glas*, (Paris, Galilée, 1974); (Paris, Denoël/Gonthier, 1981).
   M Jacques Derrida, *Margins of Philosophy*, trans. Alan Bass (Chicago, University of Chicago Press, 1982); (Brighton, Harvester Press, 1982); [*Marges de la philosophie* (Paris, Minuit, 1972)].
   O Paul Valéry, *Oeuvres*, volumes I and II (Paris, Gallimard, 1957).
  OA Jacques Derrida, *L'Oreille de l'autre* (Montréal, VLB Éditeur, 1982).
   S Jacques Derrida, 'Sending: On Representation', trans. Peter and Mary Ann Caws, *Social Research*, vol. 49, 1982, pp. 294–326; ['Envoi', *Actes du XVIIIe Congrès des Sociétés de Philosophie de Langue Française*, 1980, pp. 6–30].
  SP Jacques Derrida, *Speech and Phenomena*, trans. David B. Allison (Evanston, Northwestern University Press, 1973); [*La Voix et le phénomène* (Paris, Presses Universitaires de France, 1967)].
  TA Jacques Derrida, 'D'un ton apocalyptique adopté naguère en

philosophie', in Philippe Lacoue-Labarthe and Jean-Luc Nancy (eds), *Les Fins de l'homme: à partir du travail de Jacques Derrida* (Paris, Galilée, 1981); [*D'un ton apocalyptique adopté naguère en philosophie* (Paris, Galilée, 1983)].

WD Jacques Derrida, *Writing and Difference*, trans Alan Bass (Chicago, University of Chicago Press, 1978); (London, Routledge & Kegan Paul, 1978); [*L'Écriture et la différence* (Paris, Éditions du Seuil, 1967)].

3 Sir Arthur Eddington, *The Nature of the Physical World* (the Gifford Lectures given at the University of Edinburgh in 1927) (London, Dent, 1935), p. 6.

4 L. Susan Stebbing, *Philosophy and the Physicists* (London, Penguin Books, 1944), pp. 49–50. All quotations are from her Chapter III.

5 Sir Isaac Newton, *Opticks*, 4th ed. reprinted (London, Bell & Sons, 1931), Bk I, Pt II, pp. 124–5, cited at Stebbing, p. 54.

6 Compare Eddington, pp. 8–9:

It is true that the whole scientific inquiry starts from the familiar world and in the end it must return to the familiar world; but the part of the journey over which the physicist has charge is in foreign territory.

Until recently there was a much closer linkage; the physicist used to borrow the raw material of his world from the familiar world, but he does so no longer. His raw materials are aether, electrons, quanta, potentials, Hamiltonian functions, etc., and he is nowadays scrupulously careful to guard these from contamination by conceptions borrowed from the other world.

7 The *Concise Oxford Dictionary* gives under 'form': 'body of type secured in chase for printing at one impression'; and under 'chase': 'iron frame holding composed type for page or sheet'. For a case of a body of type not fully secured against decomposition, see John Llewelyn, *Derrida on the Threshold of Sense* (London, Macmillan, 1986); (New York, St Martin's Press, 1986), p. ix, where the author's initials were no proof against the eventuality of certain words ('France on sabbatical leave to work on this study, and the Directors and staff of the Institut Français d'Ecosse for enabling') that were present following line 13 of the page proofs being disseminated outside their frame and failing to complete the journey to the page of the book. But in any case 'the presence of what is gets lost . . . the words come apart'. The frame is always broken.

CHAPTER 9 JOHN McCUMBER: PHILOSOPHY AS THE
HETERONOMOUS CENTER OF MODERN DISCOURSE: JÜRGEN
HABERMAS

1 Jürgen Habermas, *Theorie des kommunikativen Handelns*, (Frankfurt
am Main, Suhrkamp, 2 vols, 1981 (hereinafter *TKH*), I, pp. 15–24/
1–7. Figures after the slash for volume I refer to Habermas, *The
Theory of Communicative Action*, trans. Thomas McCarthy (Boston,
Beacon Press, 1984); translations from volume II are my own. Also
cf. Habermas, 'Die Philosophie als Platzhalter und Interpret,' in
Habermas, *Moralbewußtsein und kommunikatives Handeln* (Frankfurt
am Main, Suhrkamp, 1983), pp. 22–6. I am endebted to Richard J.
Bernstein and Thomas McCarthy for their comments on earlier
versions of this paper; its conclusions and (if distinct) its errors
remain my own.
2 Maurice Merleau-Ponty, 'Philosophy and Non-philosophy since
Hegel', *supra*, p. 83.
3 Cf. Habermas' remarks on, and abjural of, his own 'philosophical'
preoccupations at *TKH* I, pp. 7f./xxxix.
4 Oedipus, for example, blinded himself with a pair of κέντρα:
Oedipus the King, 1318.
5 The radius of a circle, for example, was τα ἐκ του κεντρου. For the
center as 'source' of the circle, see Plato, *Parmenides*, 137e; Aristotle,
Rhetoric, III.b, 1407b27. It is noteworthy that Euclid, in definition
15 of the *Elements*, avoids such locutions.
6 The συμφυτον πνευμα to be found, he thought, in their hearts:
Aristotle, *de Motu Animalium*, 698a-b, 703a.
7 Plotinus, *Ennead*, IV.1.24ff.
8 The ego thus becomes a mathematical center when man, as
Heidegger argues, becomes ground: Martin Heidegger, 'Die Zeit
des Weltbildes,' in Heidegger, *Holzwege*, (Frankfurt am Main,
Klostermann, 4e Aufl., 1963), pp. 69–104.
9 Immanuel Kant, 'Was Heißt: sich im Denken Orientieren?' in
Whilhelm Weischiedl, (ed.), Kant: *Werkausgabe* V, (Frankfurt am
Main, Suhrkamp 1958), pp. 267–83.
10 Hugh J. Silverman, 'Re-reading Merleau-Ponty,' *Telos*, 39, 1979,
p. 113. Also *Inscriptions: Between Phenomenology and Structuralism*
(London: Routledge & Kegan Paul, 1987), ch. 8.
11 Maurice Merleau-Ponty, *Consciusness and the Acquisition of Language*,
trans. Hugh J. Silverman (Evanston, Northwestern University
Press, 1973), pp. 3–7; Jacques, Derrida, 'Structure, Sign and Play
in the Discourse of the Human Sciences,' in Derrida, *Writing and
Difference*, trans. Alan Bass (Chicago, University of Chicago Press,
1978), pp. 278–80; for Habermas' version of this, cf. Jürgen

Habermas, 'Überbietung der temporalisierten Ursprungsphiloso-
phie: Derridas Kritik am Phonzentrismus,' in Habermas, *Philosophische Diskurs der Moderne* (Frankfurt am Main, Suhrkamp, 1985),
pp. 200f.

12 For a description of such shields, see Anthony M. Snodgrass, *Early
Greek Armour and Weapons* (Edinburgh, Edinburgh University Press,
1964), pp. 37–51; see esp. plate 37, which very clearly illustrates
the 'offensive' use of the shield.

13 G. F. W. Hegel, *Wissenschaft der Logik*, George Lasson (ed.)
(Hamburg, Felix Meiner, 2 vols, 1934 II), pp. 371–4.

14 Cf. Maurice Merleau-Ponty, pp. 43–4.

15 Austin's speech act theory, I suggest, is 'defensive' in so far as the
examples it analyzes are 'institutionally bound,' for which cf. Jürgen
Habermas, 'What is Universal Pragmatics?' in Habermas, *Communication and the Evolution of Society*, trans. Thomas McCarthy, (Boston,
Beacon Press, 1979), p. 38f. For Habermas' critique of Gadamer's
view that 'on-going tradition and hermeneutic inquiry merge to a
single point,' cf. Jürgen Habermas, 'A Review of Gadamer's *Truth
and Method*,' in Fred R. Dallmayr and Thomas A. McCarthy (eds),
Understanding and Social Inquiry, (Notre Dame, IN, University of
Notre Dame Press, 1977), pp. 356–61.

16 *TKH* I, pp. 201, 336f./140, 247; Jürgen Habermas, 'Wozu noch Philosophie,' in Habermas, *Philosophisch-politische Profile* (Frankfurt am
Main, Suhrkamp, 1981), p. 36f.

17 *TKH* I, pp. 201f./140.

18 That Hegel, with respect to the state, was not true even to the
modest critical capacities of his own philosophy is argued in my
'Contradiction and Resolution in the State: Hegel's Covert View,'
forthcoming in *CLIO*.

19 *TKH* I, p. 201/140.

20 *TKH* I, pp. 65f., 320–31/39f., 233–42; II 584f.

21 *TKH* II, pp. 549f.

22 *TKH* I, p. 458/342; II, p. 584f.

23 Diogenes Laertius, *Lives of Eminent Philosophers* III, pp. 5–6; *Iliad*
XVIII, pp. 392f.; *TKH* I, pp. 19–22/4–7.

24 Habermas' most vigorous defense of modernity is perhaps his
'Modernity: an Incomplete Project' in Hal Foster (ed.), *The Anti-
Aesthetic: Essays on Postmodern Culture* (Port Townsend, WA, Bay
Press, 1983), pp. 3–15.

25 *TKH* I, pp. 339f./249.

26 *TKH* I, pp. 39–44, 71, 141–55, 410–15/19–22, 94–101, 305–10.

27 *TKH* II, pp. 171–228.

28 *TKH* II, pp. 586, 588; also cf. Jürgen Habermas, 'A Reply to my

Critics,' in John B. Thompson, and David Held, *Habermas: Critical Debates* (Cambridge, MA, MIT Press, 1982), pp. 239f.; 'Die Philosophie als Platzhalter und Interpret,' pp. 25f.

29 *TKH* I, pp. 16, 38f., 327/2, 18f., 239; II, pp. 550, 562.

30 As in his claim that post-Hegelian philosophy, from logic to aesthetics, exhibits a convergence upon the theory of the formal conditions of rationality, or as shown by his claim that the mutual differentiation of validity-spheres in modernity has now 'meta-differentiated' itself into various centripetal moments of culture, all re-converging upon the theory of communicative action: *TKH* I, pp. 16, 504/2, 376f.; II, pp. 16, 86, 586.

31 As is the case with system-theory and action theory, *TKH* I, p. 460/343f.; II, pp. 303, 550.

32 *TKH* II, p. 298.

33 *TKH* I, pp. 172–6/117–20.

34 Jürgen Habermas, 'Wozu noch Philosophie,' pp. 34ff.

35 Cf. *TKH* I, pp. 17, 198–203/2f., 138–41; II, pp. 550, 562–83.

36 Martin Heidegger, 'Die Sprache im Gedicht,' in Heidegger, *Unterwegs zur Sprache* (Pfullingen, Neske, 4e Auflage, 1971), pp. 37f; I have modified Hofstadter's translation which, among other things, deletes the reference to the spear: *On The Way to Language* trans. Albert Hofstadter (New York, Harper & Row, 1971), pp. 159f.; also cf. Habermas, 'Die Philosophie als Platzhalter und Interpret', p. 23.

37 Cf. Otto Pöggeler, 'Heidegger's Topology of Being,' in Joseph Kockelmans (ed.), *On Heidegger and Language* (Evanston, Northwestern University Press, 1972), pp. 107–35.

38 Among the works in English concerned with this general issue, cf. Richard J. Bernstein, *Beyond Objectivism and Relativism* (Philadelphia, University of Pennsylvania Press, 1983), pp. 182–97; Raymond Geuss, *The Idea of a Critical Theory* (Cambridge, Cambridge University Press, 1981); Thomas McCarthy, *The Critical Theory of Jürgen Habermas* (Cambridge, MA, MIT Press, 1978), pp. 126–271; John McCumber, 'Reflection and Emancipation in Habermas,' *Southern Journal of Philosophy*, 22 (1984), pp. 71–81; and the essays in John B. Thompson and David Held (eds), *Habermas: Critical Debates* (Cambridge, MA, MIT Press, 1982), especially those by McCarthy, Mary Hesse, John B. Thompson and Steven Lukes, together with Habermas' response.

39 *TKH* II, p. 189.

40 Cf. *TKH* I, pp. 456–8/340–2; Jürgen Habermas, 'Exkurs zur Einebnung des Gattungsunterschieds zwischen Philosophie und Literatur,' in Habermas, *Philosophische Diskurs der Moderne, op. cit.*, pp. 242f.

41 *TKH* II, pp. 589–91.

42 *TKH* II, p. 225.

43 Cf. Hugh J. Silverman, 'Rereading Merleau-Ponty,' pp. 108f.; Jürgen Habermas, 'Exkurs zur Einebnung des Gattungunterschiedes zwischen Philosophie und Literatur,' *op. cit.*, p. 244.

44 *TKH* I, p. 259/184.

45 *TKH* I, pp. 197–203/137–141; also cf. Jürgen Habermas, 'Moralbewußtsein und kommunikatives Handeln,' in Habermas, *Moralbewußtsein und kommunikatives Handeln, op. cit.*, pp. 127ff.

46 *TKH* II, pp. 586f.

47 *TKH* I, p. 197/137.

48 *TKH* II, pp. 586f.

49 Immanuel Kant, *Kritik der Urteilskraft*, Berlin Academy Edition, pp. 212f.; page numbers to this edition are given marginally in *Kant's Critique of Judgment*, trans. James Creed Meredith (Oxford, Clarendon Press, 1952).

50 J. L. Austin, *How to do Things with Words* (J. O. Urmson, ed.) (New York, Oxford University Press, 1965), pp. 99–101.

51 Richard J. Bernstein, *Beyond Objectivism and Relativism* (Philadelphia, University of Pennsylvania Press, 1983), pp. 184f., 192ff., 223–31.

52 Jürgen Habermas, 'Questions and Counterquestions,' in Richard J. Bernstein (ed.), *Habermas and Modernity* (Cambridge, MA, MIT Press, 1985), pp. 195f.

53 Though not in the aesthetic: cf. Pierre Aubenque, 'La prudence chez Kant,' *Revue de métaphysique et de morale*, 80 (1975), pp. 156–82.

54 Richard J. Bernstein, *Beyond Objectivism and Relativism*, pp. 118–26, 154–65.

55 My account of Kant here relies on the Berlin Academy edition of the *Critique of Judgment*, pp. 179f., 183–5, 210, 216, 232–5, 284f., 286f.

56 *TKH* I, p. 114/75; II, pp. 561f., 593; I will leave open here the question of whether other disciplines which Habermas calls 'reconstructive,' such as Chomskyan linguistics, can be construed in terms of Kantian reflective judgment.

57 *TKH* I, pp. 157ff./106f.

58 *TKH* I, pp. 229–31, 326f./160f., 238; Thomas McCarthy, 'Reflections on Rationalization in *The Theory of Communicative Action*', in Bernstein, *Habermas and Modernity*, pp. 176–91.

59 McCarthy, *op. cit.*, pp. 187–9; Jürgen Habermas, 'Walter Benjamin: bewußtmachende oder rettende Kritik,' in Habermas, *Philosophisch-politische Profile*, pp. 336–76.

60 *TKH* II, pp. 559f.

61 *TKH* I, p. 327/239; McCarthy, p. 191.

62 Jürgen Habermas, 'Moral Development and Ego Identity,' in Habermas, *Communication and the Evolution of Society*, trans. Thomas McCarthy (Boston, Beacon Press, 1979), pp. 88ff.; this is why Habermas can refer to learning processes as 'independent' (*selbstständig*): Habermas, 'Exkurs zur Einebnung des Gattungsuntershieds zwischen Philosophie und Literatur,' p. 241.
63 *TKH* II, p. 593.
64 For which cf. McCarthy, *op. cit*, pp. 181f.
65 Habermas, 'Die Philosophie als Platzhalter und Interpret,' pp. 26f.
66 Elisabeth Young-Bruehl, *Hannah Arendt: For Love of the World* (New Haven, Yale University Press, 1982), pp. xvii, 324, 327.

CHAPTER 10   ROBERT BERNASCONI: LEVINAS: PHILOSOPHY
AND BEYOND

1 *Emmanuel Levinas, Le temps et l'autre* (Paris, Presses Universitaires de France, 1983), pp. 20–2 (henceforth cited as *TA*). Richard Cohen is in the course of preparing a translation for publication.
2 Levinas distinguishes *autre* from *autrui* and both are sometimes spelled by him with an initial capital letter. Following the convention among translators of Levinas, I shall reserve 'Other' for *autrui*, the 'other man,' as Levinas says, or, as I would prefer, 'the other human being,' even though the latter phrase returns to the order of being that which in Levinas transcends being. But faced with the choice between sexist or ontological language – and it has to be admitted that the two are more usually found together – the latter is preferable.
3 Emmanuel Levinas, *Totalité et Infini* (The Hague, Martinus Nijhoff, 1961), p. 247; trans. A. Lingis, *Totality and Infinity* (Pittsburgh, Duquesne University Press, 1969), p. 269. (Henceforth cited as *TI*; page numbers after the slash indicate the translation.)
4 There is some equivocation in Levinas as to the extent of the dominance of 'ontology' within Western philosophy. Should it be said that it has 'most often been an ontology' (*TI*, p. 13/43) or does primacy of the same 'define the whole of Western philosophy' (*TI*, p. 16/45)? This uncertainty could be construed as a consequence of Levinas's failure to pursue the question of the history of philosophy with sufficient resolve. On the other hand, it will be seen that when he does address this question it is not to resolve the ambiguous status of Western philosophy, but to affirm it. The word 'metaphysics' is also used unambiguously as, for example, in the section on 'Separation and Absoluteness' where Levinas reverts to its more

traditional sense, construing it as a knowledge which suppresses separation (*TI*, p. 75/102).

5 Emmanuel Levinas, 'L'ontologie est-elle fondamentale?' *Revue de métaphysique et de morale*, 1951, vol. 56, pp. 88–98.

6 Emmanuel Levinas, 'Martin Buber et la theorie de la connaissance,' *Nom Propres* (Montpellier, Fata Morgana, 1976), p. 49 (henceforth *NP*). 'Martin Buber and the Theory of Knowledge,' P. A. Schilpp and M. Friedman (eds), *The Philosophy of Martin Buber* (La Salle, University of Illinois Press, 1964), p. 149.

7 Emmanuel Levinas, *De l'existence a l'existant* (Paris, Vrin, 1947), p. 168; trans. A. Lingis, *Existence and Existents* (The Hague, Martinus Nijhoff, 1978), p. 97. (Henceforth *EE*.)

8 Emmanuel Levinas, 'Martin Buber, Gabriel Marcel et la philosophie,' *Revue Internationale de Philosophie*, 1978, vol. 32, no. 126, p. 502.

9 Martin Heidegger, *Die Frage nach dem Ding* (Tübingen, Max Niemeyer, 1962), p. 93; trans. W. B. Barton and V. Deutsch, *What is a Thing?* (Chicago, Henry Regnery, 1970), p. 119. Cf. 'The Separation Out (*Abhebung*) of What is Superior from What is Inferior,' *Wegmarken* (Frankfurt, Klosterman, 1967), p. 334; trans. T. J. Sheehan, 'On Being and Conceptions of *Physis* in Aristotle's Physics b, 1,' *Man and World*, 1976, no. 9, p. 241.

10 Ethics in Levinas does not take the form of a series of obligations or a collection of duties or virtues, but resides in the *impossibility* of denying the Other. So Levinas will say that it is impossible to kill the Other. This is not to be understood to mean that one is factually unable to commit violence on the Other as Other, which would reduce violence to the order of being. On Levinas's understanding, violence can only be directed against the Other. The other human being is the only being I can intend to kill. But if my aim in killing the Other is to eradicate him or her, I inevitably fail because I will remain haunted by that face, as Macbeth was haunted by the ghost of Banquo (*EE*, p. 101/62).

11 For example, Emmanuel Levinas, 'Transcendence et Hauteur,' *Bulletin de la Societé française de Philosophie*, 1962, vol. 3, p. 94. But here too it is acknowledged that philosophy is 'born of an allergy,' p. 95. (Henceforth *TH*.)

12 Emmanuel Levinas, 'Ethique comme philosophie première,' *Justifications de l'éthique* (Bruxelles, Editions de l'Université de Bruxelles, 1984), pp. 41–51.

13 Jacques Derrida, *L'écriture et la différence* (Paris, Seuil, 1967), p. 117; trans. A. Bass, *Writing and Difference* (London, Routledge & Kegan Paul, 1978), p. 79. (Henceforth cited as *ED*.)

14 The English translation reads 'metaphysics' instead of this 'it.'

However, if Derrida did indeed mean 'metaphysics' (the most natural reading grammatically) he has gone further astray than is likely. The passage in Levinas on which Derrida is drawing also suffers from a proliferation of feminine pronouns not clearly identified, and it is also grammatically possible that these could be construed as 'metaphysics' as well, although 'ontology,' 'theory', and 'critique' are more plausible candidates. Derrida would appear to mean this 'it' to be 'ontology.' And yet a careful reading of the passage in *Totality and Infinity* would require one to challenge Derrida's interpretation of it, if it is Derrida's. In this section of the book Levinas distinguishes two senses of theory, one ontological and a second which respects alterity. It is this latter sense which is relevant here, a theory which 'delineates another structure essential for metaphysics.' I understand Levinas to be saying that theory in this sense is concerned with critique, a critique which calls ontology into question, even to the point where theory and critique itself is called into question, 'the inversion of critique' as he calls it elsewhere (*TI*, p. 59/87). At this point critique gives way to ethics or metaphysics, so rendering only provisional the identification of ethics and critique. On this reading ethics 'accomplishes the critical essence of knowledge,' by no longer being knowledge or critique. Levinas does not write that metaphysics is critique, but proposes an analogy between them: 'And as critique precedes dogmatism, metaphysics precedes ontology' (*TI*, p. 13/43).

15 I have taken up this issue in 'The Trace of Levinas in Derrida,' *Derrida and Difference* (Coventry, Parousia Press, 1985), pp. 17–44.

16 Emmanuel Levinas, *Difficile liberté* (Paris, Albin Michel, 1976), pp. 76–7 (henceforth cited as *DL*).

17 Derrida refers the argument to 'a Greek,' because its source, which traditionally was attributed to the *Protrepticus* of Aristotle, is now disputed. See Anton-Hermann Chroust, *Aristotle: Protrepticus. A Reconstruction* (Notre Dame, University of Notre Dame Press, 1964), pp. 48–9.

18 Derrida does not list the passages in which Levinas distances himself from empiricism (*TI*, pp. 126/153, 130/157, 148/173). Derrida's attempt to refer Levinas to empiricism should be seen in the context of Derrida's other discussions of this term. See Marion Hobson, 'Deconstruction, Empiricism and the Postal Services,' *French Studies*, 1982, vol. 36, pp. 290–314.

19 Emmanuel Levinas, *Autrement qu'être ou au-delà de l'essence* (The Hague, Martinus Nijhoff, 1974); trans. A. Lingis, *Otherwise than Being or Beyond Essence* (The Hague, Martinus Nijhoff, 1981) (Henceforth cited as *AQ*.) For a helpful review of this book see Adriaan

Peperzak, 'Beyond Being,' *Research in Phenomenology*, 1978, vol. 8, pp. 239–61.

20 Emmanuel Levinas, *De Dieu qui vient a l'idée* (Paris, Vrin, 1982), p. 94 (henceforth cited as *DVI*). Trans. R. Cohen, 'God and Philosophy,' *Philosophy Today*, 1978, vol. 22, p. 127 (henceforth cited as *GP*).

21 The kinship between philosophy and non-philosophy is not conceived by Levinas purely formally with reference to the argument that negation remains determined by that which it opposes. 'The refusal of presence is not pure negation' ('Amour et révélation,' *La charité aujourd'hui* (Paris, SOS, 1981), p. 145). Compare this 1962 account of non-philosophy:

> The failure of philosophy lies in this resistance of the other to the same. Non-philosophy is the tyranny of Opinion where the Same submits to but does not find in itself the law of the other; thus the obscurity of the imagination where the knowing subject is lost – the for-itself, the Same or the I loses itself and goes astray; it is the heteronomy of inclination where the person follows a law which it has not given to itself; it is the alienation where one loses oneself without noticing it; it is the inauthenticity where being flees from its identity toward anonymity. (*TH*, p. 92)

Quoted according to an unpublished translation by Tina Chanter.

22 Emmanuel Levinas, 'De la Conscience à la veille,' *Bijdragen*, 1974, vol. 35, pp. 235–49. Reprinted in *DVI*.

23 Martin Heidegger, *Zur Sache des Denkens* (Tübingen, Niemeyer, 1969), p. 25; trans. J. Stambaugh, *On Time and Being* (New York, Harper & Row, 1977), p. 24.

24 Jacques Derrida, *Marges de la Philosophie* (Paris, Minuit, 1972), p. 22; trans. A. Bass, *Margins of Philosophy* (Chicago, Chicago University Press, 1982), p. 21. (Henceforth cited as *M*.)

25 Emmanuel Levinas, 'La pacte (Traité *Sota* 37a–37b),' *L'au-delà du verset* (Paris, Minuit, 1982), pp. 105–6.

26 Exodus 3:4; Samuel 1, 3:4.

27 Derrida discusses the saying and the said, as well as a number of other aspects of Levinas's thinking that I have taken up in this essay, in his second major essay on Levinas: 'En ce moment même dans cet ouvrage me voici,' *Textes pour Emmanuel Levinas*, ed. François Laruelle (Paris, Jean-Michel Place, 1980), pp. 21–60.

28 There are some exceptions to saying. In an interview in 1981 Levinas said that lying is a non-saying. R. Kearney, *Dialogue with Contemporary Continental Thinkers* (Manchester, Manchester University Press, 1984), p. 65 (henceforth cited as *DK*). This remark made in

the course of an interview should be placed alongside the observation in *Totality and Infinity* that the language of the eyes is impossible to dissemble. 'The alternative of truth and lying, of sincerity and dissimulation, is the prerogative of him who abides in the relation of absolute frankness, in the absolute frankness which cannot hide itself' (*TI*, p. 38/67). What is called 'sincerity' in *Otherwise than Being* and in 'God and Philosophy' would seem to correspond to the 'absolute frankness' of *Totality and Infinity*.

29 And at times Levinas also shows his indebtedness to Greek ethics. He would not anyway seem to accept the way Derrida at the end of 'Violence and Metaphysics' presents Greek and Jew as extremes, alternatives with the radically different values of philosophy and non-philosophy. So, for example, he observes that in the West we have been nourished on the Bible as much as on the so-called pre-Socratics and our understanding of each has been influenced by the other. *Humanisme de l'autre homme* (Montpellier, Fata Morgana, 1972), p. 96.

30 Emmanuel Levinas, 'A propos de Buber: quelques notes,' *Qu'est-ce que l'homme? Philosophie/Psychanalyse, Hommage à Alphonse de Waelhens (1911–1981)* (Bruxelles, Facultés Universitaires Saint-Louis, 1982), p. 133.

31 T. S. Eliot, 'East Coker,' *Collected Poems 1909–1962* (London, Faber & Faber, 1974), p. 203.

32 'Idéologie et idealism,' *Archivio di Filosofia*, 1973, pp. 135–45. Reprinted in *DVI*. Trans. A. Lesley, 'Ideology and Idealism,' *Modern Jewish Ethics*, ed. Marvin Fox (Athens, Ohio, Ohio State University Press, 1975), pp. 121–38 (henceforth cited as *MJE*).

33 The essay, originally published in 1973 in a special issue of *L'Arc* (no. 54) devoted to Derrida, is reprinted in *Noms Propres*. Quotations are based on an unpublished translation by Olivier Serafinowicz.

34 See also the essay, 'Façon de parler,' extracted from 'De la signification du sens,' *Heidegger et la question de Dieu*, eds R. Kearney and J. S. O'Leary (Paris, Grasset, 1980). Perhaps more boldly than elsewhere, Levinas there acknowledges the inherent contradiction in affirming the independence of ethical intelligibility in relation to the theoretical thought of being. This affirmation is itself theoretical, although, as he says, it is from first to last the way of his own work (*DVI*, p. 266).

35 Jacques Derrida, *La voix et le phénomène* (Paris, Presses Universitaires de France, 1967), p. 3; trans. D. B. Allison, *Speech and Phenomena* (Evanston, Northwestern University Press, 1973), pp. 4–5. (Henceforth *VP*.)

36 There would appear to be a third sense of doubling which can be found in Levinas's comment that language understood as the saying without a said 'loses its superfluous and strange function of doubling up thought and being' (*DVI*, p. 122/GP, p. 141), which would seem to refer to the relation of correspondence in Western ontology.

37 In his 1981 interview with Kearney, Levinas gave unambiguous answers to the questions of whether there was still a role for philosophy today and whether philosophy had not reached its end. He said that philosophy in its traditional forms as ontotheology and logocentrism had come to an end, but not philosophy in the sense of critical speculation. Furthermore, he saw new lease of life in the contemporary, and to his mind speculative, discourse of overcoming and deconstructing metaphysics (*DK*, p. 69). Levinas's reply is no doubt an accurate representation of much of what he says in his published works on this topic, but it is also worth remembering Levinas's comment in the Preface to *Totality and Infinity* that 'philosophical research does not answer questions like an interview, an oracle, or wisdom' (*TI*, p. xviii/29). What is lacking from this answer is his account of the ambiguity of philosophy, as expressed for example at *AQ*, p. 56/44: the philosopher's saying is both 'an affirmation and a retraction of the said.'

CHAPTER 11   JACQUES DERRIDA: THE DEATHS OF ROLAND BARTHES

1 Derrida's original title is *'Les Morts de Roland Barthes.'*
2 Derrida plays here on a number of different meanings of *accorder*: to bring into harmony or accord; to concede, grant, admit, or avow; to put in grammatical agreement; to tune; etc.
3 *La loi du nom* (the law of the name) suggests *la loi du nombre* (the law of the number; the rule of the masses).
4 *Plus de* means both 'more' and 'no more.' This indecidability is discussed by Alan Bass in a translator's note in Derrida's *Margins of Philosophy* (Chicago: University of Chicago Press, 1982). p. 219.
5 Roland Barthes, *Writing Degree Zero*, trans. Annette Lavers and Colin Smith (New York, Hill & Wang, 1983) pp. 9–10 (henceforth cited as *WDZ*).
6 Roland Barthes, *Camera Lucida*, trans. Richard Howard (New York, Hill & Wang, 1981), p. 94 (hereafter *CL*). We have referred to this translation throughout, though the context of Derrida's essay has sometimes necessitated a retranslation of particular words and a return to the original text, *La chambre claire* (Paris, Seuil, 1980). All

differences between our translation and Howard's are indicated in
the text.

7 The French word here is *studieux* which is usually translated as
'studious.' We have opted for 'studied,' meaning 'of or related to
the study – the *studium*.'

8 Maurice Blanchot, *Le livre à venir* (Paris, Éditions Gallimard, 1959),
p. 25.

9 The phrase here is *tourner autour du point* which is a play on *tourner
autour du pot* (to beat around the bush).

10 Roland Barthes, *Roland Barthes by Roland Barthes*, trans. Richard
Howard, (New York, Hill & Wang, 1977), p. 142 (henceforth cited
as *RB*).

11 Maurice Blanchot, *L'amitié* (Paris, Éditions Gallimard, 1971),
pp. 326–30. As Derrida later alludes to, both the book and the last
section of the book bear the title *L'amitié*. Also, the entire five-page
section is italicized in the original, though we, following Derrida,
have omitted the italics in the following quotations.

12 Blanchot begins *Le livre à venir* with two epigraphs from Bataille.
We have translated them as follows: 'my close friendship: this is
what my whole disposition brings to other men'; 'a friend even
until that state of deep friendship where an abandoned man, abandoned by all his friends, meets in his life the one who will
accompany him beyond life, himself without a life, capable of a
free friendship, released from all attachments.'

13 Derrida is referring here to his own text. First published in *Poétique*
in September 1981, this essay was apparently written about a year
before that, approximately six months after Barthes' death in March,
1980.

14 Like so many other things that do not survive translation, the
passage on the back of *La chambre claire* has been omitted in *Camera
Lucida*. We thus restore here this 'gesture around what we believe
to be the essential writing':

> Marpa was very shaken when his son died, and one of his
> disciples said to him, 'You have always said that everything
> is an illusion. Is not the death of your son an illusion as well?'
> And Marpa responded, 'Certainly, but the death of my son is
> a super-illusion'
> –a practice of the Tibetan Way

15 We have referred to the French text here because the handwritten
lines of Barthes appear in black on a white background in the
English edition and have been incorporated into the opening and
closing pages of the text rather than being retained on the front

and back inside covers. Howard translates these two inscriptions as follows (going from front to back):

It must all be considered as if spoken by a character in a novel.

And afterward?
–What to write now? Can you still write anything?
–One writes with one's desires, and I am not through desiring.

16 Roland Barthes, 'Analyse textuelle d'un conte d'Edgar Poe,' in *Sémiotique narrative et textuelle*, ed. Cl. Chabrol, Larouse, coll. 'L,' 1973.
17 This phrase is indecidable and thus defies translation since it can be read as 'returning to the letter,' 'literally returning,' 'ghost to the letter,' and perhaps even 'literally a ghost.'

BIBLIOGRAPHY

BARTHES, ROLAND

1953

Writing Degree Zero. Trans. Annette Lavers and Colin Smith. Pref. by S. Sontag. New York, Hill & Wang, 1968.
Le degré zéro de l'écriture. Paris, Seuil, 1953.

1954

Michelet. Paris, Seuil, 1954, 1974.

1957

Mythologies. Selected and trans. Annette Lavers. New York, Hill & Wang, 1972; London, Jonathan Cape, 1972.
Mythologies. Paris, Seuil, 1957, 1970.

1963

On Racine. Trans. Richard Howard. New York, Hill & Wang, 1964; Octagon Books, 1977.
Sur Racine. Paris, Seuil, 1963, 1967, 1979.

1964

Critical Essays. Trans. Richard Howard. Evanston, Northwestern University Press, 1972.
Essais critiques. Paris, Seuil, 1964.
The Eiffel Tower and Other Mythologies. Trans. Richard Howard. New York: Hill & Wang. 1979.
La Tour Eiffel. Paris, Delpire, 1964.

1965

Writing Degree Zero, and Elements of Semiology. Trans. Annette Lavers and Colin Smith. Pref. by S. Sontag. Boston, Beacon Press, 1968.

344

Le degré zéro de l'écriture, suivi de: Eléments de sémiologie. Paris, Gonthier, 1965.

1966

Criticism and Truth. Trans. Katrina Pilcher Kenneman. Minneapolis, University of Minnesota Press, 1987.
Critique et vérité. Paris, Seuil, 1966.

1967

The Fashion System. Trans. Richard Howard. New York, Hill & Wang, 1983.
Système de la Mode. Paris, Seuil, 1967.

1970

Empire of Signs. Trans. Richard Howard. New York, Hill & Wang, 1982; London, Jonathan Cape, 1982.
L'Empire des signes. Paris, Flammarion, 1970; Genève, Skira, 1970.
S/Z. Trans. Richard Miller. New York, Hill & Wang, 1974; London, Jonathan Cape, 1975.
S/Z. Paris, Seuil, 1970.

1971

Sade, Fourier, Loyola. Trans. Richard Miller. New York, Hill & Wang, 1976; London, Jonathan Cape, 1976.
Sade, Fourier, Loyola. Paris, Seuil, 1971.

1972

New Critical Essays. Trans. Richard Howard. New York, Hill & Wang, 1980.
Le degré zéro de l'écriture, suivi de: Nouveaux essais critiques. Paris, Seuil, 1972. (Second part of a volume of which *Le degré zéro de l'écriture* was the first part.)

1973

The Pleasure of the Text. Trans. Richard Miller. New York, Hill & Wang, 1975; London, Jonathan Cape, 1975.
Le plaisir du texte. Paris, Seuil, 1973, 1982.

1975

Roland Barthes. Trans. Richard Howard. New York, Hill & Wang, 1977; London, Macmillan, 1977.
Roland Barthes. Paris, Seuil, 1975, 1979.

1976

Et la Chine? Paris, Bourgeois, 1976.

1977

A Lover's Discourse: Fragments. Trans. Richard Howard, New York, Hill & Wang, 1978, 1981.
Fragments d'un discours amoureux. Paris, Seuil, 1977.
Image, Music, Text. Essays selected and trans. Stephen Heath. New York, Hill & Wang, 1977; London, Fontana, 1977, 1984.
Leçon inaugurale faite le vendredi 7 janvier 1977. Paris, Collège de France, 1977.

1979

Sollers écrivain. Paris, Seuil, 1979.

1980

Camera Lucida. Reflections on Photography. Trans. Richard Howard. New York, Hill & Wang, 1981.
La chambre claire: note sur la photographie. Paris, Seuil, 1980.

1981

A Barthes Reader. Ed. with introd. by Susan Sontag. New York, Hill & Wang, 1981.
The Grain of the Voice: Interviews 1962–1980. Trans. Linda Coverdale. New York, Hill & Wang, 1985.
Le Grain de la voix: entretiens 1962–1980. Paris, Seuil, 1981.

1982

The Responsibility of Forms: Critical Essays on Music, Art and Representation. Trans. Richard Howard. New York, Hill & Wang, 1985.
L'Obvie et l'obtus. Paris, Seuil, 1982.

1984

Le Bruissement de la langue. Paris, Seuil, 1984.

1986

L'Aventure sémiologique. Paris, Seuil, 1986.

DELEUZE, GILLES

1957

Mémoire et vie. Paris, Presses Universitaires de France, 1957, 1963.

1962

Nietzsche and Philosophy. Trans. Hugh Tomlinson. New York, Columbia University Press, 1983; London, Athlone Press, 1983.
Nietzsche et la philosophie. Paris, Presses Universitaires de France, 1962, 1967, 1970, 1973, 1977.

1963

Kant's Critical Philosophy: the Doctrine of the Faculties. Trans. Hugh Tomlinson and Barbara Habberjam. London, Athlone Press, 1984; Minneapolis, University of Minnesota Press, 1984.
La philosophie critique de Kant: doctrine des facultés. Paris, Presses Universitaires de France, 1963, 1967.

1964

Marcel Proust et les signes. Paris, Presses Universitaires de France, 1964.

1965

Nietzsche. Paris, Presses Universitaires de France, 1965, 1977, 1983.
Nietzsche: sa vie, son oeuvre, avec un exposé de sa philosophie. Paris, Presses Universitaires de France, 1965.

1966

Le Bergsonisme. Paris, Presses Universitaires de France, 1966.

1967

Présentation de Sader Mashoch, le froid et le cruel. Avec le texte intégral de la Vénus à la fourrure, trad. de l'allemand. Paris, Minuit, 1967.

1969

Logique du sens. Paris, Minuit, 1969.

1973

Anti-Oedipus: Capitalism and Schizophrenia. Trans. Robert Hurley, Mark Seem, and Helen Lane. New York, Viking Press, 1977; Minneapolis, University of Minnesota Press, 1983; London, Athlone Press, 1983, 1984.
L'Anti-Oedipe. Capitalisme et schizophrénie. Avec Félix Guattari. Paris, Minuit, 1973, 1980.

1975

Kafka: Toward a Minor Literature. Trans. Marie McLean. Baltimore, Johns Hopkins University, 1985. Trans. Dana Polan. Minneapolis, University of Minnesota Press, 1986.

Kafka. Pour une littérature mineure. Avec Félix Guattari. Paris, Minuit, 1975.

1977
Dialogues. Avec Claire Parnet. Paris, Flammarion, 1977.

1980
Empirisme et subjectivité. Essai sur la nature humaine selon Hume. Paris, Presses Universitaires de France, 1980.
Mille Plateaux. Capitalisme et schizophrénie. Avec Félix Guattari. Paris, Minuit, 1980. Translated excerpts in *On The Line.* Trans. John Johnston. New York, Semiotext(e), 1983.

1981
Francis Bacon. Logique de la sensation. 2 vols. Paris, Différence, 1981.

1983
Cinema. Trans. Hugh Tomlinson and Barbara Habberjam. Minneapolis, University of Minnesota Press, 1986.
Cinema 1. L'Image mouvement. Paris, Minuit, 1983.

DERRIDA, JACQUES

1962
Edmund Husserl's Origin of Geometry: an Introduction. Trans. John Leavey. New York, Great Eastern Books, 1978.
L'Origine de la géométrie. Paris, Presses Universitaires de France, 1962.

1967
Of Grammatology. Trans. Gayatri Spivak. Baltimore, Johns Hopkins University Press, 1976.
De la grammatologie. Paris, Minuit, 1967.
Speech and Phenomena, and Other Essays on Husserl's Theory of Signs. Trans. David B. Allison. Evanston, Northwestern University Press, 1973, 1979.
La voix et le phénomène: introduction au problème du signe dans la phénoménologie de Husserl. Paris, Presses Universitaires de France, 1967, 1972, 1976, 1979, 1983.
Writing and Difference. Trans. Alan Bass. Chicago, University of Chicago Press, 1978; London, Routledge & Kegan Paul, 1978.
L'écriture et la différence. Paris, Seuil, 1967, 1979.

1972

Dissemination. Trans. Barbara Johnson. Chicago, University of Chicago Press, 1981; London, Athlone Press, 1981.
La dissémination. Paris, Seuil, 1972.
Margins of Philosophy. Trans. Alan Bass. Chicago, University of Chicago Press, 1982; Brighton, Harvester Press, 1982.
Marges de la philosophie. Paris, Minuit, 1972, 1975.
Positions. Trans. Alan Bass. Chicago, University of Chicago Press, 1982.
Positions. Entretiens avec Henri Ronge, Julia Kristeva, Jean-Louis Houdebine, Guy Scarpetta. Paris, Minuit, 1972.

1974

Glas. Trans. John Leavy and Richard Rand. Lincoln, University of Nebraska Press, 1986.
Glas. Paris, Galilée, 1974; Denoël, 1982.

1975

Adami. Paris, Galerie Maeght, 1975.

1976

The Archaeology of the Frivolous: Reading Condillac. Trans. John Leavey. Pittsburgh, Duquesne University Press, 1980.
L'Archéologie du frivole. Paris, Denoël, 1976.
La carte postale: de Socrate à Freud et au-delà. Paris, Flammarion, 1976.
Cryptonymie: le verbier de l'Homme aux loups. Paris, Flammarion, 1976.

1978

Spurs: Nietzsche's Styles. Trans. Barbara Harlow. Chicago, University of Chicago Press, 1979.
Eperons. Les styles de Nietzsche. Paris, Flammarion, 1978.
Titus Carmel (The pocket size Tlingit Coffin). Paris, Centre Pompidou, 1978.
La vérité en peinture. Paris, Flammarion, 1978.

1980

Glyph 7. Baltimore, Johns Hopkins University Press, 1980.

1982

Affranchissement du transfert et de la lettre: colloque autour de la *Carte postale* de Jacques Derrida, 4 et 5 avril 1981. Paris, Confrontation, 1982.
The Ear of the Other: Otobiography, Transference, Translations; Texts and

Discussions with Jacques Derrida, Trans. Peggy Kamuf. New York, Schocken Books, 1985.

L'oreille de l'autre: otobiographies, transferts, traductions: textes et débats avec Jacques Derrida. Paris, VLB, 1982.

1983

D'un ton apocalyptique adopté naguère en philosophie. Paris, Galilée, 1983.

1984

Otobiographies: l'enseignement de Nietzsche et la politique du nom propre. Paris, Galilée, 1984.

Signéponge/Signsponge. Trans. Richard Rand. New York, Columbia University Press, 1984 (parallel French and English transl.).

1985

Droit de regard. Paris, Minuit, 1985.

La faculté de juger. Paris, Minuit, 1985.

1986

Choréographies. Jacques Derrida and Christie V. McDonald. Ann Arbor: Xerox University Microfilm, 1985.
  (Originally published in *Diacritics*, Vol. 1, 1982).

Droits de regards. Photographies de M. F. Plissart. Suivi d'une lecture de Jacques Derrida. Paris, Minuit, 1985.

La faculté de juger. Paris: Minuit, 1985.
  (Communications by Jacques Derrida et al. Includes six papers presented at Cerisy-la-Salle in July–August 1982).

Les sauvages dans la cité: auto-émancipation du peuple et instruction des prolétaires au XIXe siècle. Avant-propos de Jacques Derrida. Seyssel, Champ Vallon, 1985.

Mémoires: for Paul de Man, trans. Cecile Lindsay, Jonathan Culler and Eduardo Cadavo. New York, Columbia University Press, 1986.

Parages. Paris, Galilée, 1986.

Schibboleth pour Paul Célan. Paris, Galilée, 1986.

1987

De l'esprit: Heidegger et la question. Paris, Galilée. 1987.

For Nelson Mandela. Ed. by Jacques Derrida and Mustapha Tilli. Trans. Philip Franklin et al. New York, H. Holt & Co., 1987.

Psyché. Inventions de l'autre. Paris, Galilée, 1987.

Ulysse gramophone: deux mots pour Joyce. Paris, Galilée, 1987.

FOUCAULT, MICHEL

1961

Madness and Civilization: a History of Insanity in the Age of Reason. Trans. Richard Howard. New York, New American Library, 1965, 1967, 1971; Vintage Books, 1965, 1973; Pantheon Books, 1965; Tavistock, 1967.
Histoire de la folie à l'âge classique. Paris, Plon, 1961; Gallimard, 1976, 1977; Union Générale d'Editions, 1971.

1962

Mental Illness and Psychology. Trans. Alan Sheridan. New York, Harper & Row 1976.
Maladie mentale et psychologie. Paris, Presses Universitaires de France, 1962, 1966.

1963

The Birth of the Clinic: An Archaeology of Medical Perception. Trans. A. M. Sheridan-Smith. New York, Pantheon, 1973, 1976; Tavistock, 1973, 1976; Vintage Books, 1975.
Naissance de la clinique. Une archéologie du regard médical. Paris, Presses Universitaires de France, 1963, 1972, 1975, 1983.
Death and the Labyrinth: the World of Raymond Roussel. Trans. Charles Ruas. Garden City, Doubleday, 1986.
Raymond Roussel. Paris, Gallimard, 1963.

1966

The Order of Things: an Archaeology of the Human Sciences. New York, Pantheon, 1970, 1971; Tavistock, 1970.
Les Mots et les choses. Une archéologie des sciences humaines. Paris, Gallimard, 1966.

1968

Théorie d'ensemble. Paris, Seuil, 1968, 1980.

1969

The Archaeology of Knowledge. Trans. A. M. Sheridan-Smith, New York, Harper & Row, 1972, 1976; Pantheon, 1972; Tavistock, 1972, 1974.
L'Archéologie du savoir. Paris, Gallimard, 1969, 1977.

1970

Anthropologie du point de vue pragmatique. Trans. from German. Paris, Vrin, 1970.

351

1971

'The Order of Discourse.' Trans. Ian McLeod. In *Untying the Text: A Post-Structuralist Reader*. Ed. by R. Young. Boston, Routledge & Kegan Paul, 1981.
L'Ordre du discours. Leçon inaugurale au Collège de France prononcée le 2 décembre 1970. Paris, Gallimard, 1970.

1972

Histoire de la folie à l'âge classique. Suivi de mon corps, ce papier, ce feu et la folie, l'absence d'oeuvre. Paris, Gallimard, 1972.

1973

This is not a pipe. With illustrations and letters by René Magritte. Trans. James Harkness. Berkeley, University of California Press, 1981.
Ceci n'est pas une pipe: deux lettres et quatre dessins de René Magritte. Paris, Fata Morgana, 1973.
C'est demain la veille. Paris, Seuil, 1973.
I, Pierre Rivière, Having Slaughtered My Mother, My Sister and My Brother; a Case of Parricide in the 19th century. Trans, Frank Jellinek. Harmondsworth, Penguin, 1978; Lincoln, University of Nebraska Press, 1982.
Moi, Pierre Rivière, ayant égorgé ma mère, ma soeur et mon frère. Un cas de parricide au 19e siècle. Paris, Gallimard, 1973; Gallimard/Julliard, 1977.
Reyberolle. Paris, Galerie Maeght, 1973.

1975

Fromanger, Le désir est partout, La peinture photogénique. Paris, Bucher, 1975.
Discipline and Punish: the Birth of the Prison. Trans, Alan Sheridan. London, Allen, 1977; New York, Pantheon, 1977; Vintage Books, 1977, 1979.
Surveiller et punir; Naissance de la prison. Paris, Editions Gallimard, 1975.

1976

The History of Sexuality. Vol. I. Trans. Robert Hurley. New York, Vintage Books, 1976.
Histoire de la sexualité. Vol. 1. La volonté de savoir. Paris, Gallimard, 1976.

1977

Language, Counter-memory, Practice: Selected Essays and Interviews. Ed. with an introd. by Donald F. Bouchard. Trans. Donald F. Bouchard and Sherry Simon. Ithaca, Cornell University Press, 1977, 1980; London, Blackwell & Mott, 1977.

Microphysique du pouvoir. Ed. by A. Fontana and P. Pasquino. Turin, Einaudi, 1977.

Politiques de l'habitat: 1800–1850. Paris, Comité de la Recherche et du Développement en architecture, 1977.

1978

Herculine Barbin: Being the Recently Discovered Memoirs of a Nineteenth-century French Hermaphrodite. Trans. Richard McDougall. Brighton, Harvester Press, 1980.

Herculine Barbin dite Alexina B. Paris, Gallimard, 1978.

1979

Michel Foucault: Power, Truth, Strategy. Ed. by Meaghan Morris and Paul Patton. Sydney, Feral Publications, 1979.

1980

L'impossible prison: recherches sur le système pénitentiaire au XIXe siècle. Paris, Seuil, 1980.

Power, Knowledge: Selected Interviews and Other Writings, 1972–1977. Ed. by C. Gordon. Brighton, Harvester Press, 1980; New York, Pantheon, 1980.

1982

Le désordre des familles. Lettres de cachet des archives de la Bastille. Avec Arlette Farge. Paris, Gallimard, 1982.

1983

Sécurité sociale: l'enjeu. Avec Bernard Brunhes et René Lenoir. Paris, Syros, 1983.

1984

The Foucault Reader. Ed. by Paul Rabinow. New York, Pantheon, 1984.

Histoire de la sexualité. Vol. 2 L'usage des plaisirs. Paris, Gallimard, 1984.

The Use of Pleasure. Trans. Robert Hurley. New York, Pantheon, 1985.

Histoire de la sexualité. Vol. 3. Le souci de soi. Paris, Gallimard, 1984.

1986

Maurice Blanchot: The Thought from Outside. Trans. Jeffrey Mehlmann and Brian Massumi. New York: Zone Books, 1987.

La pensée du dehors. Paris, Fata Morgana, 1986.

HABERMAS, JÜRGEN

1954

Das Absolute und die Geschichte von der Zwiespältigkeit in Schellings Denken. Bonn, Bouvier, 1954.

1961

Student und Politik; eine soziologische Untersuchung zum politischen Bewusstsein Frankfurter Studenten. Neuwied, Luchterhand, 1961, 1969.

1962

Strukturwandel der Öffentlichkeir. Untersuchungen zu einer Kategorie der bürgerlichen Gesellschaft. Neuwied, Luchterhand, 1962, 1979.

1963

Theorie and Practice. Trans. John Viertel. Boston, Beacon Press, 1973. *Theorie und Praxis: sozialphilosophische Studien.* Neuwied, Luchterhand, 1963; Frankfurt, Suhrkamp, 1971, 1972, 1978.

1968

Antworten auf Herbert Marcuse. Frankfurt, Suhrkamp, 1968.
Knowledge and Human Interests. Trans. Jeremy Shapiro. London, Heinemann Educational, 1978.
Erkenntnis und Interesse. Frankfurt, Suhrkamp, 1968, 1973, 1979.
Die Linke antwortet Jürgen Habermas. Frankfurt, Europäische Verlagsanstalt, 1968, 1969.
Technik und Wissenschaft als 'Ideologie.' Frankfurt, Suhrkamp, 1968, 1979.

1969

Toward a Rational Society; Student Protest, Science and Politics. Trans. Jeremy Shapiro. Boston, Beacon Press, 1970. (The first three essays were published in *Protestbewegung und Hochschulreform.* Frankfurt, Suhrkamp, 1969. The last three essays were published in *Technik und Wissenschaft als 'Ideologie.'* Frankfurt, Suhrkamp, 1968, 1979.)

1970

Über Sprachtheorie. Einführende Bemerkungen zu einer Theorie der kommunikativen Kompetenz. Wien, Verein Gruppe Hundsblume, 1970.

1971

Philosophical-political Profiles. Trans. Frederick G. Lawrence. Cambridge, MA, MIT Press, 1985; London, Heinemann, 1983.
Philosophisch-politische Profile. Frankfurt, Suhrkamp, 1971.

Theorie der Gesellschaft oder Sozialtechnologie. Frankfurt, Suhrkamp, 1971.

1973
Arbeit, Freizeit, Konsum: frühe Aufsätze. s'Gravenhage, Van Eversdijck, 1973.
Kultur und Kritik: verstreute Aufsätze. Frankfurt, Suhrkamp, 1973, 1977.
Legitimation Crisis. Trans, Thomas McCarthy, London, Heinemann, 1976.
Legitimationsprobleme in Spätkapitalismus. Frankfurt, Suhrkamp, 1973, 1979.
Zur Logik der Sozialwissenschaften. Materialen. Frankfurt, Suhrkamp, 1973.

1974
Können komplexe Gesellschaften eine vernünftige Identität ausbilden? in: *Zwei Reden.* Frankfurt, Suhrkamp, 1974.

1976
Communication and the Evolution of Society. Trans. Thomas McCarthy. Boston, Beacon Press, 1979.
Sprachpragmatik und Philosophie und Zur Rekonstruktion des Historischen Materialismus. Frankfurt, Suhrkamp, 1976.

1978
Politik, Kunst, Religion: Essays über zeitgenössige Philosophen. Stuttgart, Reclam, 1978.

1979
Das Erbe Hegels: 2 Reden aus Anlass der Verleihung des Hegel-Preises 1979 der Stadt Stuttgart an Hans-George Gadamer am 13. Juni 1979. Frankfurt, Suhrkamp, 1979.
Observations on the 'Spiritual Situation of the Age': Contemporary German Perspective. Ed. by J. Habermas. Trans. Andrew Buchwalter. Cambridge, MIT Press, 1979.
Stichworte zur geistigen Situation der Zeit. Frankfurt, Suhrkamp, 1979.

1981
Theorie des Kommunications Handeln. Frankfurt, Suhrkamp, 1981.

1985
Philosophical Discourse of Modernity. Cambridge, MA, MIT Press, 1987.
Der philosophische Diskurs der Moderne. Frankfurt, Suhrkamp, 1985.

HEIDEGGER, MARTIN

1927

Being and Time. Trans. J. Macquarrie and E. Robinson. New York, and Harper Row, 1962.
Sein und Zeit, in *Jahrbuch fur Philosophie und phänomenologische Forschung,* Band VIII, ed. E. Husserl. Tübingen, Niemeyer, 1927.

1929

Kant and the Problem of Metaphysics. Trans. J. Churchill. Bloomington, Indiana University Press, 1962.
Kant und das Problem der Metaphysik. Bonn, F. Cohen, 1929.

1949

Essence of Reasons. Trans. Terrence Malik. Evanston, Northwestern University Press, 1969.
Vom Wesen des Grundes. Jahrbuch für Philosophie und phänomenologische Kritik. Frankfurt, Klostermann, 1949.
Existence and Being. London, Vision Press, 1949, 1956, 1968; New York, Regnery, 1949, 1962, 1965, 1968; Gateway, 1976, 1979, 1986.

1950

Hegel's Concept of Experience. New York, Harper & Row, 1970.
Hegels Begriff der Erfahrung. In *Holzwege.* Frankfurt, Klostermann, 1950, pp. 105–92.

1953

An Introduction to Metaphysics. Trans. R. Manheim. New Haven, Yale University Press, 1959.
Einführung in die Metaphysik. Tübingen, Niemeyer, 1953.

1954

What is called Thinking? Trans. Glenn Gray and Fred Wieck. New York, Harper & Row, 1972.
Was Heißt Denken? Tübingen, Niemeyer, 1954.

1956

The Question of Being. Trans. W. Kluback and J. T. Wilde. London, Vision, 1959.
Zur Seinsfrage. Frankfurt, Klostermann, 1956.
What is Philosophy? Trans. W. Kluback and J. T. Wilde. New Haven, New College and University Press, 1958.
Was ist das-die Philosophie? Pfullingen, Neske, 1956.

1959

Discourse on Thinking. Trans. J. M. Anderson and Hans Freund. New York, Harper & Row, 1969.
Gelassenheit. Pfullingen, Neske, 1959.
On the Way to Language. Trans. P. Hertz. New York, Harper & Row, 1971.
Unterwegs zur Sprache. Pfullingen, Neske, 1959.

1961

Nietzsche. The Will to Power As Art. Vol. I. Trans. by David Krell, New York, Harper & Row, 1979.
Nietzsche, Vol. I. Pfullingen: Neske, 1961.
Nietzsche. The Eternal Recurrence of the Same. Vol. II. Trans. David Krell. New York, Harper & Row, 1984.
Nietzsche. Vol. I. Pfullingen, Neske, 1961.
Nietzsche. The Will to Power as Knowledge and as Metaphysics, Vol. III. Trans. J. Stambaugh and F. Capuzzi. New York, Harper & Row, 1985.
Nietzsche. Vol. I. Pfullingen, Neske, 1961.
Nietzsche. Nihilism. Vol. IV. Trans. F. Capuzzi. New York, Harper & Row, 1982.
Nietzsche. Vol. II. Pfullingen, Neske, 1961.

1962

What is a Thing? Trans. W. B. Barton and V. Deutsch with an analysis by Eugene T. Gendlin. South Bend, Indiana: Regnery/Gateway, 1967.
Die Frage nach dem Ding. Tübingen, Niemeyer, 1962.

1969

On Time and Being. Trans. J. Stambaugh. New York, Harper & Row, 1972.
Zur Sache des Denkens. Tübingen, Niemeyer, 1969.

1971

Schelling on Human Freedom. Trans. J. Stambaugh. New York, Harper & Row, 1978.
Schellings Abhandlung über das Wesen der menschlichen Freiheit (1809). Tübingen, Niemeyer, 1971.

1975

The Basic Problems of Phenomenology. Trans. Albert Hofstader. Bloomington, Indiana University Press, 1982.
Die Grundprobleme der Phänomenologie. Frankfurt, Klostermann, 1975.

Early Greek Thinking. Trans. David Krell and Frank Capuzzi. New York, Harper & Row, 1975.
(English translation of four essays ('Holzwege,' 'Logos,' 'Moira,' 'Aletheia.')
Poetry, Language, Thought. Trans. A. Hofstadter. Includes 'The Origin of the Work of Art,' 'Language,' 'Building,' 'Dwelling,' 'Thinking,' 'The Thing,' 'Poetically Man Dwells.' New York, Harper & Row, 1975.

1976

The Piety of Thinking: Essays by Martin Heidegger. Includes 'Language,' 'Building,' 'Dwelling,' 'Thinking,' 'The Thing,' 'Poetically Man Dwells'. Trans. K. Hoeller, J. G. Hart, J. C. Maraldo. Bloomington, Indiana University Press, 1976.

1977

Basic Writings. Ed. by David Krell. Includes 'The End of Philosophy' and 'The Task of Thinking', 'What is a Thing?' 'Building, Dwelling, Thinking,' 'The Origin of the Work of Art,' 'On the Essence of Truth,' 'Letter on Humanism,' 'What is called Thinking?' 'What is Metaphysics?' 'Being and Time' (Introduction). New York, Harper & Row, 1977.
The Question Concerning Technology and Other Essays. Trans. W. Lovitt. New York, Harper & Row, 1977; Garland, 1978. (Translations of essays which originally appeared in *Die Technik und die Kehre*, *Holzwege*, and *Vorträge und Aufsätze*.)

1979

History of the Concept of Time: Prolegomena. Trans. Theodore Kisiel. Bloomington, Indiana University Press, 1985.
Prolegomena zur Geschichte des Zeitbegriffs. Frankfurt, Klostermann, 1979.
The Metaphysical Foundations of Logic. Trans. M. Heim. Bloomington, Indiana University Press, 1984.
Metaphysische Anfangsgründe der Logik im Ausgang von Leibniz. Frankfurt, Klostermann, 1979.

For further references on Martin Heidegger, please consult *Martin Heidegger: Bibliography and Glossary* by Hans Martin Sass which contains over 6,350 entries in sections covering Works by Heidegger, Lists of Translations, Works on Heidegger, Heidegger Conferences, and a comprehensive Heidegger Glossary.

LACAN, JACQUES

1932

De la psychose paranoïaque dans ses rapports avec la personnalité. Doctoral thesis. Paris, Le François, 1932, Seuil, 1975, 1980.

1933

Le crime des soeurs Papin. Paris, Le Minautore, 1933.

1966

Écrits. A Selection. Trans. Alan Sheridan. London, Tavistock, 1977; New York, Norton, 1977.
Écrits. 2 vols. Paris, Seuil, 1966, 1970, 1971.

1968

The Language of the Self: Speech and Language in Psychoanalysis, Trans. Anthony Wilden. (Originally published as *Fonction et champ de la parole et du langage en psychanalyse,* Vol. I (Paris, 1956) and in the author's *Écrits,* 1966. Originally published in English as *The Language of the Self: The Function of Language in Psychoanalysis,* in 1968.) Baltimore, Johns Hopkins Press, 1968, 1981; New York, Dell, 1975.

1973

The Four Fundamental Concepts of Psychoanalysis, Trans. Alan Sheridan. New York, Norton, 1973, 1978, 1981: London, Hogarth Press, 1977, 1978; Harmondsworth, Penguin, 1977, 1979.
Le Séminaire. Vol. XI: *Les Quatre concepts fondamentaux de la psychanalyse.* Paris, Seuil, 1973.
Le Séminaire. Vol. I: *Les écrits techniques de Freud.* Paris, Seuil, 1973.

1974

Télévision, Paris, Seuil, 1974.

1975

Le Séminaire, Vol. XX: Encore, 1972–1973. Paris, Seuil, 1975.

1976

Marguerite Duras, Étude sur l'oeuvre littéraire, théâtrale et cinématographique de Marguerite Duras. With Maurice Blanchot. Paris, Albatros, 1976.

1977

Lacan: Théorie et pratiques. By Robert Georgin. Lausanne, Editions l'Age d'Homme, 1977.

1978

Propositions du 9 octobre 1967, première version. Paris, Navarin, 1978.
Le Séminaire. Vol II: *Le moi dans la théorie de Freud et dans la technique de la psychanalyse, 1954–1955*. Paris, Seuil, 1978.

1981

Le Séminaire. Vol. 3: *Les psychoses*. Paris, Seuil, 1981.

1982

Feminine Sexuality: Jacques Lacan and the École Freudienne. Ed. by Juliet Mitchell and Jacqueline Rose. London, Macmillan, 1982; New York, Pantheon and Norton, 1982, 1985.

1984

Les Complexes familiaux dans la formation de l'individu: essai d'analyse d'une fonction en psychologie. Paris, Navarian, 1984.

LEVINAS, EMMANUEL

1930

The Theory of Intuition in Husserl's Phenomenology. Trans. André Orianne, Evanston, Northwestern University Press, 1973.
La Théorie de l'intuition dans la phénoménologie de Husserl. Paris, Alcan, 1930; Vrin, 1963, 1978.

1947

Existence and Existents. Trans. Alphonso Lingis. The Hague, Nijhoff, 1978.
De l'existence à l'existant. Paris, Fontaine, 1947; Vrin, 1981, 1984.

1949

En découvrant l'existence avec Husserl et Heidegger. Paris, Vrin, 1949, 1967, 1974, 1982.

1960

Totality and Infinity. An Essay on Exteriority. Trans. Alphonso Lingis. Pittsburgh, Duquesne University Press, 1969.
Totalité et infinité. Essai sur l'extériorité. The Hague, Nijhoff, 1960, 1965.

1963

Difficile liberté; essais sur le judaïsme. Paris, Michel, 1963, 1976, 1983.

1968

Martin Buber. L'Homme et le philosophe. Bruxelles, Editions de l'Institut de Sociologie de l'Université Libre de Bruxelles, 1968.

Quatre lectures talmudiques. Paris, Minuit, 1968.

Le renouveau de la culture juive. With Moshe Davis, Shahul Esh, and Max Gottschalk, Bruxelles, Editions de l'Institut de Sociologie de l'Université Libre de Bruxelles, 1968.

1972

Humanisme de l'autre homme. Paris, Fata Morgana, 1972.

1974

Otherwise Than Being; Or, Beyond Essence. Trans. Alphonso Lingis. The Hague, Nijhoff, 1981.

Autrement qu'être; ou au-delà de l'essence. La Haye, Nijhoff, 1974.

1975

Sur Maurice Blanchot. Paris, Fata Morgana, 1975.

1976

Jean Wahl et Gabriel Marcel. With Xavier Tilliette and Paul Ricoeur. Paris, Beauchesne, 1976.

Noms propres. Paris, Fata Morgana, 1976.

1977

Du sacré au saint; cinq nouvelles lectures talmudiques. Paris, Minuit, 1977.

La révélation. With Paul Ricoeur and Edgar Haulotte. Bruxelles, Facultes Universitaires Saint-Louis, 1977.

1979

Le temps et l'autre. Paris, Fata Morgana, 1979; Presses Universitaires de France, 1979.

1982

L'Au-delà du verset: lectures et discours talmudiques. Paris, Minuit, 1982.

De Dieu qui vient à l'idée. Paris, Vrin, 1982.

De l'évasion. Paris, Fata Morgana, 1982.

Ethics and Infinity. Conservations with Philippe Nemo. Trans. Richard A. Cohen. Pittsburgh, Duquesne University Press, 1985.

Ethique et infini. Dialogues avec Philippe Nemo. Paris, Fayard, 1982, 1984.

1984

Emmanuel Levinas, Textes rassemblés par Jacques Rolland. Lagrasse, Verdier, 1984.

Transcendance et intelligibilité. Suivi d'un entretien. Geneva, Labor et Fides, 1984.

1986

Collected Philosophical Papers of Emmanuel Levinas. Trans. Alphonso Lingis. Dordrecht, Nijhoff, 1986.

LYOTARD, JEAN-FRANÇOIS

1954

La Phénoménologie. Paris, Presses Universitaires de France, 1954, 1959, 1964, 1967, 1969, 1976.

1971

Discours, figure. Un essai d'esthétique. Paris, Klincksieck, 1971, 1974, 1978, 1985.

1973

Dérive à partir de Marx et Freud. Paris, Union Générale d'Editions, 1973.
Les Dispositifs pulsionnels. Paris, Union Générale d'Editions, 1973; Bourgeois, 1980.

1974

Economie libidinale. Paris, Editions de Minuit, 1974.

1975

Toil. Paris, Bourgeois, 1975.

1977

Instructions païennes. Paris, Galilée, 1977.
Récits tremblants. With Jacques Monory. Paris, Galilée, 1977.
Rudiments païens. Genre dissertatif. Paris, Union Générale d'Editions, 1977.
Les Transformateurs Duchamp. Paris, Galilée, 1977.

1979

Just Gaming. Trans. Brian Massumi, Minneapolis, University of Minnesota Press, 1985.
  Au juste, Conversations. With Jean-Loup Thébaud. Paris, Bourgeois, 1979.
Le Mur du Pacifique. Paris, Galilée, 1979.
The Post-modern Condition: a Report on Knowledge. Trans. Geoff

Bennington and Brian Massumi. Minneapolis, University of Minnesota Press, 1984; Manchester, Manchester University Press, 1984.
La Condition post-moderne: rapport sur le savoir. Paris, Editions de Minuit, 1979.

1981

Ciels: nébuleuses et galaxies: les confins d'un dandysme. Paris, Galerie Maeght, 1981.
Les Couleurs: sculptures; les formes; peintures. Paris, Centre National d'Art et de Culture Georges Pompidou; Les Presses du Nova Scotia College of Art and Design, 1981.
Sur la constitution du temps par la couleur dans les oeuvres récentes d'Albert Aymé. Paris, Traversière, 1981.

1983

Adami: peintures récentes. Paris, Galerie Maeght, 1983.

1984

L'Assassinat de l'expérience par la peinture, Monory. Paris, Castor, 1984.
Le Différend. Paris, Editions de Minuit, 1984.
L'Histoire de Ruth. With Ruth Francken, Paris, Castor, 1984.
Tombeau de l'intellectuel et autres papiers. Paris, Galilée, 1984.

1985

L'Art des confins: mélanges offerts à Maurice de Gandillac. With Annie Cazenave. Paris, Presses Universitaires de France, 1985.
Traitement de textes: cartes et brouillons. Paris, Bedou, 1985.

1986

Le post-modernisme expliqué aux enfants, Correspondence 1982–1985. Paris, Galilée, 1986.

MERLEAU-PONTY, MAURICE

1942

The Structure of Behavior. Trans. Alden L. Fisher. Boston, Beacon Press, 1963, 1967; London, Methuen, 1965.
La Structure du comportement. Paris, Presses Universitaires de France, 1942, 1949, 1953, 1960, 1963.

1945

Phenomenology of Perception. Trans. Colin Smith. New York, Humanities Press, 1962, 1974, 1976, 1978; London, Routledge & Kegan Paul, 1962, 1967, 1981.

Phénoménologie de la perception. Paris, Gallimard, 1945.

1947

Humanism and Terror: an Essay on the Communist Problem. Trans. John O'Neill. Boston; Beacon Press, 1969, 1985; London, Greenwood Press, 1980.
Humanisme et terreur, essai sur le problème communiste. Paris, Gallimard, 1947, 1972.

1948

Sense and Non-Sense. Trans. Herbert L. Dreyfus and Patricia Allen Dreyfus. Evanston, Northwestern University Press, 1964.
Sens et non-sens. Paris, Nagel, 1948, 1958, 1963, 1965, 1967.

1953

In Praise of Philosophy. Trans. John Wild and James M. Edie. Evanston, Northwestern University Press, 1963.
Éloge de la Philosophie, leçon inaugurale faite au Collège de France, le jeudi 15 janvier 1953. Paris, Gallimard, 1953, 1960, 1965.
Éloge de la Philosophie et autres essais. Paris, Gallimard, 1960.
Éloge de la Philosophie. Paris, Gallimard, 1965.

1955

Adventures of the Dialectic. Trans. Joseph Bien. Evanston, Northwestern University Press, 1973; London, Heinemann, 1974.
Les Aventures de la dialectique. Paris, Gallimard, 1955, 1967, 1977.

1956

Les Philosophes célèbres. Paris, Mazenod, 1956.

1960

Signs. Trans. Richard C. McCleary. Evanston, Northwestern University Press, 1964.
Signes. Paris, Gallimard, 1960, 1967.
The Primacy of Perception, and Other Essays on Phenomenological Psychology, the Philosophy of Art, History, and Politics. Edited by James M. Edie. Evanston, Northwestern University Press, 1964.
Les Sciences de l'homme et la phénoménologie. Paris, Centre de Documentation Universitaire, 1958, 1967.
L'Oeil et l'esprit. Paris, Gallimard, 1964.

1964

The Visible and the Invisible; followed by working notes. Trans. Alphonso Lingis. Evanston, Northwestern University Press, 1968.

Le Visible et l'invisible; suivi de notes de travail. Paris, Gallimard, 1964, 1979.

1968

Themes from the Lectures at the Collège de France, 1952–1960. Trans. John O'Neill. Evanston, Northwestern University Press, 1970.
Résumés de cours, Collège de France, 1952–1960. Paris, Gallimard, 1968, 1982.
L'Union de l'âme et du corps chez Malebranche, Biran et Bergson, Notes prises au cours de Maurice Merleau-Ponty. Paris, Vrin, 1968, 1978.

1969

The Prose of the World. Trans. John O'Neill. Evanston, Northwestern University Press, 1973.
La Prose du monde. Paris, Gallimard, 1969, 1978.
The Essential Writings of Merleau-Ponty. Edited by Alden L. Fisher. New York, Harcourt, Brace & World, 1969.

1971

Existence et dialectique. Paris, Presses Universitaires de France, 1971.

1973

Consciousness and the Acquisition of Language. Trans. Hugh J. Silverman. Evanston, Northwestern University Press, 1973.

1974

Phenomenology, Language and Sociology: Selected Essays of Merleau-Ponty. London, Heinemann Educational, 1974.

1981

Approches phénoménologiques. Paris, Hachette, 1981.

SARTRE, JEAN-PAUL

1939

The Emotions, Outline of a Theory. Trans. Bernard Frechtman. New York, Philosophical Library, 1948.
Esquisse d'une théorie des émotions. Paris, Hermann, 1939, 1948, 1960, 1961, 1965, 1969.

1943

Being and Nothingness: An Essay on Phenomenological Ontology. Trans. Hazel Barnes. New York, Pocket Books, 1956, 1966; Citadel Press,

1964, 1965, 1969; Washington Square Press, 1968, 1969; London Philosophical Library, 1956; Methuen, 1968.

Existential Psychoanalysis. (Translation of selected essays from *L'être et le néant.*) Trans. Hazel Barnes. Chicago, Gateway Editions, 1962, 1986.

The Wisdom of Jean Paul Sartre; a Selection. (From *L'être et le néant.*) Trans. Hazel Barnes. New York, Philosophical Library, 1956.

L'être et le néant: essai d'ontologie phénoménologique. Paris, Gallimard, 1943, 1953, 1976, 1981, 1983.

1946

Descartes, 1596–1650. Paris, Trois Collines, 1946.

Existentialism and Humanism. Trans. Bernard Frechtman. New York, Haskell House, 1947, 1977. Trans. Philip Mairet. London, Methuen, 1973.

L'Existentialisme est un humanisme. Paris, Nagel, 1946, 1962, 1963.

Anti-Semite and Jew. Trans. George Becker. New York, Schocken Books, 1948, 1965; Grove Press, 1960, 1962.

Portrait of an Anti-Semite. Trans. Mary Guggenheim. New York, Partisan Review, 1946.

Réflexions sur la question juive. Paris, Morihien, 1946, 1947; Gallimard, 1954, 1985.

1948

Pour et contre l'existentialisme: grand débat. Paris, Atlas, 1948.

Literature and Existentialism. Trans. Bernard Frechtman. New York, Citadel Press, 1965, 1980.

Qu-est-ce que la littérature? Paris, Gallimard, 1948, 1972.

1949

Entretiens sur la politique. Avec David Rousset. Paris, Gallimard, 1949.

1953

L'Affaire Henri Martin. Paris, Gallimard, 1953.

1955

Literary and Philosophical Essays. Trans. Annette Michelson. (From *Situations II* and *III.*) New York, Collier Books, 1955, 1965; Criterion Books, 1955; Rider, 1955; London, Hutchinson, 1968.

1960

Critique of Dialectical Reason. Vol. I: Theory of Practical Ensembles. Trans. Alan Sheridan-Smith. London, Verso, 1976, 1982.

Critique de la raison dialectique, précédé de Questions de méthodes. Vol. I Théorie des ensembles pratiques. Paris, Gallimard, 1960.
Search for a Method. Trans. Hazel Barnes. New York, Vintage Books, 1963.
Questions de méthode. Paris, Gallimard, 1960. (First published under *Existentialisme et Méthode*, 1960, 1980.)

1962

Between Existentialism and Marxism: Sartre on Philosophy, Politics, Psychology and the Arts. Trans, John Mathews, New York, Pantheon Books, 1974, 1983.
Marxisme et existentialisme. Controverse sur la dialectique. Paris, Plon, 1962.
Imagination: a Psychological Critique. Trans. Forrest Williams. Ann Arbor, University of Michigan Press, 1972.
L'Imagination. Paris, Presses Universitaires de France, 1962, 1963, 1983.

1963

Essays in Aesthetics. Selected and trans. Wade Baskin. New York, Philosophical Library, 1963; Citadel Press, 1963.

1964

The Communists and Peace. With a reply to Claude Lefort. New York, Braziller, 1968; London, Hamish Hamilton, 1969.
Les Communistes et la paix. (From *Situations VI and VII.*) Paris, Gallimard, 1964.

1965

Essays in Existentialism. (First published under title *Philosophy of Existentialism*, 1965.) Ed. and trans. Wade Baskin. New York, Citadel Press, 1965, 1974.
The Philosophy of Jean-Paul Sartre. Ed. by Robert D. Cumming. London, Methuen, 1965; New York, Vintage Books, 1972.
Literature and Existentialism. Trans. Bernard Frechtman. New York, Citadel Press, 1965, 1980.
Qu'est-ce que la littérature? Paris, Gallimard, 1965.
Situations. Trans. Maria Jolas. New York, Braziller, 1965.
The Transcendence of the Ego; an Existentialist Theory of Consciousness. Trans. Forrest Williams and Robert Kirkpatrick. New York, Farrar, Strauss & Giroux, 1957; Noonday Press, 1957; Octagon Books, 1972.
La transcendence de l'ego. Esquisse d'une description phénoménologique. Paris, Vrin, 1965, 1978, 1985.

1968

On Genocide. And a Summary of the Evidence and the Judgments of the International War Crimes Tribunal. Boston, Beacon Press, 1968.

1972

Plaidoyer pour les intellectuels. Paris, Gallimard, 1972.

1974

The Writings of Jean-Paul Sartre. Compiled by Michel Contat and Michel Rybalka. Trans. Richard C. McCleary. Evanston, Northwestern University Press, 1974.

1977

Life/Situations. Trans. Paul Auster and Lydia Davis. New York, Pantheon, 1977.

1983

Cahiers pour une morale. Paris, Gallimard, 1983.

1984

Le scénario Freud. Paris, Gallimard, 1984.

1985

Critique de la raison dialectique, précédé de Questions de méthode. Vol. I: Théorie des ensembles pratiques. Texte établi et annonté par Arlette Elkhaïme-Sartre. Paris, Gallimard, 1985.
Critique de la raison dialectique. Vol. II (Inachevé): L'Intelligibilité de l'histoire. Paris, Gallimard, 1985.

NOTES ON CONTRIBUTORS

Robert Bernasconi

Robert Bernasconi is lecturer in philosophy at the University of Essex and the editor of the *Bulletin of the Hegel Society of Great Britain*. Educated at the University of Sussex, he is author of *The Question of Language in Heidegger's History of Being* (Humanities Press, 1985) and editor of a collection of Gadamer's writings on aesthetics entitled *The Relevance of the Beautiful* (Oxford University Press, 1986). He is currently completing a book concerned with the relation between Levinas and Derrida.

Peter Caws

Peter Caws was educated at the University of London and at Yale University. He taught at the University of Kansas and at Hunter College before joining the faculty of the George Washington University as University Professor of Philosophy in 1982. His publications include *The Philosophy of Science: A Systematic Account* (Van Nostrand, 1965), *Science and the Theory of Value* (Random House, 1967), and *Sartre* (Routledge & Kegan Paul, 1979; second printing with additional material, 1984; in the series 'Arguments of the Philosophers').

Jacques Derrida

Jacques Derrida is director of studies at the *École des Hautes Études en Sciences Sociales* in Paris. From 1975 to 1986 he was Visiting Professor of Humanities at Yale University and is now visiting professor at the University of California at Irvine.

English translations of his many writings include: *Margins of Philosophy* (Chicago University Press, 1972), *Speech and Phenomena and Other Essays on Husserl's Theory of Signs* (Northwestern University Press, 1973), *Archeology of the Frivolous* (Chicago University Press, 1973), *Of Grammatology* (Chicago University Press, 1976), *Writing and Difference* (Chicago University Press, 1978), and *Spurs: Nietzsche's Styles* (Chicago University Press, 1979).

Alphonso Lingis

Alphonso Lingis is professor of philosophy at the Pennsylvania State University. He is author of *Excesses: Eros and Culture* (State University of New York Press, 1983), *Libido: The French Existential Theories* (Indiana University Press, 1985) and *Phenomenological Explanations* (Martinus Nijhoff, The Hague, 1986). His translations include Merleau-Ponty's *The Visible and the Invisible* and Levinas' *Totality and Infinity*.

John Llewelyn

John Llewelyn is reader in philosophy at the University of Edinburgh. Educated at Oxford and the University of Edinburgh, he has also taught at the University of New England in Australia. He is author of *Beyond Metaphysics?* (Humanities Press, 1985) and *The Thresholds of Sense* (St Martins, 1986) and has published articles on continental philosophy in numerous journals.

John McCumber

John McCumber, assistant professor of philosophy at Northwestern University, has also taught at the Graduate Faculty, New School for Social Research and at the University of Michigan at Dearborn. He is author of numerous articles including: 'Reflection and Emancipation in Habermas,' 'Hegel's Anarchistic Utopia: The Politics of his *Aesthetics*', and 'Critical Theory and Poetic Interaction.'

Maurice Merleau-Ponty

Maurice Merleau-Ponty was born in Rochefort, France in 1908. He was professor at the Sorbonne from 1949 to 1952, when he took the Chair of Philosophy at the Collège de France. He held that position until his death in April of 1961. He was one of the founders of *Les Temps Modernes*. English translations of his works include: *Structure of Behavior* (Beacon, 1963), *Phenomenology of Perception* (Humanities Press, 1962), *The Visible and the Invisible* (Northwestern University Press, 1968), *Adventures of the Dialectic* (Northwestern University Press, 1973), and *Consciousness and the Acquisition of Language* (Northwestern University Press, 1973).

Tony O'Connor

Tony O'Connor is lecturer at University College in Cork, Ireland. His published articles include 'Merleau-Ponty and the Problem of the Unconscious' in *Research in Phenomenology* and 'Ambiguity and the Search for Origins' and 'Categorizing the Body' in the *Journal of the British Society of Phenomenology*.

William J. Richardson

William J. Richardson, SJ is professor of philosophy at Boston College. He has held the position of Director of Research at the Austin Riggs Center and is a practising psychoanalyst. He has published many articles concerning psychoanalysis and contemporary continental philosophy. He is author of *Heidegger: Through Phenomenology to Thought* (Martinus Nijhoff, The Hague, 1963), and (with John Muller) *Lacan and Language* (New York, International Universities Press, 1982).

John Sallis

John Sallis, currently Schmitt Professor of Philosophy at Loyola University of Chicago, was Chairman of the Philosophy Department at Duquesne University. He is author of *Being and Logos: The Way of Platonic Dialogue* (Duquesne University Press, 1975; 2nd edition, 1986), *The Gathering of Reason* (Ohio University

Press, 1980), *Delimitations: Phenomenology and the End of Metaphysics* (Indiana University Press, 1986) and *Spacings – of Reason and Imagination* (Chicago University Press, 1987). He is also editor of *Research in Phenomenology*.

Stephen H. Watson

Stephen H. Watson is associate professor of philosophy at Notre Dame University. He has published a number of articles on contemporary French philosophy including: 'The Closure of Modernism,' 'Merleau-Ponty's Involvement with Saussure', and 'Abysses.' He is currently working on a translation of Merleau-Ponty's Sorbonne Lectures which will be published by Ohio University Press.